Where These Memories Grow

Where These Memories Grow

Memories Grow

History, Memory, and Southern Identity

Edited by W. Fitzhugh Brundage

The
University
of North
Carolina
Press

Chapel Hill
and London

Library of Congress Cataloging-in-Publication Data

Where these memories grow : history, memory, and southern
identity / edited by W. Fitzhugh Brundage.

p. cm. Includes index.

ISBN 0-8078-2572-7 (cloth: alk. paper)

ISBN 0-8078-4886-7 (pbk.: alk. paper)

1. Southern States—Civilization. 2. Southern States—History—
Philosophy. 3. Memory—Social aspects—Southern States.
4. Group identity—Southern States. 5. Southern States—
Social conditions. 6. Minorities—Southern States—History.
7. Social classes—Southern States—History. 8. United States—
History—Civil War, 1861–1865—Influence.

I. Brundage, W. Fitzhugh (William Fitzhugh), 1959–

F209.W47 2000   975—dc21   00-026211

Catherine W. Bishir, "Landmarks of Power: Building a South-
ern Past in Raleigh and Wilmington, North Carolina, 1885–
1915," was originally published in slightly different form as
"Landmarks of Power: Building a Southern Past, 1885–1915,"
Southern Cultures, Inaugural Issue (1993). Copyright © 1993
Duke University Press; all rights transferred in 1996 to the
UNC Center for the Study of the American South, the pub-
lisher. Used by permission of the publisher.

Laurie F. Maffly-Kipp, "Redeeming Southern Memory: The
Negro Race History, 1874–1915," was originally published in
slightly different form as "Mapping the World, Mapping the
Race: The Negro Race History, 1874–1915," *Church History* 64
(December 1995). Used by permission of the publisher.

04 03 02 01 00   5 4 3 2 1

For H. A. W.

Te traeré de las montañas flores alegres, copihues
avellanas oscuras, y cestas silvestres de besos
Quiero hacer contigo
lo que la primavera hace con las cerezos.
—Pablo Neruda

contents

illustrations and maps

MAPS

acknowledgments

Many debts were incurred during the writing of this book. It had its inception while I was the beneficiary of two blessings, an all-too-brief stay at the National Humanities Center (NHC) and a semester as the Kirk Visiting Scholar at Agnes Scott College. At the NHC, Bob Connor, Kent Mulliken, and the rest of the staff gave me a glimpse of the Promised Land. Special thanks are in order for Eliza Robertson and Jean Houston, who tracked down the obscenely large number of articles and books that laid the foundation for this collection. At Agnes Scott, Michele Gillespie and Katherine D. Kennedy of the Department of History were exemplary hosts. Indeed, I owe a special debt to my students and faculty colleagues at Agnes Scott because my experiences there convinced me of the need for this collection. I also am grateful to the contributors for their enthusiasm and creativity during the long gestation of this project. I am indebted to Lewis Bateman and Paula Wald of the University of North Carolina Press for guiding the manuscript to publication and give special thanks to Stevie Champion, whose superb copyediting may partially compensate for my editorial lapses. Finally, I salute the contributors who deftly juggled their ongoing scholarly creativity and child rearing.

Where These Memories Grow

No Deed but Memory

W. Fitzhugh Brundage

In 1890 William P. Trent, a historian at the University of the South, wondered whether "the cause of history [is] practically dead at the South." After a survey of the paltry resources devoted to the enterprise, he concluded, "It is obvious that there is no overwhelming zeal for historical studies at the South."[1] Nearly a half century later E. Merton Coulter, in his 1935 presidential address to the newly founded Southern Historical Association, protested that "Other sections of the country have written almost the minutest details of their history, even to magnifying the Boston Tea Party and Paul Revere's Ride into an importance which has permeated the national consciousness, while the South has permitted its history to lie unworked and many of its major figures and movements to remain to this day unhonored and unsung."[2]

These laments about the "want of history" in the South, in fact, coincided with the flowering of the Confederate tradition, the glorification of the Old South, the onset of a southern literary renaissance absorbed with the past, and the emergence of academic historical scholarship in the region. By the time of Coulter's presidential address, the southern past *had* insinuated itself deeply into the national consciousness. Few present-day observers are likely to parrot Trent's or Coulter's accusations that southerners suffer from amnesia about their past. Instead, like the distinguished writer V. S. Naipaul, we may be inclined to characterize the southern past as "a wound."[3] The contemporary circumstance is not that the southern past is neglected, but that it is raw and sensitive. Disputes over the region's history appear regularly, sometimes in unexpected places and jarring ways. For the foreseeable future, ongoing contests over the meanings of that history will ensure that the southern past remains an open wound.

The remembered past and debates about it have a deep significance for both public life and regional identity in the American South. Southerners, after all, have the reputation of being among the most historically oriented of peoples and of possessing the longest, most tenacious memories. The notion that the South is a place saturated with history is self-evident, commonsensical. Allen Tate had in mind this vision of a terrain hallowed by the past when he wrote in the "Ode to the Confederate Dead":

> Of a thousand acres, where these memories grow
> From the inexhaustible bodies that are not
> Dead, but feed the grass, row after rich row.[4]

By invoking the inexhaustible Confederate dead, Tate summons images of an equally limitless southern (white) memory and of a landscape imbued with that memory. The evocation of the past is evident in other enduring symbols of the South. What azalea festival in the region is complete without its southern belles dressed in ersatz antebellum attire and what self-respecting southern county is satisfied without a statue of a stern Confederate soldier poised for battle in front of the courthouse?

The question of how and why the supposed essence of the South has become tied to certain elements of regional history cannot be answered simply by responding that the region is exceptionally rich with a distinctive history. To claim that the American South is historically richer than other regions of the United States is sophistry. Any locale that has been occupied by humans arguably can be ascribed significance in human history; the relative importance attached to one region or another reflects only the historical narratives told about it, not any inherent, "objective" significance. As Stuart Hall has observed, the past nowhere has inherent meaning, "only that which is imposed upon it by language, by narrative, by discourse."[5] Moreover, the presence of "history"—public monuments, restored homes, forts, and so forth—is no less conspicuous elsewhere in the United States than in the South.

We should not take for granted, then, the inevitability of the contemporary southern landscape dense with invocations of the past. The historical South that exists today is the consequence not of some innate regional properties, but of decades of investment, labor, and conscious design by individuals and groups of individuals who have imagined themselves as "southerners." If characterizations of southern memory are to be meaningful, attention should be given to what kind of history southerners have valued, what in their past they have chosen to remember and forget, how they have disseminated the past they have recalled, and to what uses those memories have been put. We need, in short, a social history of remembering in the South.

In recent years scholars in various fields have shown increasing interest in historical memory. Informed by anthropology, psychology, linguistics, literary criticism, and cultural studies, recent studies of historical memory have achieved considerable theoretical and analytical sophistication. To date, however, surprisingly little work has been done on the historical memory of the South. This collection is intended to fill, if only partially, that gap by exploring and assessing the significance of particular manifestations of historical memory in the South. This introduction offers an overview of some of the theoretical assumptions that undergird the collection. Another goal of this introduction is to underscore that our understanding of southern historical memory will be enriched by adopting the broadest comparative and historical perspective. A further aim is to extend the discussion beyond the scope of the individual essays by speculating about both the contemporary significance of historical memory for the region's public life and the possible evolution of contemporary controversies over the southern past.

Southerners share with other humans a seemingly universal impulse to shield memory from being swallowed into what Vladimir Nabokov called "the ooze of the past." Memories, however, defy preservation because they are innately elusive and ephemeral. They are, as Guillaume Apollinaire observed, like "hunting horns whose sound dies on the wind."[6] Challenged by this fleeting quality, individuals resort to all manner of techniques, ranging from diaries and photographs to genealogies, in their heartfelt attempts to cling to some of the past.

Societies likewise seek to remember by creating "attics of memory." Since the 1920s, when Maurice Halbwachs, a French sociologist, proposed the concept of collective memory, it has become conventional wisdom that all memory is inextricably bound up with group identity.[7] Memory, he posited, is not principally an expression of the autonomous individual psyche. Unlike Sigmund Freud, who contended that the obscure world of the unconscious psyche was a repository for all past experiences, Halbwachs urged scholars to focus on the conscious memory expressed in social contexts. Even apparently personal memories, he asserted, are shaped by social circumstances and hence private memory imperceptibly incorporates collective memory. Nearly all personal memories, then, are learned, inherited, or, at the very least, informed by a common stock of social memory.[8]

Collective memory consists of those shared remembrances that identify "a group, giving it a sense of its past and defining its aspirations for the future."[9] For individuals and groups alike, memory forms an essential component of their social identity. By definition, collective memory involves sharing, discussion, negotiation, and often conflict. Remembering consequently becomes implicated in a range of activities that have as much to do with identity, power, authority, cultural norms, and social interaction as with the simple act of conserving and recalling information. Groups invariably fashion their own image of the world and their place in it by establishing an accepted version of the past, a sort of genealogy of identity. Although collective memories may trace a chronology readily recognizable to people outside the group, events within that narrative are assigned an importance distinct from the significance ascribed to them by outsiders. In addition to providing a singular ordering of the past, a group's social memory, like the myth described by Roland Barthes, addresses pressing concerns of identity; "it purifies them, it makes them innocent, it gives them natural and eternal justification, it gives them a clarity which is not that of an explanation but that of a statement of fact."[10]

The recent history of the Cajuns of southwestern Louisiana provides one conspicuous illustration of the link between a claimed past and collective identity. The highly assimilated French ethnic population of southwestern Louisiana would be indistinguishable from other white Americans were it not for some residual folkways and, most important, their acute sense of ethnic identity rooted in history. Beginning in the nineteenth century and continuing to the present, descendants of the French settlers who were evicted from British Canada in the eighteenth century have affirmed a collective identity rooted in the trauma of expulsion. Although the ousting of the French Acadians is a comparatively minor occurrence in the conventional narrative of British North American imperial policy, the expulsion is the defining event in the Cajun hierarchy of memory. Indeed, the traditional criterion for distinguishing Cajuns from other Louisianans is descent from the expelled refugees. During the 1930s politicians, raconteurs, and Cajun enthusiasts labored to root Cajun identity in a narrative centered around the eighteenth-century expulsion of the Acadians from Canada. Through paeans to the Acadian historical experience, "pilgrimages" of Cajuns to Canada, campaigns to "preserve" the Acadian French idiom, and various commemorative activities, the

Acadian boosters proposed an inventory of the past that now comprises an essential element of the Cajun "imagined community."[11]

The act of remembering the past and of assigning levels of significance to it, as the example of Cajuns illustrates, is an act of interpretation. No longer can we presume the existence of fixed images of the past that we retrieve intact through acts of memory. Recently, older notions of memory as a passive process of storing and retrieving objective recollections of lived experiences have given way to an understanding of memory as an active, ongoing process of ordering the past. "Remembering," Frederick Bartlett explains, "appears to be far more decisively an affair of construction rather than one of mere re-production."[12] Collective memories, like personal memory, are constructed, not simply reproduced.

Historical memory, consequently, transmits selective knowledge about the past. By discerning patterns in the past and by attaching significance to events, groups create interpretative frameworks that make "the flux of experience comprehensible."[13] Events, as both Stuart Hall and Marshall Sahlins have pointed out, acquire historical importance only when they are incorporated into a cultural scheme.[14] The arrival of Cajuns in eighteenth-century Louisiana, for instance, takes on significance only when integrated into a saga of exile and perseverance. Inherent in the transmission of historical memory, therefore, is the active labor of selecting, structuring, and imposing meaning on the past rather than the mere reproduction of inherent historical truths.

Collective memory self-evidently should not be mistaken for an "objective" record of the past. English dramatist Harold Pinter warned that "The past is what you remember, imagine you remember, convince yourself you remember, or pretend to remember."[15] The pursuit of objectivity, as Pinter pointed out, may have been a central tenet of the academic study of the past but it is not essential to collective memory. Even so, in order for a historical narrative to acquire cultural authority, it must appear believable to its audience. Precisely because groups care whether their historical narrative is "true" or "false," they strive to distinguish it from fiction by affirming its authenticity. They consequently establish standards of credibility against which they test their narratives. But those standards may vary greatly over time and from group to group, from society to society. Professional historians, followers of a religious faith, and members of a fraternal society, for example, may all apply substantially different measures of verisimilitude to their understandings of the past. Moreover, whether provoked by slowly changing circumstances or sudden controversy, groups periodically experience the need to apply new tests of credibility to differentiate what happened from what is said to have happened.[16]

In the study of historical memory, the important question is not how accurately recollections describe an "objective" historical reality. As Frederick Corney explains, to pit the constructed past against the supposed historical reality of the past "in order to expose falsification and political manipulation is to ignore the complex process involved in the efforts of any group or polity to construct a reality in which to exist."[17] Our focus of attention should be on how historical actors fashion and test the credibility of memories in a certain way at a particular time.[18]

One conspicuous manifestation of both the interpretative character of historical memories and standards of credibility is the propensity of groups to suppress as well as to recall portions of the past. Within collective memories a dialectic exists between the willfully recalled and deliberately forgotten past. Campaigns to remember the past by forgetting parts of it have occurred in many times and places. Shortly after the murder of Julius Caesar, for instance, Cicero declared in the Roman Senate that all memory of the previous tumult should be consigned to eternal oblivion. In Restoration France during the early nineteenth century, civil officials, following orders from Paris, pursued an explicit policy of "forgetting" the previous twenty-five years of history. First, revolutionary mementos were burned in elaborate public spectacles, and then, subsequently, authorities held annual commemorations of the executions of Louis the XVI and Marie Antoinette during which, curiously, the government forbade any explicit reference to the event being commemorated.[19] More recently, Austrians of Kurt Waldheim's generation recounted a past in which they were innocent victims of, rather than willing participants in, Nazi aggression. And the newborn nation of Israel has diligently transformed the traditional depiction of the defenders of Masada in ancient times from a sect of suicidal Jewish zealots into role models for Zionist defenders of the modern Jewish state.[20]

Historical silences likewise were prominent in the depictions of slavery produced by white southerners during the late nineteenth and early twentieth centuries. In autobiographies, essays on contemporary issues, nostalgic recollections published in magazines, and historical novels, whites elevated to cliché the moonlight-and-magnolia imagery of plantation life, with its benign portrait of slavery. Taken together, these depictions achieved a kind of classic purity. Regardless of whether the setting varied from the Revolution to the Civil War, the accounts were brimming with idealized renderings of dashing and honorable white planters, beautiful and refined plantation mistresses, and contented black slaves. This idealization of slave life and glorification of the loving and faithful black slave, especially the mammy, sought to conceal alternative memories of violence, exploitation, and cruelty. Slave auctions, beatings, and uprisings, much less more mundane hardships, had no place in this white historical memory. Not until recent decades when activists and scholars imposed new standards of credibility was this representation of the Old South substantially revised.[21]

As the white memory of slavery suggests, the creation of historical memory harnesses the energies of groups and individuals in what Michel-Rolph Trouillot calls "historical production."[22] The creation of influential historical narratives is as likely to take place outside of academia as within it. Only a small portion of what most groups or societies understand of history is generated by professional historians; politicians, antiquarians, artists, and writers are at least as important custodians of the remembered past as scholars. Indeed, scholarship only recently has exerted influence over social memory in the American South. Until well into the twentieth century trained historians were so few in number and so limited in influence that they could not exert broad cultural authority over matters past. Even when their influence began to increase, trained historians did not quickly discard interpretative conventions inherited from their amateur predecessors and contemporaries.[23]

Reflecting the diversity of constituencies that often have a hand in historical production, societies employ varied formal and informal techniques to transmit collective memories. The resources that any group has available to it dictate the medium of expression used to impart the recalled past. Each mode has its own possibilities and idiosyncracies. Preliterate societies and technologically advanced, literate societies typically use different methods to record and transmit their histories. A society's possession of literacy has important implications for its historical memory. By no means is the ability of a group to convey its social memory in logical and articulate form dependent on the possession of writing. The ancient Greeks, precolonial Sub-Saharan Africans, and Native Americans are just a few of the societies that developed complex orally transmitted social memories. And even in literate societies, collective memory continues to be shaped by both oral and written forms. But where literacy prevails, including in the American South, the fusion of written expressions of memory and technology makes possible a dizzying range of historical representations, such as school texts, historical novels, highway historical markers, monuments, and museums, to name only a few.

Indeed, an important theme in the social history of collective memory in the South during the past century and a half has been the relentless expansion of media used to define the region, its past, and its heroes.

Southerners, no less than others, have displayed great creativity in employing material objects to record their past. Because memories are transitory, people yearn to make them permanent by rendering them in physical form. By erecting monuments or marking off sacred places, groups anchor their memories in space and time. Objects become infused with commemorative qualities, and thereby serve as physical markers of memory that preserve the past in the present, underscoring the connectedness of past and present.[24] Social memory accordingly becomes associated as much with material culture as with intangible images of the past.

The collections of museums and historical societies in the turn-of-the-century South, which were chock full of totemic relics, demonstrate this impulse to transcend the chasm of time and to experience the past through contact with objects. The Trinity College Historical Society boasted that it possessed the "Limb of [a] mulberry tree" under which British general Cornwallis "ate dinner while in North Carolina." The Arkansas State Historical Museum displayed another evocative tree branch from an apple tree at the site of the Confederate surrender at Appomattox, Virginia, as well as a Book of Prayer, molded out of clay gathered from the site of the Civil War battle of the "Crater" at Petersburg, Virginia. As one contemporary explained, these relics were "speaking witnesses" that related "a story of past life." Over time, the multiplication of these and other physical catalysts of memory in the South (and the rest of the nation as well) created a physical and cognitive landscape dense with symbols of the recalled past.[25]

Seldom satisfied with mere mute physical representations of historical memory, groups (whether based on geography or interest) often employ a fusion of narrative and performance to give added meaning to the past. Public ceremonies, such as elaborately staged pageants to celebrate the unveiling of monuments, mock colonial balls hosted by patriotic societies, or induction ceremonies for historical associations, are powerfully didactic performances that act out group identity and put historical consciousness into words.[26] Elaborate and immense rites of white memory in the American South, for example, regularly punctuated the late nineteenth century after the United Confederate Veterans emerged as the preeminent veterans' organization. Through a variety of rituals, especially reunions, Confederate veterans carried their interpretation of the Civil War to vast audiences of white southerners. For example, 100,000 visitors massed in Richmond for the 1896 reunion. Of the 140,000 who attended the 1902 Confederate reunion in Dallas, only 12,000 were former soldiers. With broad participation from every conceivable white club and organization, Confederate reunions exerted a cultural influence far greater than mere parades or gatherings of decrepit old soldiers. Such ritual observances are central to historical memory because, by both eliciting and shaping memories, they provide a framework within which individual and collective memories acquire broader meaning. By participating in commemorative events, people "learn what to remember and what it is to remember as part of a social enterprise."[27]

Expressions of historical memory require precise articulation. Culturally influential historical narratives typically acquire an accepted form that is free of the idiosyncracies and nuances that shade personal memory. Memories that deviate too much from convention are unlikely to be meaningful to large audiences or to be spread successfully. Consequently, groups labor to create stable social memories that are resistant to eccentric or unsanctioned interpretations. For instance, the Nazis in Germany created a series of commemorative ceremonies that, according to Paul Connerton, rapidly assumed "a canonical form" that was both regulated and total. In France, Bastille Day, which was initiated in 1880, developed into a carefully ritualized reassertion of French revolutionary nationhood. And in the American South, women's and veterans' groups fashioned a script for Confederate Memorial Day so that it became an annual rite during which white southerners made manifest their veneration of the Confederacy.[28]

The repetition of these observances, like all ritualized expressions of historical memory, established continuity with the past. Unlike occasional festivities that may only imply a connection with history, these rituals explicitly asserted historical continuity. For example, beyond reminding participants about the past, the Confederate Memorial Day festivities—parades of veterans, military drills by local militia, and the marking of graves—re-presented the past so that participants became, if only temporarily and symbolically, contemporaries with mythical events. Such routinized performances are essential to the diffusion and enduring cultural authority of historical memory.

Yet in any collective memory there is an inherent dialectic between stability and innovation. This characteristic of memory almost certainly is what Eudora Welty had in mind when she observed that "memory is a living thing—it too is in transit."[29] The identity of any group goes hand in hand with the continuous creation of its sense of the past. No enduring social memory can be entirely static. Each time a tradition is articulated, it must be given a meaning appropriate to the historical context in which it is invoked. For a historical memory to retain its capacity to speak to and mobilize its intended audience, it must address contemporary concerns about the past. Consequently, although the crafters of historical memory often resolve to create a version of the past that is impervious to change, their very success depends on its ongoing evolution.

One illustration of the adaptation of collective memory to changing circumstances is the rise of historical tourism in the South. In the late nineteenth century public representations of the past were intertwined with civic culture. Volunteer historical enterprises, which purportedly represented the "public will" of mobilized communities, were the driving force behind public expressions of memory. The state rarely bestowed monuments, historical displays, or public commemorations on communities. Instead, private groups proposed and funded them (and only then, in the case of monuments, donated them to the state for safekeeping). This tradition of historical voluntarism underwent considerable change in the early twentieth century. Beginning in the 1920s, the popularity of automobile touring began to alter both how and to whom historical memory was transmitted. As increasing numbers of tourists escaped the rigors of northern winters by exploring the southern hinterland, the promotion of tourism became a central concern of both business groups and state policy across the South. Since then, much of southern heritage has been conceived from the perspective of the tourist. Commercial interests and state and local governments have eagerly contributed to, and increasingly have taken the lead in creating, public sites intended to entertain as much as to edify. The advent of automobile tourism has led to a commercially oriented celebration of southern architecture, landscape, and history, and in turn historical memory in the South has come to reflect the ubiquitous influence of tourism.

Changes in the social and political circumstances of groups similarly propel the evolution of historical memories. Because power and access to it are central to the creation and propagation of historical memory, changes in the relative power of groups invariably has far-reaching consequences for what of the past is remembered and how it is remembered. The transformation of the status of African Americans in the South illustrates this process. When placed against the backdrop of black political empowerment, the ongoing disputes over public displays of Confederate symbols, monuments to contested historical figures and events, and the commemoration of the African American past become understandable. For a century after the Civil War public representations of southern history conspicuously ignored any recognition of the recalled past of blacks. African Americans created their own understanding of their past, but whereas white social memory was both public and universal in its claims, the black countermemory was neither. Through the activities of African American fraternal lodges, churches, schools, and civic groups, blacks certainly imagined their history. But these expressions were either ignored by or were largely invisible to whites. Not until the 1960s did blacks command the political power necessary to insist on a more inclusive historical memory for the South. Then, black southerners acquired the necessary leverage to displace white ideas about the past that had the cultural authority of tradition and habit.

As many of the essays in this collection make clear, the evolution of historical memories merits careful scrutiny because it highlights the connections between historical memory and the exercise of power. An essential characteristic of collective memory is the cultural authority attached to it. Representations of history are instruments of, and may even constitute, power. Groups routinely sort the past in a particular way to legitimize their current power or aspirations. Not only do social memories often incorporate claims to factual legitimacy but they also may invoke or come to be viewed as authoritative traditions. The depth and tenacity of a historical memory within a society may serve as one measure of who exerts social power there. Struggles between groups to define some social memories as authoritative and others as trivial fictions are also contests over who exercises the power to make some historical narratives possible and to silence others. Whether in Russia, China, Africa, or Great Britain, political elites have been preoccupied with making "themselves the master[s] of memory and forgetfulness."[30] The interpretation of history, as Michel Foucault has insisted, is a conspicuous form of domination.[31] That the struggle to forge historical memory is a contest over discourse does not diminish its gravity. "The stakes in debates over social memories," David Blight explains, "are quite real; material resources, political power, and life chances may all be at stake."[32]

This fusion of cultural and political power has emerged repeatedly during the past two centuries of southern history. During the heated political contests of the 1890s, for example, white Democratic elites in the region faced both Republican challengers and Populist insurgents. The Democrats responded by claiming for themselves the mantle of defenders of the Confederate tradition against these threats. Not by coincidence did the Democratic Party send forth Confederate veterans as candidates. Nor was it happenstance that many Democratic politicians joined in the glorification of the Confederacy and the South's traditional elites. Democratic handbills and speakers proclaimed that a vote for either the Republicans or the Populists was an act of treason against southern traditions and the white race, especially southern white womanhood. Although Democratic elites also employed fraud, intimidation, and violence to retain power, their skillful appeals to historical memory undergirded their success.[33]

While historical narratives like those projected by white Democrats in the 1890s legitimated the prevailing distribution of power, alternative narratives could become sites of contestation. The Fourth of July and Emancipation Day festivities in the New South, for instance, rather than reaffirming the southern racial and political hierarchy, instead provided an opportunity for African Americans to share visions of liberation. When blacks gathered to celebrate the Declaration of Independence or the abolition of slavery, they not only represented symbolically their past and present status, but they also envisioned a utopian future in which they attained meaningful equality and self-determination. In these commemorations of freedom, blacks expressed the otherwise unsaid and unsayable in the Jim Crow South. That white southerners, after the tumult of Reconstruction, often mocked or ignored altogether black civic festivities should not diminish the significance of these rituals as a forum for black protest. To the contrary, the white response reveals an important pattern in the relationship between contested memories. Southern whites, like all dominant groups seeking to claim unanimity among themselves and consent among subordinates, purposely sequestered black dissent out of their sight. Blacks simultaneously had good reason to preserve the public facade of willing compliance with white dictates; to do otherwise in the Jim Crow South could be literally lethal and might have led to the outright suppression of the comparative autonomy that blacks enjoyed, if only briefly, in their festivities. Thus, the ideological resistance that black counternarratives represented was often cryptic, muted, and veiled.[34]

Just as subversive versions of the past are regularly obscured, so too are the workings of historical memory—how it is created and disseminated—often intentionally concealed. Architects of historical memory usually work hard to sustain the fiction that they are merely agents of a more universal collective whose shared memory they seek to express. Invariably insisting that they speak for "the people" or "their people" as a whole, crafters of memory are eager to erase the origins of the memories they promote. They instead contrive representations that conceal the very process that gives meaning to and disseminates them. Memorialists also present their narratives as timeless, as free of historical contingency. This discursive sleight of hand, Michel de Certeau contends, "is rather sly: the discourse gives itself credibility in the name of the reality which it is supposed to represent, but this authorized appearance of the 'real' serves precisely to camouflage the practice which in fact determines it. Representation thus disguises the praxis that organizes it."[35]

The construction of historical monuments in the nineteenth-century South (and elsewhere in the United States) illustrates these fictions. Public monuments were portrayed by purportedly voluntary associations (which, in fact, often had close ties to officialdom) as spontaneous expressions of popular enthusiasm and reverence. Such groups invariably summoned the public to contribute funds and provide support for commemorative projects. Eventually, after months, even years, of fund-raising, sculptors were hired, designs approved, and then the completed monuments unveiled before the gathered public. The monuments that emerged from this process frequently were testimonials to popular enthusiasm, but neither was the enthusiasm spontaneous nor the "public" necessarily one people united by shared memory. Yet once the monuments were erected, the origins and struggles over the sponsorship and design of public monuments receded into the background (until some latter-day controversy exposed them). Whatever the particular motivations of the promoters of the memorials, their monuments to Confederate soldiers, loyal slaves, Revolutionary-era patriots, and local dignitaries became sacrosanct and in time defined the enduring image of the "public" that purportedly erected them.[36] Only by piercing the appearance of immutable collective memory can the struggles over the power to define, include, excise, and interpret the past be seen.

In addition to the important insights that the study of collective memory sheds on the role of power in the production and uses of history, it also clarifies the links between personal and group identity. So tightly bound together are collective memory and self-identification that memory is the thread of personal identity. It is at the personal level that collective memory is sustained by what Jacquelyn Dowd Hall calls "the everyday performance of self."[37] The narrative conventions of a group's historical memory provide individuals with a framework within which to articulate their experience, to explain their place, in the remembered past. When appealing to a collective memory, individuals necessarily define themselves in relation to inherited conventions and hierarchies. Consequently, justifications of status, privilege, and authority, like a mnemonic device that derives its efficacy from repetition, often are recurring elements in both personal and social memory. Any attempt to revise the public memory almost inevitably compels a revision of existing hierarchies, whether they relate to race, class, gender, ethnicity, or religion.

The profusion of historical activities undertaken by white women at the close of the nineteenth century, for example, was bound up in the evolving notions of gender in the American South. White women assumed the leadership in erecting monuments, preserving historic sites, creating historical displays. Likewise, women's organizations supplied classroom materials, conducted classes to "Americanize" immigrants, funded college scholarships, and crusaded for the teaching of "true history" of the South, especially with regard to slavery and sectional strife. White women of the New South, in sum, asserted a cultural authority over virtually all representations of the region's past.[38]

The essential point is that many white middle-class and elite women found in history an instrument for self-definition and empowerment. Within the boundaries imposed by the prevailing beliefs of the era, the meaning of the collective memory of the white South was open to multiple readings which in turn allowed white women to use it for varied purposes. The historical activities of white women legitimated contradictory claims for power, some reactionary, others emancipatory. For many white women, their gendered identities could not be separated from their ties to the past—not just their personal, familial past, but also the collective "History" of the South. Beset by the transformations of the New South, elite white women found in history a resource with which to fashion new selves without sundering links to the old. The study of historical memory, then, forms an important element of any understanding of the construction of social identities.[39]

The salience of memory for class identity is a persistent thread in many of the essays in this collection. Georgia artisans in the early republic, Michele Gillespie explains, viewed themselves as a group united by their historical contributions to the founding of the republic. Later in the century, as several essayists describe, southern white elites labored to make their claims to power and wealth appear to be a natural and inviolable part of history. At the same time, the southern Populists invoked a rich language and corpus of historical metaphors, informed by Jacksonian and Jeffersonian ideologies, to explain the contemporary plight of farmers and other "producers." The Populists did not so much look to the past for solutions to the economic and political distress of their age, but rather as a reference point from which to trace their deteriorating circumstances. Finally, perceptions of southern millworkers during the first half of the twentieth century, especially those held by union activists, reflected notions about the grip of inherited traditions and the past on the southern working class. The perceived reticence of millworkers to join labor unions, some observers concluded, could be traced to ancient folkways of self-sufficiency. Other observers presumed that the force of history would impel southern workers to follow in the footsteps of industrial workers elsewhere who had embraced labor unions and demanded social justice. Thus, assumptions about class consciousness among southern workers in part reflected assumptions about the historical experiences that were prerequisites for worker solidarity.[40]

Finally, the social history of collective memory in the South sheds light on the possible future evolution of southern regional identity. In recent decades, scholars and pundits alike have debated the persistence of southern distinctiveness. Some scholars point to the inevitable dilution of southern distinctiveness as a result of the dismantling of legal racial discrimination, the in-migration of outsiders, and the economic transformation of the region. Others insist that distinctive southern culture(s) endure and are observable in southerners' purported affinity for an unhurried pace of living, "good manners," patriotism, stock car races, capital punishment, fundamentalism, and trailer homes, among other things. Perhaps more compelling evidence of enduring regional distinctiveness are the ongoing disputes over the southern past.

These controversies over what of the past should be remembered provide the crucible for future definitions of any meaningful southern identity. By engaging in debates over historical representations, contemporary southerners give meaning to their abstract collective identities as southern whites, blacks, Latinos, men, women, and so forth. Southern identity, in short, will endure as long as people imagine themselves within a southern historical narrative.

For the foreseeable future, prior renderings of the southern past will continue to shape representations of the region. At first glance, both white and black southerners have felt the tension between "what was" and "what ought to have been" in their pasts. For different generations of whites the Civil War and then more recently the economic and social transformation that C. Vann Woodward has called the "Bulldozer Revolution" have broken the ribbon of time, severing the present from preceding eras. Twice over the white past has been rendered obsolete. The traumas of the southern past, as Woodward has explained, ensured that white southerners could not easily depict their history as one of unbroken success and progress. Yet the appearance of abrupt and wrenching change, especially the modern civil rights movement, has enabled white southerners to see parts of their past as conveniently obsolete. This eagerness to forgive the past for the sins of the past is encouraged by

regional boosters, southern politicians eager to erase the stigma of provincial-
ism, and a tourist industry that promotes nostalgia.

Black southerners, in contrast, have ample reason to see history as an
unresolved, ongoing process. For them, the past is a living past bound up in
the present, one neither exotically different nor obsolete. Most important, the
black historical memory has a distinctive orientation toward the future. The
black memory has legitimated struggle and has been a vision of the future.
This idea of a purposeful past is what W. E. B. Du Bois had in mind when he
wrote in his *Autobiography*, "Teach us Forever Dead, there is no Dream but
Deed, no Deed but Memory." For Du Bois the past is prologue, and the
future is the fulfillment of hopes anticipated, inspired, and urged on by past
sacrifices. A covenant with the past links the struggles of contemporary
African Americans and their ancestors; it informs their identity as black
southerners and their enduring hopes.[41]

If the contemporary understandings of the southern past remain as different as I have suggested, the contemporary debates about them pose important questions for the prospects for an inclusive civic culture in the South.
Can the previously hidden memories of blacks, Latinos, and other marginalized groups be incorporated into the public life of the South? And can these
diverse historical memories coexist in the public arena? Some commentators
have called for the recognition of the "common attachment to something
meaningful and enduring" and "composite culture" that unite southerners.
But in fact no "common cultural canopy" exists in the South.[42] To the extent
that the memories of groups in the South diverge, they can share neither
experiences nor assumptions.

The legacy of the earlier hegemony of white memory is a landscape and
public culture packed with symbols of white privilege and virtually barren of
images endorsed by blacks. Many important historical places, symbols, and
events evoke such sharply divergent responses among southerners that no
reconciliation of memories seems feasible. To take but one example, the 1987
National Association for the Advancement of Colored People (NAACP) resolution advocating the removal of Confederate flags from statehouses and state
flags has provoked angry complaints from many whites that they are being
asked to surrender and repress their heritage. The former president of the
Confederate Society of America sees the campaign to disown the Confederate flag as a fundamental threat to southern identity: "There is a distinct
nature of the South that cannot be applied to any other part of the country.
Northern states want to impose this sameness about the country. That's why
we need to protect the Confederate symbols." Insisting that opponents of the

Confederate flag distort its historical meaning, many defenders of the flag reject any historical associations with slavery or white supremacy. That the white memory of secession or a white understanding of southern identity should be incorporated into public symbols and spaces is taken for granted and apparently tolerates no scrutiny.[43]

Control over the Alamo in San Antonio, Texas, is another flash point of contested memory in the contemporary South. Since 1905, the Daughters of the Republic of Texas (DRT) have retained custody over the state-owned portions of the Alamo mission compound, the scene of the much mythologized battle between Texans and Mexican troops in 1836. The Daughters, who claim direct descent from the founders of the Texas Republic, vigilantly preserve the site as a shrine to the heroism of the men who died there. The tours they conduct and the history they endorse focus on the thirteen days of the siege of the Alamo by General Santa Ana's troops and especially such Anglo heroes as Jim Bowie, William Travis, and Davy Crockett. In recent years the DRT's hagiographic presentation of the history of the Alamo increasingly has come under criticism. The waning of elite Anglo political control in San Antonio and the simultaneous rise of Mexican American political influence have precipitated an ongoing debate over the appropriate social and ethnic imagery at the Alamo. Some Mexican Americans in San Antonio demand that the Alamo be recast to acknowledge the role of their ancestors, alongside the celebrated Anglo heroes, in defending the mission. Others resent the condescending, even racist depictions of Mexicans in the Alamo saga. Finally, some critics question the Daughters' reasons for concentrating on only a brief moment in the long and rich (Spanish) history of the Alamo mission site. Some Anglos, in turn, have dismissed these attacks on the Daughters and their custodianship of the Alamo as baseless assaults on hallowed traditions and as shrill ethnic grandstanding.[44] The Daughters, meanwhile, have vigorously defended their control of the site and have made only small concessions to their critics.

In a real sense the Daughters of the Republic of Texas and the champions of the Confederate flag are continuing to claim the cultural authority to define the public memory. The memory they promote is exclusionary and inherently (almost certainly intentionally) omits any alternate African or Mexican American memories. As Mary Peeler, executive director of the NAACP in North Carolina, asks, just what is being memorialized by modern-day Confederate zealots? "The Civil War was not a period for America to celebrate. It was a time when the American union was torn. When black folks were still in bondage. When they were treated as less than human. So I see no reason for celebration there."[45] The simmering controversies over the Confederate flag and the Alamo may appear to be merely symbolic, ephemeral spats. To the contrary, both are the harvest of a century of insidiously narrow representations of the southern experience.

Controversies in the South will continue not only over what parts of the past should be memorialized but also how to do so. We have only begun to ask whether African American and other marginalized forms of memory will resonate with other communities. Museums admittedly have made strides in introducing audiences to the pasts of America's minorities. Yet difficult challenges remain. Objects wrenched from their intended setting and exhibited in apparently neutral spaces may lose some of their function and acquire new meanings not intended by their creators. Native Americans in the South and elsewhere have complained that sacred Indian objects have been trivialized and dishonored by being placed in public and secular displays. This problem of changed context and altered meaning may be magnified when performances as well as objects are involved. How, for instance, can history museums adequately convey the full meaning of African American religious observances as forums for all manner of black expression? If displays of African American religious objects almost certainly cannot communicate the complexities of black religion, can mock religious ceremonies or documentary films do any better? Finally, the preponderance of artifacts of elite whites and the comparative paucity of remnants of nonelite southerners of all races impedes the creation of inclusive museum collections. Creative reinterpretations of material culture at Colonial Williamsburg and elsewhere have not succeeded in conferring comparable nuance and gravity to the white and nonwhite pasts. Consequently, we should not exaggerate the capacity of museums to incorporate in an adequate or meaningful fashion the history of previously excluded southerners.[46]

Questions also remain about whether the pasts of blacks and others can be incorporated into the whole range of cultural expressions that transmit public memory. Blacks and other minorities, as they have gained a measure of power, have influenced some public expressions of memory. Other representations of the past, however, remain resistant to revision. For instance, the past has become a valuable commodity and is one of the South's largest wealth producers. Incorporating the memories and experiences of blacks and other previously marginalized groups into touristic renderings of the past is an enormous and as yet barely begun undertaking. One wonders if cities such as Charleston, Savannah, Natchez, and San Antonio, to name only the most obvious examples, can acknowledge *fully* the African or Mexican American past without subverting their carefully nurtured images of gentility, romance, and nostalgia. To recognize that past would raise contentious questions about the legacies of discrimination and poverty as well as current race relations. An incorporation of the minority past risks dissolving the complete separation of the past and present that is so appealing and soothing to contemporary tastes.

Are there no alternatives to these pessimistic predictions about the course of contemporary debates over the southern past? Indeed, there are. Small steps such as the removal of offensive historical monuments (for instance, a United Daughters of the Confederacy monument at Harpers Ferry National Historical Park and a monument to Reconstruction-era white supremacists in New Orleans) hold out the promise of a southern landscape that may be less alienating to some southerners. The proliferation of historical tourism focused on formerly ignored groups of southerners may partially ameliorate the effects of the moonlight-and-magnolia southern tourism industry. And the erection of a statue commemorating the black tennis star Arthur Ashe along an avenue otherwise most notable for its Confederate monuments in Richmond, the centennial observation of the Wilmington, North Carolina, Race Riot of 1898, and the opening of museums of African American history in Savannah and of civil rights history in Greensboro, Memphis, and Birmingham all are examples of efforts to fill some of the silences in past narratives of southern history. African Americans have been the instigators, planners, and even curators at some of these sites. Even places that seemingly defy a redemptive, inclusive reinterpretation are now presented in innovative ways. A few antebellum slave plantations, most famously Somerset Plantation in North Carolina, have hosted annual reunions of the descendants of slaves and masters.[47] Any similarities between these reunions and turn-of-the-century celebrations of aged former slaves and mammies are superficial. Instead, present-day descendants have occasion to ponder the history that both divides and unites them. Similarly, as Holly Beachley Brear forecasts in her essay in this collection, a reinterpretation of the Alamo appears imminent. Almost certainly Mexican Americans will play a significant role in the future interpretation of this site, and at last the "Second Battle of the Alamo" may end. Even if a "community of memory" does not exist in the South, the public representations of the region's past are more inclusive than at any previous time.[48]

Although the future debates over the southern past cannot easily be predicted, there is every reason to believe that they will be a persistent element of public life because of the stakes involved. The prospects for an enduring civic culture in the South depend to a very considerable degree on the acknowledgment of the region's heterogeneous memories. As competing pasts have proliferated, sometimes fierce conflicts have emerged between claims vying for dominance. As long as this contestation occurs within a democratic setting, it is altogether healthy. Mary Ryan has reminded us that during the early nineteenth century Americans nurtured a robust and, yes, contentious public culture that recognized (if not always fully tolerated) all manner of difference.[49] Civic tumult, of course, is not an end in itself. But neither should our goal be to suppress or appease argument over the past. Without a recognition of the diversity of memories, without pondering all of the traces of the past, there can be no recognition of difference, no tolerance for the rich complexities of personal and cultural, political and regional identities.

Southerners face, then, an exceedingly difficult task. The creation of a community of memory in the South will require stamina, experimentation, and tolerance. And it will require all these from southerners far removed from academic settings. Historians alone cannot be the physicians of southern memory. They possess neither the power nor the wisdom to mold and remold singlehandedly a cultural attribute of such profound importance as collective memory. Instead, the struggle to decide what should be revered, what should be acknowledged, and what should be forgotten must incorporate the full breadth of southerners. Almost certainly this debate will continue in a haphazard and unpredictable fashion. But as long as southerners do not succumb to nostalgia, do not idealize an imagined past when a single collective memory prevailed, and do not presume the inherent value of a regional identity, much good almost certainly will come from ongoing contests over southern memory. In time the shadows of recalled pasts may dissolve, redeeming at last the dreams, deeds, and memories of the peoples of the South from either willful exploitation or slow atrophy.

While contemplating the mysteries of ancient ruins in Ceylon, John Still mused that "The memories of men are too frail a thread to hang history from."[50] Memory, he charged, is a capricious source of knowledge that cannot withstand the erosion of time. With due respect for Still's admonition, the contributors to this collection share the conviction that the thread of memory is far stronger than Still has allowed. By bringing together a broad sample of research on historical memory in the American South, they hope to demonstrate both the vitality of memory and the value of scholarly attention to the interplay of memory and history.

The authors also hope that this collection will be a constructive addition to present-day discussions of the southern past. By demonstrating that histor-ical memories are crafted intentionally by people for specific reasons, and by exploring how and why collective memories have been crafted, these essays may contribute to a new awareness of the nature and influence of southern public memory. To the extent that the collection offers new insights and contributes to a greater understanding of how southerners have developed their sense of the past and how it has affected their present and may shape their future, the essayists will have made a contribution to the renewal and perhaps redemption of southern historical memory.

With essays that range in time from the early nineteenth century to the present day and in places from Texas to Virginia, this volume attempts to explore a diverse range of representations of the southern past. This collec-tion, which includes two recently published essays along with work pub-lished here for the first time, joins the growing number of studies of collective memory that help us to refine, deepen, correct, and if necessary replace vitally important ideas about southern history, conflicts over control over history, and the nature of historical memory in all societies.

Most of the essays are devoted to the postbellum era, in large part because it was then that historical memory came to play an especially conspicuous part in defining regional and ethnic identities in the South. Four essays draw our attention to how groups before and during the Civil War looked to the past to inform their sense of community and future purpose. Although the focus is on the American South, we also speak to the expression and the so-cial and political uses of collective memory that have parallels in societies throughout the world. By tracing the complex relationship between personal and collective memory, these essays offer insights into the relationship be-tween individual and group identity that have relevance far beyond the Amer-ican South.

The essays in this volume do not exhaust the subject. Many aspects of historical memory in the American South remain to be investigated. Too little is known about the role of institutions in buttressing social memory in the South. For instance, what role did formal education and schools in the South play in the propagation of collective memory across the centuries? We need to know much more about the curriculum and pedagogy that touched on the past. Similarly, only scattered scholarship on the Confederate tradition and various denominations addresses the role of southern churches in shaping and disseminating social memories. Almost certainly the rise and evolution of religious organizations committed to, for example, millennial Evangelicalism, Pentecostalism, or Fundamentalism have had broad implications for how southerners of all faiths and ethnicities have interpreted the past. And in our deracinated age it is perhaps difficult to recall the earlier influence of fraternal societies. While scholars continue to explore the organization and impact of women's associations, fraternal societies still remain beyond the historians' gaze. This scholarly oversight is especially egregious with regards to African American fraternal societies, which were focal points of black community organizing throughout the nineteenth and twentieth centuries. Finally, historians of Europe, Great Britain, and elsewhere have revealed the important function of museums, archives, and other institutional repositories of memory in forging a collective understanding of the past. To date, no comparable (let alone cursory) histories of museums in the South exist.

The recovery of previously suppressed versions of the past is yet another rich vein for future work. This collection bears the mark of Philippe Ariès's insight that the study of memory can challenge the conventions of history writing by providing access to facets of the past long since obscured by the dominant versions of history. To date, the recovery of the countermemories of marginalized groups in the South has only just begun. Contributor John Howard and others have taken the first steps in reconstructing the historical memory of gay/lesbian identity in the South, but a plethora of questions about sexual identity in the region await their muse. While southern queer (especially lesbian) literary history is undergoing a renaissance, the social history of gay and lesbian southerners remains in its infancy.[51] Much also remains unclear about the role of historical memory in the maintenance of class structures and the reactions of different groups of southerners to representations of their region's past. How has the fusion of work, status, gender, and ethnic identity informed the historical memory of different communities of southerners? What content and form have the collective memories of union members in the South taken? Have these memories evolved substantially over time along with the fortunes of the union movement in the region?[52] And how have the Mexican Americans in Texas, Italian Americans in Louisiana, and German Americans in the Valley of Virginia, to take just a few examples, each imagined themselves as groups with a shared past? As long as these countermemories remain only poorly understood, discussions of collective memory in the South will continue to be shaped by the enduring force of the past propagated by elite white southerners.

A full understanding of the diverse memories of the South will require a sophisticated grasp of the interrelationship of the different memories. The recalled past of all societies is inherently relational; no group fashions its memory without reference to others. In the South, for instance, African

American memory emerged from an ongoing process of fusion and adaptation, as well as contestation of white memory. A similarly complex but still largely uncharted process of synthesis and repudiation has shaped the recollected past of Native Americans in the South, culminating in a historical memory that is at once distinctive from but not autonomous of white memory. Another illustration of mnemonic adaptation that merits careful study is the curious reconciliation of upcountry southern whites to the symbols of the Confederacy. How can we explain the conspicuous popularity of Confederate symbols in a region that was noted for widespread Unionist sentiment during the Civil War and that subsequently resisted the memorialization of the Confederacy during the apogee of the "Lost Cause" movement? Answers to these and similar questions will clarify the symbiotic relationships that often exist between the remembered past of dominant groups and the countermemories of the marginalized.

The study of collective memory has blossomed in recent years, leading at least one scholar to propose that collective memory can serve as "a general category of knowledge."[53] The contributors to this volume assign a more humble import to collective memory; there are important historical questions that almost certainly cannot be resolved through the study of social memory. But, at the same time, we contend that many pressing concerns about personal and regional identity, about social interaction, and about the exercise of cultural authority and power in the American South depend on an understanding of how the recalled past has been woven into southern life. This claim, on the face of it, may appear altogether prosaic. After all, have not William Faulkner and C. Vann Woodward emphasized the power that the past exerts on the present-day South? But to date we have explored, and haphazardly at that, only a small fraction of the remembered past below the Mason-Dixon line. Rather than treating social memory as a periodically salient element of history—say, as a symptom of dislocation or anxiety—historians should treat memory as a central and enduring feature of the human condition. We present this collection in the hope that it brings together useful and thought-provoking work that will reveal the scope of research done so far and, above all, will stimulate further efforts to understand the uniquely human impulse to remember.

NOTES

1. William P. Trent, "Notes on the Outlook for Historical Studies in the South," *Papers of the American Historical Association* 4 (October 1890): 384.

2. E. Merton Coulter, "What the South Has Done about Its History," in George B. Tindall, ed., *The Pursuit of Southern History: Presidential Addresses of the Southern Historical Association, 1935–1963* (Baton Rouge: Louisiana State University Press, 1964), 3.

3. V. S. Naipaul, *A Turn in the South* (New York: Knopf, 1989).

4. Allen Tate, *Collected Poems, 1919–1976* (New York: Farrar Straus Giroux, 1977), 20.

5. "The Narrative Construction of Reality: An Interview with Stuart Hall," *Southern Review* 17 (March 1984): 15.

6. Vladimir Nabokov, *Strong Opinions* (New York: McGraw-Hill, 1973), chap. 195; Guillaume Apollinaire, "Cors de Chasse," in *Apollinaire: Selected Poems*, trans. Oliver Bernard (London: Anvil Press Poetry, 1986), 102.

7. Richard Condon, *A Talent for Loving* (New York: McGraw-Hill, 1961), 142. The terms "historical," "social," "public," and "collective" memory elude precise definition. Whereas some scholars have expressed concerns about their expansive and vague meaning, I believe that all four terms can apply to any organized, explicitly public representation of the past. See N. Gedi and Y. Elam, "Collective Memory—What Is It?" *History and Memory* 8 (1996): 30–50; Jeffrey K. Olick and Joyce Robbins, "Social Memory Studies: From 'Collective Memory' to the Historical Sociology of Mnemonic Practices," *Annual Review of Sociology* 24 (1998): 105–40; and Barbie Zelizer, "Reading against the Grain: The Shape of Memory Studies," *Critical Studies in Mass Communications* 12 (June 1995): 234–35.

8. For valuable discussions of Halbwachs's work, see Jan Assman, "Collective Memory and Cultural Identity," *New German Critique* 65 (Spring–Summer 1995): 125–33; Patrick H. Hutton, "Collective Memory and Collective Mentalities: The Halbwachs-Ariès Connection," *Historical Reflections* 15 (1988): 311–22; and Zelizer, "Reading against the Grain," 215–17. For a concise introduction to "memory studies," see Olick and Robbins, "Social Memory Studies."

9. James Fentress and Chris Wickham, *Social Memory* (London: Blackwell, 1992), 3. Assman asserts that collective memory "comprises that body of reusable texts, images, and rituals specific to each society in each epoch, whose cultivation serves to stabilize and convey that society's self-image. Upon such collective knowledge, for the most part (but not exclusively) of the past, each group bases its awareness of unity and particularity." Assman, "Collective Memory and Cultural Identity," 130, 133.

10. Roland Barthes, *Mythologies* (New York: Hill and Wang, 1972), 143.

11. James H. Dorman, *The People Called Cajuns: An Introduction to an Ethnohistory* (Lafayette: Center for Louisiana Studies, 1983); Dudley Joseph LeBlanc, *The True Story of the Acadians* (Lafayette: Privately published, 1932); Robert Lewis, "L'Acadie Retrouvée: The Re-making of Cajun Identity in Southwestern Louisiana, 1968–1994," in Richard H. King and Helen Taylor, eds., *Dixie Debates: Perspectives on Southern Cultures* (New York: New York University Press, 1996), 67–84.

12. Frederick C. Bartlett, *Remembering: A Study of Experimental and Social Psychology* (Cambridge: Cambridge University Press, 1964), 205.

13. Louis O. Mink, "Narrative Form as a Cognitive Instrument," in Henry Kozicki and Robert H. Canary, eds., *The Writing of History: Literary Form and Historical Understanding* (Madison: University of Wisconsin Press, 1978), 131.

14. Marshall Sahlins, *Islands of History* (Chicago: University of Chicago Press, 1985), xiv; "Narrative Construction of Reality."

15. Pinter quoted in David Lowenthal, *The Past Is a Foreign Country* (New York:

Cambridge University Press, 1985, 1990), 193 (page citation is to the reprint edition). Similarly, William Ralph Inge observed: "What we know of the past is mostly not worth knowing. What is worth knowing is mostly uncertain. Events in the past may roughly be divided into those which probably never happened and those which do not matter." Inge, "Prognostications," in *Assessments and Anticipations* (London: Cassell and Co., 1929), 104–5.

16. On narratives and objectivity, see Jacques Rancière, *The Names of History: On the Poetics of Knowledge*, trans. Hassan Melehy (Minneapolis: University of Minnesota Press, 1994), 13–16.

17. Frederick C. Corney, "Writing October: History, Memory, Identity, and the Construction of the Bolshevik Revolution, 1917–1927" (Ph.D. diss., Columbia University, 1997), 7.

18. In a discussion of the uses of tradition, Jack Zipes explains that his aim is not to expose the manipulation or invention of tradition by the powerful, but rather the way tradition enables "people to sustain their life-worlds and give their endeavors some sense of meaning. In other words, how have people been using their traditions . . . to make sense of their existence." Zipes, "The Utopian Function of Tradition," *Telos* 94 (Winter 1993–94): 27.

19. Sheryl Kroen, *Letting Tartuffe Be Our Guide: Practicing Politics in an Age of Counterrevolution, France, 1815–1830* (Berkeley: University of California Press, 2000).

20. Tony Judt, "The Past Is Another Country: Myth and Memory in Postwar Europe," *Daedalus* 121 (1992): 83–118; Guenter Bischof and Anto Pelinka, eds. *Austrian Historical Memory and National Identity* (New Brunswick, N.J.: Transaction Publishers, 1997); Nachman Ben-Yehuda, *The Masada Myth: Collective Memory and Myth-Making in Israel* (Madison: University of Wisconsin Press, 1995). The campaign of public authorities in Mexico to forget the bloody repression of student protests in 1968 is discussed in Sergio Auayo Quezada, *1968: Los Archivos de Violencia* (Mexico City: Grijalbo/Reforma, 1998).

21. Catherine Clinton, *Tara Revisited: Women, War, and the Plantation Legend* (New York: Abbeville Press, 1995), 191–204; Elizabeth Grace Hale, *Making Whiteness: The Culture of Segregation in the South, 1890–1940* (New York: Pantheon, 1998); Jessie W. Parkhurst, "The Role of the Black Mammy in the Plantation Household," *Journal of Negro History* 23 (July 1938): 349–50; Kirk Savage, *Standing Soldiers, Kneeling Slaves: Race, War, and Monument in Nineteenth-Century America* (Princeton: Princeton University Press, 1997), 155–61; Cheryl Thurber, "The Development of the Mammy Image and Mythology," in Virginia Bernhard, Betty Brandon, Elizabeth Fox-Genovese, and Theda Purdue, eds., *Southern Women: Histories and Identities* (Columbia: University of Missouri Press, 1992), 87–108; Micki McElya, "Monumental Citizenship: Reading the Mammy Commemoration Controversy of the Early Twentieth Century" (Ph.D. diss., New York University, forthcoming).

22. Michel-Rolph Trouillot, *Silencing the Past: Power and the Production of History* (Boston: Beacon Press, 1995), esp. chap. 1.

23. On how "scientific history" distinguishes itself from "other" forms of discourse, see Rancière, *Names of History*, 38–39, 89–90. For assessments of academic history at southern institutions across the twentieth century, see Joseph J. Mathews, "The Study of History in the South," *Journal of Southern History* 31 (February 1965): 4; William K. Boyd, "Southern History in American Universities," *South Atlantic Quarterly* 1 (July 1902): 238; Stephen B. Weeks, "On the Promotion of Historical Studies in the South,"

Publications of the Southern History Association 1 (January 1897): 24–25; and Frederick W. Moore, "The Teaching of History in the South," *Vanderbilt University Quarterly* 3 (January 1903): 9.

24. Pierre Nora explains that memory "relies on the materiality of the trace, the immediacy of the recording, the visibility of the image." Nora, "Between Memory and History: Les Lieux de Memoire," *Representations* 26 (Spring 1989): 13. See also Nathan Wachtel, "Memory and History: Introduction," *History and Anthropology* 12 (October 1986): 212, and L. S. Vygotsky, *Mind in Society: The Development of Higher Psychological Processes* (Cambridge: Harvard University Press, 1978), 51.

25. Nannie M. Tilley, *The Trinity College Historical Society, 1892–1941* (Durham: Duke University Press, 1941), 27; Dallas T. Herndon, *The Arkansas History Commission Catalogue* (N.p., 1923), 7, 8; *Trinity Archive* (January 1898): 177–87. Apparently, the precise historical significance of the "Cornwallis" tree branch was not clear. Elsewhere, the tree branch was identified as part of a tree to which Cornwallis tied his horse. On the materials of history and fetishism, see Bonnie G. Smith, "Gender and Practices of Scientific History: The Seminar and Archival Research in the Nineteenth Century," *American Historical Review* 100 (October 1995): 1170–71.

26. Public ceremonies, according to Emile Durkheim, enable a group or society to "renew the sentiment which it has of itself and its unity." Emile Durkheim, *The Elementary Forms of the Religious Life* (New York: Free Press, 1965), 420.

27. David Middleton and Derek Edwards, introduction to Middleton and Edwards, eds., *Collective Remembering* (Newberry Park, Calif.: Sage Publications, 1990), 8. On Confederate veterans and their rituals, see Gaines Foster, *Ghosts of the Confederacy: Defeat, the Lost Cause, and the Emergence of the New South, 1865 to 1913* (New York: Oxford University Press, 1987), 127–44.

28. Paul Connerton, *How Societies Remember* (Cambridge: Cambridge University Press, 1989), chap. 2. On the "generic" quality of early American nationalist rituals, see David Waldstreicher, *In the Midst of Perpetual Fetes: The Making of American Nationalism, 1776–1820* (Chapel Hill: University of North Carolina Press, 1997), 35.

29. Eudora Welty, *One Writer's Beginnings* (Cambridge: Harvard University Press, 1984), 104.

30. Jacques LeGoff, *History and Memory*, trans. Steven Rendall and Elizabeth Claman (New York: Columbia University Press, 1992), 54.

31. Michel Foucault, *Language, Counter-Memory, Practice: Selected Essays and Interviews*, ed. Donald F. Bouchard (Ithaca: Cornell University Press, 1993), 150.

32. David W. Blight, "W. E. B. Du Bois and the Struggle for American Historical Memory," in Geneviève Fabre and Robert O'Meally, eds., *History and Memory in African-American Culture* (New York: Oxford University Press, 1994), 68 n. 16.

33. The best discussion of the fusion of racial and historical identity in public life in the postbellum South is Glenda Elizabeth Gilmore, *Gender and Jim Crow: Women and the Politics of White Supremacy in North Carolina, 1896–1920* (Chapel Hill: University of North Carolina Press, 1996), esp. 31–118.

34. One illustration of white repression of black traditions is the nineteenth-century suppression of the John Canoe festival in the Carolinas. See Elizabeth A. Fenn, " 'A Perfect Equality Seemed to Reign': Slave Society and Jonkonnu," *North Carolina Historical Review* 65 (April 1988): 127–53, and Raymond Gavins, "North Carolina Black Folklore and Song in the Age of Segregation: Toward Another Meaning of Survival," *North*

Carolina Historical Review 66 (October 1989): 417–18. On expressions of resistance, see James C. Scott, *Domination and the Arts of Resistance: Hidden Transcripts* (New Haven: Yale University Press, 1990), esp. chaps. 4–5. Scott clarifies the public roles of the powerful and the powerless and the forms that contests between them can take. His conclusions about the role of protective social spaces as breeding grounds for dissent has important implications for the study of historical memory, especially African American memory in the South.

35. Michel de Certeau, *Heterologies: Discourse on the Other*, trans. Brian Massumi (Minneapolis: University of Minnesota Press, 1986), 203.

36. See Savage, *Standing Soldiers, Kneeling Slaves.*

37. Jacquelyn Dowd Hall, "'You Must Remember This': Autobiography as Social Critique," *Journal of American History* 85 (September 1998): 439–53.

38. See the histories of the various women's historical organizations: Peggy Anderson, *The Daughters: An Unconventional Look at America's Fan Club* (New York: St. Martin's Press, 1974); Karen L. Cox, "Women, the Lost Cause, and the New South: The United Daughters of the Confederacy and the Transmission of Confederate Culture, 1894–1919" (Ph.D. diss., University of Southern Mississippi, 1997); Wallace Evan Davies, *Patriotism on Parade: The Story of Veterans' and Hereditary Organizations in America, 1783–1900* (Cambridge: Harvard University Press, 1955); Margaret Gibbs, *The DAR* (Holt, Rinehart, and Winston, 1969); Mrs. Joseph Rucker Lamar, *A History of the National Society of the Colonial Dames of America* (Atlanta: National Society of the Colonial Dames of America, 1934); Lucile E. Laganke, "The National Society of the Daughters of the American Revolution: Its History, Politics, and Influence, 1890–1949" (Ph.D. diss., Western Reserve University, 1951); Stuart McConnell, "Reading the Flag: A Reconsideration of the Patriotic Cults of the 1890s," in John Bodnar, ed., *Bonds of Affection: Americans Define Their Patriotism* (Princeton: Princeton University Press, 1996); and Francesca Morgan, "Home and Country: Women, Nation, and the Daughters of the American Revolution, 1890–1939" (Ph.D diss., Columbia University, 1998), esp. 151–218.

39. See W. Fitzhugh Brundage, "White Women and the Politics of Historical Memory in the New South, 1880–1920," in Glenda E. Gilmore, Jane Dailey, and Bryant Simon, eds., *Race and Politics in the New South* (Princeton: Princeton University Press, forthcoming).

40. Bruce Palmer, *"Man over Money": The Southern Populist Critique of American Capitalism* (Chapel Hill: University of North Carolina Press, 1980), esp. conclusion; Dolores Janiewski, "Southern Honor, Southern Dishonor: Managerial Ideology and the Construction of Gender, Race, and Class Relations in Southern Industry," in Ava Baron, ed., *Work Engendered: Toward a New History of Men, Women, and Work* (Ithaca: Cornell University Press, 1991), 70–91; Robert H. Zieger, "From Primordial Folk to Redundant Workers: Southern Textile Workers and Social Observers, 1920–1990," in Robert H. Zieger, ed., *Southern Labor in Transition, 1940–1995* (Knoxville: University of Tennessee Press, 1997), 273–94.

41. For a cogent survey of African American representations of the past, see Faith Davis Ruffins, "Mythos, Memory, and History: African American Preservation Efforts, 1820–1990," in Ivan Karp, Christine Mullen Kreamer, and Steven D. Lavine, eds., *Museums and Communities: The Politics of Public Culture* (Washington, D.C.: Smithsonian Institution Press, 1992), 506–611.

42. Edward L. Ayers, "What We Talk about When We Talk about the South," in Edward L. Ayers, Patricia Nelson Limesick, Stephen Nissenbaum, and Peter S. Onuf,

eds., *All over the Map: Rethinking American Regions* (Baltimore: Johns Hopkins University Press, 1996), 62–81; James C. Cobb, "Community and Identity: Redefining Southern Culture," *Georgia Review* 50 (Summer 1996): 24.

43. *Raleigh News and Observer*, 28 April 1996, 18A.

44. Holly Beachley Brear, *Inherit the Alamo: Myth and Ritual at an American Shrine* (Austin: University of Texas Press, 1995).

45. *Raleigh News and Observer*, 28 April 1996, 18A.

46. See James Clifford, *Routes: Travel and Translation in the Late Twentieth Century* (Cambridge: Harvard University Press, 1997), and Richard Handler and Eric Gable, *The New History in an Old Museum: Creating the Past at Colonial Williamsburg* (Durham: Duke University Press, 1997).

47. On the reinterpretation of Somerset Place and other sites, see Jeffrey J. Crow, "Interpreting Slavery in the Classroom and at Historic Sites," *Perspectives* 36 (March 1998): 23–26, and Dorothy Spruill Redford, *Somerset Homecoming: Recovering a Lost Heritage* (New York: Doubleday, 1988).

48. On memory as an essential component of community, see Robert N. Bellah, William M. Sullivan, and Steven M. Tipton, eds., *Habits of the Heart: Individualism and Commitment in American Life* (Berkeley: University of California Press, 1985), 185.

49. Mary P. Ryan, *Civic Wars: Democracy and Public Life in the American City in the Nineteenth Century* (Berkeley: University of California Press, 1997), esp. epilogue.

50. John Still, *The Jungle Tide* (London: W. Blackwood and Sons, 1930), 117.

51. John Howard, ed., *Carryin' On in the Lesbian and Gay South* (New York: New York University Press, 1997). Howard's *Men Like That: A Rural Queer History* (Chicago: University of Chicago Press, 2000) undoubtedly will establish the standard for the field.

52. For a model study of working-class memory, see John Bodnar, "Power and Memory in Oral History: Workers and Managers at Studebaker," *Journal of American History* 75 (March 1989): 1201–21.

53. Barry Schwartz, "The Reconstruction of Abraham Lincoln," in David Middleton and Derek Edwards, eds., *Collective Remembering* (Beverly Hills, Calif.: Sage Publications, 1990), 81.

part one

Varieties of Memory
in the Old South

Although any chronological starting point in a discussion of historical memory in the American South is to some extent arbitrary, the post–Revolutionary South is a defensible beginning. The American Revolution self-evidently was a defining moment in American history; out of it emerged both the enduring institutions that have given shape to American life and the historical narratives that have informed Americans' sense of themselves as a distinct people. The Revolution was the touchstone for much of the nation's public life until at least the Civil War. It also elevated awareness of regional distinctions and prompted curiosity about the historical origins of those distinctions. This interest found expression in history writing and the founding of antiquarian societies and museums across the South. Curiosity about the past, of course, was not limited to such elite activities. Indeed, the two essays in this section underscore that all southerners, black and white, had a stake in coming to terms with the Revolutionary past.

The focus of Michele Gillespie's essay is on historical memory and class identity in Georgia during the early republic. Until recently, historians interested in class typically defined it in terms of such purportedly objective measures as income or job classification. Now many scholars insist that class, like gender and race, is a contingent and subjective category. As an act of social imagination, class identity comes into being when individuals perceive that they share distinct economic concerns or status aspirations. Collective memories often provide essential components of such anxieties and hopes. In

early nineteenth-century France, for example, tradesmen had an acute sense
of their status, which was bound up in their notions of the historical privileges and rights of their predecessors. When workers in Lyon or Paris
imagined themselves as united by grievances or aspirations, they did so not
only because they shared similar relationships to the means of production but
also because they shared a similar understanding of how history had shaped
their opportunities. These notions about class identity often become woven
into narratives about historically significant events.[1]

Understandings of the past, Gillespie stresses, informed the class identities
of white southerners in the early republic. She reconstructs the struggles of
Georgia artisans to assert political rights and to claim status by "remembering" their contributions to the founding of the American republic. By invoking their role in the American Revolution in print and in public ceremonies,
artisans staked their claim to a place in what Mary Ryan has described as the
young nation's "heterogeneous but associated democracy." The civic rituals
of the early nineteenth century promoted a vision of society composed of
"people in association," not isolated individuals or undifferentiated masses.[2]
Thus, when artisans claimed a place in public life, they did so collectively.
The remembered past provided them with a precedent for collective political
mobilization at a time when they were otherwise a disparate group. At least in
the short term, the artisans successfully staked their claim to a place in the
public realm. But as Gillespie explains, their unity waned as their identification with the American Revolution and artisanal traditions subsided in the
early nineteenth century. More than just an important contribution to southern labor history, Gillespie's essay also is a model study of how the conjunc-
tion of class identity and historical memory can have important and tangible
social and political consequences.

The implications of the American Revolution also are at the center of
Gregg Kimball's essay on black Virginians in the early republic. Recently, historians have revealed the diverse ways that southern blacks preserved a sense
of their African heritage and identity. Scholars also have traced how African
Americans asserted their claim to the rights secured by the Revolution. By
deftly tapping scant and scattered sources, Kimball reveals the complex interplay between these various impulses. According to Kimball, blacks in Virginia
felt the tug of their identities as Africans, Americans, and Virginians. Poised
between two worlds, black Virginians simultaneously sought the rights and
privileges enjoyed by whites while continuing to identify with African American cultural traditions. Many blacks, he insists, explicitly asserted their African identity even while they also claimed, to the extent that they could in a

slave society, the natural rights that they believed they had helped secure in the American Revolution. What emerges from Kimball's subtle account is a complex and contradictory African American memory in which understandings of the past urged on blacks' common pursuit of freedom and dignity but in different directions. For some, the memory of Africa led them to Liberia. For more, memory and hope drew them to Canada. And for others, Kimball explains, memory led to a complex affiliation with white patrons. We are mistaken if we presume that blacks' historical memory made easier the decisions of African Americans who confronted often painful choices and limited options. But for a people caught in the thralldom of American slavery, historical memory helped them to understand their circumstances and to imagine what had preceded and what might follow their captivity.

NOTES

1. William H. Sewell, *Work and Revolution in France: The Language of Labor from the Old Regime to 1848* (Cambridge: Cambridge University Press, 1980). The role of the "working class" in the Russian Revolution is a case in point of the weaving together of class identity and memory. Only through the act of interpretation did the Russian Revolution become a "workers' revolution." For the Bolsheviks and their sympathizers, the legitimacy of the revolution rested on explaining the event as the will of the working class. Thus, the Soviet government labored diligently to weave notions of class and workers into the revolutionary narrative. In response, many participants in the confusing events of the revolution came to interpret their memories in a manner consistent with the *Bolshevik* narrative. In this process, understandings of the event, of class identity, and of collective memory became almost inseparable. Participation in the revolution attested to one's proletarian credentials, which, in turn, established the working-class origins of the event itself. Frederick Corney, "Writing October: History, Memory, Identity, and the Construction of the Bolshevik Revolution, 1917–1927" (Ph.D. diss., Columbia University, 1997), esp. chap. 6; Stephen Kotkin, "One Hand Clapping: Russian Workers and 1917," *Labor History* 32 (Fall 1991): 618–19.

2. On mid-nineteenth-century street parades as "performances of people in association," see Mary P. Ryan, *Civic Wars: Democracy and Public Life in the American City in the Nineteenth Century* (Berkeley: University of California Press, 1997), 58–93.

Memory and the Making
of a Southern Citizenry

Georgia Artisans in the Early Republic

Michele Gillespie

White artisans in the slaveholding towns of Savannah and Augusta proudly boasted that tradesmen and mechanics like themselves, from carpenters and tailors to silversmiths and carriage makers, had helped secure Americans' independence from England and shaped the political contours of the new republic. This "remembering" of past deeds, which took place at mechanics' meetings, celebrations, and parades throughout the 1790s, served a critical function for free white men who worked with their hands in a slave society that revolved around unfree labor and the authority of a planter elite. Georgia artisans pressed their communities to recall artisans' pivotal role in the patriots' struggle and then used that memory to establish a unique identity for themselves as artisan-citizens in a slaveholders' world. Promoting the historical memory of the American Revolution allowed artisans in Georgia not only to lay claim to the past but also to reshape the present.[1]

How Georgia artisans used memory is interesting in and of itself, especially since artisans generally have been ignored in the history of the South, but their actions at the close of the eighteenth century were not unique. Their construction of a class consciousness and a community identity based on the past was part of a larger movement among American artisans in the 1790s. What does make these Georgia artisans unique was their willingness, unlike most artisans elsewhere in the nation, to part with this identity by the 1820s. This break from broader national developments among workers was significant. Understanding why artisans in Georgia separated from the national norm helps explain not only what made southern social relations distinct at the beginning of the antebellum era but also why the South in subsequent decades could build such a powerful regional identity in the face of mounting political challenges from the North. In this sense, memory became a critical tool among artisans in particular and southerners in general as competing groups and regions clashed over the definition of "the nation" in the early republic. These clashes would culminate in civil war a half century later.[2]

It is not surprising that many artisans in Georgia during the 1790s shared the same set of beliefs as their brethren to the north. Most artisans in Savannah, a key distribution center in the Atlantic economy for rice, hides, lumber, tobacco, and cotton, and in Augusta, a busy trade center for upcountry tobacco and cotton, were not native Georgians. They hailed from cities, towns, and villages on both sides of the Atlantic. On completing their apprenticeships elsewhere, they went to Georgia to seek their fortune, often with little more than the tools of their trade. Although some artisans simply sought steady work as journeymen, the majority hoped in time to own their own shops and call themselves master craftsmen. Some hoped for even more. Short-term events like the Savannah fire of 1796, which created a desperate need for carpenters and other artisans in the building trades, and long-term developments, especially the spread of short-staple cotton in the upcountry, that generated a rising demand for artisan goods and services, made such ambitions, which included landholding and slaveholding, tenable between 1790 and 1820.[3]

Despite widening opportunities for social mobility in the slaveholding South, migrant artisans understood that to ensure their inclusion in this world, they needed to convince fellow white southerners of their social and political worth. Although Georgians had been sympathetic to white artisans' unique circumstances as skilled free laborers in a slave labor economy, going so far as to eliminate property-holding qualifications for mechanic voters in the state constitution of 1777, artisans in Georgia, unlike artisans in many other colonies, had no sustained political organization or identity during the Revolutionary era.[4] In the 1790s, however, they crafted a strong political voice for themselves by invoking a collective memory about the important role of artisan patriots in the American Revolution. Ironically, these same men came to discard this newly established identity despite its important links to a glorious past and the moral authority it gave them in the present. Their artisan consciousness, reinforced in their mechanic organizations and activities during the 1790s, had put artisan leaders into public office. During the first decades of the nineteenth century, expanding economic opportunities along with their newly won political power allowed them to leap into the ranks of the planter class. As landholders and slaveholders, they quickly cast aside their identity as artisan patriots in the process.

Prior to this transformation, Georgia artisans had embraced the same political ideology as their skilled brothers in more northern urban settings like New York, Philadelphia, Boston, and Baltimore. This shared artisan republicanism gave political and social meaning to post–Revolutionary artisan experience and helped earn them respect as artisan-citizens.[5] Like most Americans in the wake of the Revolution, mechanics believed that republican thought rested on a set of political conceptions considered vital to the welfare of the new republic. Citizens must participate in politics, work to preserve the commonwealth, subordinate private ends on behalf of the public good, and establish their independence from the political desires of others. But artisans more than any other social class in the early republic pushed these key republican beliefs further by criticizing increasingly inegalitarian social relations brought on by the market revolution. Artisan republicanism in the late eighteenth century used the memory of the American Revolution and the republican ideals it spawned to champion artisans' right to equal representation and the dignity of labor.[6] They would continue to borrow from this Revolutionary tradition through the Jacksonian era, evident in the Boston workingmen's embrace of shoemaker George Robert Twelves Hewes, for example, whose well-known experiences in the American Revolution inspired artisans' and workingmen's visions of a more truly democratic society in the 1830s.[7]

Artisans in Augusta and Savannah, like artisans elsewhere in the United States, employed this artisan republicanism to build a political voice for themselves in the new republic. Mechanics in seaboard cities up and down the Atlantic coast had begun to recognize their shared interests as a class when they mobilized against Great Britain following the Stamp Act of 1765. Commitment to nonimportation of British goods in 1769 further strengthened their collective identity. As key participants in protests against British imperial power and as a critical force in the Sons of Liberty, they quickly assumed leadership positions in the patriots' movement. In the wake of the war, mechanics acquired significant political weight. Not only had their important actions actually helped to ensure the patriots' success, they also came to symbolize the new nation's recognition of all its citizens, not just the prosperous and powerful.

Despite the political identity and social memory artisans had constructed for themselves during the Revolutionary era, artisans throughout the new republic and certainly in Georgia were a disparate group of men who failed to coalesce neatly into one social class for any length of time. Artisan class identity was constantly challenged by ethnic, religious, and political identities, as well as critical economic considerations. The difference between a master craftsman and a merchant could at times be indiscernible, whereas the difference between a master craftsman and the men who labored for him as journeymen, apprentices, and, in some cases, slaves could be enormous. Nowhere was this more true than in the slaveholding South. Crafting a class consciousness was no easy task here.

Relying on the historical memory of the American Revolution, artisans in Georgia nonetheless built a collective identity for themselves in the 1790s. They used it both to critique leading members of their community and to secure their inclusion in that community as political actors. This identity reminded Georgians of the critical roles artisans had played in the American Revolution—as members of the Sons of Liberty, as signers of petitions and authors of lists of grievances against the king, as willing participants in nonimportation, as printers of broadsides and pamphlets, and as soldiers. Georgia artisans then used their reputation as artisan-patriots to establish their own mechanics' organizations and to participate as a class in local politics and festivities. The public celebrations of their societies that ensued, as well as their participation in parades and other forms of street theater, were important political acts.[8]

Ultimately, these men appropriated the language and ideology of the American Revolution, applied it in the public arena through their participation in public rituals, and shaped it to their contemporary world to make a place for themselves in this new slaveholders' republic.[9] They were not alone in their efforts, although their circumstances increasingly differed in important ways from those of northern artisans. As in mechanics' societies, benevolent organizations, and fraternal orders around the country, Georgia artisans celebrated their investment in the new American nationalism of the early republic and broadcast their political principles through a wide array of public acts. They used public space and national celebrations to confront, challenge, and redefine who had power in the political sphere.[10]

In 1790 the town of Augusta held a special election intended to challenge a corrupt city council composed of British merchants and their allies. A tailor named Edward Shoemaker was elected to the vacant seat and mechanics and other residents celebrated this victory by bearing Shoemaker on a makeshift throne through the town. During this parade they stopped to hurl insults at each of the incumbent councilmen's doors.[11] Shoemaker's election marked an important victory to those residents, including mechanics, who believed that the previously elected British merchants had entertained little respect for the ideals of the Revolution. "The privileges of a free people have been violated, arrogance encountenanced, and the public good sacrificed for private interest," proclaimed an editorialist in the *Augusta Chronicle and Gazette of the State*.[12] To these children of the American War of Independence, the state's unwillingness to protect the citizens' interests against those of the British merchants was damning. "Ill-fated Americans! Are these the effects of your memorable struggle to liberty?" demanded "An Examiner." "To what purpose is it that your exertions, added to the will of Providence, have left you in a state of freedom and independence, if you are still to be controlled by the adherents of that government which exerted its utmost strength to bind you and your children in lasting slavery?"[13] This invocation of Revolutionary principles should not be surprising. People generally embrace a specific past and the values it seems to represent—in this case, fair elections and a virtuous citizenry—when that past seems most at risk.[14]

The mechanics of Augusta were particularly sensitive to this risk. After this special election and amid clarion calls to protect the principles of the American Revolution, they built an artisan community with its own leadership and following. This community took formal shape a little over a year later when fifteen artisans (six of whom had signed a petition to the governor protesting the corrupt city council) organized the Mechanics Society of Augusta (MSA).[15] For the next thirteen years, virtually all of these men served as the elected leadership of the MSA, which held quarterly meetings, elected officers, hosted dinners, marched in public festivals, and routinely celebrated their society's anniversary, St. Tammany's anniversary, and the Fourth of July. By 1800 they had even financed and erected their own Mechanic Hall.[16] These men were using their public rituals and festivities to equate themselves with

the American republican tradition. In this way they forced the political community to recognize them as citizens.[17]

Members drank celebratory toasts at called meetings in honor of "the
[mechanic] arts" and "mechanism and the sciences," proclamations that
underlined their independence and their class identity.[18] At the same time,
such toasts at public gatherings enabled artisans to cement their allegiance
not only to each other but also to the new nation.[19] Although not all mechanics owned land, slaves, capital, or stock-in-trade, all owned their tools
and their skills, forms of property that, in the tradition of the American
Revolution, entitled all mechanics—including white journeymen who labored alongside slaves—to citizenship and respectability. Thus they were
laying claim to their republican birthright.[20] Referring to themselves as "the
Sons of Liberty" and "the Sons of America," these artisans sought to establish their right to participate in the political sphere as independent, virtuous
men and gain recognition as the true heirs of the American Revolution. They
pledged at their meetings and in their toasts to support struggles for political equality and to challenge local and state political actions they deemed
corrupt.[21]

At every MSA gathering, members honored the president of the United
States, Congress, the governor, and Georgia. They also celebrated the men
who fought and fell "in defense of American freedom" during the American
Revolution. As war veterans and as militiamen themselves, the mechanics actively sought to preserve the independence and liberty they had defended on
the battlefield and prepared to defend by practicing on the muster ground.[22]
Moreover, like the members of the democratic-republican societies that proliferated from 1793 to 1800 (which also were principally composed of artisans
who considered themselves the successors to the Sons of Liberty), the members of the MSA pledged to protect citizens' liberties from unjust and corrupt
leaders. "May the genuine principles of rectitude and philanthropy in future
govern all legislative, judicial, and executive bodies," they toasted at their
meetings.[23] One of the central concerns of the MSA, as expressed in the
republican pledges these artisans made to each other at their gatherings, was
the preservation of public morals: "May merit always prevail in every public
or private dispute. . . . May the *honest* hearts never want. . . . Disappointment
to those who would exchange the cause of their country for selfishness and
sordid gain."[24] That these toasts were subsequently published in the local
newspapers illustrates the degree to which these artisans understood that
their meetings and toasts represented an important challenge to the traditionally elite leadership of Augusta.

The members of the MSA also championed political equality. Their society embraced the French Revolution for its commitment to liberty and equality. Initially adopting a moderate stance, toasting both the king and the National Assembly at a meeting in 1791, the artisans moved to a more radical position by 1793, borrowing from the language of the American Revolution to proclaim, "May the hard fate of Louis the XVI be a lesson to kings, monarchs, and emperors."[25] In this sense, Augusta artisans wanted to connect the democratic and even radical events of the French Revolution to the more conservative American Revolution.

The principles advocated by the artisans frequently became the subject of moral and political debate in Augusta, which should not be a surprise since this was the artisans' intent. When the former general of the Revolutionary army and the first president of the republic, George Washington, borne across the state in his immaculate and ostentatious white coach-and-four, visited Augusta in the spring of 1791, state politicians concluded the president's three-day tour with a subscription ball.[26] The beloved president had spent much of 1789 and the current year touring the country not only to build a renewed sense of national pride but in effect to teach Americans how to sentimentalize their new nation and its origins. At the same time, his tours bore a striking resemblance to a royal procession. In city after city, town after town, including Augusta, Washington stepped from his coach a few miles from his destination, mounted his white horse with its gleaming saddle and royal blue saddle cloth, and, guided by local officials, greeted the crowds that had turned out alongside the road into town to see the noble republican for themselves. Washington then spent the evenings attending dinner parties and balls offered by the local elite.[27]

The dinner party and ball in Augusta were hosted by some of the wealthiest men in Georgia. Mechanics were expressly forbidden to attend. The decision to exclude Augusta mechanics, those "honest and industrious men" with "unspotted characters" according to one editorialist, became a cause célèbre for mechanics who, after all, had contributed mightily to the war that had transformed Washington into a hero. A flurry of letters to the editor of the *Augusta Chronicle* soon followed this event. Penned by artisans and their allies, the letters painted those Georgia elite in attendance at the ball as enemies of the people, more closely aligned to the pro-British, Federalist political faction in the city than the sturdy, honest republicans who had not been invited. Washington himself was championed as a kind of popular sovereign who would never have excluded the artisan class had it been his call. Thus artisans and their allies used the public ritual of Washington's visit to highlight and challenge the local elite's discriminatory notions of citizenship and nationhood.[28]

Politicians subsequently learned to capitalize on the idea of artisans as virtuous men rather than ignore and exclude them. Indeed, ambitious candidates soon were eager to court the votes of such a relatively large group of townsmen. Another exchange of letters in the *Augusta Chronicle* shows how competing candidates tried to claim for themselves the Revolutionary principles now ascribed to artisans to secure their votes. R. Dickenson, the inferior court clerk for Richmond County, running for a state assembly seat in 1793, accused his opponent, Philip Clayton, "You are giving Barbecues in the country for electioneering purposes, feasting the *honest* mechanicks in town, . . . and holding forth every specious allurement for favour and popularity." To which Clayton replied, "The mechanicks of this town are not like *yourself*; they stand on too *respectable* a footing for any man to offer them a *bribe*." Clayton, by championing mechanics as the most virtuous of all citizens, won the seat.[29]

MSA leader William Dearmond, a carpenter by trade as well as a small slaveholder, found himself relying on the respectability now accorded artisan-patriots when he was called before a military tribunal in 1798. Accused of neglectful duty, contemptuous and willful disobedience, and even mutiny after failing to process his troops as ordered during a parade, the captain of the Richmond Light Horse was forced to explain his conduct to his superiors.[30] Apparently, Dearmond had not received the orders to move his troops forward. His explanation for his failure to act had been terse at the time, and his superior officer had been displeased by his attitude. To defend himself at his trial, Dearmond cited his exemplary service to the nation as patriot, soldier, and artisan: "In closing my defense I can say that I feel neither hatred[,] malice [n]or revenge but at the same time I must say that my feelings had been much injured. These feelings you must yourselves possess and thus feeling you will receive me in a proper light[.] Having served my country faithfully both as a Soldier and a Mechanick in the worst of times and for many years I did hope that my character as both was irreproachable, nor do I know to the contrary." Dearmond alluded to the importance of the work of the American Revolution and the fragility of the new republic by concluding, "These are not the times to erect fudes [feuds] among citizens but to cultivate harmony. . . . [W]hich of these fall to my lot is for you to say." Although the outcome of the tribunal has not been preserved, Dearmond certainly believed that his fine mechanic's character, as well as his service to the nation as a soldier in the American Revolution, established the quality of his character and his obvious innocence.[31]

The mechanics' newly earned respectability helped them gain political office. Over half of the MSA leaders became involved in local politics between 1790 and 1810. Machinist and inventor William Longstreet was elected alderman in 1792, 1798, 1808, and 1809 and state legislator in 1794, as well as appointed justice of the peace.[32] Silversmith John Catlett was named justice of the peace in 1805 and chosen president of the Augusta Jockey Club (a position of great social prestige) in 1806. He was elected alderman and appointed mayor in 1808.[33] Carpenter Robert Cresswell sat on the city council in 1798 and 1806.[34] For many years shoemaker Francis Vallotton served as district poll manager. MSA charter member, Thomas Bray, was appointed clerk of the market. Carpenters William Dearmond and Baxter Pool and shoemaker Joseph Stiles, all MSA officers, were elected militia captains, a traditional route to political office. Isaac Wingate and Thomas Bray, both MSA charter members, sat on the board of the Richmond Academy.[35]

Savannah artisans followed a similar path, crafting an artisan class consciousness that was reinforced with their establishment of a mechanics society that helped propel its leaders into political office as well. Despite the obvious demographic and economic differences between the two urban centers, the strategies and ideologies of these two groups of artisans largely mirrored each other. Tax-paying mechanics, at least a third of the adult white male population in Savannah by 1798, also comprised an important block of votes.[36] Accordingly, planters, shopkeepers, *and* mechanics were all viewed "worthy of judgement as citizens," according to local officials.[37] At the same time, Savannah mechanics, like Augusta mechanics, were often viewed as political peacemakers able to surmount individual differences in the interest of republicanism, as the words to this "Mechanics Song," published in Savannah's *Georgia Gazette* in 1789, suggest:

Ye merry mechanicks come join in my song;
And let the brisk chorus come bounding along;
Tho' some may be poor, and some rich there may be,
And yet all are contented, and happy and free. . .
Each tradesman turn out with his tool in his hand,
To cherish the arts
And keep peace through the lands.[38]

Local politicians and civic leaders who sought the support of white artisans in Savannah looked upon them as a unified political force that championed freedom and peace and deserved full participation in the public sphere, a perspective that the mechanics had worked hard to cultivate. A series of events with profound political repercussions during the 1790s persuaded some Savannah mechanics to put the politicians' lofty rhetoric to the test by running for office themselves. In the process, some of these artisans discovered that their newfound political strength could be used to augment their individual public influence and growing private wealth.

The Savannah Mechanics Association (SMA) was organized in 1793 in the wake of an infamous local event known as "The Nelson Incident." As in Augusta, Englishmen controlled many Savannah merchant houses. And also as in Augusta, this reality did not endear the British to many Savannah residents. These same Savannah residents were more likely to be supporters of the French Revolution, even after the execution of Louis XVI. On 31 January 1793, for example, two hundred Savannah citizens, with many mechanics among them, assembled at the courthouse to rejoice over "the late happy events in favor of the freedom of France."[39] Six months later, on 20 July, French privateers off the Georgia coast were captured and brought into the city by British supporters. Three of the men were jailed; the fourth was released but delivered to a pro-British mob that tarred and feathered him.[40] Offended by this "stain on Georgians who purportedly value republicanism and honor," pro-French supporters accused the pro-British men of "mak[ing] a mockery of republicanism" by publicly shaming the French privateer named Nelson without a trial.[41]

The Nelson affair quickly became a watershed of sorts in Savannah politics, cementing the reality of two political camps in Savannah: Federalist-inclined British merchants, speculators, and their sympathizers and republican mechanics, professionals, and planters. This split was not unique to Savannah. Across the nation, more radical republicans were eager to link the American Revolution to the French Revolution, in an effort to underline the possibilities for increasing democratic transformation in America. The fledgling Federalists were far less eager to recognize this relationship, which resulted in partisan public rituals in urban America by 1794, even as expressions of national republicanism exploded.[42]

In Savannah, the Nelson Incident, which provoked five months of public debate, helped instigate formal recognition of the Savannah Mechanics Association. The association was chartered by the state in December 1793 but had been meeting informally for several years before its official formation.[43] Except for carpenter William Lewden, the first president of the SMA as well as a three-term city councilman, and cabinetmaker Gabriel Leaver, who owned a large plantation, the twenty-eight other original SMA petitioners were unremarkable men of moderate to no wealth with little previous involvement in local politics.[44] Whereas Lewden's three-term election to the city council suggests that Savannah artisans had already formed a loose union at the polls, the creation of the Mechanics Association signaled a more sophisticated effort toward politicization by a self-selected group of tradesmen. Like the MSA, the SMA met quarterly, held elections, and participated in public events. Indeed, both organizations bore a strong resemblance to the democratic-republican societies proliferating throughout America at this time because of their shared emphasis on egalitarian principles as well as their strident avowals of nationalism.

Within two years of the SMA's incorporation, an event larger and more profound than the Nelson affair, the Yazoo crisis, pushed Savannah's artisans more firmly into the local political world. In 1794 four land companies had bribed the Georgia assembly to pass a bill selling them 50 million acres of Georgia's western land claims for the sweet bargain of half a million dollars. Once this law, which virtually gave away Georgia's "Yazoo" lands, became public knowledge, the state's citizens were outraged.[45] Savannah residents spearheaded the protest against Yazoo in the spring of 1795 by sending re-monstrances to the legislature demanding that their "servants correct acts . . . designed to benefit private members . . . in a measure so momentous to the common rights and interests of the People."[46] SMA mechanics were some of the strongest leaders of this protest. Newly elected city councilman Bal-thasser Shaffer, a tailor, authored a circular intended for "the honest and industrious Mechanics and Planters of Chatham County" that criticized their representatives' role in Yazoo. After identifying this corrupt group as "the Free and Easy Club," Shaffer asked citizens to elect the popular democratic leader General James Jackson. Jackson had promised to resign from the U.S. Senate, run for a seat on the Georgia assembly, and, if elected, force the state to rescind the hated Yazoo Land Act.[47]

A series of letters to the editor apparently written by artisans reiterated Shaffer's points and show the degree to which artisans identified themselves as watchmen in the tradition of the American Revolution. "A Mechanic" warned citizens that "if the speculators succeed, we shall not much longer be freemen, for the legislature may as well sell us as sell our rights." "A Real Mechanic" agreed. Yazoo speculators "would ruin the country, without re-garding oaths or the principles of honor, to make their own fortunes." Savan-nah artisans did not simply argue their positions in circulars and editorials, however. They also organized among themselves. On 5 November 1795 a committee representing "a considerable portion of the citizens of Chatham County" requested General Jackson's resignation, "knowing his moral heart

[is] in the right place." The committee was comprised of five men, four of them leaders of the SMA; two of these four, Shaffer and Lewden, were also city councilmen. Jackson officially agreed to their request and was subsequently elected to the state legislature. The following year, after the Yazoo Land Act was declared void and the papers were burned, a relieved "Free Man" boasted that "each industrious man enjoys the fruits of his own labor, in security and peace."[48]

As the Yazoo crisis suggests, Savannah's mechanics had been among the most vocal and organized of oppositions throughout the 1790s. They were rewarded for their efforts with the responsibility of community leadership. For example, when news of George Washington's death reached the city, a funeral procession was arranged, with judges, civic leaders, officers, lodge members, *and* the SMA leading the rest of the citizens through the streets.[49] This public mourning demonstrates the degree to which Savannahians could join together across their class differences to honor the life and loss of a key Founding Father and pay homage to the ideals of the American Revolution. This ceremony was an important reminder of the high political road artisans had won for themselves as citizen-republicans. In Savannah and Augusta, where British merchants continued to hold political and economic power, notwithstanding republican critiques spearheaded by artisan-patriots, such public actions displayed people's efforts to construct a powerful historical memory to mold the present. The funeral procession for Washington in Savannah, like other civic rituals such as the public burning of the rescinded Yazoo Land Act or the procession that bore tailor Edward Shoemaker through Augusta, helped cement Georgians' sense of themselves as inheritors of the Revolution's legacy, even as they boosted artisans' respectability. Taken together, these rituals of civic theater contributed to the forging of an American identity and challenged the pro-British, Federalist merchant faction that dominated the political and economic life of both Savannah and Augusta. Again and again, artisans participated in these public acts as a class, pressing for recognition as significant members of the citizenry.[50]

Accordingly, the citizens of Augusta and Savannah had come to recognize the artisans in their communities as bona fide patriots. These skilled free laborers had earned respectability through their public commitments to republicanism. As a consequence, their political opinion now mattered. This new fraternity that extended across class differences was not unique to Georgia. Throughout the country members of the elite acknowledged that artisans had become "full participants in the virtuous, orderly, patriotic republic." Disparate classes now joined together in festivities, parades, and dinners, where they made toasts in honor of the new nation. At the same time, however, artisans in Georgia and around the republic used these public opportunities to highlight their political differences.[51]

In the intervening years since the Savannah Mechanics Association had been incorporated, the twenty-eight unremarkable charter members had begun to acquire political stature. Between 1791 and 1820 almost no year passed without an artisan alderman in office. Moreover, artisans also served as election superintendents in many of the wards. In 1800 and 1801 William Eppinger, Balthasser Shaffer, William Lewden, and William Spencer, all SMA members, were selected to monitor Heathcote, Percival, Derby, and Warren wards respectively.[52]

This phenomenon of artisan leaders turned local politicians helps explain why the MSA and the SMA, as well as expressions of artisan republicanism, declined precipitously during the early years of the nineteenth century. The MSA held no more meetings after 1804 until the 1820s, when a new generation of Augusta merchants, claiming to be artisans, rechartered the society and met off and on for several years. They took part in no public rituals whatsoever. The SMA disappeared from the historical record in 1809, not to appear again until the 1850s.[53]

Whereas artisans in the North used their new respectability to critique economic changes wrought by the early inroads of industrialization, artisans in Georgia could now align themselves politically and economically with the planter class. The unwillingness of these artisan leaders to sustain their artisan identity over time arose from their ability to transform themselves from craftsmen into planters, merchants, and speculators. Many mechanics, in a variety of trades, accrued substantial landholdings during the early republic. William Longstreet, a machinist and an inventor, for instance, built and sold cotton gins and engines and earned money from the operation of two cotton gins and a sawmill. His stock-in-trade from these ventures was valued at a hefty $5,000 by 1809, and he bought and sold over 1,200 acres of upcountry land and town property during his twenty-five years in Augusta.[54] Silversmith John Catlett glided into the ranks of the planter class after running a "wet-goods" store and a tinsmithing shop and engaging in a variety of real estate transactions, including appraisals, rentals, and sales.[55] By the early 1800s he had invested in the newly formed Planter's Bank, operated a plantation with the help of fifty-three slaves, and owned about 5,000 acres in three upcountry counties that produced upward of 150 bales of cotton by 1810.[56]

Although few artisan leaders in Augusta could match Longstreet's success as a speculator or Catlett's as a planter, other MSA officers also enjoyed

prosperity.⁵⁷ Slave ownership proved another equally important route to
wealth and status in the slaveholding South. At least eleven of the sixteen MSA
leaders owned slaves between 1790 and 1810, though half owned only one or
two. By comparison, only about half of Augusta taxpayers owned slaves in
1800.⁵⁸

Savannah artisan leaders also achieved considerable financial success. The
wealthiest was probably William Spencer, who at his death owned eleven
slaves and an estate valued at $4,000. Three members acquired taverns
or grog shops during their careers.⁵⁹ John Miller, a shoemaker, possessed
enough capital by 1800 to switch his business to the importation of ready-
made shoes, which he sold to upcountry shopkeepers. The majority of
Savannah artisans owned more taxable property in 1806 than in 1798. Moreover, at least nine had each acquired a few hundred acres of land.⁶⁰ In short,
though none of these men had joined the ranks of the wealthiest Georgia
planters and merchants, almost all of them had made great financial strides
during the early republic. These men, who had once tied their fortunes to
their trade, had become in many instances landholders and slaveholders.
They had exchanged their class identity from that of skilled free laborers in
an unfree world to planters-in-the-making and thereby accepted the terms of
social mobility, economic gain, and political authority that were beginning to
characterize the emerging cotton kingdom in Georgia.

In contrast, artisans in the North were feeling the pinch caused by early
industrialization and the rise of the market. In trades like shoemaking and
tailoring, the introduction of mechanization and output work turned skilled
journeymen into low-paid wageworkers, while more fortunate master craftsmen with access to capital became manufacturers and speculators. The creation of this new working class and the resultant low wages and limited social
mobility it caused led to trade union organization and eventually a political
movement among workingmen in the 1820s and 1830s. Encouraged by the
spread of manhood suffrage, free laborers not only organized strikes and
protests; they also formed workingmen's parties. They borrowed and reshaped the principles of the American Revolution and the artisan republicanism they had forged during the late eighteenth century into more radical
critiques that included the right to fair pay and a family wage, shorter work-
days, better conditions, and even the redistribution of property. With the
establishment of the second party system, workingmen's parties died out, but
both the Whig and Democratic Parties were forced to recognize the power of
workingmen as voters and to incorporate some of their critiques into their
platforms.⁶¹

While the North was on the verge of remapping the relationships between social structure, political ideology, and the party system in response to early industrialization, the South was moving in a very different direction at the close of the early republic. Slavery had long set the South apart from the rest of the nation. The invention of the cotton gin in 1793 set in motion a revolution in commercial agriculture that served to wed the region to slavery all the more. Southerners' growing knowledge of cotton cultivation and rising demand for the staple crop from England's textile industry made cotton king in Georgia and South Carolina in the early decades of the nineteenth century. Cotton quickly spread westward into Alabama, Mississippi, and Tennessee. A democratic staple crop, cotton was easier and cheaper to cultivate than tobacco, rice, or sugar and easier to transport to market. Young men who labored hard could often turn enough profit to acquire new wealth, especially in the form of slaves and land, and in time to enter the planter class. Artisans in Georgia during the early republic benefited in significant ways from this new cotton economy. Growing numbers of farmers and planters sold their crops in Savannah and Augusta in exchange for cash and credit. They used their returns to purchase a new array of consumer goods from shopkeepers and artisans. Artisans used these proceeds to buy land and slaves.

While northerners slowly but surely distanced themselves from the memories of the American Revolution, replacing their political ideology with a new brand of egalitarianism by the Jacksonian era, southerners continued to cling to those republican ideals forged in the Revolutionary era. The heroes of the American Revolution had fought England's enslavement of the colonies to establish independence. Southerners, who understood the institution of slavery intimately, did not take the notion of independence lightly in the early republic. White men knew that their social and economic independence, which they believed could be guaranteed only through property holding, rested in large part on the enslavement of a racially distinct class of subordinates—Africans and African Americans. They also were beginning to understand that their political independence could be jeopardized by new developments at the national level.[62]

Given their special circumstances, including a thriving cotton economy, a labor system based on racial slavery, and a political system based on Jeffersonian notions of independence, artisans who viewed themselves as planters-in-the-making had little reason to press for a distinct artisanal identity rooted in memories of the American Revolution any longer. The region's growing sense of its own unique identity in relation to the nation took precedence. By the 1820s leading planters and politicians in Georgia and throughout the

South, intent on creating a regional identity that served their interests best, pressed all white southerners to remember and celebrate the independence they had first claimed for themselves in 1776.[63]

In this sense, artisans in Georgia had contested the meaning of the American Revolution long enough to ensure their inclusion in the social and political worlds of the South. They had laid claim to their right to the legacy of the meaning of the struggle for independence and their role in it through their organizations and public actions, all of which had emphasized their class identity and moral authority. This identity was no longer necessary once artisans were included in the political order as voters and elected officials.[64] This new experience of political leadership, along with widening economic opportunity, helped artisans transform themselves into slaveholding farmers and planters.[65] Once this transformation occurred, these men no longer needed to promote the memory of artisans in the American Revolution but instead could embrace the dominant collective memory of white southerners. Thus artisans in Georgia had laid claim to respectability as an idealized republican citizenry and won it, at least for the foreseeable future. Artisans elsewhere in the nation would continue to struggle for this respectability and identity throughout the antebellum era.

In the end, a series of interlaced developments in Georgia promoted a shared social and political identity for all white men at the expense of a separate artisan community. White Georgians' opportunities for political and economic mobility, along with a political cohesiveness hatched in the wake of the Yazoo scandal, seriously discouraged internal divisions along class lines. Together these developments suggest how the making of a shared social identity based on the memory of artisans' contributions to the American Revolution was briefly important but eventually no longer necessary. Historians have traditionally assumed that the slave labor system and the rise of the plantation economy prevented the emergence of an artisan class in the Old South. In fact, artisans in Augusta and Savannah actively constructed a political voice for themselves based on the collective memory of artisan roles and artisan political consciousness in the American Revolution. They used that voice to launch mechanic societies, communicate their political concerns, and secure local office for themselves. But widening economic opportunities along with this political identity enabled artisan leaders to establish their own shops; accrue capital, land, and slaves; speculate; and transform themselves into substantial middling men and even planters with an important measure of political power. With the emergence of a distinct southern economy and society, they willingly cast aside their more radical artisan republican beliefs, forged in the American Revolution and honed in the early republic, to create a place for themselves, not as artisans, mechanics, or craftsmen, but as property-holding white men—citizens—in a slaveholding society bent on protecting the independence southerners believed they had secured in the American Revolution.

NOTES

I wish to thank Fitz Brundage for his forbearance and helpful comments.

1. In this essay the words "mechanic," "artisan," and "craftsman" are used interchangeably to refer to all skilled workers who practiced a trade; these men would have identified each other as mechanics or by their specific craft: butcher, baker, tanner, saddler, miller, furniture maker, turner, tinner, blacksmith, etc. On claiming the past to create historical memory, see Raphael Samuel and Paul Thompson, eds., *The Myths We Live By* (London: Routledge, 1990), 15–21. On how Americans interpreted the language and events of the Revolutionary era to redefine citizenship in a more truly democratic fashion, see Gordon S. Wood, *The Radicalism of the American Revolution* (New York: Knopf, 1992).

2. On the significance of competing groups defining the nation, see David Waldstreicher, *In the Midst of Perpetual Fetes: The Making of American Nationalism, 1776–1820* (Chapel Hill: University of North Carolina, 1997), 8–9.

3. On migrant artisans and urban economies in Georgia, see Michele Gillespie, *Free Labor in an Unfree World: White Artisans in Slaveholding Georgia, 1789–1990* (Athens: University of Georgia Press, 2000), chap. 1.

4. Albert B. Saye, *A Constitutional History of Georgia, 1732–1968* (Athens: University of Georgia Press, 1948), rev. ed. 1970, 106, 142–45.

5. Alan Dawley, *Class and Community: The Industrial Revolution in Lynn* (Cambridge: University of Cambridge Press, 1976); Susan E. Hirsch, *Roots of the American Working Class: The Industrialization of Crafts in Newark, 1800–1860* (Philadelphia: Temple University Press, 1978); Bruce Laurie, *Working People of Philadelphia, 1800–1850* (Philadelphia: University of Pennsylvania Press, 1980); Howard B. Rock, *Artisans of the New Republic: The Tradesmen of New York City in the Age of Jefferson* (New York: New York University Press, 1979); Sean Wilentz, *Chants Democratic: New York City and the Rise of the American Working Class, 1788–1850* (New York: Oxford University Press, 1984); Charles Steffan, *The Mechanics of Baltimore: Workers and Politics in the Age of Revolution, 1763–1812* (Urbana: University of Illinois Press, 1984); Steven J. Ross, *Workers on the Edge: Work, Leisure, and Politics in Industrializing Cincinnati, 1788–1890* (New York: New York University Press, 1985); Ronald Schultz, *The Republic of Labor: Philadelphia Artisans and the Politics of Class, 1720–1830* (New York: Oxford University Press, 1993).

6. Alfred Young, "The Mechanics and Jeffersonians: New York, 1789–1801," *Labor History* 5 (1964): 247–76; David Montgomery, "The Working Classes and the Pre-Industrial American City, 1780–1830," *Labor History* 9 (1968): 3–22; Wilentz, *Chants Democratic*, 34–39; Charles Sellers, *The Market Revolution: Jacksonian America, 1815–1846* (New York: Oxford University Press, 1991).

7. Alfred F. Young, "George Robert Twelves Hewes (1742–1840): A Boston Shoemaker and the Memory of the American Revolution," *William and Mary Quarterly*, 3d ser., 38 (October 1981): 561–623.

8. Susan G. Davis, *Parades and Power: Street Theatre in Nineteenth-Century Philadelphia* (Berkeley: University of California Press, 1988), 5–6.

9. Artisans were certainly not alone in their efforts to impress upon others their right to citizenship and all that it entailed. In many respects, their battle was far easier than that of African Americans, who used public ritual in a similar fashion and for the same purposes with less promising results. See Shane White, " 'It Was a Proud Day': African Americans, Festivals, and Parades in the North, 1741–1834," *Journal of American History* 81 (June 1994): 13–50.

10. Davis, *Parades and Power*, 6–7; Waldstreicher, *In the Midst of Perpetual Fetes*, 7–8.

11. Reported in *Augusta Chronicle and Gazette of the State* (hereafter *AC*), 13 February 1790.

12. *AC*, 23 January 1790.

13. *AC*, 6 March 1790.

14. On the creation and meaning of memory and heritage, see David Lowenthal, *Possessed by the Past: The Heritage Crusade and the Spoils of History* (New York: Free Press, 1996), chap. 1.

15. The society was organized prior to 7 May 1791, when the *Augusta Chronicle* announced the MSA's first meeting. Fifteen mechanics petitioned the state legislature to incorporate the MSA three and half years later. Executive Department Minutes, 24 December 1794, Georgia Department of Archives and History, Atlanta (hereafter GDAH). The petitioners were William Longstreet (machinist/inventor), John Catlett (silversmith), Thomas Bray (jeweler), Robert Cresswell (carpenter), Conrad Liverman (carpenter), Hugh Magee (miller), William Dearmond (carpenter), Baxter Pool (carpenter), John Cook (tailor), Joseph Stiles (silversmith), John Stiles (saddler), and Edward Primrose, Isaac Wingate, Angus Martin, and Hiel Chatfield (occupations unknown).

16. On MSA meetings and activities, see *Augusta Chronicle*, 7 May, 23 July 1791; 28 January, 24 April, 5 May, 14 July 1792; 27 January, 20 April, 3 May, 27 July, 10 August 1793; 25 January, 14 March, 1 May 1794; 25 April, 7 November 1795; 16 April, 29 October 1796; 22 April, 6 May, 22 July, 27 October 1797; 25 January, 10 March, 17 April, 1 May, 17 May, 28 August 1798; 26 January, 13 April, 27 July, 26 October 1799; 1 February, 26 July 1800; 31 January 1801; 7 May 1803; and 28 July 1804 (the last announcement about MSA activities until the institution reorganized itself under new leadership in 1823). It is impossible to determine MSA membership. Whereas incomplete records of MSA officeholders have been preserved through newspaper records of election results, membership lists have not.

17. Sean Wilentz, "Artisan Republican Festivals and the Rise of Class Conflict in New York City, 1788–1837," in Michael H. Frisch and Daniel J. Walkowitz, eds., *Working-Class America* (Urbana, Ill., 1983), 37–77.

18. *AC*, 4 May 1793, 5 May 1792.

19. Waldstreicher, *In the Midst of Perpetual Fetes*, 26.

20. Thomas J. Schlereth, "Artisans and Craftsmen: A Historical Perspective," in Ian M. G. Quimby, ed., *The Craftsman in Early America* (New York: Norton, 1984), 35–39.

21. *AC*, 7 May 1791, 5 May 1792. On the tradition of artisan promotion of political equality, see Wilentz, *Chants Democratic*, 93–97.

22. MSA leaders who served during the American Revolution included Captain Baxter Pool (*General Index to Compiled Military Service Records of Revolutionary War Soldiers*, part of War Department Collection of Revolutionary War Records, Record Group 93, M-860, roll 0041, National Archives, and "Georgia Military Affairs" [hereafter GMA], typescript, Georgia Department of Archives and History, Athens, 1:164, 168, 174–75); John Cook (Alfred D. Candler, [ed.], *The Revolutionary Records of the State of Georgia* [Atlanta: Franklin Turner Co., 1904–16], 3:169); and Hugh Magee, who was listed on the militia muster rolls between 1773 and 1793 (GMA, 1:23). William Dearmond served as captain of the Richmond Light Horse in the 1790s (GMA, 2:424). John Catlett, John Cook, and William Longstreet were each listed on the militia muster rolls between 1791 and 1813 (GMA, 1:300, 3:46, 142). On the relationship between political ambitions and militia leadership, see George Lamplugh, *Politics on the Periphery: Factions and Parties in Georgia, 1783–1806* (Newark: University of Delaware Press, 1986), 22. On the connections between popular societies and militia in the United States, see Eugene Perry Link, *Democratic Republican Societies* (New York: Octagon Books, 1965), 52, 111–12, 179–84.

23. *AC*, 5 May 1792, 4 May 1793.

24. *AC*, 7 May 1791, 5 May 1792, 4 May 1793.

25. *AC*, 4 May 1793.

26. For a description of Washington's visit, see Archibald Henderson, *Washington's Southern Tour* (Boston: Houghton Mifflin, 1923), xxv, 238, 242, 245–49, and Charles C. Jones Jr., *Memorial History of Augusta, Georgia: From Its Settlement in 1735 to the Close of the Nineteenth-Century* (Syracuse: D. Mason and Co., 1890), 141–42.

27. Henderson, *Washington's Southern Tour*, 245–46; Waldstreicher, *In the Midst of Perpetual Fetes*, 120–21, 124–25.

28. *AC*, 28 May, 11–18 June 1791; Lamplugh, *Politics on the Periphery*, 96; Waldstreicher, *In the Midst of Perpetual Fetes*, 124–25.

29. *AC*, 10 August 1793; Lamplugh, *Politics on the Periphery*, 108, 136.

30. GMA, 2, pt. 2:363–82, 424–25, 428.

31. Ibid., 377–80 (quotations, p. 380).

32. *AC*, 5 May 1792, 11 April 1807, 9–16 April 1808, 25 March 1809; John Donald Wade, *Augustus Baldwin Longstreet: A Study of the Development of Culture in the South* (New York: Macmillan, 1924), 3–11; Jones, *Memorial History of Augusta*, 135–36, 163.

33. *AC*, 2 August 1805, 6 December 1806, 31 October 1807, 16 April 1808; Jones, *Memorial History of Augusta*, 166–67.

34. *AC*, 20 March 1798, 19 April 1806; Jones, *Memorial History of Augusta*, 135.

35. *AC*, 20 March 1798, 28 March 1801 (Vallotton); *Southern Centinel and Gazette of the State*, 13 February 1794 (Bray); *AC*, 12 April 1788; *Georgia Gazette* (hereafter *GG*), 7 April 1798, and Executive Department Minutes, 2 July 1795, GDAH (Dearmond, Pool, and Stiles); Telamon Cuyler Collection, Richmond County, box 36, 3 June 1797, Hargrett Library, University of Georgia (Wingate and Bray).

36. Calculation based on data from Chatham County Tax Digest, 1798, GDAH (microfilm).

37. *GG*, 2 October 1789.

38. *GG*, 19 February 1789.

39. *GG*, 31 January 1793.

40. *AC*, 20 July 1793.

41. *GG*, 3 August 1793.

42. Waldstreicher, *In the Midst of Perpetual Fetes*, 128–31.

43. Act of the Georgia General Assembly, 16 December 1793, in H. Marbury and W. H. Crawford, *Compilation of the Laws of Georgia* (Savannah: Seymour, Woolhopter and Stebbins, 1802), 145–46.

44. City of Savannah, City Council Minutes, 1791–96, GDAH; Will M. Theus, *Savannah Furniture, 1735–1825* (N.p., 1967), 58–63.

45. Kenneth Coleman, ed., *A History of Georgia* (Athens: University of Georgia Press, 1977), 96–97.

46. *GG*, 19 March 1795.

47. Circular published in *GG*, 25 July 1795.

48. *GG*, 10 September, 1 October, 5 November 1795; *Columbian Museum and Savannah Advertiser*, 23 September 1796.

49. *Columbian Museum*, 17 January 1800.

50. On this conflict between the American Revolution as the origin of a newly constructed American identity and the overwhelming impact of British imperial heritage on that identity, see David Lowenthal, *The Past Is a Foreign Country* (Cambridge: Cambridge University Press, 1985), 105–6.

51. Waldstreicher, *In the Midst of Perpetual Fetes*, 105–7.

52. *GG*, 16 June 1800, 25 June 1801.

53. Gillespie, *Free Labor in an Unfree World*, chap. 2.

54. *The Story of Georgia: Biographical Volume* (New York: N.p., 1938), 683; Jones, *Memorial History of Augusta*, 146–47; Wade, *Longstreet*, 10–13.

55. Alfred D. Candler, *Colonial Records of Georgia* (Atlanta: Franklin Turner Co., 1904–16), 10:14, 75, 215, 628; George Barton Cutten, *The Silversmiths of Georgia, 1733–1850* (Atlanta: Pigeonhole Press, 1958), 136; *AC*, 23 April 1791, 28 January, 12 May, 13 June 1792; Richmond County Ordinary Tax Digest (hereafter RCOTD), 1807, GDAH ; Richmond County Probate Records, Richmond County Courthouse, 1811.

56. *AC*, 12 April 1811, 8 December 1810, 6 February 1808; RCOTD, 1809, GDAH.

57. For example, Robert Cresswell, a carpenter by trade, owned five houses and lots as well as 1,750 acres in Washington County valued at $23,000 at his death in 1816. In addition to their urban properties, which included at least one house and lot for all but one of the MSA leaders, twelve owned significant amounts of upcountry land. Silversmith Thomas Bray held nearly 1,000 acres, tailor John Cook 260 acres, carpenter William Dearmond 200 acres, carpenter Conrad Liverman over 2,000 acres, miller Hugh Magee nearly 3,000 acres, Angus Martin 600 acres, carpenter Baxter Pool 1,100 acres, Edward Primrose over 200 acres, and shoemaker Francis Vallotton 700 acres. *AC*, 4 July 1801 (Bray); RCOTD, 1800, GDAH, and *Index to the Headright and Bounty Grants of Georgia, 1756–1909* (Vidalia, Ga., 1970) (hereafter *IHRBG*), 127 (Cook); RCOTD, 1800 (Dearmond); RCOTD, 1800 (Liverman); *IHRBG*, 402, RCOTD, 1795, 1809, and Richmond County Probate Records, 8 September 1812 (Magee); *IHRBG*, 409, and RCOTD, 1800 (Martin); *IHRBG*, 526, and *AC*, 2 February 1800, 12 August 1809 (Pool); *AC*, 29 October 1808, and *IHRBG*, 534 (Primrose, who may have been a brewer, given the items, such as casks, crockeryware, vinegar, and scales, sold at his estate sale); RCOTD, 1800, 1807 (Vallotton).

58. RCOTD, 1800, GDAH.

59. Chatham County Estate Records, 1805–23, GDAH (Spencer); Theus, *Savannah*

Furniture, 63–64 (Peter Miller in 1797); *Columbian Museum*, 3 January 1800 (Thomas Palmer in 1800).

60. *Columbian Museum*, 4 April 1800 (Miller); Chatham County Tax List, 1798, 1806, GDAH.

61. Wilentz, *Chants Democratic*, 114–84.

62. William J. Cooper, *Liberty and Slavery: Southern Politics to 1860* (New York: Knopf, 1983), 49–64.

63. It should not be surprising that northerners and southerners remembered the American Revolution in such different ways. Michael Kammen points out that Founding Fathers were already bemoaning the lack of written documentation and the proliferation of inaccurate memories of the Revolution by the early 1800s. Kammen, *Mystic Chords of Memory: The Transformation in American Culture* (New York: Knopf, 1991), 44–45, 48–49.

64. Successful artisans in the North pursued a similar path in that they not only transformed themselves into entrepreneurs and owners of factories, but also carved out considerable political and cultural authority for themselves among the new northern middle class. See, e.g., Gary J. Kornblith, "Becoming Joseph T. Buckingham: The Struggle for Artisanal Independence in Early-Nineteenth-Century Boston" (123–34), and William S. Pretzer, "From Artisan to Alderman: The Career of William W. Moore, 1803–1886" (135–52), both in Howard B. Rock, Paul A. Gilje, and Robert Asher, eds., *American Artisans: Crafting Social Identity, 1750–1850* (Baltimore: Johns Hopkins University Press, 1995).

65. On the importance of economic, political, and cultural markers of planter status, see Drew Gilpin Faust, *James Henry Hammond and the Old South: A Design for Mastery* (Baton Rouge: Louisiana State University Press, 1982), 14–18.

African, American, and Virginian

The Shaping of Black Memory in Antebellum Virginia, 1790–1860

Gregg D. Kimball

In the late 1930s Works Progress Administration (WPA) interviewer Susie R. C. Byrd asked two elderly former slaves for their recollections of slavery. Sarah Wooden Johnson responded: "What in de world is you gwine do wid all dis here longy, longy go stuff you scrapin' up in dis here lightin' time? Gal, what is you doing? Ha, ha, ha. Say you is writin' hist'ry? Lord, Lord, po' nigger ain't got much fer you to git 'cause in dem times he longst to de white man. A slave ain't had no say so of his own 'til de 'render come and he was sot free. Glory, glory, gal! Us ain't had no book larning."[1] Arthur Greene, in contrast, met Byrd's questions with a question of his own: "Lord, Lord, chile, what make you folks wait so long 'fo' you git dis stuff 'bout way bac' yonder? All us fellers 'most done gone to tother world. Well, God done spared a few o' us to tell de tale."[2]

The reactions of Sarah Wooden Johnson and Arthur Greene to Byrd's inquiries about slavery were clearly at odds. Greene told his story willingly, whereas Johnson implored Byrd to let the "back stuff" be. Greene told of harsh punishment, "paterrollers," and runaways. He defended stealing by slaves as necessary to survival and described furtive slave religious meetings sheltered by brush arbor. He clearly viewed the telling of his tale as a way to publicly remember the repression that slaves had suffered and their ability to persevere. Johnson, a free woman, related stories of her family, the Civil War, and her religious conversion, but she did not dwell on the harshness of African American life. Her discomfort with a discussion of slavery times, even with another black woman, suggests the potential social shame created by bondage—a stigma that probably prevented many potential witnesses from testifying about their past.

These two statements reveal distinctly different concepts of history and the past. According to Johnson, African Americans, who were owned by others and devoid of "book larning," were powerless to shape "history," that is, the written, formal history privileged in a world dominated by elite and literate whites. She related her own story but apparently considered it insignificant as formal history. Greene envisioned another type of history, a hidden narrative of oppression and resistance that needed to be expressed publicly. And, indeed, now both Greene's and Johnson's stories are a part of the public narrative, recorded for posterity in the works of the Virginia Writers' Project and subsequent scholarship.

Any accounting of African American memory in the antebellum era must face squarely the problem of how and where slaves could discuss their ideas about the past. As James Scott has argued, those under domination may appear in the public realm to be subservient to the system that oppresses them. But, he argues, there is a "hidden transcript" of resistance created among the oppressed that sometimes peeks out from behind the facade of conformity. Moreover, those thought to be "powerless" often find ingenious ways to affect the "public transcript." In more than a few cases, as we will see, glimpses of the hidden transcript of African American memory in antebellum Virginia were revealed to public view.[3]

For historians who study the lives of slaves in the nineteenth century, the implications of Scott's argument extend to the very sources that form the basis of their work. Historians must constantly assess the language and perspective of sources created or sanctioned by those in control, including newspapers and government records, as well as the "public documents" written by African Americans, such as legislative petitions. Rarer, but not impossible to find, are private letters and life accounts written during and after slavery that help balance the public record.

Slaves and free blacks in antebellum Virginia also disclosed glimpses of their collective memories when they participated in and remembered momentous events—international wars, insurrections, and large-scale migrations. The American Revolution, Gabriel's and Nat Turner's Rebellion, and the experiment of African colonization all influenced African Americans' views about their past and present as well as the possibilities of the future. Black Virginians worked out ideas about liberty and slavery against this historical backdrop even as white Virginians struggled with the same ideas. Through memory some African Americans laid claim to a prominent place in the story of Virginia, and thus America, and at the same time made sense of their membership in the African diaspora. At the very least, rural slaves integrated the lessons of revolutionaries into the everyday sayings and strategies that allowed them to survive in a hostile world.

Many recent authors have emphasized the way that African Virginians subverted the authority of whites through their understanding of the tenets of the American Revolution and their recollections of slave insurrections. In contrast, scholars writing on the Liberian experience have highlighted the conservative caste of the Americo-Liberians' views, especially their inability to understand or approve of the behavior of the native African peoples with whom they came in contact. My perspective falls somewhere in the middle. There is no doubt that the revolutionary movements of the late eighteenth century inspired many African Americans to seek freedom in a multitude of ways. But those who gained positive benefits for their Revolutionary service from the state, especially freedom or financial support, then had to adapt to living free in a slave society dominated by whites, with all the negotiations and concessions attendant on such an existence. Likewise, there is no doubt that African Virginians believed in an abstract racial, even biblical, connection to their African heritage, largely born out of a shared experience of oppression. It is just as true, however, that their culture and mores had been shaped in contact with European Americans for at least several generations, making the transition to life in Africa a jarring experience.

Black Virginians began constructing a memory of their role in the struggle for human liberty and freedom as soon as the guns fell silent at Yorktown, if not before. The memory of the black Revolutionary role was kept alive in many ways. Immediately after the war a number of slaves petitioned the legislature for their freedom, couching their pleas in the language of revolution and liberty. Aged veterans themselves were living proof of black participation in the Revolutionary struggle, and those in reduced financial circumstances vigorously pressed their claims for state support. Thomas Evans, of Lunenburg County, for instance, was one of many black veterans who appealed to the legislature. Despite having been turned down for a federal pension, Evans successfully petitioned Virginia's lawmakers, who approved his request for aid.[4]

The best-known story of a black Revolutionary—then and now—was that of James, a slave belonging to William Armistead of New Kent County. James spied on General Cornwallis in his camp, reporting British activities to the Marquis de Lafayette. Lafayette gave James a certificate testifying to his service, which James attached to his freedom petition to the Virginia legislature.[5] The legislature granted James's request, and the ex-slave took the surname Lafayette in honor of his old patron. James Lafayette's service entered the historical consciousness of Virginians in the ensuing years through newspapers, novels, and public rituals. When the Marquis de Lafayette visited Yorktown during his triumphal tour of the United States in 1824, he glimpsed James Lafayette in the crowd along the line of procession. The *Richmond Enquirer* noted that the two old veterans embraced. A few years later state auditor James Heath made James Lafayette a minor, but heroic, character in his novel *Edge-Hill*, set during the American Revolution. Heath probably had met James Lafayette, since, as state auditor, his office dispensed the pension that Lafayette received annually beginning in 1819. However Heath became aware of the freedman's saga, he concluded his novel with an account of the Yorktown reunion and a transcription of the Marquis de Lafayette's testimonial.[6]

The public recognition accorded James Lafayette by whites in the 1820s flew in the face of the increasing repression of free blacks and slaves in Virginia. For instance, the published "Order of the Day" for Lafayette's visit to Richmond stated that "No intoxicated or colored person will be permitted to enter the [Capitol] Square."[7] Yet elites could easily reconcile James Lafayette's story with the dominant public culture. For whites, rewarding a few black patriots did not threaten the system of slavery but, on the contrary, emphasized the loyalty of African Americans, who, without hesitation, took up arms to defend Virginia's society and institutions. Legislators also reinforced their perception of themselves as magnanimous and liberal men willing to reward merit and patriotism, for, in the view of elite whites, black Revolutionary soldiers had simply proved themselves superior to most of their race.

Because of whites' acceptance of black patriots and because petitioners couched their missives in the unassailable language of the Revolution, veterans often took the liberty of asserting rights far more sweeping than the legislature intended. James Lafayette's petition publicly stated more than his individual claim to freedom. While emphasizing his "honest desire to serve this country in its defence," James also asserted the universal right to human liberty in his petition. He was "persuaded of the just right which all mankind have to Freedom, notwithstanding his own state of bondage," a conclusion easily substantiated by the declarations and publications that flowed from the pens of Virginia Revolutionary leaders.

Other memorials to the General Assembly revealed a subtle understanding of the politics of the war and slavery. Saul, a slave of George Kelly, chose to soldier and spy for the Americans despite the "Invitation, trumpeted forth by British Proclamations, for slaves to Emancipate themselves by becoming the assassins of their owners," an offer that Saul knew many slaves had accepted.[8] Saul's veiled invocation of the specter of slave insurrection in his petition served to put the Virginia authorities on notice that a people who had fought with the implicit promise of freedom were unlikely to accept anything less. Such petitioners expressed the ideals and aspirations of African Americans— glimpses of the hidden transcript—but did so from the relative safety of their positions as patriots and in the language of republicanism.

Most white Virginians probably considered the language of freedom petitions mere rhetorical excess, but the fruits of these ideas among slaves became readily apparent. The American Revolution was not the only successful revolt against colonial rule in the Americas during the late eighteenth century. In the 1790s slaves on Saint Domingue rose up, threw off the yoke of the French, and by 1804 created a black republic. Because Virginia was part of an elaborate network that tied together a transatlantic black world, knowledge of the insurrection quickly reached the Old Dominion. Black seamen and émigrés from the West Indies in towns like Norfolk, where officials complained of the many slaves and free blacks who had accompanied fleeing French planters, spread firsthand accounts of the successful slave insurrection. (Indeed, insurrectionary scares periodically focused on émigrés from the former French colony.) Black boatmen and draymen as well as hired-out slaves then carried news of the revolt to blacks in the countryside.[9]

Notions of freedom and liberty derived at least in part from recent events in Saint Domingue were the catalyst for the first of two great slave insurrections in nineteenth-century Virginia—Gabriel's planned revolt in 1800. Virginia authorities, aided by informing slaves, suppressed the conspiracy and executed its leader, Gabriel, along with approximately twenty-five conspirators. The intentions of the insurrectionists make clear their debt to the overheated political rhetoric of the day, when Democratic-Republicans and Federalists in Virginia argued about the proper extent of liberty and debated the legacy of the French, American, and even Haitian Revolutions. Gabriel himself intended to carry a flag into Richmond during his uprising that would bear the words "death or Liberty," a clear reference to Patrick Henry's famous Revolutionary appeal. One captured insurgent allegedly announced that "I have nothing more to offer than what General Washington would have had to offer, had he been taken by the British and put to trial." If the relative importance of artisanal republicanism and religion in the origins of the rebellion remains in dispute, there is no question of the influence of either the Saint Domingue uprising or the contemporary debates over the Revolutionary inheritance.[10]

The memory of Gabriel and his insurrection lived on throughout the antebellum era in both song and story. Abolitionist and pan-Africanist Martin Dulaney incorporated him into a novel, as did white Virginia author Mary Virginia Hawes Terhune (writing under the pen name Marion Harlan). Although neither of these sources probably circulated among Virginia's African American population, another tale of Gabriel most certainly did. Two related songs about him appear to have enjoyed wide circulation during the antebellum era.[11] One song, "Gabriel's Defeat," is described in the northern abolitionist paper, the *Liberator*, and the other, quite similar, in an 1840 novel entitled *Poor Jack*. Neither song tells the story of Gabriel's insurrection but instead relates his capture by Virginia authorities. James Sidbury argues that the version of "Gabriel's Defeat" from *Poor Jack* "accepted the terms in which Governor James Monroe had originally chosen to tell the story of the conspiracy, by focusing not on the conspiracy itself but on its repression." He also asserts that the song's emphasis on the intense security around Gabriel and the generous reward for his capture highlighted the seriousness of white concerns and fears. The version described in the *Liberator* conflates Gabriel and Denmark Vesey, the leader of a slave insurrection in Charleston, South Carolina, in 1822 and adds other details, however inaccurate, that link Gabriel to a larger revolutionary consciousness. Interestingly, it includes a speech by Gabriel that draws a connection between the "tyranny of the king of England" and black oppression. Gabriel offers himself as a "martyr to liberty," proclaiming that his example "will raise up a Gabriel, who will, Washington-like, lead on the Africans to freedom." The two versions of the song reveal the multiple meanings that blacks attached to the songs. One version, which might be sung before a black audience outside the gaze of whites, was a heroic portrayal of black aspirations and sacrifice. The other version, suited to public performance in the presence of whites, including Virginia's political and social elite, was a cautionary tale of failure and repression. Taken together, both accounts taught valuable lessons to black listeners.[12]

"Gabriel's Defeat" apparently was widely performed in Virginia. The report on the song in the *Liberator* claimed that it had become a "favorite air in the dances of white people." The author of *Poor Jack* ascribed the song to a black fiddler with a repertoire of songs based on the music of Virginia and North Carolina.[13] Further corroboration of the circulation of songs about Gabriel comes from a profile of Titus, a black Virginian who was described as the "Original Banjo-Man." Although this account does not provide the content of the song's words, it does suggest the context within which it was performed. Titus apparently died around 1818, but his fame was sufficiently durable for an article to appear about him in 1852 in the *Richmond Dispatch*. Titus played regularly at the Fairfield racecourse just north of the town, regaling sportsmen, including such leading white citizens as John Marshall, with songs of the race. The article's author lamented that most of Titus's songs had not been written down and thus immortalized. But among the few sagas preserved was "an entire piece giving a true and graphic account of the capture of the 'nigger general,' as he calls him, Gabriel." That Titus's song described Gabriel's capture, rather than his attempted rebellion, almost certainly indicates that it was a version of the ballad documented in the *Liberator* and *Poor Jack*.[14]

The social position of the transmitters of the tale—free black and slave musicians—raises interesting questions about the passing on of tradition and memory among African Americans. Although there was undoubtably a "hidden" version of the Gabriel song, musicians worked under a system of constraints and rewards that probably discouraged many of them from singing potentially subversive songs to their fellow African Virginians. Musicians like the slave Blind Billy, a popular Lynchburg fifer, played at both martial events and private dances and balls at the homes of the region's elite. African American musicians depended on these associations for financial security as well as protection from the arbitrary exercise of black codes against them.[15] Moreover, musicians played for white militia companies that had an explicit role in controlling black people, especially suppressing slave disturbances and insurrections. The tradition of black musicians accompanying militias was itself a legacy of the fact that African Americans were stripped of the right to bear arms in the eighteenth century.[16] Though free blacks continued to perform in fife and drum bands and at celebrations of American freedom and other national holidays, such events were increasingly segregated.

The history of the "Blues Band" in Richmond highlights the role and position of free black musicians and artisans in antebellum Virginia. In 1829 the Richmond Light Infantry Blues, a white volunteer militia, "proposed to try the expedient of raising a band of free colored men, and for this purpose have caused inquiries to be made, from which it appears by a list furnished and hereto attached that thirteen men of the above class have signified their consent to serve the company two years for their instruction." Among the musicians recruited were prominent free black barbers and artisans, including George W. Ruffin, Lomax B. Smith, and Benjamin W. Judah.[17] After the band no longer was officially affiliated with the company, band members nonetheless continued to march with the Blues Band and attend their events. The Richmond papers reported that after John Brown's raid on Harpers Ferry in 1859, Lomax Smith proposed to raise a company and "shear the ears" of the abolitionists. Several members of the Blues Band apparently followed the company during the Civil War, and Benjamin W. Judah's wife Judith presented flowers in 1866 "as an offering to the gallant dead of the Richmond Light Infantry Blues, of which my husband was once a musician, and who fell in the service." At the company's 1866 anniversary, three members of the former "colored band" were praised by former governor Henry A. Wise for not taking part in the first Emancipation Day celebration on 3 April in Richmond and for knowing "their position." Indeed, Lomax Smith regularly opposed black activists during Reconstruction. Although we cannot accept at face value the comments of white newspapers and politicians, there is enough evidence here to suggest that some free black musicians who might have been influential transmitters of subversive historical memory did align themselves closely with powerful whites.[18]

African Americans understood the difficulty of the free black's position in antebellum society. Many of the ex-slaves interviewed in the 1930s noted the reluctance of free blacks to associate with slaves, and, in one remarkable case, a former slave related the complexity of pre–Civil War race relations through the story of a black military figure. In 1937 a WPA field-worker recorded a story about James Bowser, who had actually been a free black Revolutionary veteran from Nansemond County. In the later retelling he was transmuted into a tragic Civil War spy. The tale recounted how slaves universally despised Bowser because he would not associate with them, although the black interviewee gave a sympathetic explanation of Bowser's conduct. The free black simply had wished to avoid the suspicions and recriminations of whites and understood that associating with slaves might cause him trouble. In the WPA story, Bowser eventually shows his true loyalty to his race by spying for the

Union army. The tale ends tragically, as Bowser's activities were exposed and he was beheaded by angry whites.[19]

The story of James Bowser explicitly recognized the difficult position of black veterans, whether of the Civil War or the Revolution, who stood between the hidden transcript of freedom and the public transcript of the faithful black servant. Military service in the American Revolution prompted soldiers to entertain broad views of human liberty and freedom, but the realities of being a black veteran in antebellum Virginia militated a certain conservatism of conduct as well. Rewarded for their role in creating freedom for whites, emancipated slaves and free black veterans often acted conservatively to defend their position, which for many rested on white patronage. Some veterans, such as Robert Cordley, the doorkeeper of the state capitol, held government sinecures, and others received financial aid through pensions. Thus, even Saul, who had pointed out successful British appeals to slave revolt, understood that the "war was levied upon America not for the Emancipation of Blacks, but for the subjugation of Whites."[20]

The coded meanings of folktales probably gets us closer to the hidden transcript of the memory of revolution for most slaves than the songs of antebellum musicians. Virginia's WPA workers recorded few explicit stories of Nat Turner's insurrection in their interviews with ex-slaves, but allusions to Turner's Rebellion were often just below the surface of folktales and language. The writers who compiled *The Negro in Virginia*, for instance, interpreted the common slave expression "can't fool ole Nat" as a tribute by former slaves to Turner's ability to elude capture. Ex-slave Cornelia Carney, of Williamsburg, related the expression to field-workers in the context of her memories of her own father's skill at evading the authorities. Thus a historical figure usually studied and discussed as part of the political controversy over slavery was for many slaves an example of successful behavior and bravery in the real world of day-to-day slave resistance. Like the protagonist of "Gabriel's Defeat," "ole Nat" was a survivor who outwitted his white pursuers, if only for awhile. He became not a heroic military figure, but a trickster eluding capture through cunning and wits. In the twentieth century, the Gabriel song would evolve into an escape narrative featuring a heroic rescuer named Billy, who carries the wounded Gabriel to safety.[21]

Although most slave men and women engaged in and approved of everyday resistance to slavery, they also drew practical lessons from the white reaction to insurrection. In a rare antebellum manuscript autobiography penned in 1847, Fields Cook wrote of his dismay and consternation after Nat Turner's Rebellion: "I was a boy about the time of Nat Turners insurrection

who had better never been born than to have left such a curse upon his nation
I say that he had better never been born: for at that time I was living in the
country and we poor colored people could not sleep at nights for the guns
and swords being stuck in at our windows and doors." We might be inclined
to censure Fields Cook for his criticism of Nat Turner, but Cook was simply
expressing his understanding of the realities of power in antebellum Virginia
society. The consequence of failure was repression that bore down on the
very slaves Turner had intended to liberate. He clearly thought that the time
was not yet ripe to "speak truth to power" and reveal the hidden transcript of
freedom. But that time would come later in his life, and Cook himself would
become a prominent political and labor leader in Reconstruction-era Richmond who proudly addressed mass meetings that would have seemed inconceivable in his youth.[22]

The destruction of slavery and the new possibilities of the post–
Emancipation world would allow a fuller and more public statement of
the black Revolutionary heritage. Black militias would become a fixture in
postbellum Emancipation Day celebrations, and the Revolutionary heritage
would form a key element in those events. Capitol Square, off-limits to blacks
before the Civil War, became a favorite place of celebration with its monuments and buildings dedicated to the Revolutionary heritage. Black militias,
such as Captain Josiah Crump's Attucks Guards, then marched through the
square in the shadow of Thomas Crawford's imposing equestrian statue of
George Washington and Thomas Jefferson's capitol building.[23]

African Virginians faced enormous challenges to maintaining memory in the
antebellum era. The breakup of families, limitations on literacy, and other
obstacles made the maintenance of a "usable past" extremely difficult. Yet,
despite these problems, as we have seen, at least some African Virginians
incorporated ideas of liberty and equality into their identity. The emergence
of this complex identity took place against the backdrop of wrenching
changes in slave family life. James Sidbury's recent survey of the development
of identity among late-eighteenth-century African Virginians argues convinc-
ingly that the dispersal of the great Tidewater holdings of the old planter class
in that era uprooted the small, "local worlds" of slave life that had been held
together for several generations by the great Virginia land barons and the law
of entail. As the center of gravity for the slave economy moved to the Piedmont and the agricultural base shifted toward grains, African Virginians
became scattered on smaller holdings across the state. In turn, extended

families and neighborhood communities were broken up. Indeed, most ex-slaves interviewed in the 1930s only remembered a generation or two into their family's past. Virginia's infamous role as an exporter of slaves in the domestic slave trade certainly took its toll on generational memory and continuity. But, perhaps because of the profound sense of loss engendered by the sale of immediate family members, the family became a centerpiece of African American life and remembrance.[24]

A rare letter from Henry Page, an enslaved coachman owned by Mann Valentine, in reply to an unexpected letter from his son, stands as one example of the tenacity of family ties among slaves. Page could neither read nor write; the letter appears (on the basis of similarities in handwriting) to have been written by one of his master's daughters. Page asked his son to "imagine the joy of a father's heart on receiving a letter from a son whom he had never expected to hear from again, or whom he thought if perhaps living had forgotten his affectionate father." Page's son obviously wrote after years of separation, and Page's reply is full of news of the family. Page praised his son for "so far cherish[ing] your Mother's memory as to name your oldest child after her." His granddaughter Sarah was not the only family member with a family name that had been passed down. Page related that his son's sister Kitty was well, and that Aunt Kitty "says she intends writing you herself." Page sent his love to his grandchildren and "hope[d] he may yet live to see them all," and relayed his "fatherly feeling" for his son's wife, "though I have never seen her." He implored his son's wife "not to let her children forget that they have a grand-father in 'Old Virginia.'" Evident throughout Page's letter is the pain of family separation under slavery and the extraordinary effort required to preserve a tenuous sense of family history.[25]

The family life of free blacks was also uncertain. State law, rather than sales or forced migration by masters, often compelled free blacks to abandon their homes and extended families. A change in state law after Gabriel's Rebellion compelled emancipated slaves to leave the state unless the legislature, or, later, local courts, granted permission to stay. The letters of those who left and the petitions of those who asked to remain reveal much about the values of black Virginians, both their concern for freedom and their attachment to the land of their birth.

The use of the term "old Virginia" carried with it the ties of family and home that bound newly emancipated African Americans required by law to leave the state. As much as the desire for freedom, the comfort of familiar faces and surroundings kept many blacks in Virginia. Peter Strange, formerly enslaved by G. H. Bacchus, for example, stated that "your petitioner is a

Black Smith by trade which he considers a useful one where he is—; that by industry it furnishes him an humble support, but that he is now about 50 years of age & in precarious health so that if he were forced into a strange land without money or friends & severed from his wife & children, who are slaves & to whom he is sincerely attached he could foresee nothing but suffering and distress." As the Strange petition suggests, ties between slave and free black men and women often complicated the decision to migrate. A population survey of the wards in Richmond in 1854, for instance, showed that there were "152 slaves owned by free persons of color" in the city, many by family members to prevent their resale outside the state.[26] Walter D. Blair supported Strange's petition, writing that Strange "for about twenty years past . . . has been the husband of a woman in my family," further noting that "I think he comes up to the standard of character (and the Blacks have their standards of character) that would be useful as an example to those of his colour around him, if permitted to remain in the commonwealth."[27]

African Americans, despite their desire for freedom and opportunities, carefully considered the benefits of freedom against the reality of leaving a familiar home and friends, traveling to a place where "thar is very few blacks in this city in deed to look hear an in some other citys that I have bin in since I left . . . thar is such a few that some times I think I left them all behind in old virginia." The members of the Scott-Pearman family, like many other African Americans, left Virginia to further their economic and social goals. Their letters eloquently attest to the concrete benefits and freedoms that free blacks anticipated in their new homes, as well as their nostalgia for family and fireside in the Old Dominion. Lucy Jarvis was freeborn in York County, Virginia, and first married a man named Pearman. Eventually she migrated from New Kent County with her second husband William C. Scott to Richmond, where she resided in 1850 with some of her children. William Scott was a deacon and Lucy a member of the First African Baptist Church.[28] Along with other relatives, the Scotts moved first to Columbus, Ohio, and then on to Brantford, Canada West. In a series of letters to "My Dear Children," the Scotts implored other relatives to join them, discussing the possibilities of life in a new place. Lucy Scott's plea to her children revealed divided feelings, telling them "I am in good hopes that this may find you all well an making up you minds to leave old virginia my marthrs home my hart morn with sorry to think that I had to seek a home in a strange land among strangers for the sack of my children." Scott knew that the separation from family and friends would be just as difficult for her children and told them so, yet she urged that "for the sack of you children you all mus part from you good friends also an come to a land whar you children can be men an women."[29]

The Scott-Pearman family and other free blacks had practical reasons to maintain their surprisingly precise sense of family based on both blood ties and legal codes. Because many free people derived their legal status from a free ancestor, the memory of that genealogical link was of incalculable significance. Many African Virginians interviewed by the WPA who had been free before the Civil War, for instance, traced their freedom to Native American ancestors who they believed (incorrectly) could not be enslaved. For free people, maintaining liberty meant constantly holding a pass from the county or city court attesting to either free birth or an act of emancipation. Family lore and documents recording a free-born heritage formed a legal bulwark against reenslavement and helped maintain family traditions.[30]

While African Virginians endeavored to maintain a memory of family and place, they also developed a larger sense of African American identity. Africa played a major role in the consciousness of black Virginians, free and slave, in the antebellum era. As early as 1776 blacks in Williamsburg organized the African Baptist Church of Williamsburg, and by the end of the antebellum era churches in Fredericksburg, Petersburg, and several other cities and towns styled themselves African churches.[31] In 1823 "a number of persons of colour residing in the City of Richmond" petitioned the state legislature for a church, noting "that from the rapid increase of population in this City the number of free persons of colour and slaves has become very considerable" and "it has been the misfortune of your petitioners to be excluded from the churches, meeting House, and other places of public devotion which are used by white persons in consequence of no appropriate places being assigned for them, except in a few Houses." The petitioners, "consisting of free persons and slaves," requested "a law authorizing them to cause to be erected within this City, a House of public worship which may be called the Baptist African Church."[32] Eighteen years passed before whites authorized the founding of the first African church in the capital city, but it was soon followed by three other Baptist churches in Richmond that described themselves as African.

The development of a larger sense of African heritage hinted in these church names had deep biblical and religious roots. The image of the biblical figure Ham and his "lost tribe" became ingrained in the consciousness of blacks in the American diaspora. The tale of Ham created a rationale for the condition of African Americans and allowed a diverse and dispersed group of people to imagine a collective identity based on biblical themes familiar to them. In 1860, for instance, Richmond police investigated a group known as the Sons of Ham. Finding the group's meeting spot, an outbuilding behind a prominent citizen's house, the police listened outside and heard a "preacher, with his Bible before him, giving a biographical sketch of Moses." Breaking into the secret enclave, the police found evidence of underground railroad activity. Although whites often interpreted the biblical story of Ham as a justification of African Americans' status as "servants of servants," this black organization obviously gave the legacy of Ham a different meaning, one more in line with Moses' release of the Israelites from bondage.[33]

The reading of a potentially subversive text—in this case, the Bible— highlights the power that slaves and free blacks invested in literacy. Education was a powerful symbol of freedom, and although some Virginia slaves learned to read by themselves, in churches or through enlightened masters such as reformer John Hartwell Cocke, it became increasingly difficult for African Americans to become literate in the antebellum era. Fields Cook noted that many slaves burned their books during the repression that followed Nat Turner's insurrection. Virginia legally limited the instruction of slaves from the 1830s until the end of the Civil War. Those teaching slaves became criminals in the eyes of the law, except masters, who were allowed to instruct their own slaves. Cook continued to keep a book in his hat and "many a time have knelt down and beged god to teach me my book and I beleave that he heard my prayers for it looked to me as if I could get any lesson that was given to me without any troble what ever and all my crave was just to know how to read the bible."[34]

Reading and writing was more than a way to gain religious understanding and knowledge; slaves used these skills as a weapon to carve out greater freedom in everyday life. From forging passes to reading newspapers, literacy opened new worlds and possibilities for Virginia's bondsmen and women. Likewise, it was a means to create a collective identity and to maintain memory in a fluid society. Literacy and a collective history became closely entwined in the black mind during the antebellum era. Sarah Wooden Johnson's lament at her lack of education, which she clearly viewed as a major barrier to a true accounting of her people's past, was echoed by many ex-slaves. In 1838, for example, a group of free blacks in Fredericksburg petitioned the legislature for a school, emphasizing their property ownership and patriotic feelings. The signers pointedly noted that "some of them [were] descendants of soldiers of the revolution—others having been personally engaged in aiding the efforts of their country in the late war with England."[35] The denial of education to African Americans and, in the South, the general lack of schools for working-class whites meant that literacy was confined largely to the white middle and upper classes. That African Americans considered attainment of these skills a sign of equality is clear; the Scotts, for instance, boasted to their other children that "your sisters elizabeth can right as [?] a hand as any of our ladys in old virginia."[36] Similarly, William Scott expressed his gratitude to "the god of all mercy for his mercies and goodness towards us, that our lot was cast in a land where we can set under our own vine & fig tree and none dare to make us afraid and oh my dear Children what a great blessing it is to have the freedom of Speech and to be where we can send our little Children to School together all taught together and that for love instead of hating each other and calling each other names to hard to be borne."[37]

The allure of a promised land, where freedom and social equality might prevail, carried the Scott-Pearman family to Canada and countless runaway slaves north to freedom. This search for a safe haven and for freedom and opportunity contributed mightily to their sense of themselves as a distinct diasporic people. This sense also was augmented by African Virginians who sought to make sense of their African heritage by returning to West Africa. The expressions of memory and identity by Virginia émigrés to Africa in the antebellum colonization movement mirror those themes fleetingly glimpsed in other documentary evidence. The grip of memory on the imaginations of Americo-Liberians would be revealed both in their enduring commitment to characteristically American ideals and in their simultaneous emotional and religious attachment to their recalled African heritage.

Their participation in the colonization movement, then, was in part a testimony to the power of African American memory to inspire the creation of an imagined community of African Americans and Africans in Liberia. The impulses that led African Americans back to Africa were varied. Many went as missionaries fueled by a desire to redeem the continent for Christ. Others spoke of "civilizing" Africa and, not surprisingly, believed that the creation of a commercial economy was essential to that enterprise. And some viewed the return to the western coast of Africa, the departure point only years before of European slave ships, as a return to a black homeland.

The image of the Liberian experiment and Africa in the minds of black Virginians was decidedly mixed. Reports from returning migrants and published accounts related high levels of mortality and illness, periodic warfare with native people, and the difficulty of making economic ends meet. Also, opposition to colonization by many African American leaders no doubt dis-

couraged some potential settlers. After some initial success in attracting migrants, the number of Virginia blacks leaving for Liberia remained relatively
low. Despite these problems, black Virginians still maintained close ties to the
West African nation. Many of the country's early officials, including the first
president of the Republic of Liberia, Joseph Jenkins Roberts, were Virginians. African churches in Virginia took an active interest in its development,
sending money, aid, and missionaries to the new country.[38]

The letters of Liberian emigrants testify to a complex set of identities and
memories of Africa, ranging from pride in their native state to a powerful
sense of African heritage. The letters of James Skipwith to his former master,
prominent Virginia colonizationist and reformer John Hartwell Cocke, and to
friends and relatives in America express the feelings of many who made the
journey to Africa. Skipwith initially had difficulty adjusting to Liberia. Eventually, however, he proclaimed it "the Best Country for the Black man that is
to Be found on the face of the Earth[.] God intended Africa for the Black
Race." Racial identity had been written into the Liberian republic's 1847
constitution, which barred whites from citizenship; indeed, voting was limited to adult black males who possessed real property.[39] In 1859 Skipwith
expressed great pride in the country's hard "contest for freedom & the
struggle for independence" and felt that now his "country stands . . . on
Commanding Ground" in the "civilized world."[40]

Skipwith's use of the expression "civilized world" was not accidental.
Although American emigrants to Liberia took pride in their new home and
belonging to Africa, they were often shocked by the manners and mores of
their African brothers and sisters. Moreover, warfare with native Africans
over land, commerce, and the slave trade brought home the vast cultural
chasm that stood between the new Liberians and the inhabitants of the
"Mother Country." Indeed, Peyton Skipwith, another former bondsman of
Cocke, wrote his former master: "It is something strange to think that these
people are called our ancestors. In my present thinking if we have any ancestors they could not have been like these hostile tribes."[41]

Black settlers more often looked to biblical allusions and stories than to any
historical notion of Africa when explaining their connection to, and mission
on, the continent. James Skipwith felt that the work of creating Liberian
society was "like Building the walls of Jerusalem" and used the term "Ethiopia" for Africa. The late eighteenth century saw the beginnings of Ethio-
pianism as an element in black nationalist thought in America, rooted in the
biblical verse "Princes shall come out of Egypt; Ethiopia shall soon stretch
forth her hands unto God." In this vision of a rising black race, African

peoples were the chosen people of God. Religious chauvinism and the urge to civilize the continent mutually supported the colonists belief in their role as the uplifters of a benighted people in a progressive historical movement that would put Africa on "commanding ground." This larger sense of destiny and mission in Africa caused black settlers to assert their racial connection to Africa in several ways, not the least of which was their active campaigns to rid the coast of slave-trading stations. Ironically, suppressing the trade brought them directly into conflict with African leaders who profited from the sale of fellow Africans.[42]

Whereas the language of settlers often invoked God's plan and a sense of Christian mission, many of the actual institutions—public and private— created by Americo-Liberians reflected American precedents. Settlers quickly established literary societies, fraternal orders, and other private associations and charities akin to those common in antebellum America. Migrants to Liberia also strove to replicate popular American institutions for self-improvement, including schools. John H. Faulcon, a manumitted slave apprenticed to a stonemason in Liberia, wrote that he struggled to attend school and "What I have Learnt was by hard night work." He subsequently joined a classical school and a junior debating society to cultivate his mind.[43] The precedent of American institutions also was evident in the structure and functions of the Liberian government and the national constitution, which were closely modeled after those of the United States. Adult males proudly participated in democratic rituals and the duties of citizenship, equating them with freedom. James Skipwith reported enjoying "som of the Privlige of a free man," serving on several juries and voting in elections.[44]

Even some aspects of Virginia culture and history remained with the black settlers from the Old Dominion. Because of the relative independence of the state colonization societies, some settlements in Liberia actually took their names and populations from certain American states, among them Virginia. Virginia families often settled together and supported each other financially and culturally, forming a substantial faction of the new country's economic and political elite. The rise of the Virginians in Liberia seems both ironic and oddly appropriate. Men like Joseph Jenkins Roberts ruled over a capital city named after a Virginian president who, while governor of their home state, suppressed a slave revolt based on principles of human freedom.

The Liberian experiment perhaps best sums up the varied influences on African Virginians before the Civil War. Black Virginians forged their identity amid revolutions and rebellions that brought concepts of human freedom and liberty to the fore. The concentrated effects of extended campaigning during the American Revolution and of two major slave revolts made Virginia's revolutionary heritage especially strong. Virginians in Liberia asserted their rights with zeal, just as their brothers and sisters in the Old Dominion would after Emancipation. Likewise, Liberian migrants maintained a respect for the institutions and ideals, if not the practice, of American liberty and democracy and instituted them in their new land. Finally, African Virginians had a strong sense of being a nation, race, and people based on a created, often biblical, idea of themselves as an African, diasporic people with a shared history of oppression.

The breakup of families, suppression of slave resistance, and denial of black autonomy by whites worked not only to control the day-to-day actions of slaves, but also to erase black historical and social memory. But just as we know that slave masters were unable to totally control real-life behavior, we also must recognize the ways that slaves reinvented ideas of liberty, family, and a biblical and racial destiny through oral tradition, genealogy, and collective community building to create memory. While acknowledging the considerable limitations of African Americans' circumstances in the early nineteenth century, the few examples given in this essay, which surely will be augmented by future research, demonstrate the existence of a robust African American memory in the slave South. Finally, the various glimpses of antebellum African American memory and the revealing comments of Sarah Wooden Johnson and Arthur Greene that open this essay alert us that African American remembrance was and is not monolithic; rather, it is a complex and evolving web of experience, culture, and memory.

NOTES

1. Charles L. Perdue, Thomas E. Barden, and Robert K. Phillips, eds., *Weevils in the Wheat: Interviews with Virginia Ex-Slaves* (Charlottesville: University Press of Virginia, 1976), 163.

2. Ibid., 123.

3. James C. Scott, *Domination and the Arts of Resistance: Hidden Transcripts* (New Haven: Yale University Press, 1990).

4. Petition of Thomas Evans, Lunenburg County, 11 November 1819, Legislative Petitions, Library of Virginia, Richmond (hereafter LVa.).

5. Petition of James, New Kent County, 31 November 1786, Legislative Petitions, LVa. See John Salmon, "'A Mission of the Most Secret and Important Kind': James Lafayette and American Espionage in 1781," *Virginia Cavalcade* 31 (1981): 78–85.

6. *Richmond Enquirer*, 29 October 1824; James E. Heath, *Edge-Hill, or The Family of the Fitzroyals: A Novel* (Richmond: W. T. White, 1828), 2:72–84, 223–24.

7. *Richmond Enquirer*, 29 October 1824.

8. Petition of Saul, Norfolk County, 9 October 1792, Legislative Petitions, LVa.

9. Tommy L. Bogger, *Free Blacks in Norfolk, Virginia, 1790–1860: The Darker Side of Freedom* (Charlottesville: University Press of Virginia, 1997), 24–31; James Sidbury, *Ploughshares into Swords: Race, Rebellion, and Identity in Gabriel's Virginia, 1730–1810* (Cambridge: Cambridge University Press, 1997), 39–49.

10. Douglas R. Egerton, *Gabriel's Rebellion: The Virginia Slave Conspiracies of 1800 and 1802* (Chapel Hill: University of North Carolina Press, 1993), 51, 102. Egerton favors artisanal republicanism as the key source of Gabriel's vision; Sidbury (*Ploughshares into Swords*) emphasizes the role of religion, which Egerton specifically rejects.

11. The only extant descriptions of either song are published, secondhand accounts. Nevertheless, there are good reasons to believe that the tunes are based on songs actually sung by pre–Civil War black Virginians. The story of these songs further highlights the difficulty of excavating the African American public and private discourses about a significant event. *Liberator*, 17 September 1831; R. Brimley Johnson, ed., *The Novels of Captain Marryat* (Boston: Little, Brown, 1896), 12:122–23.

12. Sidbury, *Ploughshares into Swords*, 256–76.

13. Ibid., 259.

14. *Richmond Dispatch*, 21 April 1852.

15. *Lynchburg News*, 12 April 1896; *Lynchburg Daily Virginian*, 21 April 1855.

16. Luther Porter Jackson, "Virginia Negro Soldiers and Seamen in the American Revolution," *Journal of Negro History* 27 (July 1942): 247–87.

17. Richmond Light Infantry Blues Minute Book, 5 August 1829, 76, and 29 January 1833, 102, LVa.

18. "A Patriotic Barber," *Richmond Daily Dispatch*, November 21, 1859; Ervin L. Jordan Jr., *Black Confederates and Afro-Yankees in Civil War Virginia* (Charlottesville: University Press of Virginia), 219; John A. Cutchins, *A Famous Command: The Richmond Light Infantry Blues* (Richmond: Garrett and Massie Publishers, 1934), 172; A. A. Taylor, "The Negro in Reconstruction Virginia," *Journal of Negro History* 11 (April 1926): pt. 1, 247.

19. Virginia Hayes Shepherd, interview, Norfolk, Va., 18 May 1937, in Perdue, Barden, and Phillips, *Weevils in the Wheat*, 259–60; also in Thomas E. Barden, ed., *Virginia Folk Legends* (Charlottesville: University Press of Virginia, 1991), 69–70.

20. *Niles' Weekly Register*, 19 February 1820, 440; Petition of Saul, Norfolk County, 9 October 1792, Legislative Petitions, LVa.

21. *The Negro in Virginia* (New York: Hastings House, 1940), 127–28; "The Escape of Gabriel Prosser," transcribed in Henry D. Spaulding, *Encyclopedia of Black Folklore and Humor* (New York: Jonathan David Publishers, 1972), 236–37.

22. Mary Jo Bratton, ed., "Fields's Observations: The Slave Narrative of a Nineteenth-Century Virginian," *Virginia Magazine of History and Biography* 88 (January 1980): 92–93; Peter J. Rachleff, *Black Labor in the South: Richmond, Virginia, 1865–1890* (Philadelphia: Temple University Press, 1984), 41, 45, 52.

23. Daniel Barclay Williams, *A Sketch of the Life and Times of Capt. R. A. Paul* (Richmond: Johns and Goolsby, 1885), 45.

24. Sidbury, *Ploughshares into Swords*, 11–49.

25. Henry Page, Richmond, to his son, 20 November 1856, Valentine Family Papers, Valentine Museum, Richmond. The 1870 census taker recorded Page as unable to read and write. The 71-year-old Page lived with his wife Maria, a 56-year-old washerwoman. U.S. Census, 1870, Clay Ward, Richmond City, p. 353, LVa (microfilm). However, Page's

obituaries in 1886 gave his age as 101. *Richmond State*, 13 December 1886; *Richmond Dispatch*, 12 December 1886.

26. *Richmond Dispatch*, 24 October 1854.

27. Petition of Peter Strange, Richmond City, 25 January 1844, Legislative Petitions, LVa.

28. Richmond City and Henrico County, Virginia, *1850 United States Census* (Virginia Genealogical Society, Special Publication No. 6, 1977), 317.

29. She enticed her offspring with the "butiful schools hear you can school you child for 25 cent per mont an mak him a man up to bisness. I lick this place better than I do Ohio tho you do not pay anything thar for schooling but you can mack a better livin in this place than in Ohio." William C. and Lucy P. Scott, Brantford, Canada West, to "My Dear Children," 29 October 1854, Norvell W. Wilson Papers, Southern Historical Collection, University of North Carolina Library, Chapel Hill.

30. On the idea that free status derived from a Native American heritage, see interviews with Octavia Featherstone, Sarah Wooden Johnson, Delia Harris, and Eliza Ann Taylor in Perdue, Barden, and Phillips, *Weevils in the Wheat*, 90–91, 130–31, 163–65, 284–85. On the preservation of family tradition and documentation of free birth, see T. O. Madden Jr., *We Were Always Free: The Maddens of Culpeper County, Virginia, a Two-Hundred-Year Family History* (New York: Norton, 1992).

31. *The Negro in Virginia*, 100.

32. Petition of free blacks and slaves, Richmond, endorsed by Mayor John Adams, 22 November 1823, Legislative Petitions, LVa.

33. *Richmond Dispatch*, 11 April 1860.

34. Bratton, "Fields's Observations:" 92–93; Janet Duitsman Cornelius, *When I Can Read My Title Clear: Literacy, Slavery, and Religion in the Antebellum South* (Columbia: University of South Carolina Press, 1991), 32–34, 79–80.

35. Legislative Petitions, Spotsylvania County, 16 March 1838, LVa. When their petition was turned down, they and other "progressive free Negroes" left the Old Dominion and headed for "Detroit, Michigan, and to other centers." Luther Porter Jackson, *Free Negro Labor and Property Holding in Virginia* (New York: Appleton, 1942), 24–25, 154. On the many ways that slaves used literacy to subvert white authority, see Cornelius, *When I Can Read My Title Clear*.

36. Richmond City and Henrico County, Virginia, *1850 United States Census*, 317; Scott to "My Dear Children," 29 October 1854, Wilson Papers. There is some variation in the spelling of "Pearman" and other names in the records. I have standardized it to avoid confusion or put the name in quotations.

37. Scott to "My Dear Children," 25 April 1859, Wilson Papers.

38. Marie Tyler-McGraw, "Richmond Free Blacks and African Colonization, 1816–1832," *Journal of American Studies* 21 (1987): 220–21; First African Baptist Church, Richmond, Minutes, 5 March 1843, 47, 6 April 1845, 77, LVa. (microfilm); Pat Matthews, "Joseph Jenkins Roberts: The Father of Liberia," *Virginia Cavalcade* 23 (Autumn 1973): 5–11.

39. Bell I. Wiley, *Slaves No More: Letters from Liberia, 1833–1869* (Lexington: University Press of Kentucky, 1980), 2.

40. James Skipwith, Monrovia, to Bertheer Edwards, 31 May 1860, and to John Hartwell Cocke, 20 August 1859, ibid., 130, 132. Background on Skipwith has been drawn

from Randall M. Miller, ed., *"Dear Master": Letters of a Slave Family* (Ithaca: Cornell University Press, 1978), 46–47;

41. Peyton Skipwith, Monrovia, to John H. Cocke, 22 April 1840, quoted in Wiley, *Slaves No More*, 52; Wilson Jeremiah Moses, *The Golden Age of Black Nationalism, 1850–1925* (Hamden, Conn.: Archon Books, 1978), 23–25.

42. Miller, *"Dear Master,"* 130, 132.

43. Wiley, *Slaves No More*, 68.

44. Ibid., 131.

part two

Finding Meaning in History
during the Confederacy
and Reconstruction

None of the various names attached to the American Civil War adequately convey the scale of disruption unleashed by the conflict. For both white and black southerners, the war acquired almost apocalyptic significance. From the outset of the Confederate experiment, white southerners attempted to assign historical significance to the risky course they had chosen. They discovered that the project of launching and defending a new nation was an immense and ultimately unsustainable undertaking that taxed virtually all of their resources and profoundly shook their society. For black southerners, the Civil War was the watershed event that marked the end of two centuries of enslavement. People who began the 1860s as chattel were by the end of the decade citizens who, in theory, enjoyed the same rights as their former owners. The magnitude of these transformations understandably left deep furrows in the historical consciousness of both blacks and whites.

The impulse of white and black southerners to turn to history to make sense of the events they were caught up in illustrates how collective memory often takes on particular significance in periods characterized by great change and turmoil. During such moments, when societies confront novel situations or sharp breaks with their past, introspection about the meaning of that past is unavoidable. The legitimacy of institutions and historical claims to political power, economic resources, and social prestige may all be called into question. Groups by necessity adapt old traditions to new conditions; familiar practices and symbols—such as folk songs, literary tropes, and rituals—may be modified to serve new purposes. And groups may fashion new traditions intended to promote the acceptance of new values demanded by contemporary circumstances.

Examples of such cultural inventiveness were rife in the Confederacy. Paradoxically, the Confederacy, a nation that barely survived four years, from its very inception claimed a long history. As Anne Sarah Rubin explains, Confederates envisioned their new nation as the legitimate continuation of the Revolutionary republic from which they had seceded. Like other members of their generation who were steeped in Revolutionary lore, Confederates felt compelled to square themselves with their Revolutionary inheritance. White southerners, however, faced the difficult task of making distinctive a past that they shared with their enemy. Only gradually during the course of the war did the Confederates manage to create a unique Confederate pantheon of heroes. Until then, the Revolutionary patriots remained conspicuous Confederate icons.

Rubin persuasively demonstrates that Confederates, like other nineteenth-century nation builders, understood the importance of employing history as a source of national identity and unity. But she, unlike some scholars who have emphasized the frailty of southern nationalism, contends that Confederates shrewdly invoked the American Revolution and the Founders as a source of unity and as a way to sidestep thorny and potentially divisive questions about slavery and the legitimacy of secession. White southerners may have been divided in various ways, but, Rubin insists, they were united in the reverence of 1776 and the Revolutionary-era patriots. The implications of her provocative conclusions about Confederate efforts to fashion a national past extend to the postwar South when Confederate apologists drew on this rich archive of associations with high principle and the Revolutionary legacy in their defenses of the "Lost Cause." Rubin's essay, in sum, is a compelling case study of the use of rituals and symbols in the service of fostering a purported shared southern white identity and of creating the appearance of historical continuity in a time of upheaval.

The project of imposing meaning on the past was equally salient for African Americans after Emancipation. In their struggles to secure equality and civil rights, blacks recognized the need to root their claims in the nation's history. As Gregg Kimball demonstrates in his essay in this collection, blacks in antebellum Virginia had already worked out a usable past that highlighted their quest for freedom and their contributions to the nation's development. Kathleen Clark, in her richly detailed essay, traces how blacks built on this inheritance in the immediate postwar years. Then, many African Americans were anxious that their understanding of the conflict be acknowledged. At stake for blacks in any debate over the war were questions about freedom, equality, and racial justice. As the wartime passions receded in the decades after the war, whites in both the North and the South emphasized sectional reconciliation and minimized the ideological origins of the conflict. Many African Americans, in contrast, insisted that the war had been a moral strug-gle. For Frederick Douglass, Henry McNeal Turner, and many other blacks, Emancipation was much more than a mere tactical ploy dictated by military pressures; it was the transcendent achievement that redeemed the war's bloodshed.

Clark recounts the ongoing struggle of southern African Americans to ascribe meaning to their freedom and the events that secured it. In an age when rituals of public participation and citizenship were accorded great importance, African Americans recognized the need for public ceremonies that gave voice to their historical memory. That celebrations of Emancipation would become focal points of black public life perhaps was inevitable. Eman-cipation Day festivities, Clark makes clear, enabled blacks to express myriad aspirations and memories. They simultaneously acknowledged their shared history as slaves, celebrated their new freedom and incorporation into the nation's public life, and underscored the centrality of their history to the nation's history.

Seventy-six and Sixty-one

Confederates Remember the American Revolution

Anne Sarah Rubin

If Thomas R. R. Cobb, a member of the Georgia delegation to the 1861 Montgomery Constitutional Convention, had gotten his way, the new southern nation would have been known as the "Republic of Washington."[1] His motion failed, and in a clear, conscious echo of the rejected United States, the country became the Confederate States of America. Both proposed names for the nation tell us something about the importance of history and continuity to Confederates. They understood the power of symbols, the hold that a name or an image could have on a people and their nation. They understood that for their new nation to establish itself in the future, it would have to draw on some version of the past.

The story of the Confederacy had its roots in the story of the American nation. As Confederates went about the work of nation building, they self-consciously drew on a ready-made myth of national origin, rejecting the recent American history of sectionalism and centralization and instead seizing on the American Revolution as the defining moment of their past.[2] Few, if any, Confederates actually remembered the Revolution, but its iconography—with its language of patriots and inalienable rights, heroes like George Washington and Light-Horse Harry Lee, stories of heroism and fortitude—gave Confederates a vocabulary and a conceptual framework on

which to base their claims for national legitimacy. In essays, speeches, newspapers, poems, and popular songs, Confederates told the story of a virtuous
nation led astray by fanatical, greedy, and power-hungry Yankees. Rather
than representing a challenge to the Founding Fathers' ideals, the Confederacy would be the perfection of their vision.

Even before the shots were fired on Fort Sumter, Confederates were chris-
tening their struggle the "Second American Revolution" and praising Jefferson Davis as a second Washington. Unionists were condemned as Tories,
Yankee soldiers as Hessians. The Revolution of 1861 was the logical completion of the Revolution of 1776. As Confederates sought first to inspire and
later to sustain their people, they drew on the patriotic example of colonists
fighting for seven years, surviving material hardship, and eventually van-
quishing a more numerous and better-equipped foe both to inspire people to
support the new nation and later to sustain them as their own struggle for
independence seemed to founder. Confederates were not destroying the
Union; they were restoring it to its earlier glory. They were not rebels, but
patriots. Their ancestors had fought a glorious revolution to create a great
nation; Confederates would do the same.[3]

Confederates thus used the language of ancestry to emphasize their connection to the past. Whether an individual southern soldier had descended
from a Revolutionary fighter was largely irrelevant. What mattered was that
Confederates, as a whole, cast themselves as a people apart. They were the
Anglo-Saxon Cavaliers to the northern Puritans and immigrants. Indeed,
northern Founders like Benjamin Franklin and Samuel and John Adams were
rarely mentioned and never emulated. It was almost as if the Revolution had
been a regional phenomenon. In this construction, the courage and fortitude
of the Revolutionary generation flowed through all Confederate veins: those
of women as well as men, yeomen as well as aristocrats, Mississippians as well
as Alabamians.

Too, when Confederates cast themselves as the guardians of Revolutionary
ideals, they avoided discussing other causes of the war, specifically slavery.
The word rarely appeared in evocations of the American Revolution, and
when it did, it was usually in the rhetorical sense of Confederates fearing
enslavement to northern masters. This silence on the subject of racial slavery
suggests that Confederates used the Revolutionary War to shift the terms of
debate, and to make the war more palatable to conditional Unionists, nonslaveholders, and outside nations. A war to re-create the glory of the Founders' nation was more honorable and less divisive than a war to protect the
slaveholding prerogatives of a small percentage of the Confederate popula-

tion. A war to re-create a virtuous America might appeal to the conditional Unionists by convincing them that the Union as it existed needed to be destroyed in order to be replaced by a better one, a Confederate one. The Revolutionary War thus gave Confederates a foundation on which to construct many different explanations and justifications.

One of the first books published in the new Confederate States was actually a reprint of a 1790s volume, *The Narrative of David Fanning*, which described the adventures of a notorious North Carolina Tory. Far from endorsing Fanning's disloyalty, the new editor, T. H. Wynne, used his exploits as an object lesson for Confederate readers. Wynne explicitly connected Fanning's experiences during the Revolutionary War with the plight that Confederates, particularly those in the border states of Virginia, Maryland, and Kentucky, faced at the hands of present-day Unionists. Indeed, he explained sadly, many of the brutal scenes related by Fanning were being reenacted, with Confederates as the victims. Wynne's preface further highlighted the connection between Confederates and their ancestors. Fanning's narrative told of southern patriots who "offered up their all" to secure American independence. But, Wynne continued:

> the patriot and the philanthropist must always regret that the struggles of those who in the contest with Great Britain shed their blood on every battle field, both in their own section and that of the North, for the freedom of the whole country, was productive only of a change of masters with them, for soon after throwing off the yoke of Old England they were, through adroit management and cunning legislation, made to assume that of New England and ere the actors engaged in the first struggle had all passed from the stage of life their children had to draw the sword to protect their homes and firesides from the foe who, having fattened upon their substance and grown insolent by successes, attempted to impose on them burdens more odious than those which they refused to bear from that nation to whom they owed their existence as a people.

In this one paragraph, Wynne encapsulated the story that Confederates told, a history of betrayal and ill-treatment, in which the southern states represented the colonies and the North became Great Britain.[4]

In the 1863 pamphlet *Our Home and Foreign Policy*, Henry St. Paul described a split between the northern and southern people that predated even the American Revolution. Northerners, St. Paul and others like him argued, were descended from the Puritans, whereas southerners were the heirs of the more dashing Cavaliers. This divided heritage, and the different values implicit in it, necessarily fostered two separate societies.[5] During the years following the Revolution the people further diverged, and "in the South, Northern stock got elevated and purified, and in the North, Southern blood became corrupt and degenerated. In less than a quarter of a Century, the North hated the South and the South despised the North." Constant association with immoral northerners, tainted by their pursuit of money and power, according to St. Paul, "debased" southern society, and the Missouri Compromise, with its limitations on the expansion of slavery, was "a standing insult and defiance." Only the moral fitness of southerners allowed them to "steer clear of northern infamy" and escape "the contagious influence of northern immorality."[6] A set of essays, collected under the title *The Confederate* and authored by "A South Carolinian," similarly blamed the present war on the sins of the North. As the author explained: "this separation would have been unnecessary, because the causes which led to, and justified it, would not have been allowed to spring into existence, if the maxims and admonitions of Washington had been heeded by the bigoted fanatics of the North."[7]

The Civil War was thus, in the words of another pamphleteer, the Reverend William Hall, a "Revolution" and "*a great historic protest, the only one of the sort in history, against philosophic infidelity and disorganizing wrong.*" It was a revolt against fanaticism framed in almost apocalyptic terms: "We are leading the great battle for the sum of modern history—for the regulated liberty and civilization of the age. It is conservative religion against atheism— constitutional law against fanatical higher law—social stability against destructive radicalism." In *Our Danger and Our Duty*, Presbyterian theologian James Henley Thornwell cast the conflict as a battle between despotism on the northern side and constitutional freedom on the southern. Confederates were not, in Thornwell's formulation, revolutionaries, but rather conservatives, resisting the North's own revolt against the Constitution. Hall agreed with this explanation, reflecting that "the epithet, *rebels*, so fiercely hurled upon us by the Northmen is sadly amusing when it is remembered, that we are simply contending for the inherent right of self-government, which was so nobly vindicated by their fathers and ours."[8]

Constitutional legitimacy was crucial to the Confederates' sense of themselves. They were fighting for their rights and the rule of law; they had not betrayed the Founders' vision. Edward A. Pollard opened his popular history of the first year of the war with a section entitled "Delusive Ideas of Union" in which he argued that the "Revolution of 1776" was never about forming a Union in the first place. Rather, the thirteen colonies worked together out of necessity alone. According to Pollard, the corruption began with the "Yankee" administration of President John Adams: "the idea predominated in the North and found toleration in the South, that the Revolution of '76, instead of securing the independence of thirteen States, had resulted in the establishment of a consolidated government to be under the absolute control of a numerical majority." Although "successfully inculcated," this doctrine was, in fact, "in direct opposition to the terms of the Constitution—the bond of the Union."[9]

Confederates repeatedly stressed that the Union of the Founding Fathers was one of separate and sovereign states. According to T. W. MacMahon in his book, *Cause and Contrast: An Essay on the American Crisis*, this distinction was one of the "well-known doctrines of the Revolutionary fathers. *They never regarded the Union other than a confederacy of states, leagued together 'for the common defense and to promote the general welfare.'*" A central tenet of this belief in the right of states to separate from the Union was the understanding that the colonies had been "separate, sovereign, and independent" when they joined together to fight and ratified the Constitution.[10] The separateness of the states and their right "to withdraw peaceably from other federated states" was acknowledged by the Declaration of Independence and secured by the Revolution. So inalienable was this right, argued a piece in the *Southern Monthly*, that "no provision, then, was implanted in the Federal Constitution explanatory of the mode by which a State might withdraw from the compact, for such it was, because the right to do so was self-evident." Confederates asserted their consistency, claiming rights intrinsic to America.[11]

Confederates pored over the debates in the Constitutional Convention and selections from the *Federalist Papers*. In early 1861, even before Virginia had voted to secede, Richmonder James Lyons devoted the first two of his *Four Essays on the Right and Propriety of Secession by the Southern States* to a detailed examination of the issue in the writings of James Madison and Alexander Hamilton. Lyons claimed that a state could dissolve the compact binding the states together if any article was breached by any party, a breach surely committed by the Yankees. Too, various of the *Federalist Papers* had argued that any political minority had the right to protect itself from the tyranny of the majority, and this was exactly what the southern states were doing.[12]

Lyons devoted his remaining two essays to less legalistic arguments in favor of secession, instead appealing to southern honor and morality. He encouraged his fellow Virginians to follow South Carolina's lead, asking "have you degenerated since the days of your fathers?" and calling on them to "in the language of James Madison, '*abolish the Union*.'" Lyons scoffed at the conditional Unionists who feared civil war on economic grounds, or because they thought slavery could best be protected within the Union, challenging:

> Are you, Virginians, the descendants of those men who pledged their "lives, their fortunes and their sacred honor" for the maintenance of a conflict for liberty, with a better, a stronger, and even more glorious government than this, and tamely bear such an insult as this? Are you so degenerate, so mercenary, as calmly to listen to, and coolly to weigh an argument which counsels you to slavery and dishonor, because it may be dangerous, and not profitable at first to be otherwise? God forbid. Spirits of Washington and Jefferson; of Madison, Marshall, and Lee; of Marion, Sumter and Moultrie, forbid.

Lyons denounced northerners as having betrayed the ideals of the Founders by threatening war against the South. The southern states were in the right; they and they alone could preserve the "principles of the revolution of '76"; they alone could save the honor of the Declaration of Independence.[13]

The language of betrayal pervaded Confederate rhetoric as southerners insisted on the essential conservatism of their actions. In his inaugural address as president of the Provisional Government in February 1861, Jefferson Davis explained that "we have changed the constituent parts, but not the system of government. The Constitution framed by our fathers is that of these Confederate States."[14] The author of "Too Much Nationality," in the *Southern Monthly*, stated simply that "the Government of the Confederate States is in conformity to that established by the fathers of the American Revolution, and a continuance of the Government they established." That government had been perverted and betrayed by the Yankee tendency to (wrongly) place the interests and power of the nation above that of the individual states. That tendency, combined with the Yankees' generally corrupt and materialistic character, led to a "national decadence" that one writer dated to "the close of the administration of the last Revolutionary statesmen," James Monroe.[15]

William Meade, the Episcopal bishop of Virginia, used this northern betrayal to argue that the new Confederate nation was in no way casting "contempt on the memory of our revolutionary fathers" and undoing "all which they so wisely did." The Founders had no way of foreseeing "all the unhappiness which has been felt for the last twenty or thirty years"; had they been able to, they surely would have provided for a means of separation. Moreover, Meade continued, if "those great statesmen" were alive to see the "failure of all their efforts and plans and warnings," they would side with the South. "Would they not rather say in tones of warning," asked Meade, "made more solemn as coming from the grave, 'Forbear this vain attempt. God himself has decreed the failure of our short-sighted devices. Yield then to his will. Still be brethren. Form a new alliance and be ready to combine against a common foe. Call not those who have departed from you rebels, traitors, conspirators, as our ancient foes did the noble fathers of our revolution; still be brethren of one great American family, honoring and being honored, and show to the world that a republic is not a failure; that it may divide, yet live and prosper."[16] Confederates' present revolution was legitimated by the past; they had no doubts that the Founders would be with them.

Noted southern polemicist George Fitzhugh also linked the Revolutions of 1776 and 1861, although with his own unique interpretation.[17] Rather than following the prevailing ideology that held the Confederate Revolution to be a continuation of the American Revolution, he claimed that it was an improvement on the first. Fitzhugh deemed the first Revolution a Reformation, one that went too far in its Lockean doctrines of "natural liberty, human equality, and the social contract." The Confederates were "rolling back the excesses" of the American Revolution, excesses that meant that "Liberty was degenerating into licentiousness." Fitzhugh, despite expressing his admiration for the English Cavaliers, stressed that he was not calling for a return to Toryism or monarchism. The general outlines of the American Constitution and the Union had worked well: "the only evil we have suffered under our institutions has arisen from our connection with the North. That connection dissolved let us preserve our government in its present form until some great and pressing evil suggests and necessitates a change." The conservative nature of the Confederacy was highlighted by the decision to keep the basic format of the American Constitution. The Constitution was not generally flawed; it was simply that the American nation had run its course, had outlived its usefulness. The next stage in the perfection of America would come under Confederate rule.[18]

All of these justifications for Confederate revolution shared an emphasis on the legitimacy of secession. In leaving the corrupted Union, Confederates were doing what God and their ancestors would have wanted, and who would dare challenge their actions? They believed that they were the wronged party in this dispute, victimized by northerners who changed the rules of politics midway through the game. The role that slavery and abolitionism had played in fostering sectional hostility, however, remained virtually unacknowledged. Confederates had no wish to engage in a debate about the rightness of slavery; that question had long been settled to their satisfaction and expounded upon by numerous proslavery theorists (George Fitzhugh and James Henley Thornwell among them). Furthermore, the Founders themselves—at least those who resided in southern states—had held slaves, and so, too, should Confederates. Nor would a war for slavery necessarily have held the same appeal to nonslaveholders as one for white liberty and the honor of ancestors. For these reasons, Confederates were happy to highlight other reasons they had to be angry with the North.

Confederates not only rewrote the history of the United States with their own distinctive slant, but they also drew on the iconography of the American past in creating the symbolic foundations of their own nation. Detailed analysis of constitutional questions was generally limited to publication in pamphlets or literary and political journals, but evocations of the American Revolution were everywhere in Confederate popular culture. In poems and songs, conversation and letters, northerners and southern Unionists repeatedly were damned as "Tories" and Union soldiers as "Hessians" (the latter a play on the many immigrants in the northern ranks).[19] These more popular forms illustrate the tremendous resonance the Revolution had among the general Confederate public. Although comparatively few readers might have been expected to wade through detailed treatises on the true intentions of the Constitution's framers, even a child could appreciate the significance of a picture of George Washington adorning a broadside or laugh at a new version of an old song. Revolutionary iconography had been a staple of political culture since the 1790s, and it provided a popular shorthand for expressing loyalty to party, state, or nation. Appropriating the instantly familiar to make the war comprehensible was a sure strategy for securing loyalty, for it meant that the new nation was not so different from the old. Holding on to the Revolution made it easier for new Confederates to reject the American present.[20]

Confederates sensitive to symbols sought every opportunity to express their continuing connection to the American past. Anonymous wags put new satirical words to familiar tunes, playing on past patriotism. "The Star Spangled Banner" became "The Stars and Bars," which began:

Oh! say do you see now so vauntingly borne,
In the hands of the Yankee, the Hessian and Tory,
The flag that once floated at Liberty's dawn,
O'er heroes who made it the emblem of glory?
Do the hireling and knave
Bid that banner now wave

O'er the fortress where freemen they dare to enslave?
Oh! say has the star-spangled banner become
The flag of the Tory and vile Northern scum?

"The Southern Yankee Doodle," illustrated with Confederate flags, mocked Major Robert Anderson for failing to hold Fort Sumter against Confederate bombardment, and "The New Yankee Doodle" expressed Confederate contempt for northerners:

Yankee Doodle had a mind
To whip the Southern traitors,
Because they didn't choose to live
On codfish and potatoes.
Yankee Doodle, doodle doo,
Yankee Doodle dandy,
And so to keep his courage up,
He took a drink of brandy.

The remaining verses described Confederates whipping Yankee Doodle at Manassas and Bull Run, all the while mocking his taste for brandy. No longer a symbol of home-grown resistance, Yankee Doodle had become a caricature of all that was weak and unmanly about Confederates' foes.[21]

Twice during the war the editor of the *Raleigh Register* lamented the lack of local Independence Day celebrations. In 1861 he complained that he could not "see any reason why the birth day of Liberty should be permitted to pass unheeded wherever Liberty has its votaries. The principles asserted on the Fourth Day of July, 1776, were those of man's competency for self-government, and the South in her late act of separation from the North has but reasserted those principles." Northerners, not Confederates, had "trampl[ed] the principles of 1776 underfoot," and Confederates had no reason to ignore the Fourth. Indeed, celebrating the holiday was a responsibility: "the accursed Yankees are welcome to the exclusive use of their 'Doodle,' but let the South hold on tenaciously to Washington's March and Washington's Principles, and on every recurring anniversary of their promulgation re-assert the great principles of human liberty." His calls appear to have gone unheeded, for two years later the *Register* printed a similar complaint, this time charging that "it is blasphemy and sacrilege for the Yankees now to name the Fourth of July. That Day, with all its glorious reminiscences, now belongs exclusively to the South, by which it should be ever honored and celebrated."[22]

While the Fourth might have been ignored in Raleigh, it continued to be a holiday in other parts of the Confederacy. Some army regiments marked it as they would have in peacetime, with speeches and barbecues, fireworks, and recitations of the Declaration of Independence.[23] In Charleston in 1861, the Fourth was celebrated "with all the respect which belongs to the day," with the traditional suspension of business, pealing of bells, lemonade and ice cream. In one concession to the times, "the blockading vessels fire the usual Federal salute at sunrise, which was answered from Forts Moultrie and Sumter by a Confederate salute."[24] Confederate civilians could also expect to be treated to Fourth of July orations, like the one given by A. W. Terrell in Austin, Texas, in 1861. Addressing a group assembled for the traditional reading of the Declaration of Independence, Terrell took as his main theme the question of whether the Confederate people had "drifted away from the faith bequeathed to us by the apostles of '76." His answer, of course, was "no"; rather, he recited the traditional story of southern betrayal at the hands of hypocritical Yankees bent on destroying the Union. Confederates, Terrell reminded his audience, in rebelling against tyranny were acting as their fathers had. They had learned well "the lessons of the past," they were right to assert their "independence of the old Union for causes before the magnitude of which the collection of a tax on tea dwindles into insignificance." Terrell urged men to enlist in the Confederate army to fight for freedom as their "grandsires" had before them, assuring his listeners that "Constitutional liberty expelled from most Governments upon earth finds now her abiding place among the Confederate States of America, and so long as they are true to the principles that now govern and control them, so long will the fourth day of July be held in grateful remembrance."[25]

Far and away the most often invoked icon of the Revolutionary War was George Washington. Throughout the antebellum period he was beloved by northerners and southerners alike and by 1861 had come to symbolize all that was virtuous and heroic about the American Revolution.[26] This love of Washington carried over into the Confederacy. Both Jefferson Davis and Robert E. Lee were dubbed "second Washingtons," and Davis consciously played up the allusions to Washington during his 1862 inauguration. Standing beside a statue of Washington on Washington's birthday, Davis invoked the Founder's values and sought his blessing, explaining that "on this the birthday of the man most identified with the establishment of American independence, beneath the monument erected to commemorate his heroic virtues and those of his compatriots, we have assembled to usher into existence the Permanent Government of the Confederate States. . . . The day, the memory, and the purpose seem fitly associated."[27]

Washington's image graced two manifestations of the Confederate government: postage stamps and the Great Seal of the Confederacy. In early 1863, as the Confederate Congress debated the seal's final design, an article in the *Southern Illustrated News* expressed agreement with the prevailing sentiment that it should bear the figure of a man on horseback—after all, southerners were known for their equestrian abilities—but argued against the man being a Cavalier. "We were not all Cavaliers, and we have no patrician order," the author argued. "Far better were it to let the horseman be the well known and revered image of George Washington, as the loftiest development of the Southern Gentleman." This rejection of the Cavalier image may seem surprising in light of Confederates' frequent evocations of the Cavalier myth. In this instance, the author appears to be making a conscious bid toward greater inclusion in the Confederate polity by proposing a figure to whom Confederates of all classes would respond with positive associations.[28]

Confederates took great pride in Washington's being a southerner and seized every opportunity to highlight his origins. Virginia was repeatedly christened the "Land of Washington," a reference not only to the land of his birth, but also to his final resting place. Confederates fought, therefore, not only for their own land and independence but also for their national heritage and for the preservation of sacred ground. Thus, Confederates were exhorted to "strike for the grave of Washington!" to "pass through a lake of fire" to retain "the remains of our Washington," and to let Washington "rest, calmly rest on his dear native shore." "The Land of Washington," sung to the popular tune "Annie Laurie," encapsulated Confederate concern for safeguarding Washington's legacy:

Mount Vernon's shrine is holy,
    Where Washington doth lie,
And to protect his ashes,
    We'll lay us down and die—
We'll lay us down and die,
    Yes ev'ry valiant son,
To save from desecration
    The Grave of Washington![29]

By claiming Washington, Confederates claimed the rightness of their arguments in favor of secession and independence. And they guarded that association jealously. "Washington a Yankee!" trumpeted a headline in a 1863 issue of the *Southern Illustrated News*, its author indignant that the northern ambassador to the Court of St. James had asserted that "if he were still alive, Washington would have been on the side of the Union." Yankees argued that Washington would have sought to preserve his Union at all costs, that he would have been horrified to see southerners trying to dismantle the nation for which he had fought, the nation that he had been proud to lead. Not so, argued this writer. To even suggest such a thing was an insult to Washington, the sort of insult that only a Yankee could conceive. In one of the few direct mentions of slavery in these sorts of writings, the author attributed Washington's loyalty to the South to his having been "a Southern man in all his feelings. He was, indeed, the very model of a Southern man . . . the owner of immense estates and a vast number of slaves." Washington's first love was Virginia and the Union "but a secondary passion"; he believed the United States to be nothing more than "an experiment" and one whose outcome was far from certain. Finally, Washington would never have sided with the North because "he never manifested any love for Yankees, but the exact contrary." Washington's distaste for Yankees, the author claimed, resulted from their cowardice under his command and their reluctance to help the southern colonies when the focus of the war shifted southward.[30]

As they sought to encourage enlistments, spur patriotism, and fight despair, Confederates tended to either appeal to heroic leaders or to call upon Confederate men to live out the patriotism of their more direct ancestors, the common soldiers of the Revolution. Both sorts of appeals resonated with men and women raised on stories of honor and bravery, courage and chivalry. Poems, songs, and stories invoked Revolutionary victories on southern soil at Yorktown, Eutaw Springs, Cowpens, and Kings Mountain and the spirits of George Washington, Henry "Light-Horse Harry" Lee, and Francis "The Swamp Fox" Marion.[31]

Confederates paid tribute to the great southerners of the American Revolution, hoping that their examples would animate the present generation. Several poems, circulated throughout the Confederacy in broadside form, urged Confederates to remember the fights of their forebears—for example:

Washington! Marion—still live in our songs,
Like them our young heroes shall spurn at our wrongs.[32]

The chorus of "The Spirit of 1861," an allusion to the "Spirit of '76," declared:

By the spirit of George Washington we swear,
The yoke of slaves we'll never, never wear!

In this poem, readers were reminded:

Our fathers's arms base tyranny defied, . . .
For freedom lived they, and for freedom died.[33]

"A Toast to Virginia," a song set to the tune "Red, White and Blue," had listeners raising their glasses to George Washington, "His Spirit, her armies commanding / Still lives in Virginia today."[34]

The authors of such appeals often compared Confederate generals to their Revolutionary counterparts, using a sort of cultural shorthand to express their fitness to lead, and biographical sketches in newspapers and journals frequently cited Revolutionary War service in a Confederate leader's heritage.[35] No Confederate general, however, had as much made of his lineage as Robert E. Lee, the son of the beloved Light-Horse Harry. A sketch of Robert E. Lee in the *Southern Punch* not only mentioned his father, but also claimed that his grandmother had been the "first love" of George Washington, thus doubling his Revolutionary "pedigree." Surprisingly, the sketch did not mention Lee's connection through his wife's family—his wife Mary Custis was the daughter of George Washington's adopted son, George Washington Parke Custis, the so-called child of Mount Vernon. The symbolism of one of the Confederacy's finest generals being the son of one of the Revolutionary Fathers was too great to ignore. One early poem assured Confederates that Virginians were coming to their rescue and that "they cannot fail, who fight for right, with the son of Harry Lee!" "The Sword of Harry Lee" related the reminiscences of "an aged man, all bowed with years" who had fought with Lee the elder and been given one of Harry's swords in thanks for his gallantry. Now the man was too old to "draw this sword again," so he passed it on to his grandson:

"Now go, and do your duty, boy,
    You bear no craven's name,
And as you dread your grandsire's curse,
    Ne'er sully it with shame.
And I, as long as life shall last,
    Within this bosom free,
Will ask God's blessing on you—and
    The son of Harry Lee."

Thus, just as the fathers had followed Harry, so would their sons follow his son to the same reward of independence.[36]

This image of the Revolutionary War soldier spurring on the younger generation pervaded Confederate calls to arms. In "The Spirit of '76—The Old Rifleman," an old man put on his buckskin suit and ventured forth to inspire the new crop of soldiers:

> We'll teach these shot-gun boys the tricks,
>   By which a war is won;
> Especially how seventy-six
>   Took tories on the run!

"Seventy-six and Sixty-one" sought to conjure up the "spirits of the glorious dead!" to lend their inspiration to their southern sons, and "The Spirit of '60" referred to a resurgence of "the old spirit of '76." When Mrs. Frank Wilson of Raleigh presented a Confederate flag to the Oak City Guards in June 1861, her husband read a poem of his own writing, encouraging "Patriots! Warriors! Freedom's Sons!" to "meet as your fathers met the foe!"[37] A poem directed at Marylanders called upon the "sons of Sires, of manly deeds, who died for love of right," to emulate their forebears and rise up in revolution against despotism. Apparently they were heeding the call, for the *Southern Monthly* reported that the Maryland regiments in the Confederate army "have adopted the title of 'the Maryland Line,' which was so heroically sustained by their patriotic sires of the first Revolution."[38]

Notions of manliness and patriotism intertwined in this Confederate rhetoric of revolution. The language of "True Sons" and "militant sires," of being "freemen" fighting for the freedoms granted in the Declaration of Independence, all spoke of a gendered call to arms, one in which Confederate honor was at stake.[39] Since their fathers and grandfathers had fought and won the prerogatives of manhood, Confederate sons were expected to do the same, as anything less would be a disgrace to both their families and their new nation. Such honor was due women as well. As a member of the New Orleans Washington Artillery wrote:

> The noble dames that gave you birth
>   Gave you the blood of braves;
> Dishonored shame would brand their brows,
>   Bore ye the yoke of slaves.
> Uprise ye, then, in Freedom's might,
>   Resistless as the waves!

Vanquish the foes of Southern rights
Or sleep in Southern graves![40]

Most of the Revolutionary War rhetoric was directed at men, at encouraging them to fight for freedom. Women were not, however, immune from social pressure; just as men were told to follow their forefathers, women were compared to their Revolutionary mothers. Newspapers frequently excerpted histories of the "First Revolution" and then made that praise applicable to Confederate women. Thus the *Southern Field and Fireside*, which quoted from Carlo (Charles) Botta's *History of the War of Independence of the United States of America*, paid "a glowing tribute to the women of South Carolina, which is no less richly deserved in their present struggle, not only by them, but by all the women of the Confederate States." Just as the women of Revolutionary War South Carolina had exhibited "a more than masculine fortitude," so too were the Confederate women praised for their patriotism, their unyielding commitment to the cause even in the face of hardship and terror, and their ability to keep their husbands from wavering. A similar passage from the novel *Horse Shoe Robinson* complimented the women of 1776 for having been "as warm for our cause as the men; and some of them perhaps a little warmer. They could be pitted against the women of any part of the aqueous globe, in bearing and forbearing both, when it is good for the country." A Confederate commentator deemed the compliment "eminently applicable to their Southern female descendants of the present day," who were "nobly holding up the hands" of the defenders of liberty.[41]

Confederate women and men both turned to the Revolutionary experience to find comfort in times of trouble. And it was there for the finding, often in the form of public exhortations compelling Confederates to keep the faith. The Civil War went on for much longer than Confederates had expected, and when the people feared that all might be lost, they were reminded of the bleak times in the Revolutionary War that eventually changed for the better. Confederates were repeatedly reassured that their ancestors had been in a much more difficult spot and had overcome far worse trials than those the Confederates presently were experiencing. The *Montgomery Mail* told readers that "in the Revolution there was more suffering and more destitution than will happen to us if the war should last for fifty years. We are in a better position for carrying on a war than almost every other people, and should not complain of hardship." A piece in the *Charleston Mercury*, after the double defeat at Gettysburg and Vicksburg in July 1863, pointedly argued that "if Generals Lee and Bragg and Johnston were to-morrow beaten in the field, we would not be in as desperate a condition as our fathers were when General Washington, vanquished at Long Island, Germantown, and White Plains, and with a handful of men under his command, attacked Princeton in the dead of winter." The American Revolution proved that selfless dedication to the cause of liberty could triumph over a more numerous and better-supplied foe, and Confederates were encouraged to keep that lesson before them at all times. "Think of the men of the Revolution," exhorted an article reprinted around the country in 1863, "when the entire South was overrun by the British and the Tories! . . . Are we any less than they?"[42]

Confederate newspapers frequently drew comparisons between the first and second revolutions by reprinting documents from the eighteenth century. In May 1862 the *Raleigh Register* ran Patrick Henry's speech of 23 March 1775 in which he proclaimed "give me liberty or give me death!" No commentary beyond the explanation that Henry was willing to *"fight and die, if necessary, for the freedom and independence of America"* was provided.[43] In a similar vein, women were to be encouraged by "A Revolutionary Heroine," the story of Miss Bishop of Halifax, North Carolina. She alone among her friends and neighbors stood up to British colonel Tarleton and took back the horse his men had stolen from her. Mrs. Susan H. Waddell penned a sketch of Benedict Arnold in response to rumors that sections of North Carolina were, in her words, "charged with want of loyalty to the Southern cause." Her hope was that "the following contrast between a true and fearless patriot on the one hand and a vile and selfish traitor on the other, may not be without its moral lesson at the present crisis."[44]

Each reprinted example conveyed a lesson about emulating the American Revolutionaries' fortitude. "The Heroes of the Revolution," appearing in the *Raleigh Register*, contained extracts from letters written by General Nathanael Greene before the battle of Eutaw Springs. Deemed to "possess interest at this time," the letters described the lack of adequate clothing and supplies among Greene's men. Needless to say, Greene's soldiers overcame their disadvantages, just as Confederates would. The *Southern Illustrated News* published a list of Revolutionary War battles along with the number of casualties suffered by the British and Americans at each one, expecting that it would "prove valuable as a table of reference at the present time." Out of twenty-three battles, the British lost more men in seventeen, the Americans in only four, and both sides lost an equal number in two battles—a clear lesson in the ability of a smaller, weaker foe to outlast one more powerful and better equipped. The *Charleston Courier* reprinted the first prayer offered up in the Continental Congress, explaining that "by substituting the Confederate

States, this prayer may be used and adopted by all who are now defending the general principles of Anglo-American Republicanism against the licentious Democracy and thieving Despotism which have usurped the once proud name of the United States."[45]

Justification, explanation, inspiration—all could be found in the American past. Confederates mined a rich and familiar vein of symbolism, producing rhetoric that immediately resonated as they sought to make secession and war comprehensible. As important as what the iconography of the American Revolution allowed Confederates to say, is what it allowed them to avoid discussing: slavery. With slavery minimized by a language that did not include it, Confederates were free to construct other rationales for fighting. Historians have long struggled to understand why nonslaveholders fought so fiercely to preserve slavery. Perhaps they fought to preserve something else: their own understanding of what a nation should be. Perhaps they fought to live up to their ancestors, to experience the thrill of revolution and the triumph of victory against a foe who, they truly believed, sought to destroy them. By talking about the American Revolution, Confederates constructed an ideal past, one in which heroic men and women stood together and defeated a more numerous and better-equipped enemy. This idealized past, Confederates thought, would provide a blueprint for their future, a future in which all Confederates could join, regardless of class or gender. But race was to have been a different matter entirely.

NOTES

1. William C. Davis, "A Government of Our Own": The Making of the Confederacy (New York: Free Press, 1994), 103.

2. On Confederate nation building and the creation of a Revolutionary myth of origin, see Drew Gilpin Faust, The Creation of Confederate Nationalism: Ideology and Identity in the Civil War South (Baton Rouge: Louisiana State University Press, 1988), 3-15, and Charles Royster, The Destructive War: William Tecumseh Sherman, Stonewall Jackson, and the Americans (New York: Knopf, 1991), 144-47, 153-54, 175-76. On the connections between culture and nationalism in general, see Richard Handler, Nationalism and the Politics of Culture in Quebec (Madison: University of Wisconsin Press, 1988), 17-19, 36-39, 50-51, and Eric Hobsbawm's introduction to Hobsbawm and Terence Ranger, eds., The Invention of Tradition (Cambridge: Cambridge University Press, 1983), 9, 13. On the specific importance of print culture, see Benedict Anderson, Imagined Communities: Reflections on the Origin and Spread of Nationalism, rev. ed. (London and New York: Verso, 1991), 25, 35, 61-64.

3. Northerners, especially Abraham Lincoln, also drew on the symbolism of the Revolutionary War as they rallied to fight to keep the Union together. They too believed themselves to be the heirs of "Revolutionary sires," they too drew on tales of Revolution-

ary fortitude to maintain support for the war. See Royster, *Destructive War*, 147–56; James M. McPherson, *Abraham Lincoln and the Second American Revolution* (New York: Oxford University Press, 1991), esp. chaps. 1 and 2. For examples of this rhetoric, see "Proclamation of Governor Curtin," *New York Herald*, 16 June 1863, and "Blessings in Disguise—The Benefits of This War," *New York Herald*, 16 November 1864.

4. T. H. Wynne, ed., *The Narrative of David Fanning (A Tory in the Revolutionary War with Great Britain), Giving an Account of His Adventures in North Carolina, from 1775 to 1783* (Richmond: Printed for Private Distribution Only, 1861), ix–x.

5. Henry St. Paul, *Our Home and Foreign Policy* (Mobile, Ala.: Printed at the Office of the Daily Register and Advertiser, 1863), 3–5. For other examples, see Rev. William A. Hall, *The Historic Significance of the Southern Revolution* (Petersburg, Va.: A. F. Crutchfield and Co., 1864), 18–20; "The Puritan and the Cavalier," an extract from the *London Times* reprinted in *Southern Cultivator* 21 (March–April 1863): 53. The definitive study of this idea is William R. Taylor's *Cavalier and Yankee: The Old South and the American National Character* (Cambridge: Harvard University Press, 1979). Taylor uses literary sources to illuminate the growth of this myth in the antebellum South. See pp. 15–22, 327–39.

6. St. Paul, *Our Home and Foreign Policy*, 5.

7. *The Confederate, by a South Carolinian* (Mobile, Ala.: N.p., 1863), 3.

8. Hall, *Historic Significance*, 12, 44, 39; James Henley Thornwell, *Our Danger and Our Duty* (Raleigh: Raleigh Register Steam Power Press, 1863), 5–6. For a brief biographical sketch of Thornwell, see Michael O'Brien, ed., *All Clever Men Who Make Their Way: Critical Discourse in the Old South* (Athens: University of Georgia Press, 1992), 420–21.

9. Edward A. Pollard, *The First Year of the War* (Richmond: West and Johnson, 1862), 18. On the importance of constitutionality, see Don E. Fehrenbacher, "The Confederacy as a Constitutional System," *Constitutions and Constitutionalism in the Slaveholding South*, Mercer University Lamar Memorial Lectures No. 31 (Athens: University of Georgia Press, 1989), 62; George Rable, *The Confederate Republic: A Revolution against Politics* (Chapel Hill: University of North Carolina Press, 1994), 46–49; Royster, *Destructive War*, 173–77.

10. T. W. MacMahon, *Cause and Contrast: An Essay on the American Crisis* (Richmond: West and Johnson, 1862), 146–47. For a similar explication, see Jefferson Davis, "Message to Provisional Congress," 29 April 1861, in James D. Richardson, ed., *The Messages and Papers of Jefferson Davis and the Confederacy Including Diplomatic Correspondence, 1861–1865* (New York: Chelsea House-Robert Hector, 1966), 1:63.

11. "Too Much Nationality," *Southern Monthly* 1 (October 1861): n.p.

12. James Lyons, *Four Essays on the Right and Propriety of Secession by the Southern States, by a Member of the Bar of Richmond* (Richmond: Ritchie and Dunnavant, Printers, 1861), 9–18. The essays were originally published under the signature "Virginius."

13. Ibid., 37, 42–43, 48–49.

14. Jefferson Davis, "Inaugural Address of the President of the Provisional Government," 18 February 1861, in Richardson, *Messages and Papers*, 36.

15. "Too Much Nationality," *Southern Monthly* 1 (October 1861): 87; "Philosophy of the Revolution," *Southern Monthly* 1 (January 1862): 321; "Twin Bigotries," *The Age* 1 (February 1864): 81–82; Pollard, *First Year of the War*, 8.

16. William Meade, *Address on the Day of Fasting and Prayer Appointed by the President*

of the Confederate States, June 13, 1861; Delivered at Christ Church, Millwood, VA, by Bishop Meade, Published by Request (Richmond: Enquirer Book and Job Press, 1861), 13.

17. Fitzhugh, a Virginian, was best known for his attacks on free labor and defenses of slavery in Sociology for the South, or the Failure of Free Labor (1854) and Cannibals All! or Slaves without Masters (1857). His writings tended to be more extreme and more sensational than those of other proslavery writers. See Eugene D. Genovese, The World the Slaveholders Made: Two Essays in Interpretation (New York: Pantheon Books, 1969); Harvey Wish, George Fitzhugh: Conservative of the Old South (Charlottesville: University Press of Virginia, 1938); and Harvey Wish, George Fitzhugh: Propagandist of the Old South (Baton Rouge: Louisiana State University Press, 1943).

18. George Fitzhugh, "The Revolutions of 1776 and 1861 Contrasted," Southern Literary Messenger (November–December 1863): 718–24.

19. For a mention of Tory in relation to East Tennessee loyalists, see Lancelot Minor Blackford to Mrs. William M. Blackford, 20 November 1863, Blackford Family Letters, Special Collections, Alderman Library, University of Virginia; for North Carolina Tories, see "The Other Side of the Picture," Raleigh Register, 6 August 1862. For instances of "Hessian," see "Country, Home and Liberty" and "Chivalrous C.S.A.," Wake Forest Broadside Poetry Collection, Wake Forest University, Wake Forest, N.C.

20. On the endurance and importance of the Revolutionary War to nineteenth-century American political culture, see David Waldstreicher, In the Midst of Perpetual Fetes: The Making of American Nationalism, 1776–1820 (Chapel Hill: University of North Carolina Press, 1997), and Michael Kammen, A Season of Youth: The American Revolution and the Historical Imagination (New York: Knopf, 1978).

21. "Rebel Poetry: The Stars and Bars" and "The Southern Yankee Doodle," Wake Forest Broadside Poetry Collection; "The New Yankee Doodle," in The Stonewall Song Book: Being a Collection of Patriotic, Sentimental and Comic Songs, 11th ed., enlarged (Richmond: West and Johnston, 1865), 29.

22. "Fourth of July," Raleigh Register, 3 July 1861, 8 July 1863.

23. Bell Irvin Wiley, The Life of Johnny Reb: The Common Soldier of the Confederacy (1943; reprint, Baton Rouge: Louisiana State University Press, 1995), 168; Reid Mitchell, Civil War Soldiers: Their Expectations and Their Experiences (New York: Viking, 1988), 20–21. On soldiers using the rhetoric of liberty and the American Revolution to explain their service in the army, see James M. McPherson, For Cause and Comrades: Why Men Fought in the Civil War (New York: Oxford University Press, 1997), 104–6.

24. Charleston Mercury, 6 July 1861.

25. A. W. Terrell, Oration Delivered on the Fourth Day of July, 1861, at the Capitol, Austin, Texas (Austin: John Marshall and Co. at the Gazette Office, 1861), 3, 15, 17.

26. On George Washington's character and the reasons why he was such a popular figure, see Gordon S. Wood, "The Greatness of George Washington," Virginia Quarterly Review 68 (Spring 1992): 189–207; Barry Schwartz, George Washington: The Making of an American Symbol (New York: Free Press, 1987); and Kammen, Season of Youth, 42, 47–48.

27. Jefferson Davis, "Inaugural Address," 22 February 1862, in Richardson, Messages and Papers, 183. For Jefferson Davis as a second Washington, see "Song of the South! Gen. Jeff Davis," Wake Forest Broadside Poetry Collection. David Waldstreicher (In the Midst of Perpetual Fetes, 112–13, 129, 214–15) has traced this association of political

104   *Anne Sarah Rubin*

speeches with Washington's birthday to its origins as a Federalist tactic in the 1790s. It fast
became a convention for all political parties.

28. "Our Flag and Seal," *Southern Illustrated News*, 12 March 1863.

29. "Patriotism," *Southern Monthly* 1 (September 1861): 16; Henry W. R. Jackson, "The
Battles of Manassas and Richmond: A Warning to Lincoln," in Henry W. R. Jackson, ed.,
Historical Register, 25; "The Grave of Washington," in *The Cavalier Songster* (Staunton,
Va.: N.p., 1865), 31; "The Land of Washington," in *Cavalier Songster*, 14–15.

30. "Washington a Yankee!" *Southern Illustrated News*, 4 April 1863.

31. J. C. W., "The South," *Southern Monthly* 1 (November 1861): 212; John R. Thompson, "A Poem for the Times," *Raleigh Register*, 22 May 1861; Henry Timrod, "Carolina,"
in William F. Shepperson, ed., *War Songs of the South, Edited by "Bohemian," Correspon-
dent Richmond Dispatch* (Richmond: West and Johnson, 1862), 87–90. Many of the
poems and songs that Shepperson collected had appeared previously in newspapers such
as the *Richmond Dispatch, Richmond Enquirer*, and the *Columbus (Ga.) Times*. Similarly,
newspapers also reprinted poems from various published collections.

32. "The Confederate States," Wake Forest Broadside Poetry Collection.

33. "The Spirit of 1861," ibid.

34. "A Toast to Virginia," ibid.

35. Kentucky raider John Hunt Morgan, known as "The 'Marion' of the War," was a
lineal descendent of Revolutionary general Daniel Morgan. Confederates were also told
that the fathers of both Leonidas Polk and Joe Johnston served in the Continental army,
and Joseph Johnston's mother was a niece of Virginia's great patriot, Patrick Henry. See
biographical sketches of Morgan, Johnston, and Polk in *Southern Illustrated News*,
20 September, 1, 15 November 1862.

36. "Daguerreotype of General Lee: His Pedigree," *Southern Punch*, 19 December
1863; "Virginia to the Rescue," reprinted in Shepperson, *War Songs of the South*, 98;
"The Sword of Harry Lee," *Southern Monthly* 1 (January 1862): 344–45.

37. Frank Ticknor, "The Spirit of '76—The Old Rifleman," from the *Richmond Dispatch*, John W. Overall, "Seventy-six and Sixty-one," from the *Georgia Crusader*, and
"The Spirit of '60," from the *Columbus Times*, all reprinted in Shepperson, *War Songs of
the South*, 57–58, 62–63, 58–59; "Flag Presentation," *Raleigh Register*, 5 June 1861.

38. "To the Maryland Sons of Revolutionary Sires!," Wake Forest Broadside Poetry
Collection; "A Song for 'The Maryland Line,'" *Southern Monthly* 1 (January 1862): 351.

39. For examples of this language, see A. J. Requier, "Independence Hymn," reprinted
in Shepperson, *War Songs of the South*, 66–67. For the connection between honor and
patriotism, see Bertram Wyatt-Brown, *Southern Honor: Ethics and Behavior in the Old
South* (New York: Oxford University Press, 1982), 112–13.

40. G. M. H., Washington Artillery, "Uprise Ye Braves," from *Richmond Dispatch*,
reprinted in Shepperson, *War Songs of the South*, 103.

41. "The Women of the First Revolution," *Southern Field and Fireside*, 13 February
1864; *Raleigh Register*, 6 November 1861. Confederate women were constantly praised for
their self-sacrificing devotion to the cause. They were hailed as "Earth Angels" and "The
Mainstay of the South," and in the tradition of "Republican Motherhood" they were seen
as the nurturers of the new, Godly, and moral Confederate nation. In recent years several
studies of Confederate women and the impact of gender on Confederate nationalism have
appeared. See George C. Rable, *Civil Wars: Women and the Crisis of Southern Nationalism* (Urbana: University of Illinois Press, 1989); LeeAnn Whites, *The Civil War as a*

Crisis in Gender: Augusta, Georgia, 1860–1890 (Athens: University of Georgia Press, 1995); and Drew Gilpin Faust, *Mothers of Invention: Women of the Slaveholding South in the American Civil War* (Chapel Hill: University of North Carolina Press, 1996).

42. "Never Say Die," *Montgomery Mail*, 18 January 1862, reprinted in Jackson, *Historical Register*, 37; "Our Cause & Our Course," *Charleston Mercury*, 17 July 1863; Letter to the editor, *Montgomery Advertiser*, 8 August 1864; "Lessons of Encouragement," in Jackson, *Historical Register*, 20, reprinted in *Southern Field and Fireside*, 28 February 1863.

43. "Speech of Patrick Henry," *Raleigh Register*, 21 May 1862. The *Southern Punch* also mentioned Henry in an article about St. John's Church in Richmond, the site of the speech. "Revolutionary Curiosity," *Southern Punch*, 12 October 1863.

44. "A Revolutionary Heroine," *Southern Illustrated News*, 13 June 1863; Mrs. Susan H. Waddell, "General Benedict Arnold," *Raleigh Register*, 14 May 1862.

45. "The Heroes of the Revolution," *Raleigh Register*, 13 November 1861; "Battles of the Revolution," *Southern Illustrated News*, 20 September 1862; "The First Prayer in Congress," *Charleston Courier*, 28 January 1862, reprinted in Jackson, *Historical Register*, 22.

Celebrating Freedom

Emancipation Day Celebrations and African American Memory in the Early Reconstruction South

Kathleen Clark

On New Year's Day, 1866, hundreds of African American men, women, and children arrived at the Springfield Baptist Church in Augusta, Georgia, in anticipation of the celebration of the first anniversary of their freedom. A reporter for the local Republican newspaper, the *Colored American*, noted that people filled the church "from floor to roof," long before the scheduled activities began. At the appointed hour, exercises commenced with a choral rendition of "Blow Ye the Trumpet," and the expectant crowd settled in for a prayer and recitation of the Emancipation Proclamation. Halfway through the proceedings, a welcome break allowed everyone to be "again refreshed and re-animated by some delicious music." The congregation returned to their seats when Henry McNeal Turner, an African Methodist Episcopal (AME) minister, began the keynote address. Turner captivated the crowd with a fiery discourse on the historical and religious significance of Emancipation, then stepped down to a storm of applause. Finally, the crowd quieted to accommodate the speeches of two white officials, who stressed the importance of working hard, being peaceable, and attempting to "cultivate friendly relations" with local whites. At the end of the day, the *Colored American*

was pleased to report that "the First Anniversary of Freedom had been a perfect success."[1]

The freedom celebration in Augusta was one of hundreds of African
American commemorative ceremonies occurring around the South in the
years following Emancipation. Just as Confederate widows paid tribute to
fallen heroes in elaborate graveyard rituals, African Americans laid the foundation for their own version of the past by commemorating the birth of
freedom. On these occasions, people crowded into local churches, paraded
through city streets, and rallied in town squares. They prayed, applauded
speeches, unfurled banners, and raised flags. One woman, surveying the
number and variety of African American ceremonies occurring around her,
predicted, "Some will look [back] upon these times as if nothing but politics,
mass meetings, drums and fifes and gilt muskets were all the go."[2]

Although African American commemorations clearly impressed contemporary observers, the growing body of scholarship on historical memory in
the post–Civil War South has left them all but invisible. Instead, historians
have concentrated on white southerners' extensive efforts to memorialize the
"Lost Cause."[3] This essay aims to reestablish the significance of African
American commemorative culture and, in doing so, to expand our understanding of the multiple and conflicting ways that all southerners employed
and displayed a "usable past" as they endeavored to shape the future of the
postwar South.[4]

The early years of Reconstruction, which are the focus of this essay,
comprised a unique period in the development of African American commemorative culture in the postwar South. African Americans reshaped local
calendars and gave new meaning to significant public spaces in communities
throughout the region. Not only southern freedpeople, but also freeborn
African Americans, as well as various groups of northern whites, collaborated
in creating and organizing diverse holidays and celebrations. The mood of
these celebrations ranged from solemn church hall ceremonies on New Year's
Day to boisterous downtown parades on the anniversary of the Confederate
defeat. Massive processions overfilled town squares and other areas that
had been off-limits to African Americans before the war. A broad range
of people—black and white, freeborn and recently freed, male and female,
young and old—took turns articulating bold new visions of the South's past,
present, and future.

As different groups struggled to redefine what it meant to be black and
American, commemorative celebrations became a meaningful arena for reflecting, enacting, and refashioning these evolving identities.[5] Through the

speeches, parades, and ceremonies that made up commemorative celebrations, former slaves recast themselves as proud members of a heroic race and worthy citizens of a revitalized nation. Making history—that is, telling stories about the role of black people in the unfolding past—was crucial to their assertion of these identities. In the celebrations, African Americans established links between the founding of the country, their own freedom, and a heritage of American heroism. Enthusiastic crowds applauded both the Declaration of Independence and the Emancipation Proclamation, while speakers outlined a freedom-loving American ancestry that commonly included such figures as Crispus Attucks, John Brown, Robert Gould Shaw, and Abraham Lincoln.

Even as the commemorative ceremonies celebrated consensus, they just as frequently served as forums for negotiation and debate. Freedpeople did not always agree on the most accurate interpretation of the past or the most advantageous direction for the future, nor did the freeborn African Americans, Union army officers, Freedmen's Bureau officials, white Republicans, and northern missionaries who also had a role in shaping black ceremonies. These separate groups viewed the achievement of black freedom disparately, and they invested the commemorative celebrations with multiple and conflicting meanings. In the unstable atmosphere of the post–Emancipation South, hierarchies of class and gender compounded disagreements between northerners and southerners, whites and blacks, former slaves and the freeborn.[6]

While African American celebrations revealed contests over the meaning of the past and the best direction for the future, they occurred in a context of even greater interracial conflict in the post–Emancipation South. As white southerners struggled to reestablish economic and political control after the war, they simultaneously endeavored to shape regional memory in their own self-image. Under the special conditions of Reconstruction, however, southern whites vied with many groups for the power to define the meaning of the region's history, just as they were forced to contend with black voting rights and the "interference" of federal officials. African American commemorative celebrations generated energetic participation and intensive debate precisely because they engaged the social, political, and cultural struggles of the post–Emancipation period.

Celebrations followed quickly on news of freedom. In the Union-occupied South, Lincoln's issuance of the Emancipation Proclamation prompted ceremonies organized by numerous groups, including federal officials, northern missionaries, and the freedpeople themselves. In Port Royal, South Carolina, General Rufus B. Saxton declared New Year's Day, 1863, "a day which is destined to be an everlasting beacon-light, marking a joyful era in the progress of a nation." Following Saxton's proclamation, African Americans commenced a daylong celebration, replete with speeches, flag presentations, prayer, dancing, and a barbecue.[7] Federal authorities were not always so supportive of black celebrations—military commanders, for instance, did nothing to stop hostile whites from assaulting African Americans engaged in an Emancipation celebration in Key West, Florida.[8] But in many areas, freedpeople took advantage of the presence of northern troops to initiate public ceremonies.[9]

At the war's close, African Americans established various holidays to commemorate northern victories and the coming of freedom. As a result, not only 1 January but also a host of other dates came to be honored by freedpeople in different parts of the South.[10] The largest postwar celebrations occurred in towns and cities and attracted hundreds of men, women, and children from the surrounding countryside. Indeed, some families traveled considerable distances—forty, fifty, even sixty miles—to attend a ceremony. The freedpeople's excursions exasperated local whites, who grumbled that men and women were "desert[ing] the farms from all parts of the country" to participate in festivities.[11] In contrast, a Union soldier applauded the exuberant spirit of African Americans who participated in an Emancipation celebration in New Orleans: "At an early hour the people began to pour into the city from the country and surrounding villages. Men, women, and children, young and old. . . . For the time being, the plantation, the farm, and workshops, hotels—and all places of labor and amusement, were deserted and forgotten. The people were out to celebrate what to them was a great epoch in the history of the race."[12]

Those traveling great distances would have begun their long trek a day or two in advance of the actual celebration. At first, there might have been only a scattering of people, spread over many miles—a family here, a group of travelers there—but as the commemorators neared their destination, the roads would have grown more crowded. Those on foot were joined by others on horseback, and wagons and carriages increased the traffic along the way. An eyewitness described just such a scene as freedpeople began arriving at a rally in Lexington, North Carolina: "[W]ith the earliest dawn of the morning, the sturdy farmer with his team—horse, mule, or ox, as the case might be— could be seen wending his way to 'the grove.' Whole families—from the . . . sire to the prattling babe [came along the way]."[13] Small groups eventually

merged with the substantial crowds that whites observed with much trepida-
tion. One white onlooker, for instance, imagined a "great black serpent,
unfolding coil after coil, dragging its slow length along," as he viewed an
assemblage of African Americans in Norfolk, Virginia.[14]

The war for southern memory was waged in hundreds of local skirmishes,
as white and black residents enacted competing versions of history in town
squares, on city streets, and at neighborhood graveyards. On an early morning in May 1866, white women assembled at the local cemetery in Augusta to
pay tribute to the Confederate dead. Some days later, students and teachers
from the local freedmen's schools attempted to ornament the graves of the
Union soldiers but suddenly were surrounded and forced to flee by a group
of armed men. In the ensuing controversy, the mayor of Augusta justified the
exclusion of African Americans from the cemetery by drawing on a prewar
ordinance; the commander of the Georgia Freedmen's Bureau, fearful of
provoking local whites, declined to support the guarantee of free access to the
graveyard by freedpeople. In the end, the Union graves went unadorned,
causing a Republican editor to lament the triumph of Confederate memorialists in Augusta: "[H]as it already come to this; that the graves of men,
who fought to overthrow our Government can be covered with flowers . . .
but that the colored friends of our brave Union boys, who have died to
save their country, can not honor their memory, by strewing flowers upon
their graves!"[15]

Local whites did not always succeed in suppressing competing memories.
The efforts of white residents of Richmond could not prevent local freedpeople from holding a massive parade on 3 April 1866, the first anniversary of the
city's surrender to Union forces. When African Americans announced their
plans for a celebration, angry whites denounced it as "a jollification on the
saddest of days" and warned that participants would be "observed and
remembered," thus making "enemies where and when they most need
friends."[16] A teacher in a local freedmen's school reported that white citizens
"have threatened and protested, and even burned the church . . . where the
preparatory meetings have been held."[17] Still, the commemoration went forward as planned. A sympathetic minister reported that thousands of people
participated in the celebration, "notwithstanding the threats 'We will throw
them all out of employment,' and 'We will wade through blood before the
nigger shall [sic] celebrate the day.' "[18]

Some white southerners held outside "interlopers" solely responsible for
the African American commemorative activities. Rather than crediting the
freedpeople themselves with sincere feelings of allegiance and affection for

the country, southern whites identified northern visitors as an alien force bent on turning otherwise loyal blacks against the South. If only outsiders would stop interfering in southern affairs, many whites reasoned, such disturbances would cease. In the spring of 1866, a reporter for the *Augusta Transcript* (a white Democratic paper) reflected this view when he took issue with a northern teacher's decision to lead black students in a performance of "The Battle Song of Freedom." The reporter predicted that the effect of the song would be "to excite [the freedpeople's] hatred against the white people among whom their lives must be spent." He noted that the piece included the verse, "Down with the Traitors! / And up with the Stars!" and was accompanied by "fierce gesticulations and a waving of flags." Finally, he wondered whether a "wise and kindly teacher" could not have chosen a different tune to "celebrate the Flag," one "less likely to give offense and produce mischief." Responding to the *Transcript's* complaint, a writer for the *Loyal Georgian* (a local Republican paper and successor to the *Colored American*) scoffed at the notion that anyone in Georgia would take offense at the performance. After all, former Confederates who sought to reclaim the rights of citizenship were not hesitating to declare their fidelity to the Union. Just who are those, he asked ironically, "that are likely to be offended when loyal voices sing, 'Down with the traitors and up with the stars?' " He continued, "Certainly *none but traitors*; and you say there are none in Georgia. There are none, therefore, to whom the 'Battle Cry of Freedom' is 'likely to give offense.' "[19]

Southern whites indulged in wishful thinking when they imagined that groups of "female disorganizers" and "damn Republicans" were responsible for the proliferation of patriotic celebrations among the freedpeople. Although northern whites did encourage certain forms of patriotic expression, African Americans unquestionably articulated their own feelings and ideas about the nation and their place within it. In fact, many groups—black and white, northern-born and native—struggled to put forward their own interpretations of African American freedom through their participation in commemorative ceremonies. At times, these respective visions shared considerable common ground, and on other occasions they diverged quite sharply.[20]

Some differences were rooted in class. The repeated urging of native leaders and visiting officials that African American celebrations be "orderly" and "dignified" disclosed a degree of unease with the high spirits and broad participation that characterized such events. By all accounts, black commemorative occasions could be large, even massive affairs. Even at lesser events, the boisterous aspects of the freedpeople's behavior challenged staid standards of decorum and respectability. Leaders and officials—black and white—

promoted "respectable" standards of behavior among the freedpeople. Ministers, teachers, and officials reinforced these efforts in their voluminous reports, which repeatedly emphasized the order and propriety of participants' actions. Such accounts of black celebrations countered southern white ridicule. But black and white elites also strained to channel the freedpeople's enthusiasm and passion toward acceptable ends, and their accounts of public observances were prescriptive as well as descriptive, reflecting their particular visions of a moderate and restrained black citizenship. A similar impulse was evident in reports on some parades. The white press pointedly remarked on the contrast between the "better class of our colored population . . . who yesterday, stepp[ed] stately, erect and well-dressed, in the front ranks of the pageant [of an Emancipation parade]" and the majority of participants. "Treading in the rear . . . mounted and dismounted, in carriages and afoot, crowding upon the heels of the 'colored gentlemen' in broadcloth, regalia, sash, baton, and belt, came the real mourners of the occasion."[21]

Divergent interests were apparent even among the organizers of African American commemorative celebrations. These conflicting motivations found expression in the spectrum of voices heard at the events, ranging from conservative and accommodationist stances to more radical demands for a thorough transformation of southern society. The political issues of the day commanded attention, including appeals to freedmen to exercise "good judgment" in upcoming elections. Some participants favored subjects that earned the approval of conservative southern whites; they warned freedpeople to work hard, to form contracts, and not to expect "free" land. Such speakers, black as well as white, urged their listeners to forget the past, to be patient, and to "prove . . . that [the] race is capable of progress."[22]

Other leaders took a more aggressive stance. A Rev. Brown, the African American minister who addressed a large crowd in Charleston on 4 July 1869, reportedly led his audience in prayer and "thanked God Almighty that they, the colored people, had got their feet upon the necks of their enemies, meaning the white men, and prayed that they might continue to keep their feet there." Other black speakers took a two-pronged approach; they expressed a measure of hopefulness regarding the potential for interracial cooperation in the future even while they condemned white sins of the past.[23]

Three speeches delivered at the Springfield Baptist Church in Augusta exemplified the range of themes sounded by leaders at African American commemorative events. Henry McNeal Turner was the first speaker to address the crowd that filled the church on the morning of 1 January 1866. Born of free black parents in 1834, Turner served as the first black chaplain in the

U.S. Army during the Civil War. When the war ended, he was assigned to the Freedmen's Bureau in Georgia; as a religious and political leader, he was a logical candidate to address the Emancipation Day celebration in Augusta.[24]

Part sermon, part history lecture, Turner's speech captured the millennial hope and fervor expressed by many African Americans in the wake of Emancipation. On this, the first New Year's Day African Americans "ever enjoyed," Turner looked back on a past filled with "gloom and fearful suspense" and looked forward to a future in which "the eternal principles of equity and freedom" would reign. Like other leading churchmen, Turner invested the anniversary of the Emancipation Proclamation with religious as well as historic significance, divining that the day would be "enshrine[d]" in African American "affections with a deathless sacredness, forever and ever."[25]

Drawing on predominant themes in African American abolitionism, Turner crafted an account of American history in which good ultimately triumphed over evil, as "America and her Democratic principles and institutions" conquered "the crime which offended heaven." Tracing the roots of black freedom to the moment of the nation's birth, Turner identified the ringing of the Liberty Bell in 1776 as a harbinger of Emancipation. The end of slavery, he emphasized, was no accident of fate; it was the inevitable destiny of a nation that "threw off the British Yoke, and trampled under foot the scepter of despotic tyranny."[26]

Dwelling on the past, Turner enumerated the crimes committed by whites against African Americans and contrasted these wrongs with a record of black accomplishments. Once again, he reflected the ongoing practice of nineteenth-century black writers and orators who highlighted both the distinct accomplishments of "the race" throughout history and the particular contributions of African Americans to the building of the nation.[27] Harkening back to the Old Testament, he reminded his audience that "Ham and his whole posterity . . . were the first great men of the world." They "founded the first cities and formed the first empires . . . they carried the alphabet first to proud Greece, and the mathematical problems of Euclid [that] still puzzle the world." Moving forward in time, he recalled that the "first blood spilt in the [American Revolution] was that of Crispus Attucks, a full-blooded negro," and that black men again proved their patriotism serving in the Union army. Moreover, African Americans, "[u]nlike the white man," fought only to attain "our rights in common with other men" and did not "desire to enslave" southern whites." Only as he neared the end of his speech did Turner adopt a more conciliatory tone. Almost as an afterthought, he concluded: "[L]et me say that I have not referred to the cruelty of slavery to incite . . . passions against the white people . . . let by-gones be by-gones . . . respect them; work for them; but still let us be men."[28]

Turner would have been a difficult act to follow under any circumstances. He was a gifted and impassioned orator, and it is hard to imagine such a speech failing to inspire and animate his listeners. Indeed, the chairman for the Augusta celebration reported that the crowd responded to Turner's "lofty" eloquence with "unbounded astonishment." Not even the whites among the audience could "conceal their admiration, [or] restrain the applause due to him, as the best orator of the day."[29] Neither John Emory Bryant nor J. N. Eils, the two white men who succeeded Turner at the podium, strayed from already well-established themes in conservative speeches. Bryant, who served as head of the local Freedmen's Bureau, advised the members of his audience to make contracts with employers, informed them that the government would not give them land, and asserted that they all must "earn an honest living." He urged the freedmen to be "honest, industrious and peaceable and in every respect, conduct themselves like good citizens." Eils, editor of the *Augusta Daily Transcript*, then rose to make "a few short and pointed remarks"; he stated that he agreed with Bryant's advice and added that, as "a Georgian by birth," he wished to assure the audience that "the Southern men were their best friends."[30]

It is difficult to imagine two more different visions of the meaning of Emancipation than those put forth by Turner, on the one hand, and Eils and Bryant on the other. Whereas Turner emphasized the tremendous import of the anniversary, portrayed Emancipation as a fate determined by both God and country, and compelled his listeners to acknowledge the proven worth of black manhood, the white speakers, adopting a paternalistic tone, concerned themselves with more mundane matters and, in particular, focused on defining specific behaviors and attitudes as the measure of black citizenship. The speeches delivered at Augusta indicate that even single events could provide the context for not only distinct but also conflicting conceptions of freedom. Moreover, both Eils and Bryant probably stressed the importance of "peaceable" relations with whites precisely because Turner had just concluded a fiery condemnation of southern slaveholders. Perhaps the prevalence of white speakers at Emancipation celebrations was one expression of a felt need to respond to the challenge of African American interpretations of freedom.

If leading spokesmen struggled over the meaning of Emancipation, African Americans nonetheless gave substance to black freedom with massive parades that surged through the streets of southern towns.[31] "Abraham Lincoln the Father of our Liberties and Savior of his country" and "Slavery and

Disunion dead!" proclaimed the banners raised above the heads of black celebrants who marched in Augusta on 4 July 1865.[32] Moving out from church halls and parade grounds, pouring through thoroughfares and congregating in town squares, black celebrants asserted their right to share equally in the public domain. Black men, women, and children who had been sentenced to "social death" now enacted their rebirth. Abandoning the pose of humility that protected them under slavery, black marchers boldly assumed the posture and attitude of full and equal citizens, and willfully transgressed the boundaries that formerly distinguished black from white, slave from free.[33]

The challenge posed by such vigorous displays of black liberty and equality was not lost on unhappy whites, who viewed the freedpeople's parades as unwelcome evidence of black agency. As they contemplated African Americans marching on the Fourth of July, whites exclaimed, "This time honored day was surrendered to the colored people," and "Cuffee takes the place of the former celebrants of the day." Those whites wishing to avoid "the spectacle" of the freedpeople's processions stayed inside or left town all together; many southern whites favored countryside picnics and rural excursions during the postwar period, as they ceded city streets and town squares to their former slaves.[34]

Of course, African Americans were hardly a new presence in southern towns, but the antebellum urban geography had embodied the hierarchical distinctions of slavery. Curfews, passes, and regulations restricted the movements of slaves and free blacks. Certain spaces were designated "whites only" and the rituals of public interaction continually inscribed social inequalities. Moreover, white residents' tireless efforts to prohibit collective association among African Americans meant that a fragile and fractured black public sphere could emerge only on the margins of white society. Opportunities for African Americans to meet, share information, and shape common strategies for combating the hardships and dangers of their lives were of necessity composed of stolen moments, stealthy communications, and clandestine gatherings.[35]

After Emancipation, fearful whites witnessed (and mourned) the refashioning of public spaces to fit the conditions of freedom. Thus, each year on the Fourth of July, white Charlestonians admitted to "vain longings in their breast for a recurrence of happy bye-gone days." Likewise, white residents of Richmond were appalled when black celebrants boldly occupied Capitol Square, an area traditionally designated as off-limits to African Americans. On 4 July 1866 sequestered whites peered out from behind closed doors and shuttered windows to see the flags of the United States and Virginia floating over the capitol and the words "Liberty and Union" printed above the state's coat of arms. But to anxious white onlookers, the most noticeable alteration of the square was the appropriation of its monuments. Black celebrants had garnished the Washington Monument with evergreens and laid a small calico flag in the hands of the statues of Thomas Jefferson and George Mason. This act unhinged a writer for the *Richmond Dispatch*, who described the modification of the statues as "a liberty which no white man ever yet presumed to take with Virginia's great work of art."[36]

Significantly, African Americans' ornamentation of the monuments in Capitol Square projected a new version of American history onto the architectural landscape of Richmond. When black celebrants decorated the statues of Washington, Jefferson, and Mason, they adopted these Founding Fathers as their own forebears and invested the birth of American freedom with new significance. Claiming Capitol Square for their own purposes, they enacted their own story of the nation's past, a story intended to rescue both the leaders and the principles of the Revolution from their slaveholding abductors. African Americans who marched through southern towns waving flags and carrying banners proclaiming "freedom and equality" projected a vision of a united nation grounded in the principles of liberty and fraternity for all.[37]

One of the most elaborate postwar parades occurred in Charleston in 1865. On 21 March a vast crowd assembled at the Citadel Green and prepared for a grand parade through the main streets of town. Significantly, the ten-acre green was an extension of the South Carolina Military Academy (also known as the Citadel), which was founded in 1842 as a bulwark against potential slave rebellions. While black marshals organized marchers into line, a band struck up a lively tune. Finally, the procession began with two decorated marshals on horseback leading the way. Next came a smartly dressed regiment of black troops and a company of schoolchildren who displayed a banner reading, "We know no masters but ourselves." Behind the marchers came a horse-drawn "car of liberty" ornamented with flags, streamers, and banners. Fifteen young women sat atop the wagon; adorned in white dresses with colorful trimmings, the women smiled and waved their handkerchiefs as spectators cheered.[38]

After the car of liberty came more marchers, including schoolchildren and white teachers, butchers, tailors, coopers, firemen, painters, blacksmiths, carpenters, masons, wheelwrights, wood-sawyers, teamsters, paper carriers, bakers, and barbers. The tradesmen all displayed emblems of their work:

butchers marched with their knives at their sides and "a good-sized porker" in front of them. Other workers were similarly well appointed: "The carpenters carried their planes and other tools; the masons their trowels; the teamsters their whips; the coopers their adzes; the bakers' crackers hung around their necks; the paper-carriers a banner, and each a copy of [the] Charleston *Courier*; the barbers their shears; the blacksmiths their hammers; the wood-sawyers their sawbucks; the painters their brushes; the wheel-wrights a large wheel; and the fire companies, ten in number, with their banners, their foremen with their trumpets." Schoolchildren hoisted a banner declaring "We know no caste or color" and sang along the way, "We'll hang Jeff. Davis on a sour apple tree! . . . As we go marching on!"[39]

A mule-drawn cart was next in line. Bearing the announcement "a number of negroes for sale," the cart contained a cast of men, women, and children who portrayed the events of a slave auction. An auctioneer appealed to the crowds that lined the street, calling out his goods for sale, while a group of women and children enacted a slave family's separation. Behind the slave cart came a hearse bearing a coffin inscribed with the statement "Slavery is dead." Fifty female mourners dressed in black "but with joyous faces" followed. Various associations brought up the rear of the parade, which extended for three miles through Charleston's main streets. After returning to Citadel Green, about four thousand marchers and six thousand spectators cheered as a group of women addressed General Saxton and his wife and presented them with bouquets of flowers.

Although the Charleston parade was unusually large and complex, its organization into various associations typified most African American parades in the postwar South. The subdivisions of these processions—from soldiers to butchers to local schoolchildren—epitomized a form of nineteenth-century ceremonial citizenship that Mary Ryan has described as "heterogeneous but associated democracy." Among white Americans, the practice of performing "people in association" peaked in the decades before the Civil War, when hundreds of civic organizations arranged themselves according to familiar programs and marched in formation through city streets.[40] Among African Americans in the South, however, vigorous displays of civic organization became a dominant form of public ceremony following Emancipation.

At the moment when African Americans performed their entrance into the national community, they did so not as individuals or as an undistinguished mass, but as members of separate associations. They elected to march, not just as freedpeople, but also as soldiers, tradesmen, ministers, civic leaders, and schoolchildren. Some parades, like the spectacle in Charleston, embodied both democratic heterogeneity and broad unity: women and men, black and white, freeborn and recently freed, skilled craftsmen, and farm laborers all had a place in such ceremonies. However, other processions expressed a more restrictive vision of civic participation: Men strode by while women and children watched from the sidelines; farm laborers were marginalized while skilled craftsmen and black professionals occupied center stage.[41]

The two groups leading the Charleston march, black militias and skilled tradesmen, dominated most other commemorative processions as well.[42] In a typical postwar parade, handsomely costumed marshals swaggered by on horseback, as regiments of black troops—frequently armed—escorted other participants through city streets. The appearance of companies of African American men decked out in full military dress, swords at their sides, "with drum and fife, banners, sabers, and tinseled regalia," drew comment from white observers.[43] White onlookers in Charleston, for instance, evinced discomfort at the sight of "[l]iberty-loving freedmen . . . bearing war-like instruments upon their shoulders, [who] looked terribly patriotic as they formed the line."[44]

Whites correctly perceived the threat of black soldiers parading through downtown streets. In fact, marching black militiamen projected a vital message to all southerners. While the war was still on, African American troops drilled and marched in the Union-controlled South, and self-organized companies continued these practices during Reconstruction. In the post–Emancipation South, the participation of quasi-military organizations in commemorative processions signified the former slaves' ongoing commitment to defend their hard-won freedom. Out on the streets, for all to see, was an armed citizenry dedicated to the protection of black rights. While African American militiamen performed for local audiences, they also reinforced the broader theme of black military service that permeated commemorative speeches, African American periodicals, and historical literature. Both the rhetorical emphasis on African Americans' defense of the nation and the consistent presence of black soldiers in parades helped to advance black claims to full citizenship.[45]

As struggles over the control of the freedpeople's labor preoccupied the South and the nation, African American commemorative celebrations inevitably addressed the nature of black labor. In the tug-of-war between white employers and black workers following Emancipation, African Americans' postwar festivities celebrated black independence. Whereas antebellum holidays had occurred under the direction of slaveholders, African Americans planned postwar commemorations without the approval of their employers.[46]

Thus, on the very days when whites accused them of negligence, African Americans celebrated their status as capable and accomplished workers. Indeed, the men and women who "deserted the hoe and ploughshare" turned out in large numbers to celebrate black labor, either by marching in parades or by cheering from the sidelines. The honored role of skilled tradesmen in particular—recall the butchers in Charleston—signified African Americans' determination to exhibit the expertise that had long provided them with the highest degree of independence in their working lives. The conspicuousness of skilled craftsmen projected a hierarchical structure onto African American citizenship. But workers and farm laborers also made their presence felt in many processions, reflecting their resolution to share equally in an expanding polity.

Like the emphasis on black military prowess, the demonstrations of black labor and skill connected local parades to broader ideologies of black patriotism and citizenship. In the years following Emancipation, proponents of black rights repeatedly invoked black workers' achievements as evidence of their patriotism and their qualification for citizenship. Indeed, African Americans fashioned standards of service and loyalty that few white Americans could ever meet. If hard work and military service were the tests of good citizenship, African Americans pointed out, then 250 years of unpaid labor and unrewarded soldiering made black men *the truest* Americans.[47]

As African Americans exercised the freedom of association they had been denied during slavery, religious, educational, and civic organizations also sprang up in southern communities. The Trinity Moral Society, the Brothers and Sisters of Love, and the Sons and Daughters of Jerusalem were just a few of the associations founded by African Americans in postwar Augusta. Similar patterns of black organization occurred throughout the South, as freedpeople rapidly extended the fragile institutional base that had been nurtured by African Americans before Emancipation. Even before the war was over, commemorative parades celebrated this expansion of independent black institutions. A missionary for the AME Church was shocked to see several black societies—including two female societies, "one literary and the other secret"—on display during a Fourth of July parade in Norfolk as early as 1864. He admitted, "[I]n this connexion [*sic*], I must certainly say that I was taken entirely by surprise. The idea of seeing literary and secret societies, that had been organized for years in the very heart of oppression and tyranny . . . and flourishing, too, was something beyond my comprehension."[48]

While the composition of African American parades and assemblies illuminates the importance of collective associations for the articulation of

African American citizenship, their organization also reflects the role of gender in shaping African American ceremonies in the post–Emancipation period. At first glance, the sheer level of women's involvement in the celebrations appears to indicate a degree of gender equality in African American
commemorative culture. Whether they marched in parades or cheered from
the sidelines, presented banners to local militias or voiced their opinions of
leading orators, black women engaged wholeheartedly in public affairs. Not
only were women out on the streets sharing in local festivities, but women's
associations were active behind the scenes, helping with the planning and
preparation that went into celebrations.

Indeed, contemporaries and historians alike have described African American women as spirited participants in community affairs after Emancipation.
That the Civil War increased white women's visibility in patriotic assem-
blages was widely recognized. But the forceful presence of African American
women in public affairs was even more conspicuous to contemporaries. To
southern whites, black women's participation in public matters was one more
indication of the social chaos wrought by the war and Emancipation. They
repeatedly remarked on the presence "of both sexes" at local events and
identified black celebrations as sites of promiscuity and licentiousness, where
"dusky daughters" cavorted with "sable gallants," and "antiquated maumas"
enjoyed illicit exchanges with "rapacious . . . promenaders."[49]

Historians, on the other hand, have suggested that black women's participation in public affairs reflected African Americans' broad-ranging vision
of an informed and engaged citizenry. In particular, Elsa Barkley Brown has
argued persuasively that African Americans in postwar Richmond embraced
a democratic vision of the public sphere that involved women in all aspects of
the political discourse, including voting. The evidence from the commemorative celebrations certainly complements Brown's portrait of a democratic
public sphere—not only African American women, but also children and
white female supporters participated alongside men of all classes and occupations in commemorative affairs. Moreover, the energetic celebrations that
overfilled churches and commandeered town squares were part of a black
political culture that involved whole communities in political discussion and
public action in the early postwar period.[50]

Yet, amid stories emphasizing the shared involvement of men and women,
one also can glimpse the workings of a gender hierarchy in African American
commemorative culture. Whereas southern whites perceived black women's
participation in public affairs as doubly transgressive—offending *their* notions of racial and gender hierarchy—the more formal aspects of black wom-

en's commemorative activities suggest that African American commemorative culture was defined and expressed in substantially gendered terms. Both men and women participated in celebrations, but they usually performed different roles. To a certain extent the separate functions of men and women suggest a partnership between them. But if African American women were engaged in many aspects of commemorative culture, men largely controlled the proceedings that occurred in church halls, on city streets, and in town squares.[51]

The gendered organization of African American commemorative celebrations began in the planning stage, as women accepted primary responsibility for fund-raising, decorations, and refreshments, whereas men took control of speechmaking and planning the parades. An advertisement appearing in an early African American newspaper clearly depicted this separation of roles. The advertisement, which publicized plans for an upcoming Emancipation celebration in Charleston, also cast African American men as the most important and authoritative actors in the planning and implementation of the event. On 16 December 1865 the *Charleston Leader* announced the creation of an all-male Committee of Arrangements for the event and called on various community organizations to provide ancillary support and assistance. The authors of the advertisement requested that "[a]ll Male Societies, Companies, Clubs, or organized bodies" send representatives to the local Union League Hall to make arrangements for the celebration. They then made a special appeal to "[a]ll the Ladies' Societies and Associations," indicating that "anything they could provide would "be happily received by the Committee" but specifying the kind of tasks they might usefully undertake: "The Committee beg to inform the ladies generally that they would be extremely happy to have their assistance in making Wreaths, Banners, etc." In their third and final appeal to the women, the authors drew a sharp distinction between men's and women's spheres in the celebration, concluding: "The Committee is well aware that they cannot get along without the ladies, except in the procession." The committee's move to exclude women from the plans for the parade is striking, coming less than a year after the procession in which Charleston women participated so conspicuously.[52]

The divergence of male and female roles in commemorative events extended to the performance as well. Men dominated the political and patriotic speechmaking at public rallies, and they took center stage in most parades. When women did march alongside men, their formal roles helped to articulate separate male and female identities. Male participants strode through southern towns as soldiers, tradesmen, and political leaders, whereas women marched as members of schools and civic associations or sat, dressed in white, atop lavishly decorated "cars of liberty." Even in the early Charleston parade, women and men enacted distinct roles. Only in the comparatively feminized spaces of the freedmen's schools and Sunday schools did the roles of men, women, and children become more interchangeable, as all three groups played similar parts in flag-raisings, memorial ceremonies, and public recitals.[53]

Outside of the schools, the contrast between male and female public roles took clearest form in women's presentations of banners, flags, and swords to militiamen. When they graciously honored black troops, African American women publicly assumed the contemporary feminine attributes of decorum and propriety—qualities that white southerners were loathe to attribute to black women. On such occasions, groups of elegantly dressed women paid tribute to African American soldiers by bestowing some gift, frequently of the women's own making. In Augusta, for instance, women unfurled three banners and awarded them to a regiment of black troops just before the men served as marshals in a local Independence Day parade. But these ceremonies also helped to cast the soldiers as the most worthy patriots and citizens—a role black fighters were similarly granted in historical writings, memorial speeches, and commemorative parades. As such, black women's most prominent public actions actually contributed to male-centered definitions of patriotism and citizenship.[54]

African Americans' embrace of an open public domain that thrived on *all* citizens' participation and engagement in public affairs ran counter to an exclusively male interpretation of democracy. But African Americans' consistent emphasis on military service and growing concern with black men's voting rights tended to restrict notions of historical agency to men. Moreover, different groups brought to commemorative events distinct and sometimes conflicting ideas about men's and women's public roles, just as they held varying conceptions about determining the right to the franchise. These tensions surfaced in the observations of a white teacher in Virginia who noted: "The freedmen are holding numerous political meetings. . . . When they take a vote, the women all take part also until they are told not to by the president." At times, the organization of public affairs demonstrated freedpeople's openness to the combined involvement of women and men; on other occasions, more conservative ideas held sway. At a Fourth of July celebration in Charleston less than three months after Appomattox, black male revelers offered up a toast to "Woman, the second gift to man." Congratulating the Charleston "ladies" on their "altered condition" since Emancipation, the men magnanimously declared, "Though from circumstances she shines not so brilliantly in public as in private, but behold her bright as a sunny day, brilliant beyond comprehension, a model of what God intended her to be."[55]

The efforts of men in Charleston to circumscribe women's public activity says as much about class as it does about gender. African Americans and their white supporters understood the vulnerability of mixed-sex gatherings to white charges of disreputable conduct. Freedwomen were to become "ladies," and ladies should not occupy too prominent a place in public affairs. Or, when they did, their presence helped to symbolize both class and gender differentiation. Committees of "tastefully dressed ladies" presented soldiers with "beautiful banners." Young girls, "costumed in white," smiled and waved graciously to appreciative crowds as they passed through city streets in horse-drawn carriages. Young women, "many of them exhibiting the graces of person and manner of the most refined ladies, and dressed with neatness and even elegance," marched together through city streets. It would be a mistake to conclude that the efforts of African American men in Charleston to identify their female colleagues as "ladies" were representative, but neither were they atypical. Instead, they illustrated one inclination among many in African American commemorative culture. Like the mixed content of celebratory speeches and the precise order of civic parades, the gender dynamics of commemorative ceremonies expressed diverse conceptions of black patriotism and citizenship.[56]

The large, heterogeneous events that characterized African American commemorative culture in the early post–Emancipation period sprang from the specific conditions of Reconstruction. In cities and towns throughout the South, African American ceremonies—and the historical narratives they generated—held center stage. White residents seeking to avoid the freedpeople's celebrations literally left town. Even then, they faced detailed reports on the celebrations in their morning paper the next day. These same white residents sought and found alternative forums for their own versions of the past and hopes for the future. But they left a sizable portion of the cultural arena to African Americans, and they were singled out as an isolated voice against northern whites as well.

Over the course of the 1870s, as Reconstruction came to an end, political and cultural circumstances combined to effect changes in African American commemorative practices. In state after state, the gradual withdrawal of northern support tipped the balance of power further in the favor of southern whites. Using a combination of terrorism and political fraud, white southerners pulled down state Republican organizations and crippled groups like the Union Leagues, which helped plan and implement the postwar celebrations. Whites also targeted black commemorations for special retributive action, killing African Americans who assembled to celebrate the Fourth of July in Mississippi and South Carolina.[57]

At the same time that the political landscape of the South underwent significant changes in the latter years of Reconstruction, the cultural terrain sustained a transformation that affected the meaning of black celebrations. Early signs of the advancement of northern and southern whites toward "national reconciliation" appeared in the 1870s, as whites in some southern cities began to tone down the earlier rhetoric of Confederate rebellion and some even maneuvered quietly to recommence celebrations of the Fourth of July. However tentatively or cynically, a number of white Americans in both the North and the South were inching their way toward a shared concept of a reunited country. The net result of their actions was a refashioning of the "imagined community" of the nation—with southern whites one fractional step closer to inclusion and African Americans just a bit further away from it.[58]

African Americans did not stop asserting their visions of themselves and the nation during the decades following Reconstruction. Indeed, commemorative events such as Emancipation Day celebrations persisted throughout the latter decades of the 1800s and in some cases endured well into the twentieth century. But the changed political and cultural context in both the South and the nation forced accommodations in African American historical memory. Intraracial political disagreements and organizational rivalries also constricted African American affairs, as did arguments over when and how to represent the past. Celebrations that formerly involved hundreds of participants were pared down to smaller numbers, and parades and assemblies that once overwhelmed the main thoroughfares of southern towns were transferred to lesser streets, outlying parade grounds, and the separate spaces of various African American civic, educational, and religious institutions. Most important, the public ceremonies that accompanied African Americans' entrée into politics now occurred alongside disenfranchisement. Even elaborate celebrations were thus emptied of much of their former significance, as is demonstrated by the support of southern whites for Emancipation ceremonies in many towns during the era of Jim Crow.[59]

Still, African Americans persisted in their efforts to promote their own interpretations of history—interpretations that variously stressed both the memory of slavery and the evolution of black progress, the contributions of African Americans to the South and the nation, and the importance of racial justice for the future of the country. The postwar celebrations provided crucial forums for African Americans to reflect, debate, and enact their own versions of history and plans for the future. Broadly based community ceremonies mobilized tens of thousands of participants and involved men, women, and children in the collaborative work of redefining black identities to fit the conditions of freedom. The white backlash against African American conceptions of history and citizenship could not extinguish the commemorative practices and collective memories established by southern blacks after Emancipation. Indeed, an editorial appearing in the black press in Savannah on 8 July 1876 was both a bitter acknowledgment of the work that white Americans had accomplished in little more than a decade since the war's end and an impressive statement of African Americans' continuing resistance to their fellow Americans' efforts to reimagine the nation as exclusively white. Surveying the ongoing celebrations of the nation's centennial, a writer for the *Savannah Colored Tribune* asserted African Americans' unequivocal right to be included in commemorations of the nation's past: "Would it not be well for us to inform some of our patriotic friends who are so gloriously celebrating the 100th anniversary of American Independence, that the first blood that was shed for American liberty was that of a negro, Crispus Attucks, who fell while nobly defending the city of Boston March 5th, 1770? And yet our Democratic friends say this is a white man's country."[60]

The "reconciliation" of northern and southern whites constituted a powerful response to the efforts of African Americans and white allies to re-form the nation as a free, interracial society created and occupied by both black and white citizens. Moreover, African Americans' insistence that the United States was never "a white man's country" reminds us that historical memory was a contested arena encompassing multiple and conflicting versions of the South and the nation. We do not have to look far to see that the same is true today. In recent years, southerners have argued passionately whether it is appropriate to name a public school in New Orleans after President—and slave owner—George Washington, whether to continue to fly the Confederate flag from the South Carolina capitol building, and whether a statue of tennis great Arthur Ashe belongs on Richmond's historic Monument Avenue. These contemporary controversies carry on a time-honored tradition in southern history.[61]

NOTES

1. *Augusta Colored American*, 6, 13 January 1866. See also *Christian Recorder*, 27 January 1866. Turner's speech, "On the Anniversary of Emancipation," is reprinted in Edwin S. Redkey, ed., *Respect Black: The Writings and Speeches of Henry McNeal Turner* (New York: Arno Press and the New York Times, 1971).

2. *Christian Recorder*, 30 January 1864.

3. Valuable studies of the "Lost Cause" include Catherine Clinton, *Tara Revisted: Women, War, and the Plantation Legend* (New York: Abbeville Press, 1995); Gaines Foster, *Ghosts of the Confederacy: Defeat, the Lost Cause, and the Emergence of the New South, 1865–1913* (New York: Oxford University Press, 1987); Nina Silber, *The Romance of Reunion: Northerners and the South, 1865–1900* (Chapel Hill: University of North Carolina Press, 1993); LeeAnn Whites, *The Civil War as a Crisis in Gender: Augusta, Georgia, 1860–1890* (Athens: University of Georgia Press, 1995); and Charles Regan Wilson, *Baptized in Blood: The Religion of the Lost Cause, 1865–1920* (Athens: University of Georgia Press, 1980).

4. On African American commemorative celebrations, see David Blight, *Frederick Douglass' Civil War: Keeping Faith in Jubilee* (Baton Rouge: Louisiana State University Press, 1989), "W. E. B. Du Bois and the Struggle for American Historical Memory," in Geneviève Fabre and Robert O'Meally, eds., *History and Memory in African-American Culture* (New York: Oxford University Press, 1994), and " 'What Will Peace among the Whites Bring?': Reunion and Race in the Struggle over the Memory of the Civil War in American Culture," *Massachusetts Review* 34 (Autumn 1993): 303–410; Elsa Barkley Brown, "Negotiating and Transforming the Public Sphere: African American Political Life in the Transition from Slavery to Freedom," in Black Public Sphere Collective, eds., *The Black Public Sphere* (Chicago: University of Chicago Press, 1995); Elsa Barkley Brown and Gregg D. Kimball, "Mapping the Terrain of Black Richmond," *Journal of Urban History* 21 (March 1995): 396–446; Mitchell Alan Kachun, " 'The Faith That the Dark Past Has Taught Us': African-American Commemorations in the North and West, and the Construction of a Usable Past, 1808–1915" (Ph.D. diss., Cornell University, 1997); Kirk Savage, *Standing Soldiers, Kneeling Slaves: Race, War, and Monument in Nineteenth-Century America* (Princeton: Princeton University Press, 1997); Leonard I. Sweet, "The Fourth of July and Black Americans in the Nineteenth Century: Northern Leadership Opinion within the Context of the Black Experience," *Journal of Negro History* 61 (1976): 266–75; Shane White, " 'It Was a Proud Day': African Americans, Festivals, and Parades in the North, 1741–1834," *Journal of American History* (June 1994): 13–50; William H. Wiggins, " 'Lift Every Voice': A Study of Afro-American Emancipation Celebrations," in Roger D. Abrahams and John F. Szwed, eds., *Discovering Afro-America* (Leiden: E. J. Brill, 1975); Mitchell Alan Kachun, "The Shaping of a Public Biography: Richard Allen and the African Methodist Episcopal Church," in James L. Conyers Jr., ed., *Black Lives: Essays in African American Biography* (Armonk, N.Y.: M. E. Sharpe, 1999; and Elizabeth Rauh Bethel, *The Roots of African-American Identity: Memory and History in Free Antebellum Communities* (New York: St. Martin's Press, 1997).

5. See Benedict Anderson, *Imagined Communities: Reflections on the Origin and Spread of Nationalism*, rev. ed. (London and New York: Verso, 1991), and Kenneth Moss, "St. Patrick's Day Celebrations and the Formation of Irish-American Identity," *Journal of Social History* (Fall 1995): 125–48.

6. See Blight, "What Will Peace among the Whites Bring?," 397, and John Bodnar, *Remaking America: Public Memory, Commemoration, and Patriotism in the Twentieth Century* (Princeton: Princeton University Press, 1992), 16.

7. *Christian Recorder*, 10 January 1863; Elizabeth Ware Pearson, ed., *Letters from Port Royal: Written at the Time of the Civil War* (1906; reprint, New York: Arno Press, 1969), 128–34. A similar ceremony was held in nearby Beaufort the following year. See *Beaufort*

New South, 9 January 1864; Elizabeth Hyde Botume, *First Days amongst the Contrabands* (1893; reprint, New York: Arno Press, 1968), 75–78; Bishop L. J. Coppin, *Unwritten History* (New York: Negro Universities Press, 1919), 155–59; Leon F. Litwack, *Been in the Storm So Long: The Aftermath of Slavery* (New York: Vintage Books, 1979), chap. 4; and George P. Rawick, ed., *The American Slave: A Composite Autobiography* (Westport, Conn.: Greenwood Publishing Co., 1972), 6:239–40, 12:262.

    8. *New York Daily Tribune*, 13 January 1865.

    9. *New York Times*, 3 January 1864; *Christian Recorder*, 16 July 1864; *American Missionary Magazine*, February 1866, 32–33.

    10. See Wiggins, " 'Lift Every Voice,' " 46–47. Numerous anniversaries sometimes led to confusion as different groups tried to sort out which day(s) to celebrate. See *Christian Recorder*, 2 May 1863.

    11. *Augusta Daily Constitutionalist*, 7 July 1867 (quotation); *Athens Southern Watchman*, 10 July 1867; *Charleston Daily Courier*, 6 July 1868; *Norfolk Virginian*, 6 July 1868; Letter of Mark Clark, 28 October 1868, Mary Clark Papers, Caroliniana Library, University of South Carolina, Columbia.

    12. *Christian Recorder*, 16 July 1864 (quotation), 22 July 1865; *New York Daily Tribune*, 12 July 1865.

    13. *Christian Recorder*, 31 August (quotation), 5 October 1867. For freed people traveling long distances to political meetings and polls, and the forms of community organization that helped make such geographic mobility possible, see Julie Saville, *The Work of Reconstruction: From Slave to Wage Laborer in South Carolina, 1860–1870* (New York: Cambridge University Press, 1994), chap. 5.

    14. *Norfolk Virginian*, 2 January 1867.

    15. *American Missionary Magazine*, June 1866, 134–35. See also Paul A. Cimbala, *Under the Guardianship of the Nation: The Freedmen's Bureau and the Reconstruction of Georgia, 1865–1870* (Athens: University of Georgia Press, 1997), 19–20, and Jacquelyn Jones, *Soldiers of Light and Love: Northern Teachers and Georgia Blacks, 1865–1873* (Chapel Hill: University of North Carolina Press, 1980), 28–29.

    16. *Richmond Whig*, 30 March 1866. A similar editorial appeared in the *Richmond Dispatch* on 30 March 1866.

    17. *Freedmen's Record* 2 (June 1866): 116.

    18. *American Missionary Magazine*, May 1866, 105 (quotation); Brown and Kimball, "Mapping the Terrain of Black Richmond," 309. Whites also attacked a procession in celebration of the Civil Rights bill in Norfolk in Spring 1866. See *Norfolk True Southerner*, 19 April 1866, and *Norfolk Virginian*, 17–21 April 1866.

    19. *Augusta Daily Transcript*, 5 March 1866, quoted in *Loyal Georgian*, 19 March 1866; *Loyal Georgian*, 10 March 1866. Distrust of northern teachers was also reported in the *American Missionary Magazine*, March 1866, 59; August 1866, 173–77; October 1866, 235–36; May 1867, 103; and July 1867, 151–52.

    20. Jones, *Soldiers of Light and Love*, 22–23. The speeches, letters, and reports of northern missionaries and teachers were full of praise and encouragement for southern African Americans' nationalistic and commemorative activities. See, e.g., *Beaufort (S.C.) Free South* 1, 8 August 1863; Rev. H. W. Pierson, *A Letter to Hon. Charles Sumner with "Statements" of Outrages upon Freedmen in Georgia, and an Account of My Expulsion from Andersonville, Ga., by the Ku Klux Klan* (Washington, D.C.: Chronicle Print, 1870), 23–28; and *American Missionary Magazine*, May 1867, 140; September 1867, 201; June

1869, 139. The level of northerners' involvement and direction varied considerably from one celebration to another. See *Christian Recorder*, 10 January, 26 December 1863, and 16 January 1864. For an interesting commentary on the efforts of white male officials to dominate some proceedings, see Mary C. Ames, "Description of the Festival, by a Lady Present," in *Addresses and Ceremonies at the New Year's Festival to the Freedmen, on Arlington Heights; And Statistics and Statements of the Educational Condition of the Colored People in the Southern States, and Other Facts* (Washington, D.C.: McGill and Witherow, Printers and Stereotypers, 1867), 37–40.

21. Edward J. Cashin, *Old Springfield: Race and Religion in Augusta, Georgia* (Augusta: Springfield Village Park Foundation, Inc.), 45; *Hampton (Va.) True Southerner*, 4 January 1866; *Norfolk Virginian*, 2 January 1867.

22. *Charleston Daily Courier*, 2 January 1869, 4 January 1866; *Charleston Daily News*, 2 January 1868; Speech of General Sickel published in *Charleston Daily Courier*, 6 July 1867. Leon Litwack stresses that black spokesmen added their voices to the chorus urging freed people to be hardworking, sober, thrifty, temperate, etc. Litwack, *Been in the Storm So Long*, 522.

23. *Charleston Daily Courier*, 6 July 1869; James Lynch, *The Mission of the United States Republic: An Oration Delivered by Reverend James Lynch at the Parade Ground, Augusta, Georgia, July 4, 1865* (Augusta 1865); *Augusta Constitutionalist*, 2 January 1870. For the breadth of thought and argument presented at the freedmen's conventions, see Litwack, *Been in the Storm So Long*, chap. 10.

24. Stephen Ward Angell, *Bishop Henry McNeal Turner and African-American Religion in the South* (Knoxville: University of Tennessee Press, 1992).

25. Turner, "On the Anniversary of Emancipation," 5–6.

26. Ibid., 6–8.

27. Nineteenth-century African American historians consistently emphasized black progress and achievements, and placed particular stress on black soldiers's loyal service in U.S. wars. See William Wells Brown, *The Negro in the American Rebellion: His Heroism and His Fidelity* (Boston: Lee and Shepard, 1867); George Washington Williams, *History of the Negro Race, 1619–1880* (New York: G. P. Putnam's Sons, 1883); Joseph T. Wilson, *Emancipation: Its Course and Progress, From 1481 B.C. to A.D. 1885, with a Review of President Lincoln's Proclamations, the XIII Amendment, and the Progress of the Freed People since Emancipation; With a History of the Emancipation Monument* (Hampton, Va.: N.p., 1882). See also Leonard I. Sweet, *Black Images of America, 1784–1870* (New York: Norton, 1976), 147–49.

28. Turner, "On the Anniversary of Emancipation," 9, 11–12.

29. *Christian Recorder*, 27 January 1866. See also Litwack, *Been in the Storm So Long*, 545–46, and *Charleston Daily News*, 3 January 1871.

30. *Augusta Colored American*, 6 January 1866.

31. The work of Elsa Barkley Brown and Gregg Kimball on the black public sphere in postwar Richmond has been especially important for my own thinking about the significance of African American commemorative parades in the early post–Emancipation period. See Brown and Kimball, "Mapping the Terrain of Black Richmond," in Kenneth W. Goings and Raymond A. Mohl, eds., *The New African American Urban History* (Thousand Oaks, Calif.: Sage Publications, 1996).

32. *National Freedman* 1 (August 1865): 230–31; Lynch, *Mission of the United States Republic*, 2.

33. Orlando Patterson, *Slavery and Social Death: A Comparative Study* (Cambridge: Harvard University Press, 1982). For contemporary commentary, see J. W. Alvord, *Letters from the South, Relating to the Condition of the Freedmen, Addressed to Major General O. O. Howard* (Washington, D.C.: Howard University Press, 1870), 7, and Elias Horry Deas of Charleston to his daughter, 12 August 1865, Elias Horry Deas Papers, Caroliniana Library, South Carolina University, Columbia.

34. *Augusta Daily Constitutionalist*, 7 July 1867; *Charleston Daily Courier*, 6 July 1869. The *Richmond Dispatch* reported that whites left the city on 4 July 1866, "partly to enjoy the day's relaxation from business and partly to avoid the spectacle which they could not have avoided witnessing had they remained at home." See also *Richmond Enquirer*, 5 July 1867; *Charleston Daily Courier*, 6 July 1868; *Augusta Constitutionalist*, 6 July 1866; and *Charleston Daily News* 4 July 1867, 4 July 1868.

35. Litwack, *Been in the Storm So Long*, 177.

36. *Charleston Daily Courier*, 6 July 1867 (first quotation), 6 July 1868, 5, 6 July 1869; *Richmond Dispatch*, 6 July 1866 (second quotation), 6 July 1868. See also *Richmond Enquirer*, 5 July 1867, and Brown and Kimball, "Mapping the Terrain of Black Richmond," 305.

37. *National Freedman* 1 (August 1865): 230–31; Lynch, *Mission of the United States Republic*, 2; *New York Daily Tribune*, 4 April 1865.

38. *New York Times* and *New York Daily Tribune*, 4 April 1865. The *Times* reported that thirteen women rode in "the liberty car," whereas the *Tribune*'s account stated that the car contained fifteen women, representing the fifteen states that held slaves at the start of the war. See also Charles Henry Corey, *A History of the Richmond Theological Seminary* (Richmond: J. W. Randolph, 1895), 30; Arthur Mazyck and Gene Waddell, *Charleston in 1883* (Easley, S.C.: Southern Historical Press, 1983), 7–8; Emma Holmes, *The Diary of Miss Emma Holmes, 1861–1866*, ed. John F. Marszalek (Baton Rouge: Louisiana State University Press, 1979), 122–23, 450; and Bernard Powers, *Black Charlestonians: A Social History, 1822–1885* (Fayetteville: University of Arkansas Press, 1994), 33, 68–69.

39. *New York Times* and *New York Daily Tribune*, 4 April 1865.

40. On mid-nineteenth-century street parades as "performances of people in association," see Mary P. Ryan, *Civic Wars: Democracy and Public Life in the American City during the Nineteenth Century* (Berkeley: University of California Press, 1997), 58–93.

41. Postwar African American urban assemblies and processions were not entirely without precedent. See Ira Berlin, *Slaves without Masters: The Free Negro in the Antebellum South* (New York: Pantheon Books, 1974), 306–10, and Ryan, *Civic Wars*, 46.

42. *Christian Recorder*, 16 January 1864, 22 July 1865; *Charleston Daily News*, 3 January, 5 July 1870, 3 January, 5 July 1871, 2 January 1872, 2 January 1873; *Augusta Constitutionalist*, 2 January 1870, 3 January 1874. On the role of military organizations in patriotic processions and Irish American St. Patrick's Day parades at midcentury, see Susan G. Davis, *Parades and Power: Street Theatre in Nineteenth-Century Philadelphia* (Philadelphia: Temple University Press, 1986), chap. 3.

43. *Richmond Dispatch*, 2 January 1868.

44. *Charleston Daily Courier*, 6 July 1867 (quotation), 6 July 1868, 6 July 1869; *Norfolk Virginian*, 2 January 1866.

45. On black quasi-military "companies," see Saville, *Work of Reconstruction*, 143–51. On the emphasis on black military contributions to American wars, see Sweet, *Black*

Images of America, 148–50. See also *Christian Recorder*, 15 July 1865; Lynch, *Mission of the United States Republic*; and Frances E. W. Harper, "An Appeal to the American People," *Christian Recorder*, 21 July 1866, and "Colored Heroes of the War," *Christian Recorder*, 12 January 1867.

46. *Augusta Daily Constitutionalist*, 7 July 1867; *Athens Southern Watchman*, 10 July 1867; *Charleston Daily Courier*, 6 July 1868; *Charleston Daily News*, 20 July 1867; *Norfolk Virginian*, 6 July 1868.

47. *Christian Recorder*, 16 January 1864; *First Anniversary of the Proclamation of Freedom in South Carolina, Held at Beaufort, S.C., January 1, 1864* (Beaufort: Free South Print, 1864); *National Freedman* 1 (August 1865): 230–31. The positions of tradesmen and laborers in commemorative parades paralleled debates over suffrage. See Saville, *Work of Reconstruction*, 151–60.

48. *Christian Recorder*, 16 January 1864. See also *Christian Recorder*, 16 July 1864, 22 July 1865, 13 October 1866, and 26 October 1867; Diane Harvey, "The Terri: Augusta's Black Enclave," *Richmond County History* 5 (Summer 1973): 60–75; and Berlin, *Slaves without Masters*, chap. 9.

49. *Atlanta Constitution*, 5 July 1868; *Charleston Daily Courier*, 6 July 1867, 6 July 1868 (quotation), 6 July 1869; Holmes, *Diary*, 441.

50. Brown, "Negotiating and Transforming the Public Sphere," esp. 111–30. Julie Saville also emphasizes freedwomen's political activities in *Work of Reconstruction*, 167–69.

51. Even after white women gained a prominent role in civic ceremonies, their participation heightened and reconstructed gender differentiation. See Ryan, *Civic Wars*, 65–68, 120, 244–51, 297.

52. *Charleston Leader*, 16 December 1865. The gendered division of labor consistently occurred in both the North and the South, as is evidenced by dozens of programs and reports from around the country published in the *Christian Recorder*. See, e.g., *Christian Recorder*, 4 February 1865, 27 January, 24 February, 3 November 1866.

53. *New York Daily Tribune*, 4 April 1865; *Christian Recorder*, 18 May 1867; Pierson, *Letter to Hon. Charles Sumner*, 23–28; *American Freedman* 1 (February 1867): 167; *American Missionary Magazine*, July 1868, 151.

54. *National Freedman* 1 (August 1865): 230–31; Lynch, *Mission of the United States Republic*, 2. See also *Charleston Daily Courier*, 18 October 1866; Holmes, *Diary*, 429; and *True Southerner*, 4 January 1866. Among northern blacks, women's presentations of flags and banners to male associations preceded the war. See *Christian Recorder*, March 1855. Ryan discusses white women's role in similar ceremonies in *Civic Wars*, 247–48.

55. *Charleston Courier*, 17 April 1865; *Hampton (Va.) True Southerner*, 7, 14 December 1865, 11 January 1866; *Savannah Tribune*, 18 March 1876; *American Missionary Magazine*, August 1867, 172 (first quotation); *Christian Recorder*, 15 July 1865 (second and third quotations).

56. Lynch, *Mission of the United States*, 2; *New York Times*, 4 April 1865; *New York Daily Tribune*, 12 July 1865. For similar conclusions on white women's symbolic presence in public ceremonies, see Ryan, *Civic Wars*, 249–50.

57. Eric Foner, *Reconstruction: America's Unfinished Revolution, 1863–1877* (New York: Harper and Row, 1988), 343, 347, 442; Alan Conway, *The Reconstruction of Georgia* (Minneapolis: University of Minnesota Press, 1966), 198–99; *Richmond Dispatch*, 5 July 1873; *Christian Recorder*, 22 July, 12 August 1875; *Savannah Colored Tribune*, 15, 22 July 1876; *Savannah Tribune*, 29 July, 5 August 1876; U.S. Congress, *Debate on the Hamburgh*

(sic) Massacre in the U.S. House of Representatives, 44th Cong., 15, 18 July, 1876; Joel Williamson, *After Slavery* (Chapel Hill: University of North Carolina Press, 1965), 268–71; Thomas Holt, *Black over White: Negro Political Leadership in South Carolina during Reconstruction* (Urbana: University of Illinois Press, 1977), 199, 210.

58. For the movement toward national reconciliation, see Foster, *Ghosts of the Confederacy*, and Silber, *Romance of Reunion*. Historians have stressed the 1880s as the pivotal period during which northern and southern whites redefined the memory of the Civil War in terms that omitted conflict over slavery and paved the way for a cultural reconciliation. The evidence from southern commemorations in the 1870s illustrates early tendencies in that direction. See *Richmond Enquirer*, 6, 8 July 1872, 4 July 1873; *Richmond Dispatch*, 4 July 1872, 5 July 1873; *Augusta Daily Constitutionalist*, 6 July 1875; *Atlanta Constitution*, 7 July 1875.

59. Brown and Kimball, "Mapping the Terrain of Black Richmond," 309; *Augusta Daily Constitutionalist*, 6 July 1870, 6 July 1872, 3 January 1873, 7 July 1874; *Norfolk Virginian*, 2 January 1869, 3, 4 January 1870; *Christian Recorder*, 28 August 1869, 3 September 1870, 30 January 1873, 10 December 1874; *Savannah Tribune*, 1, 15 July 1876, 8, 15, 29 December 1894, 26 December 1896; *Charleston Daily News*, 4, 5 July 1870, 2 January 1873.

60. *Savannah Colored Tribune*, 8 July 1876.

61. *New York Times*, 12 November 1997; *Washington Post*, 11 July 1996, 20 February 1997; *Wall Street Journal*, 22 May 1998.

part three

The Past in the New South

In the late nineteenth and early twentieth centuries southerners evinced an acute concern about their historical memory. The conditions in the New South—wrenching economic transformation, political turmoil, and chronic racial tensions—seemed to demand new means to create social cohesion, express identity, and structure social relations. The past offered a framework of sorts and an inspiration for various groups of southerners as they sought to secure new sources of cultural authority. White elites, who were anxious to establish their unchallenged power, labored to establish new bonds of loyalty among themselves and among those they sought to rule. Meanwhile, African Americans struggled to defend the boundaries of their freedom in the face of white hostility, in part by building up community institutions and recounting their own version of history.

Catherine Bishir's essay, which reveals her nuanced understanding of architectural history and keen sensitivity to the motivations of North Carolina's white elite, traces the links between power, memory, and the built landscape. As much as any region, the South has become associated with characteristic architectural motifs. Bishir explains the origins of some of these associations by tracing the conscious efforts of elites in North Carolina to use architecture and public spaces to proclaim their vision of the South's past and future. The urban spaces of Raleigh and Wilmington in particular became the focal point of their ambitions. There elites built monuments to their rule and tastes. The landscape they created vouched for their unmistakable claim by birthright to political and cultural dominion over the state.

Bishir's essay also clarifies the social and political networks that elites used to craft public memory. In Europe and elsewhere in the late nineteenth century, the state increasingly shaped both the content and the expression of historical memory. But state governments in the South could not assume a comparable role in part because they were part of a federal system dominated by the victors of the Civil War. Moreover, southern state governments were weak and impoverished. Thus, voluntary organizations and civic associations, as much as southern public officials, oversaw the organized work of historical memory. Private groups typically worked in partnership with public officials in campaigns to build commemorative landscapes. As Bishir demonstrates, these alliances were facilitated by the ties of marriage, family, and class. Of course, it would be foolish to suggest that white elites in the South during the late nineteenth century relied exclusively on the manipulation of historical memory to secure power. They also employed, Bishir emphasizes, fraud, intimidation, and violence in their pursuit of power. Nevertheless, their skillful appeals to historical memory undergirded their success and created cultural motifs that have endured long after their control over the South ended.

The increasingly restrictive social climate and public spaces of the late nineteenth century, as Kathleen Clark and Catherine Bishir make clear in their essays, imposed daunting obstacles in the way of efforts by African Americans to give public expression to their history and hopes. Intent on establishing a dominant version of history, southern white elites sought to marginalize and even silence dissenting views. In this climate, African American understandings of the past necessarily became more furtive and inward focused. Even so, white memory never achieved anything approximating hegemony. Black countermemories persisted, especially within black churches. As the most robust institutions under African American control, black churches served as congenial environments for the open discussion of ideas that could not be safely expressed within white earshot.

Laurie Maffly-Kipp's essay deepens our understanding of the role of black ministers not just as leaders of vital black institutions but also as the creators of historical memory. According to Maffly-Kipp, a generation of black ministers in the late nineteenth century pondered and debated the meaning of the saga of African Americans. She highlights the complex synthesis of "thoroughly Protestant" and "thoroughly African American" beliefs that formed the worldview of these undeservedly overlooked thinkers. By fusing the millennial tradition, which exerted such a powerful grip on nineteenth-century American Protestantism, with a nascent Afrocentric interpretation of history, these ministers and historians concluded that the past could be read as a record of black achievement and especially of God's special plans for African Americans.

That some blacks, especially ministers, would interpret slavery and emancipation in spiritual terms in not surprising. But Maffly-Kipp's findings that black ministers wove the ancient annals of Africa and the more recent chronicles of Freemasonry into their histories are unexpected. They demonstrate that Afrocentric thought, which has only recently attracted widespread public attention, has a long pedigree. But, despite the sweep and power of the prophetic vision of the race historians, Maffly-Kipp explains why it ultimately proved fragile. By the second decade of the twentieth century, African Americans interpreters of the past seldom invoked scriptural authority or proffered millennial predictions. Instead, they, along with their white counterparts, now looked to "scientific methods," rather than religion, as the foundation of historical authority, and the rich tradition of religiously grounded "race histories" came to an end. Even so, these race histories merit close study because they highlight the efforts of African Americans to employ their most potent cultural resources in their quest to reimagine both their community and history itself during the so-called nadir of American race relations.

The role of memory in defining community also is at the center of John Howard's imaginative essay on a little remembered murder and trial in Mississippi. At first glance, the murder that Howard describes—of one well-born white Mississippian by another—seems to be curious but hardly exceptional. But Howard meticulously uncovers dimensions of the event that illustrate how intertwined collective memory and sexual orientation are. Unconventional behavior, including particular sexual orientations, almost inherently calls into question existing hierarchies (whether they relate to race, class, gender, ethnicity, or religion) and in turn challenges historical justifications of those hierarchies. Given the prevailing values of the South in the late nineteenth century, homosexuality contradicted bedrock assumptions about masculinity, honor, and authority. Certainly, open acknowledgment of male homosexuality in Mississippi was almost inconceivable. And yet, at the same time, he explains, contemporaries relied on a catalog of historical associations and memories of celebrated scandals associated with homosexuality to discuss homosexuality. An elaborate body of code words and oblique yet specific allusions enabled Mississippians, and presumably other Americans, to define homosexuality. Howard's essay, then, offers compelling evidence of how—how completely—some events can be erased from memory.

The autobiographical dimensions of Howard's essay testify to one of the principal concerns of gay and lesbian historiography: subjectivity. More explicitly than any other essayist in this collection, Howard makes clear that his essay about memory is itself an act of historical memory. That Howard weaves himself into his essay is not simply so that he can reveal his personal concerns and politics. Rather, it reflects his belief that "memory is about different times in conversation with each other." As a queer historian well rooted in the local community about which he writes, and as an out gay man from Mississippi, he is anxious to connect contemporary lesbian and gay persons and politics to earlier queer figures and events. Thus his essay is at once a reconstruction and a reclamation of memory.

Landmarks of Power

Building a Southern Past in Raleigh and Wilmington, North Carolina, 1885–1915

Catherine W. Bishir

In 1901 the speaker at the dedication of the Olivia Raney Library in Raleigh drew attention to three landmarks in the city. First was the old state capitol, "symbolizing the commonwealth's loyalty to constitutional liberty." Near it stood two new landmarks. "Our handsome Confederate monument" on the capitol grounds offered "a token of our loyalty to the memory of our fallen heroes who laid down their lives in defense of those principles for which Washington so successfully fought." And the library, given by a local businessman in memory of his wife, provided "a memorial of the highest type of our cultured Christian womanhood"—a classically detailed building in which "the simplicity and elegance of its graceful proportions and unpretentious appearance" evoked its namesake's exemplary character, while its proximity to the war memorial recalled "that noble band of women" (including Mrs. Raney) "to whose untiring efforts we are chiefly indebted for our Confederate monument."[1]

In this address, the Reverend M. M. Marshall of Raleigh's Christ Episcopal Church identified some of the important landmarks that gained dominion throughout the turn-of-the-century South. In addition to revering antebellum

View of Hillsborough Street, Raleigh, ca. 1903, looking west from Union Square. Seen
left to right: Olivia Raney Library, Confederate monument, and Raney House. Photo,
North Carolina Division of Archives and History, Raleigh.

buildings, leaders of his generation employed the twin arts of sculpture and
architecture to assert their definition of the past and its relationship to the
present and the future. As Marshall's comments demonstrated, these new
landmarks represented a set of interlocking beliefs about the place of the
vindicated South in the American mainstream, the rightness of the Confederate cause, and the association of classical architecture with idealized southern virtues.

Seen in the context of its times, the creation of symbolic sculpture and
architecture by members of the North Carolina elite functioned as part of
their reclamation of regional and national power. As they placed monuments
in prime civic spaces, whether commemorating the heroes of the Confederacy, the patriotic women of colonial Edenton, or the Revolutionary fighters of
the Cape Fear region, these leaders spelled out a saga of patrician Anglo-
Saxon continuity, order, stability, and harmony. The location of monuments
in the state's principal civic places lent authority to the version of history they
represented, while at the same time the monuments claimed those public
spaces and thereby defined the setting for public life. And just as monuments

commemorated specific heroes and events, so architecture commemorated and asserted the renewed continuity of the values and way of life those heroes represented. In public and institutional buildings, classicism universally reiterated the ideal of a venerable and stable hierarchy, while in residential architecture the Colonial Revival style symbolizing "the big-heartedness and hospitality which are the rightful heritage of the southern people" re-created in modern terms the deferential social relations that the antebellum plantation represented.[2] As the southern elite took control of the political process during the decades spanning the turn of the century, it also codified a view of history that fortified its position in the present and its vision of the future.

Throughout America in the decades just before and after 1900, political and cultural elites drew on the imagery of past golden ages to shape public memory in ways that supported their authority. By commissioning monumental sculpture that depicted American heroes and virtues in classical terms, and by reviving architectural themes from Colonial American, classical Roman, and Renaissance sources, cultural leaders affirmed the virtues of stability, harmony, and patriotism.[3] The principal shapers of public memory and patrons of public sculpture and architecture in Raleigh and Wilmington, centers of political and cultural activity in the state, were members of an established elite. They were akin to aristocrats throughout the nation and they were well acquainted with national cultural trends. They also shared certain backgrounds, experiences, and values. All were Democrats, and, with a few notable exceptions, they were members of families of long-established social and economic prominence. Many boasted colonial ancestry and had traditions of service in the Revolutionary and Confederate causes. Their families, moreover, were interlaced by ties of ancestry, marriage, education, and religion.

However much they had in common with patricians elsewhere, these North Carolinians had both their own concerns and their own version of history. As southerners, they alone among American elites had experienced impoverishment and devastating military and political defeat. They recalled a golden age before the Civil War when "Southern statesmen directed the policies of the nation," when "aristocratic" southern society was led by "the wisest, the strongest, the most learned," and when their families had constituted the elite in a hierarchical slave society. Although many of them had opposed secession, they nevertheless had sacrificed family members and fortunes to the southern cause. During Reconstruction, they had seen their political power and wealth shrivel, as "democracy" replaced "aristocracy" and power passed into the hands of black and white citizens who were "not so able or cultured." But in the mid-1870s, white conservatives regained political power and revived the Democratic Party. Calling themselves "Redeemers" and led by onetime Civil War governor Zebulon Baird Vance, they rolled back many of the egalitarian measures of Reconstruction.[4]

Along with recapturing political dominance, members of the old aristocracy gradually adjusted to a new economy. Some remained agriculturalists, but many moved to town to engage in business or a profession. As they adapted economically, the leading families still perpetuated their customary social networks. Almost in inverse relationship to their threadbare circumstances, they revitalized elaborate social rituals and public rhetoric, which they adorned with carefully polished silver and phrases. And they entered into cultural and patriotic pursuits that affirmed their accustomed political, economic, and social dominance.

In their hands, the creation of symbolic landmarks unfolded in two primary phases, punctuated by political events. In the 1880s and early 1890s, patrician Democrats began to call for a rehabilitation of state and southern history and the erection of civic monuments dedicated to that history, transforming the cult of defeat into the dominant culture of power regained. At the end of the century, the turbulent political campaigns of 1898 and 1900 riveted public attention and generated new themes in the Democrats' use of history. After 1900 the reentrenched elite turned with unprecedented energy and conviction to the shaping of public memory and the creation of official symbols, which quickly established a codified tradition and transformed the setting of public life.

In 1883 Samuel A'Court Ashe, a Raleigh newspaper publisher, politician, and historian, returned from a trip to Boston fired up by New Englanders' commemorative zeal. Soon afterward he ran a series of articles in his *News and Observer* urging North Carolinians to celebrate their own history and patriotic shrines. As a Confederate veteran, a native of the Wilmington area, and a descendant of colonists and Revolutionary heroes of the Cape Fear region, Ashe typified the historical penchant of North Carolina's elites by collecting and publishing state history.[5]

In the same spirit, Alfred Moore Waddell addressed the Raleigh Ladies Memorial Association on Confederate Memorial Day in 1885. Waddell, a former Confederate officer and a descendant of Cape Fear colonists and

Revolutionary War officers, was a Wilmington resident and former congress-
man who had become one of the state's most popular public speakers. The
Ladies Memorial Association, formed in 1866, was one of many founded after
the war to ensure proper burial of Confederate soldiers and to mark their
graves. Waddell used his oration to call for the memorialization of the state's
heroes and to lay out an agenda for action. He proclaimed that the period of
mourning after the war was over, as was the era of poverty that excused failure
to build monuments. He pointed out that whereas "every civilized land" had
monuments to its greatest sons to inspire and instruct natives and visitors,
North Carolina had none:

> Go to the Capitol at Washington and enter the . . . Hall of Statuary. There
> is a place reserved in it for two statues from each State. . . . Look around
> for North Carolina's contribution. It is not there. Go to any other State
> Capitol, and if its public grounds do not contain some statue or monument
> in commemoration of its great men, its legislative halls at least are hung
> with portraits of its Governors. Then come back here to Raleigh—go into
> your own State Capitol—see at the base of the rotunda those four empty
> niches—pass through the corridors—enter the Legislative Halls and look
> around! No monument, no statue, no bust, not even a portrait to remind
> you that North Carolina ever produced one man that she thought worthy
> of remembrance.

Waddell acknowledged the importance of Confederate monuments in cemeteries across the state, but he insisted that the memory of the Confederate
dead also deserved civic monuments to reflect "a sentiment alike jealous of
the honor of North Carolina, and tenderly grateful to her heroic sons."[6]

In the next three decades, the civic memorial movement followed precisely
the course Waddell laid out. In the 1890s Civil War memorializing shifted
from funereal markers placed in cemeteries to monuments of southern patriotism located in courthouse greens and town squares. The North Carolina
Confederate Monument was one of the state's earliest and certainly its most
imposing monument of this new type. It was the project of the North Carolina Monumental Association, led by socially prominent women with links
to the older Ladies Memorial Association. Proclaiming that "a land without
monuments is a land without memories," the Monumental Association organized a statewide fund-raising campaign. By 1895 these women, with assistance on practical matters from "experienced gentlemen," oversaw the completion of the state's official monument to the Confederate soldier.[7]

On 20 May 1895 about thirty thousand people from across the state gathered for the unveiling of the seventy-five-foot monument that rose at the western end of Union Square, the most prominent public site in the state. The granite column, flanked by bronze figures of a North Carolina cavalryman and artilleryman, and topped by a bronze infantryman, stood on an axis with the western portico of the capitol and faced Hillsborough Street, the premier residential avenue and one of four axial streets that defined the city plan. The Monumental Association's president, Nancy Haywood Branch Jones, and other distinguished personages presided over elaborate ceremonies in which the seven-year-old granddaughter of General Stonewall Jackson pulled the cord that let the draperies slide from the monument like "the garments of Elijah." The orator of the day was Alfred Moore Waddell.

Again Waddell set forth an agenda—the "true" history of the Confederate cause and North Carolina's role in that story. His hour-long oration was headlined in the *News and Observer* as "A Masterly Defense of the Cause for Which They Fought—In History's Clear Light." It promoted the retelling of southern history then sweeping the region. Waddell began by observing that a southerner reading history written by northern men could not but recall "what Froude said about history generally, namely that it seemed to him 'like a child's box of letters with which we can spell any word we please. We have only to select such letters as we want, arrange them as we like, and say nothing about those which do not suit our purpose.' "[8]

He laid out "the causes of and the responsibility for the war in which men to whose memory this monument is erected, were sacrificed." This was necessary because for thirty years past "my countrymen, kinsmen and my friends have been pilloried before the world as ignorant, barbarous, cruel traitors and rebels, who, without the slightest justification or excuse, sought to destroy the best government under the sun, and deluged a continent in blood." To counter this "monstrous perversion of the truth," Waddell presented the southern cause as part of the heroic tradition of American patriotism.

The speech and the monument reinforced the meaning of each other. Drawing first on the North Carolina state seal on the monument, with its date of 20 May 1775, Waddell lauded "the men of Mecklenburg" who "on this day one hundred twenty years ago" declared their independence from British tyranny. He referred to the Mecklenburg "Declaration of Independence," an event disputed by historians but popularly revered. Indeed, North Carolina had seceded from the Union on 20 May 1861, and the secession convention had authorized a state flag emblazoned with the two dates to affirm the link between the two declarations of independence.[9] The choice of 20 May 1895 as the day to unveil the state's Confederate monument reinforced the link between the Confederate and Revolutionary causes. Next, Waddell traced the nation's early history from a southern perspective, stressing the retention of states's rights, including secession, under the Constitution. He recited the saga of North Carolina's long and valiant soldiering as a source of state pride—"First at Bethel, Last at Appomattox" read the monument. The state's men had proved themselves "worthy of their Revolutionary sires."[10]

Waddell's oration struck sympathetic chords. Fellow Wilmingtonian and business leader James Sprunt wrote: "You were first in the hearts of your countrymen yesterday. . . . [O]n all sides the speech is said to be the best ever delivered in North Carolina." Sprunt predicted that "the eloquent words of your masterful address on probably the last occasion of such public honours to the Lost Cause will be repeated from generation to generation by those who look with reverence and admiration upon the beautiful shaft in Raleigh." Democratic spokesman Henry Groves Connor of Wilson praised Waddell for his "setting forth of our side of the question," noting that "we must preserve our integrity and make our fight in the struggle now confronting us. It behooves us to purify our hearts and educate our minds to meet the common enemy."[11]

Connor alluded to political developments then gaining momentum in North Carolina, which in the mid- and late 1890s absorbed the energy of the state's cultural, business, and political leaders. Throughout the South, Democrats faced challenges from Populists and Republicans, but only in North Carolina did they lose control of the state. By the 1890s the Democrats were perceived increasingly as the allies of moneyed interests and railroad magnates. Amid nationwide economic woes, the Populist movement gained strength from white farmers disillusioned with Democratic policies. After the Democrats rebuffed calls for reform, North Carolina's Populists forged a "Fusion" ticket with the Republicans. With support from both white and black voters, the Fusionists in 1894 and again in 1896 won a majority of seats both in the state legislature and in Congress. Republican candidate Daniel Russell also won the governor's office in 1896. As well, more Republicans (including some blacks in the eastern plantation region) and Populists won office in local and state governments.[12]

To recapture political power by splitting the opposition, the Democrats launched a "White Supremacy Crusade." The crusade tore aside the veil of gentility that normally shrouded public discourse and exposed the specter of violence. Organized by Furnifold M. Simmons, chairman of the Democratic Party, and led by Charles B. Aycock, Robert Glenn, and Francis Winston, the campaign played upon fears of "Negro domination" to pull white voters away from the Fusionist ticket and caused Democrats across the state to put aside old intraparty differences. Josephus Daniels, now editor and publisher of the *Raleigh News and Observer*, made it "the militant voice of White Supremacy." So violent was the campaign of 1898 that, as Daniels later recalled, it was "sometimes difficult for readers of the *News and Observer* to tell which was the bloodier, the war against Spain or the war to drive the Fusionists from power."[13]

The epicenter of violence was Wilmington. Businessman James Sprunt recalled that the city had a growing number of black citizens "whose attitude towards the whites had become unbearable" and, since the Fusionist victory, a city council that included black and white Republicans who were "not at all responsive to enlightened opinion." As Democratic leaders and prominent businessmen strove to regain control of city government, they looked to the heroic actions of their ancestors as precedent. In 1897, when Democrats sought unsuccessfully to have the city council removed, they declared that "it was quite in the order of things for Wilmington to be resisting the infamous legislation by which her citizens are deprived of local self-government, for it was the citizens of this city who first resisted the odious British Stamp Act."[14]

During the following year tensions in Wilmington mounted.[15] In October 1898 Alfred Moore Waddell gave a "sizzling talk" to a packed house of white men and women at the municipal theater. As a contemporary recalled, in this campaign Waddell was "an American Robespierre." After blasting "negro domination" and asserting Anglo-Saxon supremacy in the region and the world, Waddell looked to the past when he invoked the spirit of the "men of the Cape Fear" to inspire his compatriots to action instead of talk. "We are the sons of the men who won the first victory of the American Revolution at Moore's Creek, who stormed at midnight the rocky face of Stony Point. . . . We are the brothers of the men who wrote with their swords from Bethel to Bentonsville [*sic*] the most heroic chapters in American annals." Proclaiming that "we ourselves are men who, inspired by these memories, intend to preserve, at the cost of our lives, if necessary, the heritage that is ours," he declared that the men of the Cape Fear could no longer abide "intolerable conditions" in Wilmington: "We are resolved to change them if we have to choke the current of the Cape Fear with carcasses."[16]

In Wilmington, election day was peaceful. There, as throughout the state, the Democratic ticket triumphed. But in Wilmington the story had not ended. The next day, 9 November, several groups of "prominent business-men" assembled to make plans to oust the city council (which was not up for election) and rid the community of certain blacks and other Republicans. On the following day, Waddell led a group to the office of the *Wilmington Record*, the local black newspaper, where they destroyed the press and burned the building. As rumors of violence spread, white men shouldered weapons and moved into the streets. Fighting broke out, and by day's end, when the con-flict ceased, an unconfirmed number of black men lay dead—Waddell put the number at twenty. That evening, Waddell and his allies forced the resigna-tion of the city council and took control of the government. The Wil-mington Light Infantry patrolled the city on horseback and rounded up black and white Republicans whom the Democrats planned to banish from Wilmington.[17]

After winning the "Revolution of 1898," the Democrats aimed at total victory in the next election. In 1900 the governorship was at stake as well as legislative seats, but the central issue was an amendment to the state constitu-tion designed to disfranchise blacks. Again Democrats employed violence and intimidation to keep blacks from the polls, and Democratic speakers and newspapers blanketed the state with calls for Anglo-Saxon unity.[18] The Dem-ocrats achieved overwhelming success in 1900. To many of them it seemed that a long chapter that began in defeat had finally ended in triumph; for some, the very violence of their victory was a catharsis of old defeat. As promised in the campaign, young Democratic leaders inaugurated an era of economic progressivism that emphasized public education, transportation, and encouragement of business. They also passed Jim Crow laws to legalize racial segregation, which they viewed as a modern, rational remedy to past ills that would "cleanse" public life and promote peaceful social and economic advancement.

Once again the vindicating muse of history was invoked, this time by Governor Charles B. Aycock in his inaugural address of January 1901. First he compared the Democrats who had waged the "combat" of 1898 with North Carolina's early heroes of the American Revolutionary cause—"that people who fought the first fight in Alamance against bad government and wrote the first Declaration of Independence in Mecklenburg." He then lik-ened the recent "revolutionary" suffrage amendment to "the war for Inde-pendence" and tied the spirit of the disfranchisement movement to "the revolutionary spirit of 1776," which "still lives in the hearts of North Carolinians . . . a glorious part of their heritage."[19]

In the politically charged context of the 1900 election the state's Democratic leaders inaugurated an era of "historical awakening." Many believed that North Carolina lagged behind other states in historical activities; now they proceeded to remedy the situation. In the fall of 1900, in Raleigh's new Olivia Raney Library, prominent Democrats organized the State Literary and Historical Association. This group worked in affiliation with kindred organizations; its reports included news from the recently formed North Carolina chapters of such hereditary and patriotic groups as the Colonial Dames of America, the Daughters of the Revolution, the Daughters of the American Revolution, the Society of the Cincinnati, the Sons of the Revolution, the United Confederate Veterans, and the United Daughters of the Confederacy. The members of these societies constituted a statewide network of men and women interested in the history of their own patrician families and of the state at large, which they usually perceived as one and the same.[20]

These men and women led a surge of patriotic, cultural, and historical activities. They collected and published historical records, wrote state histories and school textbooks, initiated "North Carolina Day" in the public schools, established and expanded historical museum collections, and, with equal fervor, marked and memorialized historic sites, events, and personages. These endeavors had less to do with an obsession with the past than with the belief that a proper understanding of history and state pride, like educational reform and literary production, was a necessary component of a modern American state. A remarkable sense of shared purpose threaded through these pursuits. Just as members of ancestral patriotic groups traced their family lineages to colonial and Revolutionary forebears to affirm their place in contemporary society, so like-minded politicians and historians traced political lineage back to those heroic ancestors to affirm political legitimacy.[21]

With competing visions of the state's past, present, and future all but silenced in official discourse, these leaders shared a powerful sense that both in politics and in the culture at large, matters had been returned to their correct alignment. They set about codifying a lasting version of the state's history that tied Old South to New, interweaving old family heritage, Anglo-Saxon supremacy, and military and political heroism.[22] The saga began with the establishment of the "first Anglo-Saxon settlement" in the New World at Roanoke in the 1580s, continued through the aristocratic families and the

Zebulon Vance Monument and North Carolina State Capitol, Raleigh, ca. 1911, looking
west from New Bern Avenue. The statue has been moved to a ground-level base south of
the capitol, facing Charles Aycock's monument. Photo, North Carolina Division of
Archives and History, Raleigh.

plantation culture they established in the colonial period, and glorified Revolutionary North Carolinians' early resistance to British tyranny. It lauded the
progress of the antebellum era, sanctified the sacrifices and patriotism of
North Carolina Confederates, and insisted that their cause enjoyed the support of the populace. Finally, the story demonized Reconstruction, ennobled
the Democratic redemption of the state, and depicted the present era as a
rebirth of southern progress and leadership in the nation.[23]

By erecting memorials to the events and heroes of this narrative, Democratic leaders transformed principal civic spaces into visual illustrations of
their saga. In both Wilmington and Raleigh, their memorial work wove
together a single epic stretching from the colonial past to the redeemed
present. Immediately after the election of 1900, for example, the Democrats
triumphantly unveiled a giant bronze figure of their hero Zebulon Baird
Vance. Sculptor Henry J. Ellicott's lifelike portrait captured Vance in a characteristic gesture of debate, a Beaux Arts sculptural technique of depicting
the subject in midgesture to intensify the emotional impact of the work.
Standing on a base that raised the eight-and-a-half-foot statue to a height of
more than twenty-five feet, the powerful monument commanded the eastward
axis of Raleigh's Union Square. Acclaimed by Democrats as the ideal of
North Carolina, Vance had governed the state during the Civil War, won the

View of Worth Bagley Memorial (right) on Union Square, Raleigh, ca. 1910 postcard. On
the left are the Raney House, Confederate monument, and First Baptist Church. Photo,
North Carolina Division of Archives and History, Raleigh.

governorship again in 1876, and served in the U.S. Senate from 1879 until his
death in 1894. Soon after his death, friends had proposed a memorial, but
funding was not forthcoming since the racially and politically divided legislature was unwilling to support such a project. After the election of 1898,
however, the triumphant Democrats promptly appropriated funds to memorialize Vance. The unveiling of the statue on 22 August 1900 was "a fitting
time," as Josephus Daniels happily observed, "for Aycock, the new Governor
was to receive it."[24]

On 20 May 1907 a bronze figure of Worth Bagley, unveiled before a huge
throng on Union Square, provided a new chapter in the saga of heroic
southern vindication. The monument, made by popular New York sculptor
Francis H. Packer, memorialized the young North Carolinian who had been
the first American officer killed in the Spanish-American War. Bagley was a
member of a prominent eastern North Carolina family, and his sister Adelaide
was the wife of *News and Observer* publisher Josephus Daniels. The Spanish-
American War, in which northern and southern soldiers fought together
under a single flag, fostered sectional reunification in the cause of American
nationalism. The young southerner's death in Cuba on 11 May 1898 was
hailed in the national press as sealing the "covenant of brotherhood between
the north and south," for now "we are all Worth Bagley's countrymen."[25]

The 1907 commemoration further expanded the meaning of Bagley's death. On the base of his monument, the inscription—"First Fallen, 1898"— linked his heroism to the nearby Confederate monument with its motto, "First at Bethel, Last at Appomattox." And the unveiling date of 20 May, as speaker Governor Robert Glenn explained, deepened the sense of continuity: already sacred as "first marking the Declaration of Independence, second as the day on which North Carolina had turned to fight for friends and kindred," 20 May now acquired further significance as "the day on which the breach of sectionalism had been healed and union had been cemented in the blood of Worth Bagley." Thus, claimed another speaker, Bagley's death signaled "a new era of Union" in which "the logical adjustment of history would again give the leadership of the nation to the South."[26]

In Wilmington as well, memorializing focused on heroes who were central to city leaders' interpretation of the past and present. The Wilmington Ladies Memorial Association had already given the city its Confederate memorial at Oakdale Cemetery in 1872. Now Wilmington women led state patriotic organizations to commemorate other heroes of the Cape Fear. The city's first civic memorial—the Cornelius Harnett Monument—was presented by the North Carolina Society of the Colonial Dames of America, whose officers were mainly patrician Wilmington women. The Dames selected a "commanding and beautiful position" in the central plaza of Market Street.[27]

The 1906 cornerstone-laying ceremony drew a large, festive crowd that reflected the overlapping circles of political and cultural leadership. The Colonial Dames invited the North Carolina chapter of the Society of the Cincinnati to participate and requested that the Wilmington Light Infantry, "the flower of Wilmington for more than a half-century," provide a military feature. They asked Francis Winston, a Masonic as well as a political leader, to lay the cornerstone and Wilmington mayor Alfred Moore Waddell to deliver an address. Extolling the "heroes and patriots of the Lower Cape Fear," he assured his listeners that despite the previous absence of monuments as "material evidence of such loyalty of sentiment," the descendants of those heroes "cling with tenacity to their traditions." The following spring the Colonial Dames presented the thirty-foot granite obelisk to Mayor Waddell; the memorial commemorated both Cornelius Harnett and "the memory of the colonial heroes of the lower Cape Fear," especially the 150 men "who made the first armed resistance in the American Colonies to the oppressive stamp act of the British Parliament February 19, 1766."[28]

On one level, this first civic monument in Wilmington simply commemorated local colonists who resisted the Stamp Act and led the Revolutionary

Members of the North Carolina chapter of the Society of the Cincinnati, gathered in
Wilmington on 20 April 1906 for the cornerstone laying of the Harnett obelisk. Among
those identified by numbers are James Sprunt (nonmember guest) (1), Marshall Delancey
Haywood (5), Bennehan Cameron (9), Joseph Blount Cheshire Jr. (10), Samuel A. Ashe
(11), Alfred Moore Waddell (15), and Julian S. Carr (nonmember guest) (17). Photo,
North Carolina Division of Archives and History, Raleigh.

cause. Since the leaders of the Colonial Dames were Wilmington residents
and descendants of colonial Cape Fear planters, the subject was a natural
choice. Yet for these women, as for most members of the audience, the recent
"Revolution" in Wilmington was fresh in memory. Indeed, in 1906 a reporter
from Raleigh observed that the residents of Wilmington who "participated in
or who flourished at the time of the post–election burning of the negro
newspaper office and in the suppression of black supremacy in the city [still]
date events from the 'Revolution.' That now is heard a good many times here
in the course of a day." The rhetoric of the "Revolution of 1898" repeatedly
linked that event with the "heroes of the lower Cape Fear" and their resistance to the Stamp Act. By erecting the obelisk, the women marked the
center of the city with a monument that underscored the continuity of heroism from their colonial ancestors to their own men of the Cape Fear.[29]

Four years later a second monument on Market Street honored George
Davis, the attorney general of the Confederacy. The Cape Fear chapter of the
Daughters of the Confederacy (which shared many members with the Colo-

George Davis Monument, Market Street, Wilmington, ca. 1911. Photo reprinted with permission from the Pearl Stevens Butler Collection, New Hanover County Public Library.

nial Dames) had conceived the idea of a memorial to Davis soon after his death in 1896 but was at the time devoting its energies to creating a Confederate museum. In 1904 the Daughters began fund-raising for the monument, but donations came slowly until 1909, when their president recruited James Sprunt to spearhead a quick and effective financial campaign. In 1911 they presented to the city a life-size bronze figure sculpted by Francis H. Packer. Like the Vance memorial in Raleigh, the statue of Davis showed its subject in midgesture, "reaching forward in a characteristic gesture of the right hand, while the left rests lightly upon the flag to which he was true to the end of his life." After the unveiling and a historical address by Democratic leader and judge H. G. Connor, a stirring rendition of a poem by Davis tied the Confederate cause to the Revolutionary War and "Mecklenburg! the proud old story!"[30]

Memorializing continued in Wilmington and Raleigh after 1911, expanding on the intertwined themes of patriotic heroism and Democratic political accomplishments. It took several years before the impulse to glorify the Confederacy was fully satisfied. As late as 1924 a private bequest funded a Confederate memorial in downtown Wilmington, designed by architect Henry Bacon with expressive figures representing courage and sacrifice, again sculpted by Francis H. Packer. In Raleigh, where Union Square had become the focus of statewide commemorative interest, two new memorials filled out the Confederate story. On 10 June 1912 the North Carolina Division of the United Daughters of the Confederacy unveiled sculptor Gutzon Borglum's dramatic bronze of Henry Lawson Wyatt, the North Carolina private who had been the "First Confederate Soldier to Fall in Battle in the War Between the States" at Bethel Church on 10 June 1861. Two years later, again on 10 June, a memorial to the North Carolina Women of the Confederacy was unveiled, the result of another private donation by a Confederate veteran. The architect for the project was Henry Bacon and the sculptor was New Yorker Augustus Lukeman. The donor, Ashley Horne, appointed a committee consisting mostly of prominent veterans to direct the project. The sculptor presented two designs for the principal figures—one portraying "an elderly woman seated, reciting to a young girl . . . the story of the War Between the States, representing the activities of the Women of the South in perpetuating the memories of the Confederacy," the other showing the same woman telling the story to her grandson, "inciting him to emulate the deeds of his fathers." The committee unanimously chose the latter.[31]

Commemoration also proceeded inside the state capitol. In 1908 the Daughters of the Revolution dedicated the first memorial in the long-naked rotunda—a bronze plaque commemorating "Fifty-one Ladies of Edenton" who, on 25 October 1774, had signed a resolution supporting the patriot cause. This early political act by American women, which became popularly known as the "Edenton Tea Party," was especially inspiring to the Daughters. They initially planned to place their memorial in Edenton, but after a "Tea Party" marker was erected there, they decided to install it in the capitol. To raise money for the plaque, the Daughters in 1901 inaugurated a popular historical series, the *North Carolina Booklet*, which featured articles by prominent historians and political and cultural leaders. Mary Hilliard Hinton and Elvira Worth Moffitt, both members of elite political families and both deeply involved in the era's full range of patriotic and cultural work, assumed the leadership in planning the memorial and editing the *Booklet*.[32] Within four years of the dedication of the Edenton commemorative plaque, the long-empty niches in the rotunda were filled with marble busts of political leaders, and these were soon followed by plaques celebrating colonial and Revolutionary heroism and by various portraits throughout the building.

The most powerful recitation of the history that took form in these years resounded through the capitol when historian, editor, and political leader Samuel A'Court Ashe—who had sparked the commemorative movement back in 1883—delivered the dedicatory address in 1909 for a portrait of the building's architect, David Paton. Speaking in the senate chamber, Ashe used the capitol itself as a text by evoking the "undying memories" that pervaded its halls. He began with the accomplishments of antebellum days and recalled the trials of the Civil War, then proclaimed: "[T]hese mute walls are witnesses of the saturnalia of Reconstruction still awaiting some Dante to portray the scenes with realistic power." As to the recent past, "these walls have witnessed the reversal of that State policy forced on an unwilling people by the mailed hand of the conquering power, and the full restoration of Angli-Saxon [sic] control. Never in history has a people been so clearly and effectually vindi-cated as those gallant souls of North Carolina, who . . . swore their children to undying opposition to those who would destroy their civilization. Let the oppressed of future ages gaze on the scene and take courage."[33]

Ashe recognized that buildings possessed the power to evoke hallowed mem-ories and to inspire future ages. For his generation of southern leaders, the architecture of the colonial and antebellum past had special meaning, as did the construction of new buildings whose form and imagery captured in modern terms the symbols of that glorious past. The South's revival of classicism in public architecture and its embrace of the Colonial Revival style in residential architecture paralleled national trends. Just as the monuments these southerners erected in civic spaces commemorated past heroes and events, so too block after block of classical and Colonial Revival architecture in downtown and residential neighborhoods commemorated the "golden age" before the war. This architecture shaped public memory of the past and defined the life of the present by asserting in physical form "the southern aristocracy's continuing legitimate authority as the dominant force in the region's political, social, and economic life."[34] And, moving beyond mere glorification of a past epoch, this architecture perpetuated and revitalized for modern daily use the deferential social values of the heirs and heiresses of the glorified tradition.

A vivid local explication of the new architecture appeared in a 1907 article in Josephus Daniels's *News and Observer*. The story was entitled, "A People Known by Way They Build: How Raleigh Has 'Found Herself' Architec-turally and the Building That Is Replacing Mistakes and Fixing Permanent Standards." Superficially, the article simply reported changing taste in Ra-leigh architecture. But just beneath the surface was the story of architecture as a marker of political and social events and values. Asserting that "Beauty in architecture sounds the signal in a community of stability," the writer

presented a brief history of architectural evolution in terms that paralleled
the publisher's own sense of recent history. Condemning previous decades'
architectural "atrocities," the writer blasted that era's "pretentious frames,
garbled ideas put together for the purpose of display." He contrasted these
errors with recent improvements that defined a time when "the community
has found itself, when the frightful begins to be pulled down; when the
pretentious becomes an eyesore, when the notion is that of harmony, of
fitness to use and right to be. Each has its place." He pointed to the present
desire for "simplicity and timeliness" as evidence that "the callow period has
passed, that the bumptious period of uncertainty has been weathered, and
that there is experience as well as confidence in the air."³⁵

The city's admirable models of architecture were either antebellum landmarks or newly constructed works of classical mien. The writer praised the
state capitol—"an anomaly of beauty [that] stood as a protest against bad
taste, over-pretension, under-estimation"—and admired Christ Episcopal
Church as a spiritually inspiring edifice in the English Gothic style. "These
two early triumphs of city-building," he asserted, "stand as . . . a reproach or
congratulation to the city that is building about them. And in recent years
there has been an effort towards the symetry [*sic*] which they speak and the
form which they glorify." The writer saw evidence of "the progress of the new
thoughts in the homes of the people, in the buildings that exactly or by relation speak the public mind." He singled out a new state college building "in
the Greek style" as "a triumph of proportion and taste," praised the "Colonial design" of buildings at Peace and St. Mary's (schools for young women),
and admired a number of churches and businesses affiliated with the local
elite. "It is in the homes of Raleigh," he concluded, "that the significance of
the building and architectural spirit may be best observed," for new homes
showed "a notable taste and an evident building for permanency."³⁶

The architecture so admired by the *News and Observer* writer shared in
the national revival of symmetry and classical themes. In the late nineteenth
century most southern cities had built more or less ornate versions of the
eclectic, picturesque styles popular throughout the nation, characterized by
irregular outlines, exuberant machine-made ornaments, and rich textures and
colors. As these variegated styles faded from fashion and tastes turned toward
balance, classical motifs, and smooth pale surfaces, the southern elite went
beyond the usual rejection of recent styles, vehemently demonizing the building of the late nineteenth century along with the political and social conditions it seemed to represent. They embraced a new vocabulary that blended
modern technological convenience with a revival of classical imagery akin to

antebellum landmarks. This architecture provided a compelling metaphor for southern leaders who promoted their region as offering the best of modern reform and race relations combined with the stable social hierarchy modeled after the Old South. Thus the new classically detailed skyscrapers and columned public buildings of southern cities represented both the South's renewed prosperity and participation in the urban American mainstream and the region's preoccupation with "harmony, fitness to use and right to be."

In residential architecture a more specifically southern image emerged, both in the nationally popular Colonial Revival style and especially in the "Southern Colonial" style. Introduced to the region in the 1890s in homes of the elite, the Colonial Revival mode swiftly won broad and lasting acceptance. The American Colonial Revival gained momentum when the 1876 Centennial Exposition sparked national enthusiasm for the American past and for "Old Colonial" (especially New England) architecture. In 1893 the grandiloquent Beaux Arts architecture of the White City of the Chicago World Exposition encouraged the shift in popular taste toward imperial classical styles, while the exhibit's individual state buildings showed visitors myriad "Colonial" styles. Initially the Colonial Revival cast a broad net, drawing on a heritage that reached from initial white settlement to the mid-nineteenth century's industrial and picturesque architecture. Increasingly after about 1915 the focus narrowed to more literal use of seventeenth- and eighteenth-century precedents. The ascendancy of the Colonial Revival was linked to rising American nationalism and Anglo-Saxon nativism in the face of massive immigration and labor and class turbulence. Popular architectural literature presented the Colonial Revival as the architecture of Americanness, patriotism, stability, longevity, and specifically "our Anglo-Saxon heritage."[37]

In the South, identification of the Colonial style with Anglo-Saxon American culture appealed not only to nativist pride but also to white supremacy. Southern bonding of Colonial architecture with Anglo-Saxon elite culture likewise extended from the first settlement to the Civil War, particularly emphasizing the flowering of plantation culture just before the war. Within the broader Colonial Revival mode, a specific Southern Colonial style emerged in the form of a large symmetrical house characterized by a portico of great white columns. National architectural writers eagerly embraced the term "Southern Colonial" along with the ideal of southern life it symbolized. In 1895 *American Architect and Building News* described a new house in St. Louis whose massive columned portico made it "more of the southern Colonial architecture than its sister style of the Northeastern States" and "somewhat of a relief from the ordinary run of Colonial houses." The columns were "part and parcel of the southern Colonial, [which] somehow or another bear with them a certain tinge of the bigheartedness and hospitality which are the rightful heritage of the southern people." The Southern Colonial house also incorporated the modern conveniences of plumbing, heating, and lighting, an apt parallel to the Democrats' carefully devised amalgam of tradition and modern reform. That the Southern Colonial house was built more often for an urban businessman than for a cotton planter only confirmed its power. Modeled around 1900 chiefly in residences of prosperous members of old families, it gained sway by 1910 among wealthy citizens of various backgrounds.[38]

In a 1903 article entitled "Revival of the Colonial Style—A Simple, Dignified Home after the Old Fashion," Charlotte architects Charles Christian Hook and Stewart Rogers laid out the meaning of the style for the South. "The civil war," they explained, "marked the change from good to bad architecture in the South, the reason for which is apparent. In antebellum days when a home was built of any pretensions the owner and designer as a rule was an educated gentleman of refinement," who, "familiar with the classics and having other colonial work as models took pains to preserve the proper proportions." But "after the great conflict and things being reversed in general, we find a greater reversal in architecture than any other sign of the times. Why was it? Because the illiterate and unrefined being new to wealth desired it more than purity, and the cultured and once wealthy were either too poor to build or were so busy during the reconstruction period they had no time to devote to art." In those evil times, architecture was handed over to "the most ignorant class of men, in fact, any jack-leg who could wield a hatchet and saw. All colonial details and proportions were discarded as being 'old timey' [and] the jack-leg-carpenter with the deadly jigsaw ran riot in the land." But now, they affirmed, "out of all this chaos we again have a revival of the Colonial, [which] in its purity expresses more real refined sentiment and more intimate associations with our history than any [other style], for it is not only an association of English history with our own but also expresses the authentic memoirs of the American people."[39]

In both Raleigh and Wilmington, the first major residential projects in the Southern Colonial style were commissioned by patrician families for whom the architectural reclamation of continuity from glorious past to redeemed present had deep associations. Such houses reinforced a way of life in which, as one resident remembered of Raleigh in 1905, "the women were fine hostesses, not only abounding in wit and delightful chit-chat but in well-ordered households" where "the relation between old Raleighites and their black friends was beautiful," for many of the servants "never left the premises and

Dudley-Sprunt House, North Front Street, Wilmington, 1905 postcard. The portico was added around 1895 for James and Luola Sprunt. Photo, North Carolina Division of Archives and History, Raleigh.

scarcely knew they had been set free." And, as the feminine domain in an era of elaborate, large-scale entertaining, the magnified version of the antebellum plantation house offered the perfect setting for hospitality, patriotism, and filiopietism—all in an urban residence larger and vastly more convenient than most plantation houses had ever been.[40]

Continuity with the past was literal in some of the earliest Colonial Revival projects, in which elite couples aggrandized existing antebellum mansions. An important early example came when Wilmington civic leaders James and Luola Sprunt remodeled the downtown residence of antebellum governor Edward Dudley. James Sprunt, a Scots-born businessman and Confederate veteran, wrote local history and endowed a series of historical monographs at the University of North Carolina. As president of the North Carolina Society of Colonial Dames, Luola Murchison Sprunt spearheaded local and state efforts to mark important colonial sites. Soon after the Sprunts bought the house in 1895, they expanded it and transformed its public visage with a monumental Corinthian portico flanked by broad porches. The resulting "handsome Colonial residence" instantly gained acclaim as one of the city's principal landmarks and the setting for Mrs. Sprunt's Colonial Dames meetings.[41]

In Raleigh, too, the first major statement in the Southern Colonial style appeared in the refashioning of an antebellum residence. In 1901 Bennehan and Sallie Cameron undertook an expansion of their house on Hillsborough Street. Bennehan Cameron, a businessman whose father and grandfather had been among the richest men in the state before the Civil War, was active in the

1898 and 1900 Democratic campaigns and later in promotion of better highways. Tracing lineage from Revolutionary heroes, he enthusiastically supported patriotic groups and commemorative pursuits. Sallie Taliaferro Mayo
Cameron, a descendant of old Virginia families, was the daughter of a wealthy
Richmond businessman who had been on Robert E. Lee's staff. The Cam-
erons obtained remodeling plans from Richmond architect William G. Noland, a prominent practitioner of revival styles. To the rear they built a large
addition with bedrooms, modern bathrooms, and a new kitchen. Sallie was
especially interested in transforming the public face of the residence. With its
towering portico of Ionic columns and curved porches at each end, the
Cameron mansion impressed Raleigh as "a fine old colonial-type residence"
that "carried one's thoughts back to the days of large plantations and baro-
nial rule."[42]

The same architectural themes also appeared in new residences. The
epitome of the Southern Colonial house and Raleigh's first and grandest
example was built in 1902 for Richard Beverly Raney. The wealthy widower
previously had erected the Olivia Raney Library as a memorial to his first
wife; in 1902, in preparation for his marriage to Kate Whiting Denson, Raney
constructed a new house on Hillsborough Street across from the library, thus
completing a symmetrical relationship with the Confederate monument.[43]

Raney's architect for the house was Charles Barrett, of Raleigh, an early
proponent of the Southern Colonial style, who, with his former partner
William P. Rose, had published an example of "a complete modern southern
home" in the *Southern Architect* in 1899. Now working on his own, Barrett
designed the Raney mansion as a full-fledged exemplar of the style and
immediately published it as the centerpiece of his *Colonial Southern Homes*
(1903). Carrying forward many aspects of antebellum plantation houses, the
symmetrically planned residence had a central hallway and flanking formal
rooms—all rendered on a vaster scale and with more rooms than its antebellum predecessors. Its modern amenities included "sanitary, scientific"
plumbing, heating, and electric lighting. The exterior presented the Southern
Colonial at its most spectacular, with two massive Ionic porticoes addressing
Hillsborough Street and the capitol. In such a house, the imagery of the old
plantation evoked family histories of lost grandeur, while its modern luxury
and prominent location expressed the Raneys' position in the city, where
they and other children of planter families had created a new urban version of
the old way of life.[44]

More and more columned residences appeared as other members of the
urban elite followed suit. Raleigh's Hillsborough Street soon was lined by a

parade of pillared porticoes on both old and new houses. In Wilmington, too, local reporters rhapsodized over the "modern," "convenient," "Colonial" residences that wealthy citizens were building. The most flamboyant example rose in 1905, when Elizabeth Eagles Haywood Bridgers—a descendant of ancient North Carolina families and the recent widow of Preston L. Bridgers, a local businessman who had been among the leaders of the 1898 "Revolution"—built a massive stone townhouse dominated by a curved portico of colossal Ionic columns and filled with the latest in luxurious modern amenities.[45] As the popularity of the style continued, an especially powerful rendition appeared in 1913, when the Cape Fear Club, bastion of the city's business and professional men, erected its new clubhouse in the form of a red brick mansion trimmed in white marble, "patterned closely after the Colonial style of architecture" and featuring "long commodious verandas, with large white columns" and reception rooms "arranged and decorated after the Colonial style of the Adams period."[46]

The Southern Colonial image also reached beyond the city into suburban enclaves. Between 1907 and 1910, Mary Bridgers, Preston Bridgers's sister, developed Carolina Heights east of Wilmington for leading industrialists and merchants, building the most imposing residences in the "Colonial" style with porticoes in every classical order.[47] At the same time, James and Luola Sprunt transformed another antebellum mansion, Orton Plantation, into a hybrid Colonial Revival composition, keeping the classical, temple-form plantation house with its grand portico as the central element to which they added conveniently appointed wings on either side. Sprunt regarded Orton as "the most attractive of all the old colonial estates on the Cape Fear," which "still maintains its reputation of colonial days for a refined and generous hospitality" and presents "one of the finest examples of pure Colonial architecture in America . . . with its stately white columns gleaming in the sunshine."[48] These landmarks inaugurated a lasting pattern. As the proliferation of suburbs embodied growing separation among races and classes, the Colonial Revival in its myriad forms came to dominate upper- and middle-class housing throughout the South, and to be identified simply and universally with traditional domesticity, respectability, and continuity.

When North Carolina Democratic leaders organized the state's official presentation at the Jamestown Tercentennial Exposition of 1907, they recapitulated themes that had recently emerged in the state's life. The exposition combined a celebration of the oldest (1607) establishment of Anglo-Saxon

Orton Plantation House, Brunswick County, mid-twentieth-century postcard. The small eighteenth-century house was incorporated into a temple-form plantation house in the antebellum period, which in turn was expanded in the early twentieth century for James and Luola Sprunt. Photo, North Carolina Division of Archives and History, Raleigh.

culture in America with a southern-sponsored reunion of blue and gray, a presentation of modern southern race relations, and a certain amount of economic boosterism. Led by Governor Robert Glenn, North Carolina set out to put on an exhibit "first-class in every respect" to attract investors and "desirable" immigrants. Business leaders presented displays touting the state's economic progress and opportunities.[49]

Charged with creating a state history exhibit, Mary Hilliard Hinton, editor of the Daughters of the Revolution's thriving *North Carolina Booklet*, worked with other prominent women to assemble a dazzling display of the recent "historical awakening in the Old North State." The exhibit began with depictions of America's first Anglo-Saxon settlement, the Lost Colony at Roanoke. Other displays included photographs of James Sprunt's collection of portraits of the Lords Proprietors, silver from various "aristocratic" families, pictures of celebrated plantation homes and furniture from a few of them, and a depiction of the Edenton Tea Party scene together with possessions of those patriotic colonial ladies.

North Carolina's chief expenditure was on its state building. With each participating state constructing an example of its "typical Colonial" architec-

The North Carolina Building, Jamestown (Va.) Exposition, 1907. The building was designed by Zimmerman and Lester of Winston-Salem and built by J. E. Elliott and Brother of Hickory. Photo, North Carolina Division of Archives and History, Raleigh.

ture, the exposition managers hoped to create a "Colonial acropolis restful to the eye and satisfying to sentiment" that would "result in a revival of interest in Colonial architecture, which is really the only distinctive American order of building." North Carolina leaders chose the Southern Colonial style that had become so popular in the state, a house built of North Carolina pine and "of large colonial design with immense columns and porches." The North Carolina Building further promoted the style by inspiring citizens who visited the exposition to copy it in their own houses. In this official display of the state's self-image, as in the Colonial Revival architecture and commemorative monuments back home, Democratic leaders set forth the values and heritage with which they intended to shape the state in the new century. Miss Hinton summed up their accomplishment: "The keynote of American life is prog- ress—an excellent and most powerful characteristic; yet harm and ultimate ruin will surely follow in its trail unless safeguarded by conservatism. No study so engenders and promotes the cultivation of this check to vandalism as does History. At last the dominant trait of the Anglo-Saxon race is asserting itself and we are becoming more like our relatives overseas, who guard sa- credly whatever bears on their glorious past."[50]

For members of the Democratic elite, the book had opened on a redeemed and progressive South that reaffirmed the social order of their antebellum heyday, while embracing a program of modern economic progress. Just as they had taken control of the political process with strategies devised to dictate the present and the future, so they took control of the region's history and defined the meaning of the past in a fashion that explained and vindicated the present. By molding public memory of the past, they also shaped the direction of the future. They engaged in a process that, while sharing some features with what has been called the "invention of tradition," might best be termed the "arranging of tradition." Rather than concocting a history to undergird their position, they employed precisely the same tactic that Alfred Moore Waddell had described in 1895, using the events of the past "like a child's box of letters with which we can spell any word we please. We have only to select such letters as we want, arrange them as we like, and say nothing about those which do not suit our purpose." Vital to this spelling out of the past was the creation of public, visible, lasting symbols of that past.[51]

Thus between 1890 and 1910 elite Democratic leaders succeeded in forging a symbolic ensemble that defined North Carolina history and public life in accord with their vision of society. Within a short time, both the history they spelled out and the social and political system they had established took on an aura of permanence, which was reinforced in the form of monuments and architecture. So effective was the combined effect of cultural and political control that for many it seemed that the hierarchical, racially segregated South had always been thus, except for the brief aberration of Reconstruction, and presumably would always remain so.

In the mid-twentieth century, challenges to the racial and political structure created by the Democrats in 1900 began to change the South. But the version of history they established endured. Although historians, starting in the middle years of the twentieth century, have begun to reexamine old assumptions, public memory has been slow to change. In the sagas told by memorials and by the seemingly unbroken continuity of colonial architecture, the old story persists. Through the powerful and lasting language of monuments and architecture, the guardians of the glorious past have continued to safeguard the past, the present, and the future.

NOTES

The author acknowledges with thanks a 1987 Henry Francis du Pont fellowship at the Winterthur Museum for initial research on this topic. The author also thanks, for critical readings and suggestions, John Bishir, Jerry Cashion, Jeffrey Crow, Catherine Hutchins, James Leloudis, Carl Lounsbury, William Price, Janet Seapker, Dell Upton, Harry Watson, Camille Wells, and Chris Wilson; and for encouragement and assistance in obtaining illustrations and information, Claudia Brown, Ned Cooke, Michael Hill, Elizabeth Reid

Murray, Beverly Tetterton, Edward Turberg, Abigail Van Slyck, Harry Warren, and R. Beverly R. Webb.

1. Rev. M. M. Marshall, "Address," in *Exercises at the Opening of the Olivia Raney Library, Held in the Library Hall on the Evening of Thursday, January Twenty-Fourth, 1901* (Raleigh: Capital Printing Co., 1901), 14–15.

2. *American Architect and Building News*, 6 April 1895.

3. This summary derives primarily from Kenneth Ames, introduction to Alan Axelrod, ed., *The Colonial Revival in America* (New York: Norton, 1983); Edward L. Ayers, *The Promise of the New South: Life after Reconstruction* (New York: Oxford University Press, 1992); John Bodnar, *Remaking America: Public Memory, Commemoration, and Patriotism in the Twentieth Century* (Princeton: Princeton University Press, 1992); Michele H. Bogart, *Public Sculpture and the Civic Ideal in New York City, 1890–1930* (Chicago: University of Chicago Press, 1989); Gaines M. Foster, *Ghosts of the Confederacy: Defeat, the Lost Cause, and the Emergence of the New South, 1865 to 1913* (New York: Oxford University Press, 1987); Michael Kammen, *Mystic Chords of Memory: The Transformation of Tradition in American Culture* (New York: Knopf, 1991); Robert W. Rydell, *All the World's a Fair: Visions of Empire at American International Expositions, 1876–1916* (Chicago: University of Chicago Press, 1984); Christopher Wilson, *The Myth of Santa Fe* (Albuquerque: University of New Mexico Press, 1997; Richard Guy Wilson, Dianne Pilgrim, and Richard N. Murray, *The American Renaissance, 1876–1917* (New York: Pantheon, 1979); and Richard Guy Wilson, "Architecture and the Reinterpretation of the Past in the American Renaissance," *Winterthur Portfolio* 18 (Spring 1983): 69–87.

4. Charles B. Aycock, "The South Regaining Its Prestige," in *Literary and Historical Activities in North Carolina, 1900–1905* (Raleigh: Publications of the Historical Commission, 1907), 1:120.

5. Harry S. Warren, "Colonel Frederick Augustus Olds and the Founding of the North Carolina Museum of History" (M.A. thesis, East Carolina University, 1988), 20–21. On Samuel A'Court Ashe, see William S. Powell, ed., *Dictionary of North Carolina Biography*, vol. 1 (Chapel Hill: University of North Carolina Press, 1979).

6. Address of Alfred Moore Waddell, Ladies Memorial Association Records, Archives and Records Section, North Carolina Division of Archives and History, Raleigh (hereafter NCDAH).

7. Undated [February 1895] clipping, Scrapbook, Branch Papers, NCDAH (first quotation). On the shift from funereal to civic memorials, see Foster, *Ghosts of the Confederacy*; similar trends took place in the North. On the North Carolina Monumental Association, see Branch Papers, NCDAH.

8. "A Masterly Defense of the Cause for Which They Fought—In History's Clear Light," *Raleigh News and Observer*, 20, 21 May 1895. In contrast to the popular mass-produced soldier figures, the figures were modeled on North Carolina regiments and fashioned by Bavarian sculptor Ferdinand Von Miller. For a similar 1895 speech by Stephen D. Lee to the United Confederate Veterans in Houston, see Fred Arthur Bailey, "The Textbooks of the 'Lost Cause': Censorship and the Creation of Southern State Histories," *Georgia Historical Quarterly* 75 (Fall 1991): 508.

9. Richard N. Current, "That Other Declaration, May 20, 1775–May 20, 1975," *North Carolina Historical Review* 54 (April 1977): 169–91; "A Masterly Defense . . .," *Raleigh News and Observer*, 20, 21 May 1895.

10. "A Masterly Defense . . .," *Raleigh News and Observer*, 20, 21 May 1895.

11. James Sprunt to Alfred Moore Waddell, 21 May 1895, and Henry Groves Connor to Waddell, 23 May 1895, Waddell Papers, Southern Historical Collection, University of North Carolina at Chapel Hill (hereafter SHC).

12. J. Morgan Kousser, *The Shaping of Southern Politics: Suffrage Restriction and the Establishment of the One-Party South, 1880–1910* (New Haven: Yale University Press, 1974); C. Vann Woodward, *Origins of the New South, 1877–1913* (Baton Rouge: Louisiana State University Press, 1971); Paul Escott, *Many Excellent People: Power and Privilege in North Carolina, 1850–1900* (Chapel Hill: University of North Carolina Press, 1985).

13. Josephus Daniels, *Editor in Politics* (Chapel Hill: University of North Carolina Press, 1941), 295, 283. Other firsthand accounts include Alfred Moore Waddell, *Some Memories of My Life* (Raleigh: Edwards and Broughton, 1908), and a 1933 interview with Furnifold Simmons in Carl Goerch, *Down Home* (Raleigh: Edwards and Broughton, 1943), 131–58.

14. James Sprunt, *Chronicles of the Cape Fear River* (Raleigh: Edwards and Broughton, 1916), 554–55; H. Leon Prather, *We Have Taken a City: The Wilmington Racial Massacre and Coup of 1898* (New York: Associated University Presses, 1984), 45.

15. In August 1898 a controversial editorial in the city's black newspaper, the *Wilmington Record*, became a rallying point for the white supremacist campaign. Alex Manly, publisher of the *Record*, wrote the editorial in response to Rebecca L. Felton's article advocating lynching black men who raped white women. Portions of his editorial were taken out of context and widely reprinted. Prather, *We Have Taken a City*; Sprunt, *Chronicles*, 554–58.

16. *Wilmington Messenger*, 25 October 1898. See also Daniels, *Editor in Politics*, 301. For responses to the speech, see George M. Tolson, Hertford, N.C., to Alfred Moore Waddell, 27 October 1898, and Rebecca Cameron to Waddell, 26 October 1898, Waddell Papers, SHC.

17. Prather, *We Have Taken a City*; Waddell, *Some Memories of My Life*.

18. Daniels, *Editor in Politics*, 368.

19. *Public Documents of the State of North Carolina* (Raleigh: Edwards and Broughton and E. M. Uzzell, 1901), vol. 1, document Ia, 2, 4, 12.

20. The qualification for membership in the State Literary and Historical Association read: "any white resident of the State, or North Carolinian residing out of the State, who subscribes to the purposes of the Association." *Literary and Historical Activities in North Carolina*, 1–3, 6.

21. From these roots emerged the state's tradition of distinguished historians as well as the fruitful relationship between historical pursuits and civic and political leaders. See William S. Price Jr., "Plowing Virgin Fields: State Support for Southern Archives, Particularly North Carolina," *Carolina Comments* 29 (March 1991): 41–47.

22. For dissenting views elsewhere in the South that were omitted or denied in the official codified saga, see Kirk Savage, *Standing Soldiers, Kneeling Slaves: Race, War, and Monument in Nineteenth-Century America* (Princeton: Princeton University Press, 1997), esp. 153.

23. See *Literary and Historical Activities in North Carolina* for representative rhetoric on these topics and such activities as Francis Winston's report (pp. 29–35) on the first "North Carolina Day" celebrations in the public schools, a project assisted by the Daughters of the Revolution and the North Carolina Literary and Historical Society. See also

North Carolina Booklet (North Carolina Society of the Daughters of the Revolution, 1901–26), and Daniel Harvey Hill, *Young People's History of North Carolina* (Raleigh: Alfred Williams, 1916).

24. *Raleigh News and Observer*, 16, 18, 19 August 1900; *Heroes and Heroines on Union Square* (Raleigh: State Capitol Foundation, Inc., 1983); Daniels, *Editor in Politics*, 369; *Literary and Historical Activities in North Carolina*. On Beaux Arts sculptor Augustus Saint-Gaudens's influential use of gesture in his celebrated Farragut (1881), see Bogart, *Public Sculpture and the Civic Ideal*, 32.

25. Quoted from *Atlanta Constitution* and *New York Tribune* in Ayers, *Promise of the New South*, 331–32. On Francis H. Packer, see Tony P. Wrenn, *Wilmington, North Carolina: An Architectural and Historical Portrait* (Charlottesville: University Press of Virginia, 1984), 203.

26. *Raleigh News and Observer*, 19, 20, 21 May 1907.

27. Wrenn, *Wilmington*, 295–97; *Wilmington Star*, 2, 3 May 1907; Rosa Chiles, "North Carolina Society of Colonial Dames in America," in Sprunt, *Chronicles*, 578–79.

28. *Wilmington Messenger*, 20, 21 April 1906, 3 May 1907; *Wilmington Star*, 2, 3 May 1907.

29. *Wilmington Morning Star*, 28 January 1906, reprinted in *Charlotte Observer*, 27 January 1906. In 1909 the Colonial Dames erected a second marker to the "Men of the Cape Fear" at Brunswick, a ruined town that was the actual site of the Stamp Act resistance.

30. *Presentation of the Statue Hon. George Davis to the City of Wilmington by the Daughters of the Confederacy*, 20 April 1911, program for the event (Wilmington: Privately published, 1910), in North Carolina Collection, University of North Carolina, Chapel Hill; Mrs. William M. Parsley, "The George Davis Monument," in Sprunt, *Chronicles*, 572–73 (first quotation); Mrs. William M. Parsley to James Sprunt, 9 January, 27 March 1909, Alexander Sprunt and Sons Papers, Rare Books, Manuscripts, and Special Collections Library, Duke University, Durham.

31. Horne Committee Papers, NCDAH. Other monuments on Union Square commemorate Democratic educator Charles McIver (1912), Charles B. Aycock (1924), Samuel A'Court Ashe (1940), three presidents North Carolina "gave the nation" (1948), Vietnam veterans (1987), and veterans of World Wars I and II and the Korean Conflict (1990).

32. The *Booklet* began in May 1901 under Miss Martha Helen Haywood and Mrs. Hubert Haywood; they were soon succeeded by Miss Hinton and Mrs. Moffitt. These women made the *Booklet* a long-lived success that helped define the emerging canon of state history. On Hinton and Moffitt, see Powell, *Dictionary of North Carolina Biography*, vols. 3, 4; Mary Hilliard Hinton Papers, SHC; and Elvira Worth Moffitt Papers, SHC.

33. *David Paton: Architect of the North Carolina State Capitol, An Address by Samuel A. Ashe* (Raleigh: Edwards and Broughton, 1916), 15.

34. Bailey, "Textbooks of the 'Lost Cause,'" 508.

35. "A People Known by Way They Build . . . ," *Raleigh News and Observer*, 6 June 1907.

36. Ibid. See also Charlotte V. Brown, "The Day of the Great Cities," in Catherine W. Bishir, Charlotte V. Brown, Ernest H. Wood, and Carl R. Lounsbury, *Architects and Builders in North Carolina: A History of the Practice of Building* (Chapel Hill: University of North Carolina Press, 1990), 298.

37. Joy Wheeler Dow, *American Renaissance: A Review of Domestic Architecture* (New

168 *Catherine W. Bishir*

York: William T. Comstock, 1904). See also William B. Rhoads, *The Colonial Revival* (Greenport, Conn.: Garland Publishing, Inc., 1977) and "The Colonial Revival and American Nationalism," *Journal of the Society of Architectural Historians* 35 (December 1976): 239–54.

38. *American Architect and Building News*, 6 April 1895. Issues of *Southern Architect* show the incorporation of Colonial motifs into houses of a variety of forms in the late 1890s and a shift to the symmetrical house with a dominant portico in 1899. Many local and regional architects worked in this style. See, e.g., Catherine W. Bishir, *North Carolina Architecture* (Chapel Hill: University of North Carolina Press, 1990), 365, 416–25; Richard Guy Wilson, "Building on the Foundations," in Charles E. Brownell, Calder Loth, and Richard Guy Wilson, *The Making of Virginia Architecture* (Richmond: Virginia Museum of Fine Arts, 1992), 116–23.

39. "Revival of the Colonial Style . . .," *Charlotte Observer*, 20 December 1903. Similar ideas were repeated in national literature, as, e.g., J. Robie Kennedy Jr., "Examples of Georgian and Greek Revival Work in the Far South," *Architectural Record* 21 (March 1907), and Russell F. Whitehead, "The Old and the New South," *Architectural Record* 30 (July 1911).

40. Robert W. Winston, *It's a Far Cry* (New York: Henry Holt and Co., 1937), 262–63.

41. Wrenn, *Wilmington*, 53–55.

42. P. H. Mayo to Sallie Cameron (17 June 1901), Sallie Cameron to Bennehan Cameron (July–October 1901), and "Alterations & Additions to Residence of Col. Bennehan Cameron," September 1901, Noland & Baskervill, Architects, Richmond, all in Bennehan Cameron Papers, SHC; Virgil St. Cloud, *Pioneer Blood* (Raleigh: Edwards and Broughton, 1948) (quotation). On Bennehan Cameron (1854–1925), see Powell, *Dictionary of North Carolina Biography*, vol. 1; Jean Bradley Anderson, *Piedmont Plantations: The Bennehan-Cameron Family and Lands in North Carolina* (Durham: Historic Preservation Society of Durham, 1985); and Bennehan Cameron Papers, SHC.

43. Culled from clippings and family memorabilia, courtesy of R. Beverly R. Webb. See Richard Beverly Raney in *Who's Who in America, 1903* (1215).

44. *Southern Architect* 10 (March 1899): 684–85; Charles Barrett, *Colonial Southern Homes* (Raleigh: N.p., 1903).

45. Wrenn, *Wilmington*, 87.

46. Leslie N. Boney Jr., *The Cape Fear Club, 1967–1983* (Wilmington: Wilmington Printing Co., 1984), 1–7.

47. S. Carol Gunter, *Carolina Heights: The Preservation of an Urban Neighborhood in Wilmington* (Wilmington: Wilmington Department of Planning, 1982), 1, 15; Wrenn, *Wilmington*, 280–84.

48. James Lawrence Sprunt, *The Story of Orton Plantation* [Wilmington]: Privately published, 1958), and James Sprunt, *Chronicles*, 57–58.

49. Mary Hilliard Hinton, *The North Carolina Historical Exhibit at the Jamestown Ter-Centennial Exposition* (Raleigh: Edwards and Broughton, 1916), 7, 9.

50. Ibid., 7.

51. See Eric Hobsbawm and Terence Ranger, eds., *The Invention of Tradition* (Cambridge University Press, 1983).

Redeeming Southern Memory

The Negro Race History, 1874–1915

Laurie F. Maffly-Kipp

In 1883 African American Baptist preacher George Washington Williams published his *History of the Negro Race in America, 1619–1880*. The book, a fundamentally optimistic account of the black presence in the New World, represented an attempt by the well-educated, northern divine to balance his commitments to an American evangelical tradition with an awareness of the ongoing oppression of his fellow African Americans at the hands of whites. "I commit this work to the public, white and black," he noted in the preface, "to the friends and foes of the Negro in the hope that the obsolete antagonisms which grew out of the relation of master and slave may speedily sink as storms beneath the horizon; and that the day will hasten when there shall be no North, no South, no Black, no White,—but all be American citizens, with equal duties and equal rights."[1] The work revealed much about Williams: his upbringing in antebellum Pennsylvania as the child of an interracial union, his training at Howard University and Newton Theological Seminary, and his work experiences at Baptist churches in New England and Ohio.[2] But this particular passage highlights the motivating force behind the book: it reveals, in anticipation of a historical narrative of over two hundred years of African enslavement, Williams's desire to recast much of the American past. His historical account was, at heart, an attempt to impart moral meaning to the present by reconstructing the historical consciousness of both blacks and whites. In this desire, Williams fit precisely Friedrich Nietzsche's characterization of "historical men," those who "believe that ever more light is shed on the meaning of existence in the course of its *process*, and they look back to consider that process only to understand the present better and learn to desire the future more vehemently."[3]

In this quest for comprehension and desire he found himself in good company. Although African Americans had been writing both personal and communal narratives for several decades before the Civil War, it was not until after the emancipation of the slaves that the genre of the "race history" emerged as an increasingly popular form of black literary expression. Between 1874 and 1915 several dozen writers authored studies of the Negro past, present, and future, in an effort, as Edward Johnson put it, to record "the many brave deeds and noble characteristics" of the race.[4] These histories also had a deep religious impact. Writing in the years prior to the professionalization of history as a "scientific" mode of discourse, many early race historians were ordained ministers; some had theological training. All were interested in the prospective possibilities of history, the potential for narrative to shape the future of the free community. As blacks and as Protestants, these writers imbued the past, present, and future of the Negro with moral and spiritual significance. These histories are important, then, not simply for what they reflect about the history of African Americans. They are even more significant for what they reveal about the wide-ranging public discourse among post–Reconstruction black leaders regarding representations of the race— representations that served both to counter white racial images and to reimagine the African American community itself on different terms.[5] For these Protestant leaders, Reconstruction and its aftermath encompassed more than social and institutional reconstitution: it also included the reconfiguration of time itself.[6]

The social production of race histories was part and parcel of the ongoing mission to ex-slaves in the late nineteenth century. As northern missionaries moved into the southern states in the years following Emancipation, they brought with them an emphasis on education as the key to morality and middle-class respectability. As Evelyn Brooks Higginbotham has argued, literacy and rational discourse allowed Protestant clergy and laity to control access to correct religious doctrine, and thus to systematically shape the beliefs and ritual lives of the ex-slaves. Literacy rose quickly in the freed population in the 1880s and 1890s, and church-sponsored presses stood ready with journals, newspapers, and books to fill the new demand for printed materials.[7] But the new religious media functioned to shape more than doctrinal correctness: they also provided widespread access to racial representations that could be used to mold character. J. Max Barber, author of *The Negro of the Earlier World: An Excursion into Ancient Negro History*, commented that "a race without traditions and without a history is most likely to be a race without backbone and without self-respect."[8] Race historians served as self-appointed leaders of the effort to provide a history, and thus a moral identity, for a people often characterized as lacking both. The African American public, in turn, had access to these depictions of moral identity through the predominantly northern, urban, and often denominationally based publishing houses that controlled their production.[9]

Historical narratives functioned somewhat differently from Sunday school tracts, exegetical sermons, or other types of written religious discourse.[10] They offered "an overall vision of the historical world," which systematically placed the story of African American suffering in a reconstructed temporal context.[11] Reconfiguring time, space, and purpose, in turn, could serve to constitute a renewed sense of social unity, a new collective identity reinforced by individuals through the act of reading itself.[12] Race histories, in the guise of objective recordings of ongoing tradition, constructed expanded notions of religious and racial communities that had persevered through time. Grounded in Protestant valuations of literacy as a moral and spiritual virtue, their dissemination encouraged by the accessibility of publishing technology through black denominational presses and increasingly through northern white-controlled presses as well, race histories fostered racial and religious commitments to an enlarged African American diasporic community.

Equipped with this newly available "technology of power,"[13] black Protestant leaders hoped to influence the development of southern freedpeople in a typically Protestant way: through conversion of the head and heart. Their various approaches reflected the contentiousness of Protestant roots as well: authors interpreted the "facts" of history in divergent ways. Race historians may have been similarly motivated by historical circumstances to create historical narratives, but they differed greatly in their diagnoses of past ills and their prognoses for future improvement.[14]

From whichever temporal perspective one chose, reformulating historical consciousness entailed confronting and resolving a number of philosophical problems in the present. One of the most pressing was the perceived political and religious apathy promoted by enslavement. For many decades black

Protestants had pondered the religious meaning of African slavery in the providential scheme: why had God allowed African enslavement? Could the terrible suffering of slavery have been part of a larger plan to bring Africans to Christ?[15] If so, race historians were not satisfied that the results had been salutary or entirely Christian. Joseph T. Wilson, in his 1882 study *Emancipation: Its Course and Progress from 1481 B.C. to A.D. 1875*, lamented the "absurd extravagancies" of slave worship that still kept blacks in a position of spiritual inferiority. Writers criticized most harshly the continuing tendency of freed men and women to trust the fatalism and superstition of their old religious practices. It was not always healthy, George Washington Williams pointed out, for blacks to rely on a "divine helper" for guidance; in passing, he also criticized Harriet Beecher Stowe's antislavery novel, *Uncle Tom's Cabin*, for the "terrible fatality" of its leading black characters.[16]

Race historians, themselves committed to the transformative social powers of organized religion, wrestled with the supernaturalism and, as they saw it, the political passivity of southern blacks. One of the most scathing indictments of black fatalism came from the pen of William Hannibal Thomas. Born in 1843, Thomas was a mixed-blood lawyer with seminary training. While growing up in Pickaway County, Ohio, he witnessed his parents' service as conductors on the Underground Railroad. After a brief preparatory school education, Thomas tried to enlist as a Union army volunteer in 1860 but was turned away because of his color. Eventually he found his way into the war, fought to the end, and after professional training at a Presbyterian seminary, headed south in 1871 to organize schools for freed blacks. In 1876 he was elected to the legislature of South Carolina.[17]

In *The American Negro*, a highly contentious work published in 1901, Thomas expressed unmitigated anger toward southern blacks. "The social side of negro life," he wrote, "has been to me an open page of execrable weakness, of unblushing shame, of inconceivable mendacity, of indurated folly and ephemeral contrition." Although well aware of the obstacles that had blocked racial progress since the end of Reconstruction, Thomas believed that much of the blame had to be placed at the door of the ex-slaves themselves. He wrote his book, he explained, out of "an intense desire to awaken the negro people out of their sleep of death." The church also had to accept a good measure of culpability, he added: "To the negro, religion is a transient impulse, a kind of hypnotic sensation, a thing entirely apart from and outside of ordinary life and duty." It "accentuates individual helplessness and emphasizes dependence on unknown forces by a prominence which it gives through songs, texts, sermons, and prayers to a weird psychic guidance."[18] Although it lay within the power of Negroes to change their situation, Thomas argued that the best means to do so would be to place blacks once again under "a superior white Christian supervision." Negroes now have the Promised Land of Liberty spread out before them, Thomas explained, but they do not know how to take it for themselves: "no Joshua was with them to part the waters, and so, turning back from visions of grandeur and high-wrought hopes, they were speedily enwrapped in the darkness of industrial servitude."[19]

Race historians may have disagreed about whether slave spirituality was something that needed to be rooted out or whether it could provide a necessary basis for the growth of "true" Christianity. These differences of opinion reflected, in part, their position as self-appointed mediators between whites and southern blacks. Like many middle-class black religious leaders in the late nineteenth century, race historians had an ambivalent relationship with the black masses for whom they wished to speak. Most were, in fact, relative outsiders to the dilemmas faced by ex-slaves: many had been educated or had lived in the North.[20] Separated from their northern colleagues by race, black Protestant leaders were thus distinguishable from southern blacks along class-based and often regional lines. Ironically, Williams's and Stanford's popular appellations as the "Negro Bancroft" and the "Negro Beecher," respectively, though intended as compliments, symbolized their distance from both other blacks and other Protestant divines. Race histories provided African American leaders with a means of rhetorically uniting the various religious, social, and racial loyalties that constituted their singular stations in life. But in doing so, ironically, their narratives often revealed division more than unity, distancing them from the people they sought to improve.

The widespread criticism of ex-slave spirituality was a case in point. Most race historians, like their missionary counterparts throughout the South, posited a normative understanding of religious faith that stressed rationality and ethical behavior as the focus of the Christian life. True religion, Thomas asserted, is characterized by "clearness of spiritual perception" and "purity of ideal." The "mass of Negro religionists" do not have this perception of the principles of truth, but are instead irrational and worship a God of "personal characteristics and human idiosyncrasies."[21] Other authors agreed with the substance of Thomas's judgment but expressed less vitriol and more optimism about the ability of ex-slaves to rise from the "extreme fanaticism" of slave spirituality to religious rationalism. George Washington Williams was another mixed-blood Civil War veteran who had fled his native Pennsylvania to enlist. He later graduated from Howard University (1871) and was the first black graduate from Newton Theological Seminary (1874). Williams, a parish minister who had served Baptist churches in both New England and Cincinnati, saw more to encourage him in the growth of Protestant institutions among ex-slaves. Black churches, as he saw it, were "the best proof of the Negro's ability to maintain himself in an advanced state of civilization." The progress of the race would come about as blacks learned to do for themselves. As a salient example, Williams pointed to the recent exodus to Kansas: "It was but the natural operation of a divine law that moved whole communities of Negroes to turn their faces toward the setting sun." In other words, the divine will was operating through human agency, and blacks would gradually lift themselves up as they learned to turn their religious piety into social action.[22] In keeping with theistic evolutionary schemes current in white liberal theology, black authors stressed the workings of providence through human processes and "higher laws." They envisioned God, not as the personal and often arbitrary judge of the Israelites who ruled his people directly—and, significantly, who comforted his people in times of struggle and affliction—but rather as an impersonal force, a natural law removed from the daily cares of the black community.

The very notion of progress assumed in the writing of race histories, all of which predicted brighter days ahead, was indebted both to liberal notions of steady advance and to the development of a documentary record in which previous historical steps could be known and evaluated with precision.[23] In this respect, Protestant authors were thoroughly influenced by the dominant liberal strains of Euro-American philosophy and history; yet, as Wilson Moses has observed about black nationalists in the same period, even this degree of cultural assimilation was put to the purpose of forming an African American collective identity, an entity called the "Negro race" that, while it may not have been united socially in the present historical moment, could be unified in narratives that traced its organic and essentially romantic nature through an expanded temporal trajectory.[24] Thus black Protestants could make sense of religious discord and diversity and still maintain the superiority and eventual triumph of their own beliefs within an organic community; they could write themselves into the same story with the black masses by pointing to historical moments of solidarity within an unfolding, progressive historical drama; and, significantly, they could attempt to exert social and cultural control over less educated blacks through the rhetorical power of collective self-definition.

Race historians used familiar tools to construct their historical narratives, but they organized them in ways that diverged from Euro-American sacred and national histories. A number of writers began their works by outlining the glorious and mighty culture of the Negro race in ancient Egypt.[25] Baptist minister L. T. Smith, born in Virginia, employed as a teacher by the Freedmen's Relief Association of Pennsylvania and later educated at Hampton Institute in the 1870s, advised readers of his 1883 history, *A Great Truth in a Nutshell*, to "Wake up! Arise from the bed of dead lethargy . . . and, as I shall draw back the curtains of time, look! if you please, twenty-five hundred years back into the grim face of antiquity and see! O! see the elevated and lofty positions of honor, integrity, and so forth, your race once occupied in the scientifical world."[26] Rufus Perry, a Baptist journalist and educator from Smith County, Tennessee, also focused on past nobility, asserting proudly that the early religions of the East, of India, and of the Greco-Roman world all had roots in Egyptian and Ethiopian thought, making the Cushites the foundation of what Perry construed as the ultimate unity of all faiths.[27] African participation in ancient history was a useful counter to the white claim that the Negro had always been, and would remain, a degraded race.

The recovery of ancient Egypt also signaled more than the placement of African figures in a previously white classical landscape. Perry, Smith, and Baptist journalist J. Max Barber all argued that Europeans and Americans had actively distorted the past by conspiring to prevent African Americans from recognizing their contributions to it. "We are taught to believe that the history of the race began with slavery," Barber observed: "The white man has tried to rob us of Egypt because Egypt is the mother of modern civilization." Perry asserted that during slavery "the white man wrote for white men; and now the black man must write for black men."[28] Nevertheless, none of these authors recommended dispensing with the Christian tradition because of its associations with the evils of a Euro-American culture and the subsequent "regression" of Africans to a condition of "barbarism and heathenism." All saw the hand of providence working even in the dimmest light. "God has a purpose in all of this," concluded Barber, "and He will bring it to pass that all men shall have their turn at the wheel." Smith similarly argued that "its purpose for good is yet veiled from our eager eyes."[29]

As prominent as the culture of ancient Egypt was in several of these accounts, and in spite of its growing importance as a symbol of cultural nationalism in the Pan-African movement, race historians generally used it as a foundation and stepping-stone to link the biblical origins of the Cushites to the Christian Era. Most of the survey histories briefly mentioned Africans in the ancient world to firmly establish the monogenetic account of human origins.[30] However, they concentrated on the Euro-American tradition, particularly on American history. In doing so, race historians did not depict the era of African enslavement, for all its moral complexities, as a period of unmitigated suffering. By restructuring American history through their narratives, Protestant leaders both lauded human heroism and simultaneously rejected the Anglo-Saxon triumphalism of white accounts. What is perhaps most fascinating about these revisions is the extent to which the narratives both sacralized the history of slavery and revised sacred history to highlight the current spiritual dilemma of the Negro. Put another way, race historians used elements of the Christian paradigm to explain the significance of black emancipation and, significantly, to indicate the dawn of a new spiritual era in the late nineteenth century.

Echoing the gospel message, some histories hinged on the acts of civil war and emancipation as the harbingers of a worldwide spiritual and social transformation. Several overtly invoked the analogy to Christ's birth. Virginia-born Joseph Wilson emphasized not merely the specifics of American military engagement, but the sustained war of which the American skirmishes were a part. He centered his story around the inexorable march of events leading to Emancipation, beginning with the assertion that "no event, save that of the coming—the birth of the Savior—is so rejoiced in as that of the abolition of slavery." While he focused his attention on the United States, Wilson also universalized the subject of enslavement, reading all of history as an ongoing struggle toward the goal of human freedom: "history proves beyond a doubt that the advancing spirit of freedom has always been met by a relentless war waged by the oppressors of mankind."[31] The climax of history, then, came with the issuing of the Emancipation Proclamation, a document included, along with the Declaration of Independence and the U.S. Constitution, in the index to Wilson's book.[32] Peter Thomas Stanford also connected the abolition of slavery to the life of Christ, claiming that the nineteenth century would be viewed by later generations as the most important since the time of Christ "in results of beneficence to human life."[33]

By setting Emancipation as the axis around which the rest of history turned, race historians also identified a host of antislavery activists and other friends of the cause of abolition as prophets of the coming new order. American history thus became a sacred drama of black activism. The chronicling of these prophets sometimes differed radically from white accounts of important American heroes, religious or otherwise. The most popular object of affection and reverence, for writers, was John Brown. Stanford hailed the leader of the Harpers Ferry revolt as a "Puritan hero, Christian philosopher," and "martyr for the slaves." Using an intriguing combination of Protestant and abolitionist titles of honor, Stanford applauded Brown's religious activism:

"Baxter and Bunyan were the men with whom he sat and talked, through their books, and the bible was his chief advisor and guide."[34] In George Washington Williams's account, Brown was a martyr who "ranks among the world's greatest heroes": "his ethics and religion were as broad as the universe, and beneficent in their wide ramification."[35]

Nat Turner also occupied a prominent place in many race histories. Edward Johnson's *School History of the Negro Race in America* called him a prophet and mused that "he was, undoubtedly, a wonderful character."[36] Williams was more guarded in his praise, owing, perhaps, to his awareness of white ambivalence toward a rebel slave who had murdered scores of women and children. Nonetheless, he too compared Turner to Moses and John the Baptist: the abolitionist was a remarkable prophet who "preached with great authority," and his early years were rendered in romantic terms as a steady stream of divinely inspired visions and spiritual growth. Perhaps trying to appeal to whites and blacks alike, Williams carefully avoided the subject of the massacre itself; in addition, he placed both the word "prophet," when referring to Turner, and the word "tragedy," when referring to the slave revolt, in parentheses, as if to buffer against criticism from either side. But his meaning was clear: he concluded by remarking that although no stone marked Turner's grave, his image was "carved on the fleshy tablets of four million hearts."[37]

Despite the generous space accorded to Turner, Brown, slave rebel Gabriel Prosser, Denmark Vesey, and other heroes of the abolitionist cause, race authors did not simply write a black-centered history of America. Most also accorded space to white harbingers of liberty. In this respect, these histories were not limited to the African American story in any easily identifiable pattern; narratives were racialized to be sure, but they were also marked by national and religious loyalties. By invoking Euro-American examples, moreover, they symbolically presented even more of a challenge to traditional renderings of American history by relativizing them. The Puritans were praised for being earnest and God-fearing, as opposed to the "idle, dissolute, and mercenary" settlers of Jamestown.[38] Several authors located Emancipation in a long line of religious struggles for independence and freedom, from the Israelites in Egypt, to the French Huguenots, to the Pilgrims.[39] And a number of works stressed the parallels between the American struggle for independence from Great Britain and the antislavery crusade. Joseph Wilson reasoned that just as whites (with the help of many blacks, he pointed out) had fought for their freedom from an oppressive power, so too had the Negro demonstrated his "unquenchable thirst for liberty." Both events, he concluded, confirmed the "religious reverence for man and his natural rights."[40] Race historians thus claimed selected events in Euro-American history as part of their own sacred heritage but subordinated them to the unfolding drama of race emancipation. Rather than assimilating African Americans into white history, these narratives incorporated the tragedies and triumphs of American life into a lengthier account of moral and spiritual struggle. Previous battles, from the Reformation to the American Revolution, served as prophetic preludes to the central drama of the black jubilee.

Peter Thomas Stanford captured well the twists of thought that many contemporary observers have dismissed as simple capitulation to white values. A child of the South, Stanford was born a slave in Hampton, Virginia, lived briefly in a home for black orphans, and was subsequently sent to the family of Perry L. Stanford in Boston. After running away to New York City at age twelve, he was converted to Christianity during a revival conducted by evangelist Dwight Moody and assisted educationally through the largesse of Harriet Beecher Stowe, Henry Ward Beecher, and Henry Highland Garnet. From then on, his life reflected both an indebtedness to white Protestant support and a commitment to the unity of African Americans. In *The Tragedy of the Negro in America*, Stanford insisted on understanding the history of slavery, the "record of iniquity," not on the temporal plane of human history, but within the realm of "God's record," in which all human history was subordinated to a recognition of the clarity of divine justice. This view compelled Stanford, he declared, to be mindful of "fairness to both black and white" in his narrative; although he condemned specific social ills such as the convict lease system and the scourge of lynching, he interpreted the evil of slavery as one of many human failings throughout sacred history: "the outrages of to-day are merely repetitions of previous outrages, the bad, poisonous fruit of seed sown in the distant and near past."[41] Stanford's focus on history as a narrative of God's dealings with humanity moved his critique away from the mere exercise of judgment over the failings of Euro-Americans. For good or for ill, Stanford's narrative of historical progress represented a distinctive religious outlook.

Although differing in detail, these stories of the abolitionist movement provided blacks with a new sacred narrative, one that extended beyond the bounds of God's dealings with his people in a land of bondage. To varying degrees, they incorporated some of the more salient features of recent Christian and American history into the account of the African American journey to freedom. They held up new saints and martyrs, and some even incorporated new documents, such as the Emancipation Proclamation, into the sacred canon. These were histories for a new community, one that had moved beyond the need for supernatural deliverance from the world's woes. Race authors, motivated by their own understandings of the progressive nature of sacred history, stressed the dawning of a distinctive era, one in which blacks would take their rightful places as equals among the races of the world.

Because most were so cognizant of the perceived failings of southern blacks, moreover, writers did not place full blame for the failures of Reconstruction on the shoulders of white southerners. Blacks had a future in the South, many of these histories implied, if only they would accept and embrace a new self-definition and a new view of history, one that could accord them the dignity, civility, and religious beliefs that northern blacks thought they lacked. History, in a real sense, could redeem southern blacks by remaking their views of the world around them.

Still other authors saw the intrinsic spiritual unity of the African American race residing more firmly in future events. Calling such prophetic accounts "histories," although it may appear to stretch the term to the point of meaninglessness, nonetheless reflects the profoundly historical nature of these accounts and their grounding in a linear narrative structure that began (implicitly) with biblical precedents. In these histories, African Americans were the chosen people who had always been unified through their accountability to God's will, and who would be united once again in a future moment when called upon to enact the final stages of the providential drama. These authors seemed to agree that the stage was set for action and that the immutable laws of progress guaranteed the race an important and glorious future.

But for African American historians, as for their northern, white Protestant counterparts, the Civil War itself raised profound questions about how God might choose to act in history. As Christians, race authors accepted the biblical prophesy that Christ would return to rule over the earth in a future "golden age" or "millennium." Although the notion of millennialism pervaded both white and black evangelical thought throughout the nineteenth century, the bloody battles of the war itself, so similar to the predicted armed engagement of Armageddon, raised the issue of whether, indeed, the war had set in motion the sacred events prophesied in the Book of Revelation. Is this how the end times would arrive? If so, what role did Christians now play in that story? As James Moorhead has suggested, the question of what might follow Armageddon loomed large for American Christians in the postbellum decades.[42]

The war, therefore, had deep and lasting effects on views of sacred history. As life settled into new routines, however, blacks and whites alike pondered how to interpret the return to normalcy—and the eruption of new societal fissures. Some historians foresaw a "postmillenial" future, in which the golden age would come about primarily through the efforts of faithful Christians to realize an ideal society here on earth; such believers, in turn, advocated Christian social efforts and often a progressive political agenda as one means to this end. Even if the war had initiated the end times, in this view, human beings still had much work left to do. For "premillennialists," the war may have foreshadowed the sacred battle to come, but it also reinforced the fact that only God could redeem the world. Christ would return to earth only after a prolonged apocalyptic battle between the powers of good and evil, one fought after the end of human history as they knew it. Thus Christians were relatively powerless to help bring about this foreordained conclusion.

The views of race historians were further complicated by their conviction that Emancipation was assuredly the work of a just God overturning past injustices. But if racial issues had initiated Armageddon, of what significance would race be in the future? Most African American authors interpreted the present and future in ways that mediated—or at least combined—premillennialist and postmillennialist views and reasserted the significance of race. Like premillennialists, they upheld the tragic vision of a world disabled without the radical intervention of a retributive God. But like postmillennialists, they also maintained that African Americans, as a community, would play a central role in the steady progress toward the end of time. Some scholars have suggested that the future golden age prophesied in millennial thought is often characterized as a restoration of a mythical past; for race authors, the ancient past invariably included a monogenetic account of human development, inasmuch as equality in the present required an affirmation of equality before God in creation. One might assume, then, that historians would posit an eventual return to a period without racial differentiation, a paradise of human equality. But writers in fact disagreed about the ultimate significance of racial distinctions and held differing views on whether they would continue into the millennium.[43]

J. Max Barber envisioned a dramatic, violent reversal of racial fortunes in the years after Emancipation, predicting a future based on the continuing moral distinctions of race. "The present is the white man's," he conceded, "but the future belongs, not to the degenerating, morally putrid and cruelly avaricious white man, but to the virile, puissant races in whose hearts there is mercy and justice."[44] Arguing a point that may have been implicit in the works of even the more moderate historians, Barber indicated that blacks were the true heirs to the American tradition of freedom and independence;

Emancipation had signaled the beginning of a new era, one in which the hierarchy of the races would be reversed. Because of their moral and spiritual superiority forged in a history of oppression, blacks would eventually occupy a correspondingly elevated social position.

The most well-known proponent of this latter theme was Theophilus Gould Steward, a journalist, educator, and member of the African Methodist Episcopal Church who had been born in New Jersey in 1843 and served as a missionary during Reconstruction. Steward's 1888 study, *The End of the World, or Clearing the Way for the Fullness of the Gentiles*, carried the notion of racial reversal to its eschatological extreme, asserting that the triumph of the Negro race was linked directly to the end times of biblical prophecy. Acknowledging that his work would most likely appear "quite novel and in some respects startling" to his audience, Steward associated the present age, the age of the Gentiles, with the rise of Euro-American power, or the Saxon race. Through consistent historical demonstrations of "acquisition and conquest, subjugation or extermination," Saxons had proven that they constituted the race that the prophet Daniel had foreseen. "The writer feels bound to believe the Saxon race has well-nigh accomplished its mission," Steward asserted. He characterized the Saxon clan as at once energetic and fierce, ingenious and cruel; he described a culture that would destroy itself through its own avaricious momentum. The "bloody wave will soon have spent its force, and then the end shall come."[45]

While he criticized the hypocritical theology of the white race, Steward also pulled the true mantle of Christianity around himself and other African Americans. The Saxon God was merely a divinity fashioned to serve the whims of a dominant race: "What a very useful God! Oh, that each of the other races had one just as good!" he noted sarcastically. The corruption of Christianity had made it impossible for the majority of the world's peoples to hear the true message of Christ. "The white races of the earth," he wrote, "have modified the Christian idea to an alarming extent by [the] clan principle, so that it has become a white man's religion, and is so recognized by the darker races." What would replace it during the end times, Steward maintained, was the superior moral power of the darker races, those peoples who were not ruled by a devotion to the principle of "clan." Once the darker races were dominant, the church could be purified and liberated entirely from notions of racial difference.[46]

Although Steward's vision sounded like a more liberal version of a premillennial apocalypse, he stressed that this racial transformation could be brought about by Christians and would take place within human history. "We may dismiss from our thoughts alarming ideas of physical catastrophe," he explained. The coming change marked not the final end of the world, but only the "completion of the current age" through a series of ordinary historical events.[47] Once again using the paradigm of Christian history, Steward, like other race historians, sacralized the social and political advance of the Negro by placing it in a religious framework.

Other writers did not match Steward's high-pitched drama, but the theme of ultimate racial triumph recurred in the writings of other prominent religious leaders. James Theodore Holly, the Protestant Episcopal bishop of Haiti, argued in the pages of the AME Church Review that racial differences would play a significant role in the final redemption of humanity. Holly took a dispensational approach to sacred history, asserting that just as the descendants of Shem and Japheth had had their turn in history and had fulfilled certain functions along the road to salvation (Shem's heirs during the "Hebrew dispensation," before the destruction of the temple, and Japheth's during the "Gospel phase," or Christian dispensation), the "millennial phase" of the sacred drama would feature the descendants of Ham. In the coming dispensation, the servant of all would become the most blessed: "When, therefore, our Savior shall be crowned and seated upon His Throne of Glory, He will doubtless remember in a peculiar manner the race whose son carried His cross for Him, and choose from that race the crowned nobles who shall minister around His person in His Royal Palace."[48] In a striking combination of Christian universalism and racial collectivism, Holly's narrative secured for African Americans a prominent place in the redemption of the world.

Perhaps the most distinctive feature of these race histories is the way that they simultaneously called attention to, and then attempted to eradicate, distinctions between southern and northern blacks. The two native-born southerners discussed here, L. T. Smith and Peter Thomas Stanford, both went north at early ages for education and training, and they quickly adopted a distinctive northern black disdain for what they saw as an inferior southern way of life. All race authors emphasized the failings of southern blacks in the decades after Emancipation and argued that if only southerners would accept their own superior religious ideas and practices, they too could become civilized members of the newly united country. Yet in remapping history, race authors also downplayed and even denied the continuing importance of regional distinctions. In the (Christian) future, they seemed to suggest, the overarching loyalties of race would eradicate any differences between northern and southern blacks. Indeed, Barber, Steward, and Holly hardly mentioned geography at all in their discussions of the destiny of the race; presumably, the acceptance of racial unity in the future, when all members of the race would be as one, would render current regional distinctions pointless.

If the current resurgence of interest in the dissemination of standardized accounts of American history is any indication, the growth of concern over the creation of race histories by postbellum African American Protestants reflected a sense of cultural fragmentation rather than its opposite. The desire for cultural unity is often articulated most forcefully in periods of perceived disunity and divisiveness. To fully appreciate the historical significance of these race histories, therefore, one would also need to assess their reception by their intended audiences and their function within the communities they addressed.[49] How, for example, did middle-class black women respond to these histories that often explicitly addressed the gendered dilemma of "black manhood"? Did southern blacks buy and read these histories? How were they received by white Protestants? Although these questions lie beyond the immediate scope of this essay, they bear on our understanding of the role of religion and collective history within the African American population as a whole.[50]

Nonetheless, these works reveal a great deal about their authors' attempts to place themselves and their own "maps of the world" at the center of debate over African American identity and destiny. Despite their many disagreements over the specific interpretation of racial history, race historians were more alike than not. Heirs to an ongoing debate in the United States about race, and newly armed with technologies and institutional networks that facilitated the ability to speak on behalf of a community, these religious leaders fashioned a novel form of historical narrative aimed at the representation of a renewed African American collectivity in the years after Emancipation. Much of their art, as they themselves knew, sprang from wishful thinking. Late-nineteenth-century blacks were far from united in their views on nationality, race, or religion. Race historians hoped that their accounts would be both self-fulfilling prophecies of racial unity and prophetic indictments of contemporary racial and religious practices. In hindsight, their fragile attempts to unite middle-class evangelical values, progressive views of history, and an appeal to the fundamental verities of scriptural authority, all within a racialized vision of the world, would soon be obsolete. As Henry Louis Gates Jr. has shown, the trope of the "New Negro," increasingly promulgated by African American intellectuals after the turn of the century, had little use for biblical paradigms or sacred histories. Few narrative accounts published after

1915 carried the same religious and racial valences. The writing of race histories, in general, was turned over to scholars trained in the "science" of historical inquiry.

In the rush toward objectivity and scientific racialism, historians of the last century have forgotten the worldview that motivated early race authors. Indeed, their self-understanding has long eluded description by even the most careful historians. Wilson Moses, in discussing the views of racial destiny espoused by black Episcopalian Alexander Crummell, candidly concluded that "I can think of no simple explanation for Crummell's optimistic view of history, his reliance on Providence, his belief in progress."[51] The key to Crummell's mystery, as well as to the puzzle provided by a generation of race historians in the four decades preceding World War I, is grounded in a historical consciousness that was at once thoroughly Protestant and thoroughly African American. Synthesized in a new way by a new generation of middle-class black Christians, this consciousness took into account a temporal sweep measured in centuries rather than decades, evaluated by providential rather than human means. This sweep frequently allowed both for the acknowledgment of universal human strengths and weaknesses and for ultimate forgiveness, as well as for an unyielding commitment to a historically specific collective destiny embodied in the suffering and future triumphs of the Negro race. Neither assimilationist nor separatist, inspired by Euro-American philosophy and African American cultural unity, this worldview was articulated in the only form that could fully represent its dependence on a linear and progressive notion of time: chronological narrative. If contemporary observers have difficulty identifying the moving force behind these self-understandings, it is perhaps attributable to the polarized racial lenses through which we ourselves view these histories, as well as to the failings of our own dichotomous discourse about race that conceives of choices, both metaphorically and literally, as being either "black" or "white."[52]

NOTES

1. George Washington Williams, *History of the Negro Race in America, 1619–1880: Negroes as Slaves, as Soldiers, and as Citizens* (1883; reprint, New York: Arno Press, 1968), 1:x.
2. On Williams's life, see John Hope Franklin, *George Washington Williams: A Biography* (Chicago: University of Chicago Press, 1985).
3. Friedrich W. Nietzsche, *On the Advantage and Disadvantage of History for Life*, trans. Peter Preuss (Indianapolis: Hackett Publishing Co., Inc., 1980), 13.
4. The term "Negro" is used throughout this essay synonymously with "black" and "African American," inasmuch as postbellum authors themselves used Negro to speak of themselves.

Edward A. Johnson, *A School History of the Negro Race in America from 1619 to 1890* (New York: AMS Press, 1911), 111; Benjamin Quarles, "Black History's Antebellum Origins," *Proceedings of the American Antiquarian Society* 88, no. 1 (April 1979): 89–122; J. Max Barber, *The Negro of the Earlier World: An Excursion into Ancient Negro History* (Philadelphia: AME Book Concern, n.d.), 5. On the use of black history as a counter against the late nineteenth-century proslavery argument, see John David Smith, "A Different View of Slavery: Black Historians Attack the Proslavery Argument, 1890–1920," *Journal of Negro History* 65 (Fall 1980): 298–311. An appropriate end point for this study is 1915, when the first two blacks to receive doctorates in history published works: W. E. B. Du Bois, the first black history Ph.D., brought out *The Negro*, a study of the race in both Africa and America, and Carter Woodson's first work, *The Education of the Negro prior to 1861*, appeared. These studies, as well as the growth of black professional historical societies that limited membership to those educationally and economically qualified, signaled the shift from denominationally based historical production to the professionalization of history as an objective science. See August Meier and Elliott Rudwick, *Black History and the Historical Profession, 1915–1980* (Urbana: University of Illinois Press, 1986); Alfred A. Moss Jr., *The American Negro Academy: Voice of the Talented Tenth* (Baton Rouge: Louisiana State University Press, 1981); and Elinor Des Verney Sinnette, *Arthur Alfonso Schomburg: Black Bibliophile and Collector* (Detroit: Wayne State University Press, 1989).

5. I am indebted to the work of Henry Louis Gates Jr., specifically to his notion of representation as racial reconstruction, for my understanding of the significance of these histories. See especially his "The Trope of a New Negro and the Reconstruction of the Image of the Black," *Representations* 24 (Fall 1988): 129–55.

6. Jonathan Z. Smith helpfully suggests that when we study religion, we are examining "one mode of constructing worlds of meaning, worlds within which men find themselves and in which they choose to dwell," as well as "the variety of attempts to map, construct and inhabit . . . positions of power through the use of myths, rituals and experiences of transformation." Smith, *Map Is Not Territory: Studies in the History of Religions* (Leiden: E. J. Brill, 1978), 290–91.

7. Higginbotham, *Righteous Discontent: The Women's Movement in the Black Baptist Church, 1880–1920* (Cambridge: Harvard University Press, 1993), 11, 44. See also Eric Foner, *Reconstruction: America's Unfinished Revolution, 1863–1877* (New York: Harper and Row, 1988), 88–102; Leon Litwack, "The Gospel and the Primer," in *Been in the Storm So Long: The Aftermath of Slavery* (New York: Knopf, 1979); and William E. Montgomery, *Under Their Own Vine and Fig Tree: The African-American Church in the South, 1865–1900* (Baton Rouge: Louisiana State University Press, 1993). From just 5 percent of the black adult population in 1860, black literacy rose dramatically to 70 percent by 1910.

8. Barber, *Negro of the Earlier World*, 5.

9. Richard Brodhead, *Cultures of Letters: Scenes of Reading and Writing in Nineteenth-Century America* (Chicago: University of Chicago Press, 1993), 193.

10. I am indebted to the work of Richard Brodhead, who emphasizes the extent to which any act of writing is culturally proscribed: "A work of writing comes to its particular form of existence in interaction with the network of relations that surround it: in any actual instance, writing orients itself in or against some understanding of what writing is, does, and is good for that is culturally composed and derived." Ibid., 8.

11. Paul Ricoeur, *Time and Narrative*, trans. Kathleen McLaughlin and David Pellauer (Chicago: University of Chicago Press, 1984), 1:162. Ricoeur (p. ix) provides a helpful definition of narrative as a semantic innovation created through employment of a plot, through which "goals, causes, and chances are brought together within the temporal unity of a whole and complete action."

12. Ibid., 151–52; David Thelen, "Memory and American History," *Journal of American History* 75, n. 4 (March 1989): 1122. On the ways shared stories and memories reinforce collective identity, see John Bodnar, *Remaking America: Public Memory, Commemoration, and Patriotism in the Twentieth Century* (Princeton: Princeton University Press, 1992); Marie-Noelle Bourguet, Lucette Valensi, and Nathan Wachtel, *Between Memory and History* (New York: Harwood Academic Publishers, 1990); James Fentress and Chris Wickham, *Social Memory* (Oxford: Blackwell, 1992); Maurice Halbwachs, *On Collective Memory*, trans. Francis J. Ditter Jr. and Vida Yazdi Ditter (1950; reprint, New York: Harper and Row, 1980); Eric Hobsbawm and Terence Ranger, eds., *The Invention of Tradition* (Cambridge: Cambridge University Press, 1983); George Lipsitz, *Time Passages: Collective Memory and American Popular Culture* (Minneapolis: University of Minnesota Press, 1990); and David Lowenthal, *The Past Is a Foreign Country* (Cambridge: Cambridge University Press, 1985).

13. Through the use of this phrase, I distinguish between the possession of historical consciousness, which antebellum African Americans surely had in the form of oral traditions and limited access to education, and the possession of a mobile and complex "representational technology" that later enabled the large-scale dissemination of ideas. See Stephen Greenblatt, *Marvelous Possessions: The Wonder of the New World* (Chicago: University of Chicago Press, 1991), 9–12. Lawrence Levine makes a case for the strength of oral narrative traditions in the antebellum era in *Black Culture, Black Consciousness: Afro-American Folk Thought from Slavery to Freedom* (New York: Oxford University Press, 1977).

14. Some accounts, such as Benjamin Tucker Tanner's *The Negro's Origin* (1869), Rufus L. Perry's *The Cushite or the Descendants of Ham* (1893), Barber's *The Negro of the Earlier World* (n.d.), and Augustus T. Bell's *The Woolly Hair Man of the Ancient South* (n.d.), concentrated on the ancient and scriptural origins of the Negro race. Others focused on the roles played by blacks in American history, as in Williams, *History of the Negro Race in America* (1883), William T. Alexander, *History of the Colored Race in America* (1887), Joseph T. Wilson, *The Black Phalanx* (1888), Peter Thomas Stanford, *The Tragedy of the Negro in America* (1898), H. M. Tarver, *The Negro in the History of the United States* (1905), and Edward A. Johnson, *A School History of the Negro Race in America* (1911). Still other authors, including William Wells Brown, *The Rising Son, or The Antecedents and Advancement of the Colored Race* (1874), Joseph T. Wilson, *Emancipation: Its Course and Progress from 1481 B.C. to A.D. 1875* (1882), L. T. Smith, *A Great Truth in a Nutshell* (1883), and William Hannibal Thomas, *The American Negro* (1901), attempted topical overviews of racial history. Several more works, including James T. Holly's "The Divine Plan of Human Redemption in Its Ethnological Development" (1884), and Theophilus Gould Steward's *The End of the World, or Clearing the Way for the Fullness of the Gentiles* (1888), forecast future events within a broad scriptural narrative framework. Evidence internal to Barber's and Bell's histories leads me to date them both in the first decade of the twentieth century, probably between 1904 and 1910.

15. Albert J. Raboteau discusses the larger context for some of these theological con-

cerns in " 'Ethiopia Shall Soon Stretch Forth Her Hands': Black Destiny in Nineteenth-Century America," in *A Fire in the Bones: Reflections on African-American Religious History* (Boston: Beacon Press, 1995), 37–56.

16. Joseph T. Wilson, *Emancipation: Its Course and Progress from 1481 B.C. to A.D. 1875* (Hampton, Va.: Normal School Steam Power Press Print, 1882), 150; Williams, *History of the Negro Race*, 2:547.

17. Thomas, *The American Negro: What He Was, What He Is, and What He May Become* (New York: Macmillan, 1901), xii–xvii.

18. Ibid., xxi, xxiv, 165, 145.

19. Ibid., 44.

20. E.g., Edward A. Johnson, Rufus L. Perry, Peter Thomas Stanford, Theophilus Gould Steward, Benjamin Tucker Tanner, William Hannibal Thomas, George Washington Williams, and Joseph T. Wilson.

21. Thomas, *American Negro*, 146–48.

22. Williams, *History of the Negro Race*, 2:464, 534.

23. Elizabeth J. Eisenstein, "Some Conjectures about the Impact of Printing on Western Society and Thought," *Journal of Modern History* 40 (1968): 25. On the connections between collective identity and the rise of print capitalism, see Benedict Anderson, *Imagined Communities: Reflections on the Origin and Spread of Nationalism* (London: Verso, 1983), 44.

24. Wilson J. Moses, *The Golden Age of Black Nationalism, 1850–1925* (New York: Oxford University Press, 1978).

25. Contemporary debates over "Afrocentricity," which often rely on black precedents in ancient Egypt, have been surprisingly neglectful of the history of those representations. Ironically, much of the nineteenth-century impetus for the study of African antiquity came from black Protestants, whose reliance on Christian tradition was subsequently rejected by Afrocentrists. See John H. Bracey Jr. and August Meier, "Black Ideologies, Black Utopias: Afrocentricity in Historical Perspective," *Contributions in Black Studies* 12 (1994): 111–16.

26. L. T. Smith, *A Great Truth in a Nutshell: A Few Ancient and Modern Facts of the Colored People, by One of Their Number* (N.p., 1883), i–ii, 9.

27. Rufus Perry, *The Cushite, or the Descendants of Ham* (Springfield, Mass.: Willey and Co., 1893), 97–98.

28. Barber, *Negro of the Earlier World*, 6, 16; Perry, *Cushite*, ix–x.

29. Perry, *Cushite*, v; Barber, *Negro of the Earlier World*, 24; Smith, *A Great Truth*, 9.

30. A fuller discussion of the nineteenth-century biblical and scientific debates over monogenetic vs. polygenetic theories of humanity lie beyond the scope of this paper. All of the race histories written by African Americans that I have consulted adhere to a monogenetic biblical interpretation. See George Fredrickson, *The Black Image in the White Mind: The Debate on Afro-American Character and Destiny, 1817–1914* (New York: Harper and Row, 1971); Steven Jay Gould, *The Mismeasure of Man* (New York: Norton, 1981); and H. Shelton Smith, *In His Image, but . . . Racism in Southern Religion, 1780–1910* (Durham: Duke University Press, 1972).

31. Wilson, *Emancipation*, 9, 99. For biographical information on Wilson, see James T. Haley, comp., *Afro-American Encyclopedia, or the Thoughts, Doings, and Sayings of the Race* (Nashville: Haley and Florida, 1895), 228.

32. Wilson (*Emancipation*, p. 72) also raised an interesting question that he never

answered: if the Emancipation Proclamation was the acme of modern history, was Abraham Lincoln an instrument of the divine will? If so, what does this reveal about white agency in the abolitionist struggle? It is intriguing, in any event, that John Brown is seen as a martyr for the slaves, but Lincoln's role is somewhat more ambiguous.

33. Stanford, *The Tragedy of the Negro in America* (Boston: By the author, 1898), 43.

34. Ibid., 62, 66.

35. Williams, *History of the Negro Race*, 2:214, 223.

36. Johnson, *School History*, 92.

37. Williams, *History of the Negro Race*, 2:86, 90–91.

38. Thomas, *American Negro*, 2–3, 12.

39. Williams, *History of the Negro Race*, 2:534–35; Wilson, *Emancipation*, 100–101.

40. Wilson, *Emancipation*, 121.

41. Stanford, *Tragedy*, iii, 9.

42. James Moorhead, *American Apocalypse: Yankee Protestants and the Civil War, 1860–1869* (New Haven: Yale University Press, 1978), 81.

43. Timothy E. Fulop, " 'The Future Golden Day of the Race': Millennialism and Black Americans in the Nadir, 1877–1901," *Harvard Theological Review* 84, no. 1 (1991): 85; Ernest Lee Tuveson, *Redeemer Nation: The Idea of America's Millennial Role* (Chicago: University of Chicago Press, 1968), 78.

44. Barber, *Negro of the Earlier World*, 28.

45. Steward, *End of the World* (Philadelphia: AME Church Book Rooms, 1888), 68–69, 7, 71. For more on Steward's views of African American destiny, see Fulop, " 'The Future Golden Day of the Race' "; Raboteau, " 'Ethiopia Shall Soon Stretch Forth Her Hands' "; and David W. Wills, "Aspects of Social Thought in the African Methodist Episcopal Church, 1884–1910" (Ph.D. diss., Harvard University, 1975). On Steward's career, see William Seraile, *Voice of Dissent: Theophilus Gould Steward (1843–1924) and Black America* (Brooklyn: Carlson, 1991).

46. Steward, *End of the World*, 76, 3–4.

47. Ibid., 14, 16–17.

48. James Theodore Holly, "The Divine Plan of Human Redemption, in Its Ethnological Development," *AME Church Review* 1 (October 1884): 83.

49. This caveat is prompted by the work of Michael McGuire, who reminds us that to understand the sociology of historical narratives we must examine not simply their authors or their contents, but also their reception by an intended audience. McGuire, "The Rhetoric of Narrative," in Bruce K. Britton and Anthony D. Pellegrini, eds., *Narrative Thought and Narrative Language* (Hillsdale, N.J.: Lawrence Erlbaum Associates, 1990), 228.

50. These questions will be taken up in the larger study of which this essay is a part. See Laurie F. Maffly-Kipp, *African-American Communal Narratives, 1780–1915* (forthcoming).

51. Moses, *Golden Age*, 78. Moses, like many other observers of nineteenth-century black nationalism, is well aware of the religious character of virtually all of its manifestations. He asserts: "In the nineteenth century, black nationalism was almost inseparable from religion. . . . Rather than thinking of religious black nationalism as one of the varieties of black nationalism, one might almost say that black nationalism is a variety of religion." Moses, *The Wings of Ethiopia: Studies in African-American Life and Letters* (Ames: Iowa State University Press, 1990), 35, 113. St. Clair Drake makes similar arguments in *The*

Redemption of Africa and Black Religion (Chicago: Third World Press, 1970). Yet neither Moses nor Drake traces the institutional means, especially the black churches, through which black nationalist ideologies were disseminated.

52. In a suggestive study that has many potential applications to the study of race and racism, Sandra Lipsitz Bem analyzes the various cultural "lenses" that govern our perceptions and articulations of gender difference in the United States. See Bem, *The Lenses of Gender: Transforming the Debate on Sexual Equality* (New Haven: Yale University Press, 1993).

The Talk of the County

Revisiting Accusation, Murder, and Mississippi, 1895

John Howard

I have no memory of the events described below. Although they took place in and around my hometown, seventy-seven years before I was born, they were never told to me. And although, at the time, they commanded newspaper headlines from New Orleans to Memphis and became "the talk of the county," that talk somehow subsided.

. . . .

"Collective memory ultimately is located not in sites but in individuals," Susan A. Crane writes. "All narratives, all sites, all texts remain objects until they are 'read' or referred to by individuals thinking historically."[1]

. . . .

On Thursday, 15 August 1895, at the Rankin County Courthouse in Brandon, Mississippi, a jury convicted Dabney Marshall, Harry Coleman, and Robert Fox of murder. The next morning the "thoroughly famous trio" returned to the scene of the crime—the Brandon railroad station—where, one week prior, R. T. "Tip" Dinkins lay dead of gunshot wounds. Under guard, the three men boarded a westbound train and traveled twelve miles to the state capital of Jackson, also home of the state penitentiary.

In a banner headline story, "They Wear Stripes," Jackson's *Daily Clarion-*

Ledger described the last leg of their trip—the principal event around which I organize this essay—in this way:

No potentate or military hero was ever accorded a more enthusiastic [or more hostile] reception on his return from foreign conquests than the people of Jackson gave the three young Vicksburgers who killed "Tip" Dinkins at Brandon last Friday morning. . . . When the train arrived at the State Street crossing several hundred men and boys were on hand eager to catch a glimpse.

Marshall was the first to appear. . . . [His] face was wreathed in a broad but sickly smile as he bowed to one or more old acquaintances in the howling, hissing mob that surrounded him. . . . Coleman, who is about as diminutive as Marshall, but not quite so effeminate, was with Marshall, in front; Fox was next, accompanied by Marshall's father, who had him by the arm; and with Sergeant Parker [of the state prison] bringing up the rear, the half mile walk to the penitentiary was begun.

Marshall and Coleman led the way, apparently unconcerned as to their surroundings and treating the now largely augmented and boisterous mob with silent contempt, but Fox wore a scared, frightened look as if he expected violence. . . . The platforms were crowded with relatives and friends and attorneys of the three once popular men.

Hundreds of people stood close up to every corner and lined the streets along which the sad procession moved at a rapid, business-like gait, the rear being brought up by a mob of other hundreds of men and boys, white and black, all scuffling for the vantage ground nearest the prisoners, pushing and jostling each other in their efforts to get a good look at them.

Old men, solid citizens of seventy-five years of age, were seen to run a block or two to catch up with or head off the procession that they might catch a glimpse of the distinguished arrivals. Offensive epithets, jibes, and jeers were heard on the sides, most of them being uttered for Marshall's express benefit, but he walked on to his destination, giving no intimation that he heard them. Buggies and carriages joined in the wild rush to the penitentiary and by the time the procession arrived there the streets were crowded with wheeled vehicles as well as a thousand or more or less curious people. The crowd did not stop at the gates, but rushed in with the prisoners, up the broad paved walk and into the hall leading to the ponderous iron doors.

Once on the inside, the three young men were treated as all new arrivals to that gloomy hostelrie are treated. They were taken in charge by Sergeant

J. W. Lary, who took them to his office, stripped them, took their descriptions, [and] dressed them in regulation suits of stripes.

The men are numbered and described as follows on the prison register:

T. Dabney Marshall, No. 32—Sentenced from Rankin County for life; crime murder; age 34, born Nov. 30, 1861; height 5 feet 5½ inches, weight 108 pounds; hair brown, eyes gray; occupation lawyer; does not use tobacco; health fairly good; native of Hinds County; no whiskers; has no wife; no children; both parents living; residence Vicksburg; habits of life good; education fair; near-sighted; wears glasses.

Robt. C. Fox, No. 28—Sentenced from Rankin County for life; crime murder; age 26, born December 9, 1869; height 5 feet 10 inches, weight 160 pounds; occupation hardware clerk; smokes tobacco; health good; born in Hinds County; wears mustache; has no wife or children; both parents living; education fair; scar in center of forehead.

Harry H. Coleman, No. 33—Sentenced from Rankin County for life; crime murder; age 23, born April 29, 1872; height 5 feet 7½ inches; weight 131 pounds; hair brown, eyes blue; occupation law student; smokes and chews; health good; native of Vicksburg; no wife or children; both parents living; habits of life good; no whiskers; education fair; first finger left hand missing.

The young men are trying hard to bear up under their misfortune, but it can be seen that their punishment is hard, all the fortitude of which they are possessed being required to nerve them to look the situation in the face. The future of Dinkins' slayers is dark indeed.[2]

Ironically, in the same issue of the newspaper, in an editorial entitled "Draw the Veil," the *Clarion-Ledger* encouraged its readers to forget the saga so dramatically told in its pages over the previous two weeks:

Is it not time to draw the veil upon their unfortunate lives and turn to things more pleasant? Let the doors that deprive the prisoners of their liberty shut off all peering eyes and gossipy tongues. Let them alone in their misfortune and misery.

These men come from good families, high minded, law-abiding people, and while they deserve no clemency, and will receive none, having committed a most foul murder, . . . they should not be pursued in their cells and tormented to appease the morbid appetite of the public.

These men have mothers whose heart-strings are now bursting with grief at the shame brought upon their families—tender-hearted old mothers who nursed them into life and prayed over them as they rocked them to sleep in babyhood days. For their sake, if for no other, let us draw the veil, and leave these misguided young men alone to their own gloomy thoughts. After today, the *Clarion-Ledger* closes its columns to the Brandon tragedy.

Ironic, indeed, is this call to forgetting. For it was the *Clarion-Ledger*'s own "gossipy tongue" that set events in motion and ultimately led to the shooting on 9 August of Tip Dinkins. According to the *Vicksburg Evening Post*, Jackson's *Daily Clarion-Ledger* was as much to blame as were the three assailants.[3] Now Jackson editors urged Mississippians to forget. Such is the ebb and flow of queer spectacle and queer erasure.[4]

In 1895 the *Clarion-Ledger*'s "Around the City" column consisted of several one- or two-sentence observations of various sorts: political prognostications, traffic mishaps, news of visitors to the city and residents' travels outside the city, church affairs, public scandals, and gossip. The 3 August edition included the newspaper's first mention of Dabney Marshall, this not-so-veiled reference to the Vicksburg attorney and aspiring politician: "A sensational report is in circulation on the Warren County candidate for floater senator, which, if proven true, will doubtless cause him to retire from the race."

Marshall felt compelled to respond. His reply became the 5 August lead story, topping all national and international reporting. Under the headline, "Marshall Denies It," his letter to the editor was printed, apparently verbatim: "In your Saturday's issue you say there is a sensational rumor afloat concerning me, which if proven true will cause me to retire from the senatorial race. I hereby denounce the rumor as absolutely and utterly false in every particular. I have never done a low, mean, or disgraceful thing in my life. The people of the whole state will bear me out in this assertion."

What, precisely, was Marshall denying? What was "It"—the ambiguous referent of the newspaper headline—that Marshall stood accused of? The exact details can never be known. As the *Clarion-Ledger* later declared, "The charges made against T. Dabney Marshall by the man he afterwards killed will perhaps on account of their filthy and abhorrent nature never find their way into print." Indeed, it seems, they never did. But it is clear that one night in mid-July, Marshall and Dinkins had shared a hotel room in Raymond, a few miles southwest of Jackson. The next day Dinkins told two friends that Marshall behaved abominably. That is, Marshall apparently made a sexual overture. "Mr. Dinkins told this [unprintable story] in the strictest confidence," the *Clarion-Ledger* reported, "but it got out, as all such things generally do, and in a few days was the talk of the county."[5]

Also unknowable are the multiple forms the story surely took in its telling and retelling, after Dinkins's disclosure to his friends. It is likely that these initial accounts circulated mostly among a white elite to which both Dinkins and Marshall belonged. Heirs of the planter class, the two men had known agrarian life but chose the professions. When floods devastated Dinkins's Issaquena County plantation, he left the area to take control of a road machinery shop in Madison, subsequently headquartered in Jackson. Although Marshall was born on his father's seven-hundred-acre cotton plantation on the Big Black River, just inside Hinds County, he practiced law in the Warren County seat of Vicksburg, as did his uncle, state senator and former representative, T. A. Marshall. Both Tip Dinkins and Dabney Marshall were well connected politically and socially. In post–Reconstruction Mississippi, the white minority ruling class was so small and insular that Dinkins knew all of his assailants. In fact, he was related by marriage—through the first of his two wives—to Robert Fox.[6]

What did or did not happen between Marshall and Dinkins that night in Raymond and how it was or was not talked about in Mississippi became questions more of honor than of criminality.[7] Though an 1839 state statute prohibited "unnatural intercourse" and though seven men were incarcerated under the law as of 1880, more than in any other state, peer group standards proved of greatest concern in the Dinkins-Marshall incident.[8] Indeed, at first, some viewed Dinkins as the more culpable of the two men for having leveled the "nasty charges." Marshall, in turn, had every right, the *Clarion-Ledger* implied, to demand a retraction. Words, it seems, were more pertinent than acts. Dinkins, in referring to the incident, had spoken in (necessarily) unbecoming ways. The talk that resulted affronted community standards, even as it was perpetuated, in carefully chosen language, by the community and by its newspapers. Given that Dinkins would not recant—because, he said, the charges were true—Marshall was justified in killing him, at least early on. Had Marshall "defended his honor . . . when the charges were first made," community members reportedly felt, "his course would have been endorsed."[9]

Weeks passed, however, before Marshall and his colleagues confronted Dinkins in Brandon, where—they learned from his Jackson boardinghouse matron—he had made a sales call to the Rankin County Board of Supervisors. Worse still, Marshall did not call for a duel, an honorable resolution; rather, he ambushed Dinkins. Coleman and Fox acted not as seconds, but as participants in the surprise shooting at the train station. Combined, the three fired a "veritable fusillade" of bullets at Dinkins.[10] Such action seemingly confirmed Marshall's cowardice and compromised his masculinity. It further implicated his associates, whose marital status the prison attendant and the *Clarion-Ledger* would duly note as single.

During the week following the murder and leading up to the conviction, Marshall resigned as the Democratic Party nominee for state floater senator from Hinds and Warren Counties. Party officials proposed an investigation of the hotel incident. And Dinkins's brothers and friends insisted that were an inquiry ordered, Marshall would be "proven the most abject craven in the state." According to the prosecuting attorneys in the case at Brandon, "half a dozen witnesses" could verify (somehow without incriminating themselves) "that Marshall had been guilty of this [again, unspecified] revolting performance on previous occasions."[11]

But Marshall had his own formidable counsel. "A splendid and forcible orator," Anselm J. "Anse" McLaurin of Brandon had been nominated unanimously for governor by the 1,500 Democratic Party delegates assembled in Jackson the week before.[12] Politics and gossip had intermingled at the convention, as party news and the Marshall scandal shared the headlines. When McLaurin accepted the Marshall case, many questioned his decision. The *Memphis Scimitar* declared a conflict of interests. If McLaurin were unsuccessful at trial, the newspaper asserted, he could pardon the assailants once he assumed office. (Given the white Democratic stranglehold on state politics, the general election later that year was a mere formality.) McLaurin demurred. As the *Clarion-Ledger* paraphrased his disingenuous response, McLaurin saw himself as "a poor man [who] had just finished an expensive campaign. . . . [He] was not Governor yet," and he had a family to support.[13]

At trial, even the "foremost criminal lawyer in Mississippi," perhaps the state's most widely known political figure, could not save Dabney Marshall from conviction.[14] In Brandon, where "nothing else [was] talked about," public opinion was said to be "strong against Marshall and his friends"— purportedly "unanimous."[15] McLaurin did secure a plea bargain, however. By confessing to the shooting, the three would not hang. Rather, they would serve life sentences. The revered Methodist bishop Charles B. Galloway advised his cousins, the Dinkins family, to consent to the agreement. Mrs. Dinkins in particular felt that her deceased son's cronies should not be executed. Thus ended "the Brandon tragedy"—what the *Clarion-Ledger* called "the most sensational case ever known in Mississippi."[16]

The *Daily Clarion-Ledger* not only reported these events. It also shaped the outcome and helped mold public attitudes toward Marshall, his rumored activities, and the murder of Dinkins. The culminating news story—the representation of the penitentiary procession—articulated possible courses of community retribution, such as mob violence, as well as potential means of viewing and delineating individuals of Marshall's type. Clearly awestruck at the masses, the reporter expected an assault on the lead prisoner, a fallen member of "the classes." Elitist contempt was registered on the faces of both Marshall and Coleman, the reporter suggested, whereas Fox seemingly understood the danger. Logically, the murder might have triggered a lynching, the paper maintained—thereby occluding the practice's racial contours while linking these sorts of white men to the worst of fates in Mississippi. That a lynching did not take place, the *Clarion-Ledger* wrongly predicted, attested to the legal profession's ascendancy and expediency and a concomitant end to extralegal executions in the state.[17] Fox's fear, though justified, clearly indicated a faintheartedness; the diminutive stature of both Marshall and Coleman spoke for itself. Their effeminacy—a term of great derision when employed by longtime *Clarion-Ledger* publisher R. H. Henry—marked the men as deviant.[18]

Today, historians of sexuality ordinarily point to the late nineteenth century as the advent of modern conceptions of homosexuality, as the emergence of an identity-based sexual being—the modern homosexual. In a mutually scripting relationship, this deviancy is said to have informed sexual normalcy, and thus the Western world simultaneously witnessed "the invention of heterosexuality."[19] That flowering of medical and legal discourses of sexuality could only partially reflect the realities of queer cultures in turn-of-the-century American cities, before the discourses and the remembrances of those cultures somehow withered into obscurity. Although scholar George Chauncey, in an important act of reclamation, skillfully outlines the workings of a "gay male world" in late-nineteenth- and early-twentieth-century New York City, he acknowledges but does not explain the fact that such worlds, since that time, have "been almost entirely forgotten in popular memory."[20] How can we account for this social amnesia? Is it possible to speak of a queer collective memory? If so, how did it fail us? Or did it? And who are among the "us" to which I refer? For whom are acts of reclamation important today?

Dabney Marshall may or may not have belonged to "a colony of male sex perverts [who] in every community of any size [were] usually known to each other and [were] likely to congregate together," as one scientist proclaimed in 1889.[21] Brandon, with roughly eight hundred residents; Jackson, with seven thousand; or even Vicksburg, with twice that in 1895, may or may not have harbored easily identifiable queer networks. As yet, traditional historical sources are of little help. Still, the Marshall incident and the subsequent talk of the county offer a useful window onto processes of remembering and forgetting homosexuality. Further, they point up the distinctive features of life in post–Reconstruction Mississippi that led to a multiplicity of queer memories, memories I seek to recover through history.

. . . .

When I grew up in Brandon in the 1960s and 1970s, our town rapidly was becoming an interstate suburb of Jackson. Nonetheless, a small, white core of old, "established" families remained in old Brandon. My family lived a few houses away from the McLaurin family, descendants of Marshall's attorney, Anselm J. McLaurin, governor of Mississippi from 1896 to 1900. My father and "Mr. John" McLaurin were lifelong friends. John's son Anse was my attorney when I asked my wife for a divorce. During all that time, I never heard about the Brandon tragedy of 1895. Nor did I hear about it after I came out as gay.

Studies of memory necessarily chart multiple historical moments. Memory is about different times in conversation with each other. My time and, with greater emphasis, that of Marshall—as well as his remembered antecedents— are among the concerns of this essay. Today's popular and scholarly impulse to connect contemporary lesbian and gay persons and politics to prior queer figures and events is problematic, presentist, and yet persistent. Many are invested in such connections. My autobiographical impulse to ancestry, as informed by feminist theory and performed via the recuperation of Marshall's historical specificity, engages this vital lesbian and gay historiographical preoccupation: subjectivity. Who are our subjects? Over this essay's chronological expanse alone, the century between Marshall's adulthood and mine, the very nature of queer subjectivity (inverts, uranians, hermaphrodites, perverts, homosexuals, transsexuals, lesbians, gays, intersexuals, transgender persons) has varied radically, proving unstable in ways that are markedly distinct from that of racial minorities, to name but one other means of categorization. The last "one hundred years of homosexuality," as David Halperin calls it, proves a vibrant period across which divergent queer identities, behaviors, and affinities have been forged.[22] Perceived ancestries are likely to be based in part on class and race—as, for example, I seem to share them with Marshall. Also, as I will argue, they are based on place.

. . . .

"The importance of history to gay men and lesbians goes beyond the lessons to be learned from the events of the past to include the meanings generated through retellings of those events and the agency those meanings carry in the present," says theorist Scott Bravmann. "Lesbian and gay historical self-

representations—queer fictions of the past—help construct, maintain, and
contest identities—queer fictions of the present."[23]

. . . .

How in 1895 could an aggressive newspaper, determined to boost sales,
balance the medium's sensationalistic tendencies against the prevailing, Victorian penchant for propriety? Under such conditions, homosexuality was
made "unmentionable."[24] And yet, as the Dabney Marshall case demonstrates, it was widely talked about. Further, it was written about—but, of
course, in particular ways.

In the *Clarion-Ledger* and in other press accounts from the period, conventions of discourse around taboo sexuality were established, observed, and
perpetually renegotiated. Memory played an important role. In none of its
voluminous coverage—from the first "Around the City" rumormongering
until the closing on the penitentiary procession—did the *Clarion-Ledger* give
an explicit account of "what transpired" between Marshall and Dinkins that
July evening in the Raymond hotel. In alluding to Marshall's "shame," the
Clarion-Ledger had to rely on readers' recall and on cognitive processes of
association.[25]

Scarcely three months prior to the Marshall sentencing, a world-renowned
writer was convicted on several counts of "gross indecency" with "male persons" in London.[26] The *Clarion-Ledger* took up this readily available, international controversy, describing Marshall's alleged behavior as "a crime similar to the one for which Oscar Wilde is now serving a term in the English
prison."[27] This referential idiom—a Victorian-era tendency to connote homosexuality only through reference to prior cases—is likewise evident in C. S.
Clark's 1898 description of Toronto street boys' sexual interactions with men:
"According to their reports . . . the crime that banished Lord Somerset from
London society is committed."[28] Such rhetorical strategies kept prior episodes alive in popular memory; but they also obscured important differences
between cases, such as disparities of age and class between the sex partners.
Further details, such as the extent of consent, coercion, and payment for the
sex act, also fell away.

Even the Wilde trials yielded press reports conspicuously silent regarding
the writer's purported offense. Of the London coverage, Ed Cohen observes
that "at no point did the newspapers describe or even explicitly refer to the
sexual charges made against Wilde."[29] Jonathan Ned Katz notes a similar
New York press "reticence concerning Wilde's exact crime." Thus if Marshall's disgrace was said to mirror that of Wilde, and yet Wilde's disgrace was
never pinpointed in print, then a confusion resulted. The referential idiom, it

seems, had no concrete referent. Wilde had transgressed, journalists ambiguously disclosed. "This ambiguity," Katz concludes, "either left readers quite in the dark about Wilde's transgression, or"—as is much more likely and as I shall explore later around the Dabney Marshall incident—it "forced them to use their imaginations to make sense of the reports."[30]

In addition to this international scandal used to describe the Marshall incident, there were local analogues as well, called up not only for their familiarity, but also for their power as cautionary tales. Marshall's actions were said to mirror those of a certain Mr. "Cowsert of YMCA fame [who] pleaded guilty and left his home in Natchez to suicide, it is reported, in Chicago." Likewise tragic—and worthy of a brief retelling here—was the case of "W. R. Sims . . . , fired out of the faculty at the State University."[31]

The Sims incident well illustrates the tensions between secrecy and disclosure, both individual and institutional, as it demonstrates varied understandings of queer desire in the American South before the turn of the twentieth century. In 1889, when William Rice Sims joined the University of Mississippi faculty in Oxford, he left behind a soiled reputation at Vanderbilt, his former employer. Somehow, news of his "vicious tendency" initially did not reach Oxford, as Chancellor Robert B. Fulton later lamented.[32] Six years passed before Sims was found out. In March 1895, under intense scrutiny, the professor of English and belles lettres confessed to having improper relations with young men from both the local community and the student body.

The matter was handled internally. Chancellor Fulton talked it over with the twelve members of the faculty. Then he relayed their deliberations in a letter to the executive committee of the Board of Trustees.

Sims, Fulton explained, was "suffering from perverted sexual mania." "Grave rumors in the community" seemed true. On the 233-student campus, Sims may have "improperly handled" 2 of the 204 males.[33] Fulton told the executive committee that although he was "fully aware of the abhorrence with which this vice is thought of, . . . it has a physical basis, either inherited or acquired." The chancellor adopted a medical rhetoric of diagnosis and consequently posited the only humane option: Sims needed "treatment as much as [any] man . . . suffering from any other mania." The faculty shared Fulton's "painful anxiety" but likewise wanted to support Sims. During their colleague's leave, other members of the faculty would teach his courses, though they "wish[ed] the salary to go to him." All agreed that this "quiet way of guarding the interests of the University" was best. They wanted to head off any "undue publicity." Fulton apologized to the committee members for

University of Mississippi faculty, 1893. At bottom right, with watch chain visible and
scrolled papers in his left hand, is William R. Sims, professor of English. Third from the
left, with mustache and white pocket handkerchief, is Chancellor Robert B. Fulton.
Courtesy of Archives and Special Collections, University of Mississippi.

having written "more freely than [otherwise] would be prudent . . . believing
that you should know all the facts."[34]

By the time Sims reached Baltimore's Johns Hopkins University Hospital,
however, the chancellor had learned of many more allegations against him,
and Fulton's goodwill was exhausted. As he wrote to Sims, "I [desired] a
quiet departure . . . in order that you might escape the violent treatment
which a sudden exposure might have brought to you from this outraged
community." Intellectual forbearance now waned: "I did not myself know of
one half of the rumors in regard to your conduct circulating in the community
[and] reach[ing] back to the first year of your connection with the University." Fulton hoped that "Divine Grace" would allow Sims to "turn your back
on the past." Nonetheless, Fulton advised Sims, he should not return to the
university.[35]

In a second letter to his superiors, this time to the entire Board of Trustees,
Fulton recommended that they accept the resignation Sims initially "placed

at my disposal," since "each day has brought some new revelation." Further, while reassuring them that the "evil . . . wrought with students" had been minimal, Fulton was impelled to explicate the nature of Sims's "awful condition." In language far more frank than that of the press, he made it clear: Sims had gratified "his sexual passions by handling the private parts of boys."[36] The chairman of the Board sent his approval of Fulton's recommendation, and on 3 June 1895 the Board voted to divide Sims's remaining salary among the three professors who had covered his classes.[37]

The "unfortunate Sims matter," though revealing relatively little about Sims's life or those of his partners, makes evident a range of beliefs regarding homosexuality. While some Oxford townspeople may have urged violent retaliation as in Jackson, the cooler heads of an educated elite ostensibly prevailed. Fulton took on the language of sexologists at the same time that he moralistically decried Sims's "vice," which could be overcome only with heavenly intervention. Despite these conflicting positions, one basic assumption underpinned all of the university correspondence and deliberation. The sharing of "expert" opinion allowed a candid discussion seemingly impossible in wider forums. University officials could ascertain with confidence Sims's condition and thus chart his fate. Although news would inevitably seep out and down to the community, to be recalled dimly in future scandals, university administrators deployed a policy of quiet containment, even as they bore the consequences of Vanderbilt's similar strategy.

Lisa Duggan, in her rigorous and compelling analysis of the trials of Alice Mitchell—a young Memphis resident who killed her lover, Freda Ward, in 1892—points up lurid press "memories of cases past" strikingly comparable to recollections of Sims and others in the wake of the Dabney Marshall affair. The Mitchell trials, however, garnered national press coverage and sparked reports of "related" incidents as much as twenty-three years past involving women.[38] Interestingly, in reporting the 1895 Marshall affair, the *Clarion-Ledger* did not recall the geographically and temporally proximate Mitchell case. This silence may reflect polarized or perhaps disconnected notions of distinctively male perversions and what was increasingly referred to as lesbianism. In Mississippi, the summoning up of exclusively male case studies around the Marshall episode may bespeak more than a traditional press overrepresentation of a gendered, male public sphere. It also suggests that the panoply of sexual practices and personages outlined by legal and medical authorities may have resulted in only a sporadic linking of male and female homosexualities in the popular imagination.

Memory served to elucidate male persons seemingly akin to Marshall: the main characters of these commonplace narratives. But although these narratives, taken together, presumably would have suggested a collectivity of queer southerners—after all, lots of these sorts of stories circulated—dominant strategies of individualization and isolation fractured collectivity through marginalizing, criminalizing, and pathologizing discourses. For queer southerners who read or heard about or were somehow involved in these scandals, group identities may have cohered, but only against formidable odds. For example, once sent away to Johns Hopkins University Hospital, William Rice Sims could not return to Oxford; Fulton insisted that his remaining possessions be shipped to him.[39] Mr. Cowsert "of YMCA fame" suffered the mythical erasure—realized or not—of suicide, a fate repeatedly offered in these "related" narratives.[40] If Marshall and company were not themselves executed, legally or extralegally, they were shunted to the margins, to jail, reinforced by the *Clarion-Ledger*'s call to forgetting, the press insistence that their lives, once fully exploited for their media value, be wiped from the public record. (And yet, those press records remain for our latter-day inspection and, perhaps, identification.)

Late-nineteenth-century scandals of homosexuality and homoaffectionalism helped construct identities through a "historical process of contested narration," as Duggan terms it.[41] In this process, varied discourses carried unequal weight and power. Sims, Cowsert, and Marshall—as well as those southerners who harbored non-normative desires and thus felt some kinship with the accused—participated in public discussions infrequently and with limited discursive resources. Framed within an evermore professionalized cult of expertise, these men became the objects of study and investigation. They achieved agency and subjectivity only through a constant reworking of dominant conceptions proliferating in medical literature, case law, and mass media. To chart the ways in which these alternative subjectivities and notions were crafted, then disrupted over time, we must inventory a range of queer memories—especially the divergent memories transmitted from a single incident such as the Marshall case. Thereby, we begin to chronicle a contested lineage of queer desire.

. . . .

Brandon. The Rankin County Courthouse square. The train station, no longer standing. The streets of Jackson. My interest in Dabney Marshall is invigorated by my personal experiences of, my queer experiences in, these places where—once upon a time, way back when—he also walked, talked, was talked about, and was made to fashion his life. But any affiliation with

Marshall on my part—or by anyone else—must necessarily be partial, tentative, gestural. His times were markedly different from my own; his circumstances were markedly different from those other turn-of-the-century southerners who, in some small, perhaps unspoken way, experienced an affinity with him. In tracking those affinities and differences, I must speculate about the myriad ways in which memories of Marshall were called up and closed off over time.

. . . .

"When I find traces of his life, and of other lives," Neil Bartlett writes of another group of turn-of-the-century queer antecedents, "I'm not sure how to react, whether to celebrate or turn away, . . . angry, angry that all these stories have been forgotten. This 'evidence' raises important questions about our own attitude to our own history. Do we view it with dismay, since it is a record of sorrow, of powerlessness, a record of lives wrecked? Or is it possible to read even these texts, written as they were by journalists, policemen, and court clerks, with delight, as precious traces of dangerous, pleasurable, complicated gay lives?"[42]

. . . .

If memories reside within individuals, as Susan A. Crane asserts, they also are anchored in physical space. Though sites may not readily give up the details of their past, human musings on the past often rely on restive, ungovernable associations of place. During and after the Marshall incident, material elements of the built environment would figure prominently in ruminations on it. But these elements would both affirm and challenge bedrock historical assumptions about homosexuality and space.

The ostensible emergence of the modern homosexual in Dabney Marshall's lifetime is linked in the historical literature to processes of industrialization and urbanization, most compellingly in John D'Emilio's influential essay, "Capitalism and Gay Identity."[43] Gay identity and community were dialectically shaped in the cities—spaces of anonymity and economic independence, seemingly free of so-called small-town values. Clearly, gayness and place have been linked in particular ways. But how might we frame queer identities and ancestries in other ways? that is, in other places? In a regionalist critique of an urban-focused American lesbian and gay history, I would like to assess queerness in the towns and small cities of the still agrarian South. Specific socioeconomic conditions there suggest specific place-based experiences of sexuality and memories thereof.

The early rumors about Dabney Marshall circulated among a privileged slice of Mississippi social and political life. That political life was all but fore-

closed to the state's African American majority when Anselm J. McLaurin
and other delegates to the 1890 constitutional convention disenfranchised
black citizens and "formalized . . . white rule."[44] Even when the rumors were
committed to print—in daily newspapers in Jackson, Vicksburg, Memphis,
and New Orleans; in weeklies published at county seats throughout the
state—relatively few learned of the Marshall affair in this way.[45] Rates of
illiteracy were high in Mississippi, especially for African Americans. Although educated blacks published a number of newspapers during this period, we cannot know their views of the Marshall affair since no copies of the
papers remain.[46]

To retrieve the varied reactions of a wide range of Mississippians, we might
instead take a metaphorical walk along the same streets of the penitentiary
procession, as so elaborately described by the *Clarion-Ledger*. For the march
that the Marshall entourage undertook that sixteenth day of August 1895 not
only occasioned a spectacle suited to the ideologies of official history, highlighted by an eventual ordering of chaos and the incarceration of the deviants.
It also fostered thoughts, desires, and perhaps actions at odds with normative
structures. The way those aberrant manifestations were carried forward in
time through memory might be suggested if we undertake what Christine
Boyer calls a "new memory walk"—if we retrace those steps and begin to
imagine the multiple narratives *generated* by, the multiple memories subsequently *transmitted* about, the 1895 procession. In this way, we might craft
"new maps that help us resist and subvert the all-too-programmed and envel-
oping messages" of both our culture today and theirs.[47] Most important, we
thereby can begin to piece together more accurate histories of consciousness
that account for diverse experiences of difference and dissent across space
and time.

People filled the streets. Though it was as hot as any August day in Mississippi, the curious were out in force, aware—from newspaper accounts, by
word of mouth—that Marshall, Coleman, and Fox had been convicted the
day before and that the three would be arriving in Jackson that morning.
Though this throng, as the *Clarion-Ledger* asserted, was largely male—a
homosocial public realm with its attendant homosexual possibilities and
anxieties—women, in boardinghouses, in shops and groceries, in any number of businesses, residences, and other establishments, likewise heard and
witnessed the spectacle, through open windows and from front porches, if
not on the frenetic sidewalks.[48]

From the train station on State Street, the penitentiary procession set out

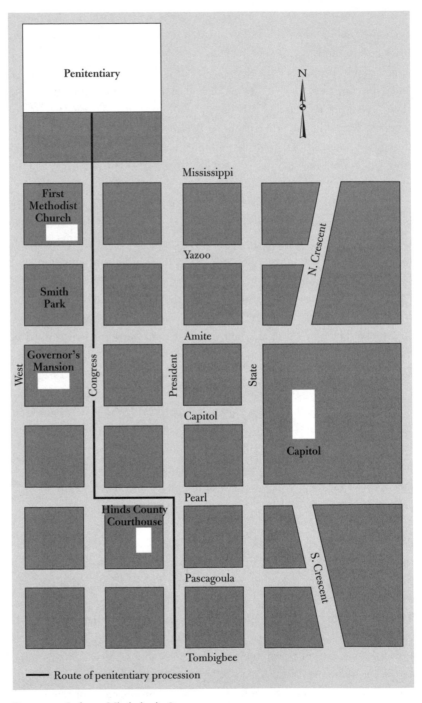

Downtown Jackson, Mississippi, 1895

on foot along the railroad tracks, after the train, just one block west to President Street. Then it headed north. It proceeded into the city center on President, turning left at the Hinds County Courthouse, built by slaves in the 1840s, and walking another block. After it turned right onto Congress Street, the group came upon the city's principal artery.

Up the grade to the right, two blocks east, Capitol Street originated at the front door of the capitol building, clearly visible. An impressive neoclassical structure completed in 1838, it occupied the focal point around which the city had been platted, a symbol of civic pride.[49] But this intersection of Capitol and Congress Streets marked the intersection of not one, but two key visual axes in Jackson. While off to the right—just beyond the Chinese laundry and other storefronts—the capitol building was perched on the city's eastern edge with its back to the Pearl River, just perceptible in the distance ahead was the penitentiary, on downtown's northernmost boundary.[50] These two mammoth structures dominated sight lines and housed respectively the state's lawmakers and lawbreakers. The buildings functioned, in turn, to craft order and contain disorder. In a stark contrast exemplified in architecture, the ominous penitentiary beckoned to the procession, as the trek continued past the elegant capitol and fashionable Capitol Street, Jackson's main street.

Yet, as Ted Ownby writes of this period, "the Southern main street" itself harbored much disorder in the form of raucous, male-dominated activities: "The competitiveness, the drunkenness, the possibility of violence, and indiscriminate mixing of all sorts of men put emotions on edge." For black men and boys, in particular, the street was rife with discord. "The element of conflict that accompanied most main-street recreations, making them exciting for some and threatening for others, was sometimes particularly intense in the postbellum years as the races mixed in new ways."[51] In the shadows of the capitol building, where sinister Jim Crow provisions passed into law, black Mississippians gauged the threat of mob violence with added investment, especially as the Marshall gawkers grew more numerous and more boisterous. As African American men looked after young boys, they no doubt instilled a caution and wariness that imbued conceptions of the event.

We can only imagine how older men—black or white, Chinese or Choctaw—responded when inquisitive youngsters asked about the reasons for the crowd's enmity, the reasons for Marshall's predicament. Or how men and boys speculated among themselves, shared stories, conventional wisdom, and opinions. Was homosexuality the topic of their talk? If so, was it framed as an elite, white phenomenon? Such a conclusion would not have been difficult to reach. Homosexual scandals often were newsworthy only to the extent that they involved newsworthy figures, such as senatorial candidate Dabney Marshall, literary celebrity Oscar Wilde, and the like. Though Wilde and others were accused of running with a more dangerous, baser class of pervert, stories of those nonelite companions frequently receded from the headlines.

Further, as guardians of the official record, newspaper editors chose, by not reporting it, to forget or obscure ordinary aspects of queer life, the everyday queer experience. If queer sexuality became a part of broad, public discourses only as a result of political scandal or social trauma, then it surely became linked in memory to scandal and tragedy. Too, sensational, moralistic representations of homosexuality among the famous, the stuff of legend, conceivably enabled ordinary Mississippians to disassociate that morality and spectacle from their own queer actions or queer neighbors. Yes, Mississippians found evidence of difference in themselves, their friends, family members, and acquaintances in the small towns and rural farming areas where most lived—and, indeed, among the crowd vying for a glimpse of the accused. But Marshall and prior referenced figures of scandal probably dominated remembrances of queer sexuality, as a phenomenon shaped in contradistinction to official ideologies and punishments.

But even official voices clashed and popular opinions differed, as local loyalties shaped understandings of the Marshall incident. Whereas the *Clarion-Ledger* and the *New Orleans Times-Democrat* reported great initial "excitement" in Brandon over the scandal, such that "nothing else [was] talked about," interest quickly faded, given that "all concerned" in the matter were out-of-towners, "comparative strangers."[52] Many Jacksonians sided with Dinkins, whose mother and siblings resided in the area. "The people of Jackson," the *Clarion-Ledger* asserted, were "very well satisfied" with the trial's outcome. Some elite Vicksburgers, on the other hand, continued to lay blame on the *Clarion-Ledger*. They sought to protect their native son Dabney Marshall, the scion of a distinguished family, and they looked down on the press antics in the smaller, younger capital city. According to the Cashman family's *Vicksburg Evening Post*, the Jackson journalists, by spreading innuendo, demonstrated both "intent and motive" to ruin Marshall.[53] His troubles were their fault. And in Vicksburg, at least, "the sympathy of the street [was] with Mr. Marshall in this deplorable affair."[54] From Rankin to Warren Counties, and no doubt even that day on the streets of Jackson, perceptions were tinged with localism.

On the streets, as the Marshall procession passed, the posturing of men and boys was enacted and situated in relation to varied displays of masculinity among the convicted. Marshall's physique and demeanor, as well as those of Coleman and Fox, took on an excess weightiness, because the referential idiom in the talk of the county—the signifying of nebulous, non-normative sexualities through aphoristic reference to related, remembered events—lacked a certain candor. Where spoken and written language failed, body language seemed to help. Not only the quality of Marshall's physical appearance ("diminutive" and "effeminate"), but also the ways in which he stepped ("lightly") and smiled ("sickly") were evaluated by the reporter and implied to be reflective or revelatory of Marshall's being. As Ed Cohen describes the related Wilde case, because "the newspapers could not offer any more concrete representation of the physical acts that were ostensibly at issue than a physical description of the actor who was legally determined to have performed them," Wilde's body became a "metonym" or sign system. The London papers "continually capitalize[d] upon the . . . appearance of the male body"—much as the *Clarion-Ledger* reporter focused on Marshall's bearing and carriage—"as a descriptive trope that personalize[d] the . . . proceedings." Thus in London, as in Jackson, observers "contextually por-tray[ed] these patterns of 'indecent' relationship as inhering in the modes of embodiment attributed to the individuals in question."[55] Whereas Marshall attempted a queer act with Dinkins that ultimately was unknowable, Jackso-nians evinced an insatiable need to know at least the form of a queer body, the telltale signs of deviancy.

Men and boys took measure of one another for any number of reasons. As the spectacle unfolded and as it was later described in innumerable conversa-tions, individuals sized each other up. They took stock of one another, in part, to gauge affinity. In any grouping or especially in any mob, a central question arose: Are we all in accord? So too in one-on-one settings, one surely wondered of the other, Are you of the same mind as I? Do you, one might have asked, view this incident as I do? As Mississippians assessed one another around the time of the Marshall incident, the myriad reactions to it were sometimes borne out more clearly than at other times. In delicate verbal dances, queer Mississippians might have identified one another through this ritual of opinion and disclosure, as counterhegemonic or reverse discourses were cautiously elaborated. Since, for a time, Marshall was all that was talked about, that talk, at least occasionally, must have offered moments of queer alliance.

At the northwestern corner of Capitol and Congress, the marchers passed on the left the stately, two-story governor's mansion with rounded front portico and Corinthian columns—where Anselm J. McLaurin would soon take over residence from John M. Stone. Further north behind the mansion on Congress, also on the left, were Smith Park and the First Methodist Church, pastored by Charles Galloway. Humbler structures also lined the street, private homes from one to two-and-a-half stories, all with wide front porches likely filled with onlookers, as the procession reached its destination at the end of Congress.

Marshall's penitentiary march, then, amounted to a community spectacle, differently discerned by different observers. It represented a generative memory walk—creating a momentous occasion and locating it in relation to both the everyday and hallowed spaces of the city. The procession bound experiences and, subsequently, remembrances of the event in discrete, spatial dimensions. Later, perhaps years after the fact, as an individual walked or drove through Jackson, or passed through on a streetcar or train, involuntary memories could be triggered by the mundane physical attributes of one particular street corner where Marshall perhaps spoke back to the crowd, or another stretch of cobblestones where an elderly man ran to catch up. Thus, it was not only the consciously commissioned and constructed monuments—such as the Confederate war memorials erected in front of the courthouse in Rankin County and throughout the South at this time—but also the ordinariness of place that could summon up past traumas and prompt recollections, particularly for marginalized peoples engaged and invested in counterhegemonic readings of those events.

For many people, however, the perceptive possibilities of the spectacle were overdetermined. Reception and judgment operated too closely, almost simultaneously, in time and space. Critical evaluation of Marshall, his crime(s), his ilk, was foreshortened by a seemingly all-consuming masculinist stance at the moment, enacted on the streets, represented in the pages of the newspaper. So too the ways of remembering the event must have been limited by the restrictive means of writing and talking about it: the referential idiom, the derisive catcalls and epithets heard on the streets, and the other narrow discourses that prescribed and proscribed the talk of the county.

Individuals who witnessed the spectacle or read about Marshall in the newspaper presumably harbored *individual* memories for a time, maybe a generation, the duration of their lifetime. But, as Dolores Hayden surmises, "*social* memory relies on story-telling."[56] The Marshall affair would be lost to memory if the story were not recounted to others. Such recountings were discouraged, likely as they were to engage taboo subject matter and to implicate the teller for exhibiting too much interest. Retellings for any purpose other than ridicule, derision, or snide entertainment were undertaken with

great care and delicacy. For this reason, the carrying forward of social memory in time clouded the circumstances of Marshall's existence. Far more than
it revealed about Marshall or homosexuality, the Marshall spectacle imparted
the protocols for engaging in the talk of the county. After Marshall was largely
forgotten, memories of these strictures would persist. But, too, the landscape
would persist, apt to elicit old and new place-bound memories.

The referential idiom, as I have called it, and its inherent instability of
referent presumably would make difficult an event's cohesion in collective
memory. The oblique language that marked this event and its protagonist as
somehow queer seemingly would close off precision in recollection. But can
memories be precise? When, if ever, are they? Might there be a liberatory
potential in just such ambiguity? I speculate that it was the very ambiguity,
allusion, and innuendo of these incidents that opened up an imaginative
space for queer southerners, those who drew particular affinities to Marshall.
The productive capacity of the ambiguous for queers allowed certain observers of this event and others who learned about it in the retelling to
imagine alternative understandings and ways of life. Thoughts of Marshall,
for some, allowed thoughts—and allegiances—of difference and dissent.

If the referential idiom rendered memories imprecise, it also destabilized
the nature of the forbidden. What exactly was proscribed? Meanings were
clouded as much by polite conventions of discourse as by the innate inability
of muckrakers, politicians, or any other surveillant authority to fully ascertain
the transgressive acts. The act of which Marshall was accused was, in effect,
inscrutable. Thus in relating it, contemporary journalistic accounts, no less
than my own history making here, inevitably engaged in conjecture and
comparison.

Yes, Marshall was a murderer. This much we know. But his actions must
be considered in the context of the violent society he inhabited. Tip Dinkins's allegations threatened Marshall's livelihood, his political career, his
income, perhaps even his life. To level such charges meant to endanger
another's very being. Often words were indeed more pertinent than acts,
in that many transgressions could be overlooked as long as they were not
talked about.

Many Mississippians shared Marshall's view that some "insults and
wrongs . . . only can be washed away in blood."[57] For some, Marshall simply
mishandled the killing. Marshall's revenge, however, should not be construed
as a flat denial of the charges of homosexuality. His carefully crafted dis-
avowal—he had never, he wrote, "done a low, mean, or disgraceful thing"—
might well have signified a distancing from lurid depictions of queer sex-

uality, not queer sexuality itself. In a culture characterized by politesse and indirection, by scrupulous shadings of language, Marshall conceivably meant to suggest that his *passions* were anything but disgraceful.

. . . .

In the early 1990s, with a group of campus activists in Tuscaloosa, Alabama, I watched a film by Gregg Araki called *The Living End*.[58] In it, two gay men, on the road, try to outrun the law and HIV. In a pivotal scene, the gun-toting partner is met on a darkened street by a group of would-be gay bashers, men with rocks and clubs ready to do harm. The man shoots them. The audience cheered wildly.

. . . .

"Fundamentally, doing queered history is a scandalous project in itself," writes legal scholar Martha Umphrey. "Queering history means acknowledging that the processes of history are unstable, the search for exemplary historical subjects always incomplete. It requires on our part a constant re-engagement, a constant questioning of our own assumptions about the 'proper' subject of history. . . . Moreover, doing queered history may require engagement with unsavory characters who . . . have an attenuated but identifiable relationship with a critique of compulsory heterosexuality."[59]

. . . .

Probably the most fundamental, tangible site of memory for the events of August 1895 was "that gloomy hostelrie" to which the murderer Dabney Marshall was confined, to which the unruly crowd accompanied him and his two accomplices. The penitentiary loomed large, a retro-Norman fortress with gatehouse, turrets, and twin towers, all topped with battlements. Situated prominently in the urban landscape, it was not simply a symbol of order and power, authority and control. It was, as well, a memory device, a potent reminder. The prison in our midst acknowledged the deviance in our midst.

And yet, only a few months after Marshall's incarceration, the prison population was relocated out of the city, to the countryside, to a work camp near Oakley in rural Hinds County. Formerly occupants of the capital city citadel, an ongoing spectacle for all to behold, the men were pushed to the margins, the hinterlands, to the site Marshall described as "a low swampy place."[60]

But Marshall had it well. Friends sent gifts of clothing and candy, and the captain at Oakley Convict Farm furnished him with "the nicest of meals."[61] Reflective of class as much as perceived gender role, Marshall received anything but the hard labor prescribed by the judge. ("Work in the field," Marshall confided to a friend, "would kill me.") Instead, he was given charge of the commissary. There, he was responsible for "the weighing out of all

The new capitol building, completed in 1903 on the former site of the state penitentiary. At left, fronting Congress Street, is the First Methodist Church, later renamed after Bishop Charles B. Galloway. Courtesy of Mississippi Department of Archives and History.

food eaten, the ordering of it when out, and the keeping of a record of the same."[62] He handled freight and mail, and during his breaks he tended his potted gardens along the building's gallery: wild violets, yellow jasmines, and petunias. Also during his free time at Oakley, Marshall wrote lengthy letters to friends and family members (letters filled with vivid descriptions that later proved useful to at least one historian of the penal system in Mississippi—a historian whose account of Marshall would suit my own inquiries into the past).[63]

Marshall endeared himself to inmates by offering legal advice, by helping them draw up petitions for the ever-elusive, all-coveted executive order: a pardon. Marshall too hoped for pardon. His father, from that very first day his son walked through the penitentiary gate, lobbied for reprieve. And in the end, Dabney Marshall proved both the *Clarion-Ledger* and the *Memphis Scimitar* wrong. The former assured its readers on that fifteenth day of August 1895 that Marshall "deserve[d] no clemency, and [would] receive none"; the latter insinuated that attorney-turned-governor Anselm J. McLaurin would surely breach ethics and free his client. It was rather the year after McLaurin left office, 1901, the year that the old penitentiary in Jackson was torn down to make way for a new capitol building—a domed structure bigger and more commanding than the one at the summit of Capitol Street, an expenditure McLaurin bitterly fought, an edifice Charles Galloway verbosely dedicated at the lavish opening ceremonies—that T. Dabney Marshall returned to Vicksburg the recipient of a full pardon.[64]

As the Jackson penitentiary was pulled down, replaced by a more magnificent monument to lawmaking and governance, some memories may have died with it. The criminal element, the outlaw, the queer in us all, edged ever further from sight, to the periphery, a geographic marginalization. Thieves and robbers, murderers and sodomites, were removed from the heavily trafficked public center, from the seat of political power. And yet such movement dispersed queer potentials, which as ever defied confinement to a single, visible urban space. Indeed, the public wanted more. On a spring day in 1896, Dabney Marshall noticed "quite a number of visitors at the camp" near Oakley—some "to see relatives," others just "seeking to feed a morbid curiosity with the sight of misfortune."[65] Marshall made a point to meet these visitors, the inquisitive, the curious, those who would not heed official calls to forgetting, those interested in learning more about Marshall and his kind.

I cannot help but wonder: Would Marshall find the latter-day curious, would he find me, you, us, as he found the visitors, "even more than usually bête and banal"? Aren't we, today's readers of the Marshall scandal, equally as engaged and implicated as his contemporaries in the production, maintenance, and perhaps reconstitution of normalcy and difference?

Indeed, I believe, we are. My unfolding of salacious details in this essay was intended to mirror and perform the voyeurism of the Marshall scandal, thereby implicating us all in the consistently sensationalized accounts and understandings of queer lives. Paradoxically, as we have seen, outlandish queer spectacle was often followed by prodigious attempts at queer erasure, both physically and discursively. Queer outlaws were exiled, sometimes killed; queer stories were renounced. Official calls to forgetting thus amounted to more than mechanisms of genteel conversation. They also were strategies of oppression. To declare particular individuals and events as unworthy of remembrance helped to assure their inferior status over time.

And yet the county did talk. The Brandon tragedy, while perpetuating notions of marginality, recirculated memories of prior queer figures. Their stories were again told—at least for a time. If the most elite of those figures such as Oscar Wilde would not be forgotten in the subsequent century, others such as William Sims and Dabney Marshall would be. Or so it seemed. How do historians prove that memories did not persist? How does anyone demonstrate any historical absence? Because I had never heard of Marshall; because I shared a certain lineage with him as a queer white Mississippian, indeed a Brandonian; because the elders and archivists I work with there likewise knew nothing of his story—I assumed it had been lost to queer collective memory. Perhaps it is no longer. We historians are beholden to the communities that support us. We must be made to answer when we declare, "I have no memory."

NOTES

1. Susan A. Crane, "Writing the Individual Back into Collective Memory," *American Historical Review* 102 (December 1997): 1381. I would like to thank Novid Parsi for his generous assistance and incisive commentary throughout this project. Thanks also go to Fitz Brundage and Elizabeth Kennedy for their very helpful suggestions.

2. *Jackson Daily Clarion-Ledger* (hereafter *CL*), 16 August 1895. Several subsequent references to *Clarion-Ledger* reports are cited, along with the date of publication, in the text.

3. *CL*, 15 August 1895.

4. In this essay, I use *queer* to broadly signify not just homosexuality but sexual non-normativities of myriad types. As Donna Jo Smith well explains, "my use of the term *queer* is meant to circumvent the limitations to our historical projects effected by the narrow model of lesbian/gay identity that has been utilized in many U.S. histories to date, so that identities and behaviors such as 'bisexual' and 'transgendered' and desires as yet unmapped and perhaps 'unmappable' can be considered within my discussion." Smith, "Queering the South: Constructions of Southern/Queer Identity," in John Howard, ed., *Carryin' On in the Lesbian and Gay South* (New York: New York University Press, 1997), 383.

5. *CL*, 9, 15 August 1895.

6. For biographical data on Dinkins, I have relied on *CL*, 14 August 1895; on Marshall, *Biographical and Historical Memoirs of Mississippi* (Chicago: Goodspeed Publishing, 1891), 400–401, and T. Dabney Marshall Subject File, Mississippi Department of Archives and History, Jackson (hereafter MDAH). In re-creating the political and social worlds of the late-nineteenth-century South, I have relied on two landmark texts: Edward L. Ayers, *The Promise of the New South: Life after Reconstruction* (New York: Oxford University Press, 1992), and C. Vann Woodward, *Origins of the New South, 1877– 1913* (Baton Rouge: Louisiana State University Press, 1951). Broad insights into constructions of sexuality are drawn from John D'Emilio and Estelle Freedman, *Intimate Matters: A History of Sexuality in America* (New York: Harper and Row, 1988).

7. The literature on honor and violence in the South is vast. Most useful for my purposes have been Edward L. Ayers, *Vengeance and Justice: Crime and Punishment in the Nineteenth-Century American South* (New York: Oxford University Press, 1984), and Bertram Wyatt-Brown, *Southern Honor: Ethics and Behavior in the Old South* (New York: Oxford University Press, 1982).

8. Jonathan Katz, *Gay American History: Lesbians and Gay Men in the U.S.A.* (New York: Thomas Y. Crowell, 1976), 37. This is a per capita calculation. Though seven men were likewise held in Tennessee, that state's larger population meant a lower incarceration rate.

9. *CL*, 9 August 1895.

10. Ibid. Sixteen bullets were found, nine in Dinkins's body. *CL*, 13 August 1895.

11. *CL*, 13, 15 August 1895.

12. *CL*, 7, 8 August 1895.

13. *CL*, 14 August 1895.

14. *CL*, 8 August 1895.

15. *CL*, 13, 14 August 1895.

16. *CL*, 15 August 1895.

17. Lynchings reached horrific proportions in Mississippi just before and after the turn of the twentieth century. "During the period from 1889 to 1945, the half century Roy Wilkins called the 'lynching era,' Mississippi accounted for 476, or nearly 13 percent, of the nation's 3,786 recorded lynchings." Of the 476 killed, only 24 were white. Neil R. McMillen, *Dark Journey: Black Mississippians in the Age of Jim Crow* (Urbana: University of Illinois Press, 1989), 229.

18. R. H. Henry, *Editors I Have Known: Since the Civil War* (New Orleans: E. S. Upton Printing, 1922), 301.

19. Jonathan Ned Katz, *The Invention of Heterosexuality* (New York: Dutton, 1995).

20. George Chauncey, *Gay New York: Gender, Urban Culture, and the Making of the Gay Male World, 1890–1940* (New York: Basic Books, 1994), 1.

21. G. Frank Lydstron, "Sexual Perversion, Satyriasis, and Nymphomania," *Medical and Surgical Reporter* 61 (1889): 254; Chauncey, *Gay New York*, 12 (quotation).

22. David M. Halperin, *One Hundred Years of Homosexuality and Other Essays on Greek Love* (New York: Routledge, 1990).

23. Scott Bravmann, *Queer Fictions of the Past: History, Culture, and Difference* (Cambridge: Cambridge University Press, 1997), 4.

24. *CL*, 15 August 1895.

25. *CL*, 9 August 1895.

26. Neil Bartlett, *Who Was That Man? A Present for Mr. Oscar Wilde* (London: Serpent's Tail, 1988), 159–60.

27. *CL*, 9 August 1895. Wilde's visit to the state in 1882 had elicited much comment from Mississippi journalists and other observers, particularly about his clothing and comportment. See Eileen Knott, William Warren Rogers, and Robert David Ward, "Oscar Wilde in Vicksburg, at Beauvoir, and Other Southern Stops," *Journal of Mississippi History* 59 (Fall 1997): 183–210.

28. Cited in Steven Maynard, "'Horrible Temptations': Sex, Men, and Working-Class Male Youth in Urban Ontario, 1890–1935," *Canadian Historical Review* 78 (June 1997): 191.

29. Ed Cohen, *Talk on the Wilde Side: Toward a Genealogy of a Discourse on Male Sexualities* (New York: Routledge, 1993), 4.

30. Jonathan Ned Katz, *Gay/Lesbian Almanac: A New Documentary* (New York: Carroll and Graf, 1983), 258–59.

31. *CL*, 15 August 1895. Allan Bérubé argues that in various parts of the United States, as early as the 1890s, "ordinary . . . bathhouses—and YMCAs—developed reputations as 'favorite spots' for men to have sex with each other. Word got out that a certain manager, masseur, employee, or police officer would look the other way when they were on duty, or that homosexuals were known to gather there at certain hours, usually in the afternoon or late at night." "The History of Gay Bathhouses," in Dangerous Bedfellows, eds., *Policing*

Public Sex: Queer Politics and the Future of AIDS Activism (Boston: South End Press, 1996), 190. Also on queer uses of YMCA facilities, see John Donald Gustav-Wrathall, *Take the Young Stranger by the Hand: Same-Sex Relations and the YMCA* (Chicago: University of Chicago Press, 1998).

32. R. B. Fulton to Donald McKenzie (each member of Board Trustees [*sic*]), 26 March 1895, Robert B. Fulton Collection, Archives and Special Collections, University of Mississippi, University (hereafter RBFC). I am grateful to Lisa K. Speer, acting curator of the Mississippi Collection, for her assistance in locating these documents.

33. On university demographics, I have consulted Dunbar Rowland, ed., *The Official and Statistical Register of the State of Mississippi, 1904* (Nashville: Brandon Printing, 1904), 267; also, *Historical and Current Catalogue of the University of Mississippi, Forty-Second Session, 1893–1894*. Of the two students allegedly involved with Sims, at least one seems to have been dismissed, though not expressly for this reason. In a letter that same month, Chancellor Fulton requested that a Crystal Springs, Miss., man "withdraw" his son from the university, given his poor academic performance: "You will see from his reports that his work is unsatisfactory except in the class in English," taught by Sims. "The members of the Faculty," Fulton added, "are convinced that he could do better work elsewhere." In a revealing final sentence, perhaps indicative of a policy of quiet containment, Fulton stated that "no censure is attached to the young man's moral character by the action which the Faculty has taken." R. B. Fulton to S. H. Aby, 16 March 1895, RBFC.

34. R. B. Fulton to Sir [members of the Executive Committee], 18 March 1895, RBFC.

35. R. B. Fulton to Dr. Wm. Rice Sims, 25 March 1895, RBFC.

36. R. B. Fulton to Donald McKenzie, 26 March 1895. Based on other references in the letters and given that university students were among them, the "boys" can be assumed to have been postadolescent. Nonetheless, this language eerily foreshadows a twentieth-century custom of conflating man-man adult consensual sex with man-boy coerced intercourse.

37. R. H. Thompson to Chancellor R. B. Fulton, 30 March 1895, RBFC; Motion of Mr. Thompson, Resolved, and Motion of Mr. Martin, Resolved, Board of Trustees Minutes, University of Mississippi, Archives and Special Collections, University of Mississippi, University.

38. Lisa Duggan, "The Trials of Alice Mitchell: Sensationalism, Sexology, and the Lesbian Subject in Turn-of-the-Century America," *Signs: Journal of Women in Culture and Society* 18 (Summer 1993): 791–814.

39. R. B. Fulton to Dr. Wm. Rice Sims, 25 March 1895, RBFC.

40. On homosexual suicide mythology and homosexual homicide mythology, see John Howard, *Men Like That: A Southern Queer History* (Chicago: University of Chicago Press, 1999), chap. 5.

41. Duggan, "Trials of Alice Mitchell," 793.

42. Bartlett, *Who Was That Man?*, 129.

43. John D'Emilio, "Capitalism and Gay Identity," in Ann Snitow, Christine Stansell, and Sharon Thompson, eds., *Powers of Desire: The Politics of Sexuality* (New York: Monthly Review Press, 1983), 100–113. See also D'Emilio's groundbreaking monograph, *Sexual Politics, Sexual Communities: The Making of a Homosexual Minority in the United States, 1940–1970* (Chicago: University of Chicago Press, 1983).

44. McMillen, *Dark Journey*, 36.

45. In the *Vicksburg Evening Post*, e.g., see 9, 10, 12–17 September 1895. References to county weeklies' coverage of the events appear throughout the Jackson and Vicksburg press accounts. Copies of those papers are no longer extant.

46. Julius E. Thompson, *The Black Press in Mississippi, 1865–1985* (Gainesville: University Press of Florida, 1993), 8.

47. Christine M. Boyer, *The City of Collective Memory: Its Historical Imagery and Architectural Entertainments* (Cambridge: MIT Press, 1994), 29.

48. My re-creation and analysis here rely on readings of contemporaneous fire insurance maps. [Map of] *Jackson, Hinds Co., Mississippi* (New York: Sanborn-Perris Map Co., Ltd., 1895).

49. On state politics and city building during this period, I have relied on both John Bettersworth, *Mississippi: A History* (Austin, Tex.: Steck Co., 1959), and James W. Loewen and Charles Sallis, eds., *Mississippi: Conflict and Change*, rev. ed. (New York: Pantheon, 1980).

50. On Mississippians of Chinese descent, see James W. Loewen, *The Mississippi Chinese: Between Black and White* (Cambridge: Harvard University Press, 1971).

51. Ted Ownby, *Subduing Satan: Religion, Recreation, and Manhood in the Rural South, 1865–1920* (Chapel Hill: University of North Carolina Press, 1990), 54–55.

52. *CL*, August 10, 13, 1895.

53. *CL*, August 15, 1895.

54. *Vicksburg Evening Post*, 9 August 1895.

55. Cohen, *Talk on the Wilde Side*, 190, 209.

56. Dolores Hayden, *The Power of Place: Urban Landscapes as Public History* (Cambridge: MIT Press, 1995), 46. Emphasis added. Hayden makes an interesting, related point in this work: "In the last forty years, civil rights marches in southern cities, women's marches to 'Take Back the Night' or win abortion rights, and Gay and Lesbian Pride parades in major cities have also established their participants in public space, as part of campaigns to achieve greater political representation. Historical changes in parades can reveal larger social transformations, such as when a group is or is not too controversial to march, or when an entire parade is overtaken by commercial interests and every float becomes an advertisement" (pp. 38–39). The transformation from penitentiary procession to Lesbian and Gay Pride parades is significant, indeed.

57. T. Dabney Marshall to Miss Alice [Shannon], 10 September 1895, Crutcher-Shannon Papers, MDAH.

58. For the screenplay of this film, see Gregg Araki, *The Living End: An Irresponsible Movie; Totally F——ed Up: A Screenplay* (New York: Morrow, 1994).

59. Martha M. Umphrey, "The Trouble with Harry Thaw," *Radical History Review* 62 (Spring 1995): 20–21.

60. T. Dabney Marshall to Miss Alice Shannon, 7 May 1896, Crutcher-Shannon Papers, MDAH.

61. T. Dabney Marshall to Mother, 13 April 1896, Crutcher-Shannon Papers, MDAH.

62. Marshall to Shannon, 7 May 1896, ibid.

63. David M. Oshinsky, *"Worse than Slavery": Parchman Farm and the Ordeal of Jim Crow Justice* (New York: Free Press, 1996), 157–61.

64. Ibid., 159.

65. Marshall to Mother, 13 April 1896.

part four

Memory and Place
in the Modern South

The concluding essays in this collection delve into significant expressions of and debates about historical memory in the twentieth-century South. Taken together, these essays demonstrate some of the links between the economic, social, and political changes of the twentieth century and the continuing evolution of southern historical memory. They also point to the myriad ways in which disputes over the southern past are interwoven with ideas about southern distinctiveness. The various invocations of the past and controversies over what should be remembered almost certainly will provide the crucible for future definitions of any meaningful southern identity. Thus, even at a time when the region has lost many of its formerly defining characteristics, southern identity will endure as long as people imagine themselves as inheritors of a southern past.

Stephanie Yuhl's elegant essay grapples with a familiar theme in discussions of southern distinctiveness—southerners and their sense of place. She explains how three prominent Charleston women wove together their personal identity, historical memory, and aesthetics of place. In the process they recast the image of their beloved city. For a brief period during the 1920s and 1930s, Charleston earned a reputation as a cultural center, a pioneer in historic preservation, and a chic tourist destination. The women who Yuhl discusses played a prominent role in all of these developments and their legacy is evident to any modern-day visitor to Charleston. Yuhl's essay is noteworthy not only because it catalogs the motivations and tangible accomplishments of these women, but also because it demonstrates that historical memory is not comprised of vague, ambient memories that individuals haphazardly adopt as their own. Rather, as the example of Charleston illustrates, the personal memories of specific individuals provide the foundation for collective memories. Here, then, is a careful case study of the process through which personal associations with place and history are codified and incorporated into the very fabric of civic culture. If individual agency too often seems to disappear in studies of historical memory, Yuhl offers a valuable corrective that highlights the profoundly personal stake that crafters of memory often have in their creations.

Yuhl's essay, along with Catherine Bishir's essay, underscores the ongoing connection between collective memory in the South and the fears and ambitions of southern white elites. But, of course, the "white" South was never homogeneous. Nor was there ever a single "white collective memory." In both North Carolina and South Carolina, white elites couched their appeals to state and local pride in explicitly ethnic as well as racial terms. Both Bishir and Yuhl stress that mantralike invocation of Anglo-Saxon greatness in elite white accounts of southern history. Other groups in the South had little if any place in these narratives. Thus, elite white memory shunted to the margins various white ethnic as well as African American historical memories.

C. Brenden Martin delves into the irony of the "discovery" of the inhabitants of the mountain South by twentieth-century tourists. Adopting a wry but empathetic perspective, Martin adeptly traces how perceptions of the peoples of eastern Tennessee and western North Carolina have become staples of the tourist industry. Fitzhugh Brundage draws attention to another group of white southerners—the Cajuns of Louisiana—who succeeded in promoting a countermemory to the familiar Anglo-Saxon and elite narratives of southern history. If Martin stresses the imposition of cultural identities on mountain southerners, Brundage emphasizes how residents of southwestern Louisiana have crafted the identities that now define them in their eyes and in the eyes of others. His essay illustrates the use of memory in the service of ethnic invention and demarcation. Ethnic identity, like collective memory, cannot be explained as a primordial attribute that is either unchanging or inherent to a group's soul. Rather, ethnicity is constantly reinvented in response to changing circumstances; ethnic boundaries are continually renegotiated and expressions of ethnicity (traditions, rituals, etc.) are invariably revised and reinterpreted. The so-called Acadian revival, which began in the 1920s, is a striking example of the invocation of memory to mobilize a group, to advance its claims to power and status, and to defend its purported cultural values.

Martin's and Brundage's essays also suggest some of the ways that historical memory and tourism have informed modern ideas about both regional and national identity. If the economic and political developments of the late nineteenth and twentieth centuries accelerated the centralization of power, wealth, and influence, they also fostered vigorous and continuing assertions of regional distinctiveness. As studies of New England tourism, of the Victorians' interest in the Middle Ages, and of collective memory of the Languedoc region of France have demonstrated, displays of nationalism in the late-nineteenth- and early-twentieth-century West often contended with robust expressions of regionalism. Thus, at the same time that the Daughters of the American Revolution and other patriotic groups were exalting the common historical inheritance of all (white Anglo-Saxon) Americans, interest in local history and tourism reinforced regional attachments. All manner of southern communities, like their counterparts elsewhere, participated in an informal cultural competition to claim the most distinguished, romantic, or exotic past. Recalling and publicizing the historical contributions of a particular region or specific locale within the South yielded communities a rich source of identity, self-esteem, and even national prestige. Also at stake in this competition, as Martin's and Brundage's essays underscore, was the promotion of destinations for tourists eager to immerse themselves in the atmospherics of history. This phenomenon had no regional boundaries; Spanish missions in the Southwest, remnants of frontier settlements in the Midwest, colonial New England towns, and Quaker meetinghouses in Pennsylvania all became part of the tourist landscape. The southern landscape, likewise, became cluttered with history. Indeed, the South became especially associated with such historical qualities as romance and timelessness. For more and more travelers during the twentieth century, the remembered past in the South surrounded and embraced them with an intensity seldom experienced elsewhere.[1]

The success of Acadian revivalists in insinuating their past into the collective memory of Louisiana demonstrates that public memory in the modern South can be revised and redefined. But, of course, not all collective memories can be easily acknowledged without significant controversy. The recent melee over the Enola Gay exhibit at the Smithsonian Institution is emblematic of the complex subtexts that continue to influence contemporary historical disputes. Holly Beachley Brear, in her account of the ongoing discord over the presentation of the Alamo, reminds us of the vehemence with which disputes over the past may be waged and the stakes involved. Past commentators, including Brear herself, have emphasized the salience of ethnic and class identity in the differing interpretations of the Alamo held by various groups in Texas. In her essay in this collection, Brear highlights the central importance of gender to the contest over the Alamo. In a perpetuation of the voluntary tradition described earlier by Catherine Bishir, the Daughters of the Republic of Texas, a voluntary and hereditary group founded at the close of the nineteenth century, continue to control the Alamo. Who will oversee the operation of the historic site in the future is unclear. Brear suggests that the Daughters probably will have their power curtailed. But, she warns, if the state asserts greater authority over the site in the name of inclusiveness, it may in fact elbow aside the women who have run the site for nearly a century. Here, then, is a compelling illustration of how contests over memory may impinge upon multiple layers of identity. In San Antonio, class, ethnicity, and gender are all central to the "Second Battle of the Alamo." With such high stakes, we should hardly be surprised that the struggle over the site has gone on so long or has generated so much heat. Instead, it may well serve as a harbinger of disputes over the past that will continue to flair elsewhere in the South.

San Antonio, Texas, and Laurens County, South Carolina, seemingly have little in common. But both communities—one a large cosmopolitan city and the other a sleepy rural district—recently have had to deal with the reconciliation of contested memories. By excavating collective memory relating to lynching and racial violence in Laurens County, Bruce Baker calls attention to some of the ways that memory is transmitted and meaning attached to it. Equipped with a folklorist's acute ear and skills, he poses important questions about the mechanics of the transmission of memory. As many of the essays in this collection demonstrate, historical memory may be expressed in sculpture, civic rituals, or printed matter. Or, as in the case of the memory of lynchings, it may be principally oral. That most expressions of the local memory of lynching in South Carolina are oral is hardly coincidental. The white memory of racial violence has been selective and cursory. Meanwhile, local blacks for most of this century have had ample reason to avoid public discussions of lynching and white violence. But, just as the antebellum blacks described by Gregg Kimball compiled a "hidden transcript" of black resistance, so too did Laurens County blacks sustain a private discourse about lynching. Only now, in the wake of the civil rights movement, has the furtive black memory of racial oppression in Laurens County and elsewhere become public.

Baker's essay is suggestive of the likely evolution of local memory now that the black memory cannot be summarily silenced or ignored. Will a community's historical memory be lost, not as a result of present-day suppression but rather as a legacy of an earlier generation's efforts to forget? Can the pasts of southern blacks be incorporated into the whole range of cultural expressions that transmit public memory? Will white southerners willingly acknowledge the past as recalled by blacks? And how can the competing memories of whites and blacks in Laurens County—the former vague and nostalgic and the latter specific and prescriptive—be reconciled? To ponder these questions is to contemplate the future of southern regional identity. Certainly any effort to redress past inequities and to build inclusive communities of memory in the South would be well advised to consider these questions.

NOTE

1. Dona Brown, *Inventing New England: Regional Tourism in the Nineteenth Century* (Washington, D.C.: Smithsonian Institution Press, 1995); Emily Chester, "The Albigensian Crusade in the Construction of Collective Memory and Identity in Languedoc," in Michael Adcock, Emily Chester, and Jeremy Whiteman, eds., *Revolution, Society, and the Politics of Memory: Proceedings of the Tenth George Rudé Seminar on French History and Civilization* (Melbourne: University of Melbourne Press, 1996), 289–94; Charles Dellheim, *The Face of the Past: The Preservation of the Medieval Inheritance in Victorian England* (Cambridge: Cambridge University Press, 1982), esp. chap. 2. See also Leah Dilworth, *Imagining Indians in the Southwest: Persistent Visions of a Primitive Past* (Washington, D.C.: Smithsonian Institution Press, 1996), esp. chaps. 2–3.

Rich and Tender Remembering

Elite White Women and an Aesthetic
Sense of Place in Charleston, 1920s and 1930s

Stephanie E. Yuhl

Forty years after Appomattox, expatriate American author Henry James conducted an extensive tour of the eastern seaboard of the United States in an attempt to understand the physical qualities and human character of his native country. During his visit to Charleston, James encountered a city still reeling from the effects of the Civil War. At every turn in the economically stagnant and socially conservative town, he detected the persistent presence of the past—"the 'old' South . . . of a vanished order," he observed, "was hanging on there." In this "city of gardens and of absolutely no men," the author noted a peculiar "softness" pervading the narrow alleys, melancholy churchyards, and dilapidated mansions. James described this mix of history and "softness" as the "feminization" of Charleston's public identity: "Whereas the ancient order was masculine, fierce and moustachioed," he concluded in 1907, "the present is at the most a sort of sick lioness who has so visibly parted with her teeth and claws that we may patronizingly walk all round her."[1]

Two decades later, the feminine continued to exert a strong influence on Charleston's public identity, but the result—a burgeoning history-based tour-

Preservation pioneer Susan
Pringle Frost, shown here in
the Manigault House, saw
the architecture of her native
city "partly through a
golden haze of memory and
association." Courtesy of
the Charleston Museum,
Charleston, South Carolina.

ism industry—was anything but a "sick lioness." During the 1920s and early
1930s, elite white women formed the backbone of an energetic cultural movement that sought to celebrate the city's historic character through the fine
arts, literature, historic preservation, and folk music.[2] Perceiving the modern
age as a threat to their way of life and connected by family ties, friendship,
class, and race, these individuals sought to preserve and enshrine Charleston
as a site for enduring American traditions. Three elite women in particular,
historic preservationists Susan Pringle Frost and Nell McColl Pringle and
visual artist Alice Ravenel Huger Smith, contributed significantly to a material expression of an idealized version of Charleston's past and present.
Bolstered by strong personal and familial associations with the city, these
women configured a civic aesthetic along gender, class, and racial lines. First,
these women bestowed a decidedly female cast to the public image they
constructed for Charleston; they infused their restored buildings and paintings with objects and images out of their own feminine understanding of
history. Thus, domestic scenes of family, women, and romance played a
prominent role in their preservation and arts activities. Second, like folklorists and regionalists active elsewhere in the 1920s and 1930s, Frost, Pringle,
and Smith depicted either explicitly or implicitly the presence of the so-called
primitive in Charleston.[3] This "primitive" was reflected through stereotypes

Artist Alice Ravenel Huger
Smith. Courtesy of the
Charleston Museum,
Charleston, South Carolina.

of laboring African Americans, depicted most often as subservient beings
close to the soil, who acted as foils for the elite white civilization these cultural
producers sought to reify. The end result was the invention of an "official"
public culture for Charleston that emphasized domesticated traditions, social
hierarchy, and racial deference.[4] This aesthetic sense of place formed the
foundation of a highly marketable commodity known as "Old and Historic
Charleston" and helped restore in the interwar years some measure of
strength to the "lioness" that had been the city.

The paintings, etchings, publications, memoirs, and personal correspondence of Frost, Pringle, and Smith reveal that their vision of Charleston was
based largely on inherited conceptions of a shared worldview.[5] Shaped by
their own childhood memories and the collective recollections of their elders,
these women's historical understanding emerged from an invented past rife
with nostalgia and longing, constituting what South Carolina cultural critic
Henry Bellamann described in 1930 as a "rich and tender remembering" of
Charleston.[6] By expressing their personal and group memories through tan-

gible artifacts—in artwork to purchase and historic homes to tour—Frost, Pringle, and Smith made their memories accessible to locals and tourists alike, thus influencing how others remembered America's self-proclaimed "Most Historic City."[7]

This female historical memory active in Charleston between the world wars differed significantly from that most commonly associated with the post–Civil War white South. These elite women's vision of Charleston did not embrace what Gaines Foster has called "the Confederate Tradition" or the concerns of the "Lost Cause."[8] Unlike their predecessors in Ladies Memorial Associations across the South, Charleston's elite female cultural producers were not interested in refighting the Civil War or mourning the southern dead. Rather, in keeping with the fashionable Colonial Revival of their day, as well as the sectional reconciliation nurtured by World War I, Frost, Pringle, and Smith fixated on the city's colonial and antebellum past.[9] In doing so, they constructed an identity for Charleston that was at once local and national, and that united elite white Americans across the country under a common aesthetic banner dedicated to their version of social order and racial harmony. By nationalizing Charleston's past and omitting potentially divisive elements from their cultural production, Frost, Pringle, and Smith practiced historical amnesia as much as historical remembering and contributed significantly to making Charleston a major American tourist attraction.

On Wednesday, 21 April 1920, a group of thirty-two white residents of Charleston—twenty-nine women and three men—gathered in the front parlors of 20 South Battery, the home of Ernest and Nell Pringle. They met at the request of Miss Susan Pringle Frost, a local realtor, friend, and in several cases, cousin. Between sips of tea and mouthfuls of mocha cake, the group listened enraptured to Frost's charismatic pleas that they organize an association that would safeguard the city's architectural jewels. A descendant of one of Charleston's oldest families, the stout and stern Frost presented a formidable figure that April afternoon. The suffragist and seasoned businesswoman knew how to motivate a crowd. She forewarned of the imminent destruction of the Joseph Manigault House, a former rice planter's mansion built in 1803 at 350 Meeting Street, and the proposed construction of an automobile garage on the site. The potential loss of such an important Charleston monument was too much for the assembly to tolerate. So, following a long tradition of public activism among local women, they founded a historic preservation group called the Society for the Preservation of Old Dwellings (SPOD).[10]

As the rallying point for the 1920 founding of the Society for the Preservation of Old
Dwellings, the Joseph Manigault House (1803) provided paying tourists with "a glimpse
into the past that will always be a charming remembrance." Courtesy of the Charleston
Museum, Charleston, South Carolina.

Women's central participation in early preservation efforts influenced the
kinds of spaces and structures that SPOD preserved, and that, in turn, helped
shape the city's public character. In their two main projects, the early republican Manigault House and the colonial Heyward-Washington House (ca.
1749), Pringle, Frost, and their colleagues selected the kind of site that was
best known to them as women, the home. In fact, Frost chose the word
"dwellings" for her organization's name specifically because it conveyed her
reverent conception of homes as reliquaries of generations of Charleston's
finest white families.[11] By singling out spaces associated with private domestic activities over commercial, legal, industrial, or financial structures more
often associated with men, the women of SPOD asserted the importance of
family and femininity in the historic landscape.

Furthermore, in an attempt to breathe life back into their preservation
projects, Charleston women went beyond financial support and inserted
themselves physically into the historic spaces.[12] They held organizational
meetings on the two properties and decorated them with their own furnish-
ings, as well as period pieces borrowed from female relatives and friends.[13]
Women SPOD members led tours of the homes, directing visitors through the

historic spaces as guides to the past. This expression of female historical understanding and spatial colonization reached its height in the early 1930s, when Nell Pringle contemplated moving into the Manigault House to limit some of the property's massive financial burden on her family. According to her husband Ernest, Nell hoped to assemble there "the best pieces of her own furniture, and those of my sister . . . and the house will become a shrine for those interested in Colonial architecture and Colonial furniture." It was hoped that the lure of Nell as "permanent hostess" would make the site more attractive, more real, more alive to visitors whose money would ensure the survival of the continually endangered home.[14]

The material culture of the Manigault and Heyward-Washington Houses, then, may be described as an expression of elite white female culture. Through these women's efforts, the sites became more than palaces built by famous, wealthy white men. They became repositories of generations of familial memory—three-dimensional theaters where the everyday drama of domestic life, comprehensible to most visitors, many of whom were women, unfolded.[15]

As founder and president of the Preservation Society, Frost was the main spokesperson for preservation sentiment in Charleston throughout the 1920s. A strong sense of ancestral worship and an evocative historical memory influenced Frost's public and private cultural activism, often clouding her practical business sense.[16] She became involved in numerous money-losing projects for the sake of their historical associations. Of her financial struggles, Frost later reflected: "I have never commercialized my restoration work, or my love of the old and beautiful things of Charleston. A friend told me once that I had too much sentiment to make money, and I think that is partly true."[17] Alston Deas, Frost's successor as SPOD president, best explained his predecessor's emotional, historically intuitive approach to preservation: "She saw it [Charleston] partly through a golden haze of memory and association, not only for its buildings, and streets, and vistas, but also for those men and women she had known, or of whom she had been told, who dwelt there, and created, through a period of many generations, the town. . . . She never lost sight of this personal feeling for the spirit of Charleston."[18]

Frost's desire to restore the eastern portion of Tradd Street, which had fallen into horrible slum conditions by the 1910s, for instance, stemmed from this "golden haze of memory and association." She purchased the Georgian mansion at 61 Tradd because it was once owned by one of her elite eighteenth-century ancestors, Jacob Motte.[19] In doing so, Frost acted on an inherited conception of the street's former glory as one of the city's oldest

The Miles Brewton/Pringle
House (ca. 1769), the an-
cestral home of Susan Pringle Frost, enjoyed prom-
inence as a "must see"
tourist site in Charleston
during the interwar years.
Photo by Keith Knight.
Courtesy of the author.

residential centers; she sought to "put it back to where it was for so many
years before my knowledge." To Frost, the *real* Tradd Street was a place
she had never experienced firsthand but understood through the stories told
by her elder kinfolk. It was the place where only "the best people" of
Charleston, as opposed to its numerous contemporary African American
residents, had resided. To bring this "elevated" past into the present, the
houses had to be restored and white occupants had to move in.[20]

Furthermore, inherited historical memory powerfully influenced Frost
in her daily struggle to preserve and maintain her own family home, an
eighteenth-century mansion at 27 King Street. Built around 1769, the stately
Miles Brewton/Pringle House figured prominently, if problematically, in
Charleston history, serving as headquarters for both the invading British
(1780) and Union (1865) armies and as the home for five generations of
Frost's family.[21] For decades, Frost and her unmarried sisters followed the
example of their spinster Aunt Susan Pringle and poured their hearts, souls,

and meager finances into preserving this family mausoleum. "We shall not change a stone or plant, you may be sure," Susan Frost wrote her cousin in 1919, "only restore it with tender hands to what it was as we remember it as chil[dren] there."[22] The "Misses Frost" were convinced of the national historic importance of their home and felt duty-bound to protect and promote its architectural legacy. The Frost sisters were, as Nell Pringle's daughter recalled, "very proud, they were emotionally bound up with [the house]. . . . They were very noblesse oblige. They had a strong and probably very pathetic, probably ridiculous sense of honor and they loved that house."[23] SPOD, then, was the logical, institutionalized extension of Susan Frost's personal devotion to visible reminders of Charleston's past.

To fund the restoration project at 27 King Street, the Frosts opened its doors to a paying public that was willing to part with one dollar to tour the mansion, or perhaps with even more money to spend a few nights within its nostalgic walls. The possibility of gaining access inside an old-family residence of this sort was alluring to many visitors seeking a purportedly "authentic" experience of the locale. "People coming to Charleston are perennially unsatisfied," local museum director Laura Bragg explained in the early 1930s, "unless they are able to penetrate what seems to them the heart of Charleston life; that is, the interior of its homes."[24] To fill this market demand and to promote their celebration of an idealized colonial past, the Frost sisters guided tourists through the halls of the Miles Brewton/Pringle House, recounting in romantic detail the family legends and history surrounding the mansion. The thousands of signatures of tourists from all over the country and abroad that filled the guest books during the 1920s and 1930s indicate the heavy traffic at this site.[25]

Some elite visitors passed parts of the winter season as boarders in the Miles Brewton/Pringle House, soaking up the history lessons of its owners. "Did you ever sleep in the Louvre or the British Museum? Well, try the Pringle House," a Pittsburgh reporter mused in 1921. "If you are recommended by royalty . . . you may be received as a guest and permitted to sleep and eat in this marvelous house."[26] For these guests, Mary and Susan Frost served as conduits to the living past in a house filled with evocative relics. "I came to *see* Charleston and I go having *felt* Charleston deeply," one female visitor wrote the sisters, "in the spirit of her people, who like you have made Charleston and her history."[27] Another guest from New York gushed to her hostesses about "the memories and realities we recalled there or that you described for us so vividly—they seemed our own experiences."[28] For many, an overnight at 27 King Street constituted time travel. "Within these classic

doorways dwelt those to whom the past was the present and the future," a
Rhode Island woman remarked wistfully. "Here were the chairs and sofas and
mirrors acquired and cherished by men who made our history. Here the
gowns and hangings and rugs of an earlier century still showed much of their
former splendour. Here the coals still glowed in their old-time grates, tended
by Georges and Sarahs as in the days of yore." The visitor concluded that 27
King Street as showcased by Frost "speaks for all Americans."[29]

To Susan Frost's cousin Nell Pringle, SPOD's first vice president, the home
was also a kind of national family reliquary—a theater of domestic performance that recalled the daily drama of love affairs, engagements, and children's play. The Bennettsville, South Carolina, native married into an old,
prominent Charleston family long concerned with the preservation of, as her
husband Ernest described it, "furniture, landmarks, tradition."[30] She felt a
strong connection with the Pringle women and was similarly preoccupied
with preserving the past, committing herself and, eventually, her health, and
her family's financial well-being to saving the Manigault House. After an
initial investment of $5,000, the Pringles assumed the Manigault House debts
of over $40,000 and became the official owners of the property in March
1922.[31] That the Pringles undertook such a massive responsibility in the
midst of a citywide depression can be explained by Nell Pringle's romantic
attachment to Charleston and her commitment to keeping the legacy of its
historical memory alive.[32]

Nell Pringle saw more in the sweeping piazza and fine mantelpieces of the
Manigault House than a gem of Adam-style architecture. A reader of Victor
Hugo and Sir Walter Scott, a devotee of the Stuarts and Bonnie Prince
Charlie, Pringle indulged in fanciful imaginings about this domestic monument to the city's slaveholding, rice planter elite.[33] She became absorbed in
the legends of the house, going so far as to paint "blood red" its secret stair-
case and to commission a waxwork "to add to the eerie atmosphere."[34] For
Pringle, this public space became the embodiment of all that was correct and
worthy of protection in Charleston's premodern past. As hostess, she shared
her interpretation of this past with her paying visitors. Tourist Sophie Coll-
man from Cincinnati confirmed the efficacy of Pringle's presentation when
she declared enthusiastically that a tour of the Manigault House provided "a
glimpse into the past that will always be a charming remembrance."[35]

An undated short story, written by Pringle probably sometime in the early
1930s, best reveals her historical understanding, romantic sensibility, anti-
modern sentiments, and intensely personal, emotional investment in the
city's fine old residence. Set in "a chaste old city being allowed to crumble

into memory as its old fashions, its old houses and its old honor are changed into a motory, modern place of grease and cheapness," it is the story of one woman's struggle to stave off the "passing of the old order of things." The protagonist, Susan Snow, a barely hidden representation of Susan Frost, fights unsuccessfully to save the "Gault" house from destruction by "a city that was lulled into contentment by money in her hands, by moving pictures, jazz and motors." As part of a cultural battle between the traditional and the modern, Pringle considers the "Gault" mansion a bulwark against "the needless trample of commercialism" taking place in Charleston.³⁶

In her story, Pringle feminizes the "Gault" house. She characterizes it as a woman, a nurturing mother of children and lovers, a witness to "a past happiness we of this generation seek for in what we call 'success' but somehow are eluded." Likewise, she bestows on each room and architectural feature a feminized, domestic referent, as she rhapsodizes:

> Standing in the Gault doorway, there came visions of children having Christmas glee around a tree in the broad old hall—of the ball held up in the drawing room for the daughters, and the wedding, where the cake and wine [that] stood for the feast were spread below in the circular dining room—a room architects have struggled in vain to copy, as well as the flying staircase, down which, with a laugh, the bride ran to join her husband, and then together they went out of the great doorway, across the piazza, down the twisted stone steps, running quickly over the flagged walks, through a quaint lodge, out far into a life of happiness.

Viewed through Nell Pringle's eyes, the Manigault House was first and foremost the repository of women's historical memory and experiences, the protective shelter of daughters and brides. "Destroying it," she concludes, "seemed like murdering an aged gentlewoman."³⁷

Gendered expressions of Charleston's historical memory in the interwar years extended beyond historic preservation to include fine arts circles, particularly the watercolor landscapes of Alice Ravenel Huger Smith. Smith shared with her cousins Frost and Pringle an unswerving commitment to the preservation of the city's architectural, artistic, social, and historical heritage and to the concomitant promotion of a cultural agenda that resisted modernization and emphasized a nationalized Low Country heritage. In Smith's mind, enshrining the source of her artistic inspiration—the culture and the historical memories of her ancestors—was synonymous with protecting Charleston's heritage.

Alice Smith was born in 1876 into an old-line Charleston family in a stately
eighteenth-century brick mansion at 69 Church Street. Due to their strained
finances, the extended Smith family lived under one roof for much of Alice's
childhood and early adulthood. Surrounded by her aunts and uncles, her
widowed father, and her paternal grandmother in an environment wedded to
tradition and manners, Smith absorbed the values and beliefs of a generation
raised before the onset of the Civil War and loyal to its own selective memory
of antebellum culture.

She learned her history primarily from her father, an amateur historian,
and grandmother, whose tales of the past, Smith recalled, "wove in and out
of our childhood." She accompanied her father on weekend walking tours of
the city and its neighboring plantations and churchyards, searching for the
homes and graves of heroes from Charleston's illustrious past. Among the
most memorable ramble was a fifteen-mile walk one Sunday afternoon to
Middleton Place, an elaborate former rice plantation on the Ashley River.
This landmark fueled Smith's historical imagination and her associations of
the past with the land. "We strolled through its paths under the great oaks
looking out across the fields and river," she recounted in her memoirs. "We
had no lack of history there. The settlement of the Colony and the growth of
its laws and government brought one noted figure after another to walk those
paths with us, and the Revolution brought another group for me to imagine. . . . I had walked a long, long way to take part in these especial gatherings
in the footsteps of great men under these especial oaks." Under her father's
tutelage, history became an intensely personal endeavor for the young girl;
she learned to take pride in having the blood of English and Huguenot
colonial settlers in her veins. Of a cemetery walk one afternoon, Smith recalled: "We would visit hero after hero, we would meet famous soldiers and
sailors, lawyers, judges, captains of industry and delightful old ladies, and
many young ones too, for he had so many stories to tell us that history
became real. It was not in a book, it was here and now."[38]

Alice Smith, who was only twelve when her mother died, was also deeply
influenced by her grandmother, who loomed large in her upbringing. "Erect
in her black dress and widow's cap, smiling but firm," Grandmother Smith
offered stories of antebellum politics and life on the plantations of her youth,
replete with female fancies such as parties, waltzes, courtships, and wed-
dings. Her recollections encompassed not only her own living memory but
also, Alice Smith contended, memories handed down from earlier generations. Infused with what Smith described as "the feeling and facts of her

parents' days," Grandmother Smith bestowed on her granddaughter a legacy of oral narratives and visual portraits that stretched from the Revolutionary War through the early twentieth century.[39]

These vivid memory-based history lessons influenced the subject matter Alice Smith depicted in her artwork. Turning to the streets of her native city, which, she declared, "carry you back to old times, with scarcely an effort on your part," Smith drew and etched the homes of Charleston's oldest families. All the while, she allowed her imagination to run free and ruminate on "those who lived within their thick walls . . . in the midst of very stirring and romantic events." In 1917, in collaboration with her father, she wrote a book-length tribute to the city's architectural and historical glory, entitled *The Dwelling Houses of Charleston*.[40] Smith also turned her sentimental gaze to the natural beauty of the surrounding South Carolina Low Country, rendering its silent swamps, grassy fields, and heron-graced marshes in the translucent watercolors that, she argued, best suited her romantic conception of those places.[41] Although these images were commercially successful and were exhibited in major galleries and museums throughout the country and abroad, by far Smith's most ambitious, personally important, and memory-infused work was a series of thirty watercolors published by the William Morrow Company of New York in 1936. Smith entitled this culmination of her artistic career, *A Carolina Rice Plantation of the Fifties*.

Accompanied by a historical essay written by yet another cousin, Charleston writer Herbert Ravenel Sass, and her father's memoirs of his plantation boyhood, Smith's magnum opus was, in her own words, "intended to be a laurel wreath for that great civilization, of the rice-planting era in South Carolina."[42] Because commercial rice cultivation had all but disappeared in South Carolina by the late 1910s, Smith sought to create a visual record of the historic importance and beauty of an extinct culture for future generations of Charlestonians and Americans to admire. "When my generation is gone," she realized, "there will be no one to pass it on pictorially."[43] Seemingly on the basis of time spent during her youth on the dying rice plantations of the Cooper and Santee Rivers and listening to family lore, she set out to represent a vanished world of which she had no firsthand experience. Nonetheless, Smith, and likely many of her patrons, considered her imagined antebellum world an authentic reproduction of the longed-for but vanished past.[44]

The "Fifties" of the book's title were the 1850s, a period in history during which Smith's father and grandmother lived on rice plantations but which predated Smith's birth by twenty years. "I threw the book back to the Golden Age before the Confederate War," she noted years later without irony, "so as to give the right atmosphere because in my days times were hard."[45] Though she possessed no firsthand experience of life on a slave plantation, Smith believed that she was an ideal spokesperson for the institution because of her family associations and inherited memories. She filtered those memories through her impressionistic painter's palette of vivid pastels and iridescent whites, constructing a material reality of a fantastic antebellum world.

Not only were the subjects and scenarios represented by Smith based on hand-me-down memory, but also the actual technique she employed to produce the images depended on mental invention. Throughout her career, she relied on a method of reproduction that she termed "memory sketches." "Memory sketches" comprised detailed, direct observation of a scene, accompanied by perhaps a few cursory drawings, then the recollection of that image in her mind, and finally, in paint, once back in the comfort of her Charleston studio. Despite her obvious reliance on imagination, Smith defended her approach as a verifiable and near-scientific method of reproduction. In her own eyes, she was the accurate transmitter, not the creative inventor, of her region's historical and physical contours. "I do not mean *guessing*," Smith explained in 1926 to a member of the Orlando Art Association, "I mean remembering. Just as there is no guessing at a history lesson or at mathematics—they have to be remembered."[46] The "history" Smith remembered, absorbed at her ancestors' knees, merged with her encounters with the South Carolina environment and her own sentimental imaginings about the past to create an art that claimed the authoritative weight of "history."

Smith's rice series, which she dedicated to the memory of her recently deceased father, preserved and promoted a sentimental and paternalistic view of Charleston's past and its people. To her credit, Smith's paintings detailed the geography of the plantation and the processes involved in the cultivation of rice, from the preparation of the fields and the first seeding to the loading of the schooners for transportation of the finished product downriver to market. Her usually impressionistic watercolorist's brush outlined with precision the fields, trunks, canals, and buildings of the plantation, and it is in these images that Smith excelled aesthetically. When depicting the plantation's human population, however, her unbridled sentimentalism is inescapable and the final artistic result notably stiff.

In the opening image of her series, entitled "Sunday Morning at the Great House," for example, Smith reconstituted in watercolors a familiar scene of the "moonlight and magnolia South." This idyllic plantation image was already etched in white America's imagination from book illustrations of the

Part of a traveling exhibition of plantation watercolors, Alice R. H. Smith's "Sunday Morning at the Great House" promoted the artist's romanticized conception of Low Country slavery during "the Golden Age before the Confederate War." © Gibbes Museum of Art/Carolina Art Association.

late nineteenth and early twentieth centuries and from Hollywood films. It was popularized further by the publication of Margaret Mitchell's epic Civil War romance *Gone With the Wind*, which appeared in 1936, the same year as Smith's rice volume.[47] The composition of "Sunday Morning" once again reinforced the standard plantation mythology: a group of brightly dressed slaves neatly lined up, each in turn greeting the master and mistress before the veranda of the plantation house on a gloriously colorful Carolina morning. An air of easy interaction and mutual affection, underscored by the friendly exchanges between the black and white children in the scene, pervades the painting. A similarly pleasant glimpse of a harmonious interracial community is conveyed in "The Stack-Yard," in which white and black children romp on large stacks of rice stalks as the plantation mistress and her smiling slaves converse. In the right foreground, a young black girl offers a gift to her white mistress's child, a handpicked bouquet of flowers in a heartfelt gesture that Smith believed symbolized the reciprocal respect inherent in the planta-tion system.[48]

In several images in the rice book, Smith visually credits African American slaves with the dignity, skill, and exertion necessary to bring a crop to fruition while, nevertheless, depicting them as generic, faceless types akin to the monumental "noble peasants" of the nineteenth-century Barbizon school of painting. Significantly, her amorphous figures tend to melt into the agricultural landscape. Although her white figures are generally better defined and undeniably individual, even within the stereotyped confines of their pictorial roles as mistress and master, Smith's slaves do not escape anonymity. They are situated as part of a nondescript mass of humanity whose life was spent, according to Sass's accompanying "historical" essay, "working cheerfully and not too strenuously" under the Carolina sun.[49] Throughout her visual tribute to the slave South, Smith omits the reality of the drabness, heat, insects, exploitative labor, the slave patrol, and, above all, the repressive violence of black bondage. For Alice Smith, the line between the real and the remembered was entirely blurred. Thus, her antebellum plantation became a selectively romantic, pastel world where affectionate relations between enslaver and enslaved were played out under moss-hung live oaks.[50] The viewer is meant to go away from her rice series believing that, as Sass declared, "Nowhere in America was slavery a gentler, kinder thing than in the Carolina Low Country."[51]

Smith effectively conveyed her particular vision of South Carolina's antebellum culture to an art-interested American public that readily consumed it through book sales and a multicity, two-year tour of her rice paintings. Critics across the country internalized Smith's claims about the authenticity and accuracy of her compositions, describing them as "valuable historical documents." The *New York Times Book Review*, for example, observed that Smith "has rendered a special historical service" through her volume, which elegantly convinced the viewer that life "in the Low Country of this period was a really delightful one." The *Washington Star* found Smith's paintings to be "without [romantic] exaggeration." "Her works," the critic continued, "are very subtle but very true; they perpetuate and make tangible the elusive and lovely." Nationally renowned cultural critic Henry Seidel Canby of the *Saturday Review* emphasized the "real historical and sociological value" of Smith's work as "a contribution to the valid memorials of our rich American past." He concluded with an expression of nostalgia that Smith herself could have written: "Here was a culture which to a high degree developed an extraordinary sense of responsibility, and which encouraged the art of living, which has since been so generally lost. And it left its mark upon a countryside which these pictures commemorate."[52]

Smith donated her rice paintings to the Carolina Art Association, the managing body of Charleston's Gibbes Museum of Art, where they continue to resonate with viewers today. In fact, as recently as the mid-1970s the first eight images from the rice book, including domestic scenes of master and slave interacting, going to church, and relaxing by the slave cabins, were reproduced in a limited edition for sale at the museum shop. Her enduring presence on the city's aesthetic map has allowed Alice Smith to retain, even in death, her position as a chief interpreter of her place and its past.

Although the cultural activities of Frost, Pringle, and Smith were limited to fashioning the aesthetic landscape of their particular locale, their impulse to give permanence to personal, familial, and status group memories reveals a more universal human power struggle over the meaning and content of community. Public representations of community identity are often rooted in material artifacts depicting events or elements from a society's past that resonate in the present. These objects, be they paintings, monuments, restored homes, or historic markers, do not emerge naturally from a disinterested "historical" database. Instead, heritage totems most often reach their vaulted status through a laborious process of selection, interpretation, and promotion on the part of individuals and groups whose particular worldview and claims to social authority are reinforced through the historical narrative that the artifacts have the potential to articulate. It is significant, for example, that Charleston preservationists worked to protect the former residences of rice planters and not the equally common, smaller dwellings once occupied by the city's white working-class and free or enslaved black population. Preservationists infused the city's elegant albeit dilapidated mansions with a conception of history and of white privilege that encouraged personal and familial memorialization as well as a sanitization of the violent reality of the slave society's past. In doing so, these cultural producers exercised historical amnesia as much as historical memory, inscribing on public spaces a tightly delineated set of allowable interpretations that reinforced the racial, political, and economic status quo. Although the content they articulated is specific to their place and region, the process through which they imposed their will on the public sphere followed a more general desire for power and permanence.

More than a mere example of the manipulation of public memory for group gain, Charleston's story also offers a rich opportunity to expand and refine our understanding of how an essentially personal memory attains salience in a collective context. The presence of the individual is too often lost in discussions of public memory. At first glance, it appears that the voluntary organizations, such as the Society for the Preservation of New England

Antiquities or the Daughters of the Confederacy, and public institutions, such as the British National Trust and the Smithsonian, that are responsible for sponsoring and maintaining much of the work of public memory are nonhuman, disembodied agencies. In fact, they are comprised of individuals armed with subjective agendas concerning the appropriate content of popular discourses about the past and, by implication, the present and future. Furthermore, these agendas are sometimes shaped by personal factors that cannot be reduced to or wholly explained by stock analytic categories, such as the subjects' race, class, or gender. Instead, deeply intimate attributes, such as family narratives and childhood experiences, can and do influence the final ideological contours of public expressions of community memory and therefore must be brought to the fore. These forces help explain why individuals in Charleston, and in turn the organizations to which they belonged, fixated on certain elements of the past and were willing to make whatever sacrifices were necessary to ensure their perpetuation in the present.

To comprehend the machinations and intent of public memory, then, the personal investment of its shapers must be mined and highlighted. The evocative writings of Frost, Pringle, and Smith illustrate vividly the workings of highly personal motivations behind material expressions of community memory. Their words and actions suggest that deeply subjective factors beyond the standard categories of race, class, and gender, such as family narratives and childhood experiences, can and do influence the construction of public identity. Access to the private writings of individuals within organizations that claim to represent a larger public will is vital to attain a more nuanced understanding of how intimate issues are writ large upon the public sphere of history, often with significant social implications.

Toward the end of her life, Alice Smith boasted of her recall ability, "I can to this day, not just *remember* but put myself there in the past where I want to be."[53] "In the past where I want to be" might just as well have been said by Susan Frost or Nell Pringle. All three women revered the people and stories of Charleston's past and manipulated their material remnants to serve a socially regressive culture of nostalgia. Locating their privilege to speak for Charleston as the inheritance promised by their bloodlines, these elite women constructed a particular, memory-based, white female aesthetic in historic preservation and the visual arts. Through the homes they preserved and opened to the public, and their paintings and publications, Frost, Pringle, and Smith transformed their selective personal or small group memories and perceptions of place into an accessible, material public identity for Charleston and the nation. Although the social, political, and racial order that

244   *Stephanie E. Yuhl*

gave birth to the world they sought to preserve did not endure beyond their lifetimes, the tangible expressions of their memory work have endured. Thus, to a considerable degree, their work achieved what they set out to accomplish—to control how others within and beyond their community remember the city and its place in American history.

NOTES

1. Henry James, *The American Scene* (London: Chapman and Hall, Ltd., 1907), 403, 414, 417. For the lingering effects of the Civil War on Charleston's economy and social attitudes, see Don H. Doyle, *New Men, New Cities, New South: Atlanta, Nashville, Charleston, Mobile, 1860–1910* (Chapel Hill: University of North Carolina Press, 1990), and Blaine A. Brownell, *The Urban Ethos in the South, 1920–1930* (Baton Rouge: Louisiana State University Press, 1975).

2. The term "elite" describing these women is not meant to connote only economic status. Rich they were not, particularly when they are considered in relation to the economic elites of other American cities in the 1920s and 1930s. In fact, these women struggled to survive financially in their chronically depressed city. Instead of a strictly economic standard, then, these cultural producers were "elite" by white Charleston's criteria—blood, marriage, family name, and the economic, social, and political status of their South Carolina Low Country slave-owning ancestors. As Charleston artist and historic preservationist Elizabeth O'Neill Verner explained in the early 1930s, "The social lines are clearly marked but they are lines of blood and breeding and have nothing to do with bank accounts." Verner, Artist's Sketchbook [pre-1 Aug. 1935], property of Elizabeth Verner Hamilton, 38 Tradd Street, Charleston.

3. For the role of primitivism in regionalism, see Leah Dilworth, *Imagining Indians in the Southwest: Persistent Visions of a Primitive Past* (Washington, D.C.: Smithsonian Institution Press, 1996); Robert L. Dorman, *Revolt of the Provinces: The Regionalist Movement in America, 1920–1945* (Chapel Hill: University of North Carolina Press, 1993); and Ian McKay, *The Quest of the Folk: Antimodernism and Cultural Selection in Twentieth-Century Nova Scotia* (Montreal: McGill-Queen's University Press, 1994).

4. In *Remaking America: Public Memory, Commemoration, and Patriotism in the Twentieth Century* (Princeton: Princeton University Press, 1992), John Bodnar defines public memory as "a body of beliefs and ideas about the past that helps a public or society understand both its past, present, and by implication, its future" (p. 15). Bodnar contends that culture becomes "official" when public memory is put forth by social leaders interested in maintaining the status quo and in reducing "the power of competing interests that threaten the attainment of their goals." Official culture "relies on the restatement of reality in ideal rather than complex or ambiguous terms. It presents the past in an abstract basis of timelessness and sacredness" (pp. 13–14). On the relationship between monuments and historical identity, see also David Lowenthal, *The Past Is a Foreign Country* (New York: Cambridge University Press, 1985), 265–69, 323–25.

5. In recent years scholars have examined the variety of ways in which memory, as a tool for recovering the past, operates to organize societies, to validate hierarchy, to invent tradition, to regulate access to or exclusion from political, social, and economic power, to create and resist consensus identities, and to control public discourse. As a category for

historical analysis, memory remains a somewhat elusive concept that is still largely in its defining stage. Nonetheless, it can provide a useful lens for examining the process through which individuals and groups fashion identities, as in the case of Charleston. For more on memory and the construction of historical identities, see Benedict Anderson, *Imagined Communities: Reflections on the Origin and Spread of Nationalism* (London: Verso, 1983); Bodnar, *Remaking America*; Paul Connerton, *How Societies Remember* (New York: Cambridge University Press, 1989); Ian Donnachie and Christopher Whatley, eds., *The Manufacture of Scottish History* (Edinburgh: Polygon, 1992); Eric Hobsbawn and Terence Ranger, eds., *The Invention of Tradition* (New York: Cambridge University Press, 1983); *Journal of American History* 75 (March 1989), special issue on "Memory and American History"; Michael Kammen, *Mystic Chords of Memory: The Transformation of Tradition in American Culture* (New York: Knopf, 1991); Lowenthal, *The Past Is a Foreign Country*; and Patrick Wright, *On Living in an Old Country: The National Past in Contemporary Britain* (London: Verso, 1985).

6. H. B. [Henry Bellamann], "Art in Charleston," *The State* (Columbia, S.C.), 14 December 1930. Bellamann deployed the phrase to describe the feelings evoked by Alice Ravenel Huger Smith's watercolors.

7. In an attempt to bolster tourism, Mayor Thomas P. Stoney in 1924 declared Charleston "America's Most Historic City." Stoney, "Mayor Stoney's Annual Address," *Year Book, City of Charleston, South Carolina* (Charleston: N.p., 1924), liv.

8. Gaines M. Foster, *Ghosts of the Confederacy: Defeat, the Lost Cause, and the Emergence of the New South, 1865–1913* (New York: Oxford University Press, 1987), 5.

9. On the Colonial Revival movement in general, see Alan Axelrod, ed., *The Colonial Revival in America* (New York: Norton, 1985). For the marketing and consumption of Colonial Revival through historical tourism, see Dona Brown, *Inventing New England: Regional Tourism in the Nineteenth Century* (Washington, D.C.: Smithsonian Institution Press, 1995), and Sarah L. Giffen and Kevin D. Murphy, eds., *"A Noble and Dignified Stream": The Piscataqua Region in the Colonial Revival* (York, Maine: Old York Historical Society, 1992).

10. SPOD became known as the Preservation Society of Charleston, which still operates as an advocacy group today. For the first SPOD meeting and the subsequent financial struggle of the Pringle family over the Manigault House, see J. Holton Fant, "Tea and Talk: A Preservation Memoir," *Preservation Progress* (Fall 1990): 1–4, 17.

11. Frost's obituary notes, "She [Frost] chose the original name to include 'dwelling' because as used in the Bible, the word implied a permanent residence passed down from generation to generation." "Rites Set Today for Miss Frost," *Charleston News and Courier*, 8 October 1960. See also William Henry Hanckel, "The Preservation Movement in Charleston, 1920–1962" (M.A. thesis, University of South Carolina, 1962), 11, and Michael Kevin Fenton, " 'Why Not Leave Our Canvas Unmarred?': A History of the Preservation Society of Charleston, 1920–1990" (M.A. thesis, University of South Carolina, 1990), 5.

12. Women in Deerfield, Mass., followed a similar path of promoting a social agenda through their control of public historical spaces and the subsequent marketing of history. Of Deerfield, Marla R. Miller and Anne Digan Lanning note: "Through the manipulation of commemorative and commercial spaces, these women promoted a romanticized colonial past in an effort to restore 'traditional' moral values, to rehabilitate Anglo-Saxon communal pride and cultural authority, and to revitalize white middle class economic life."

Miller and Lanning, "'Common Parlors': Women and the Recreation of Community Identity in Deerfield, Massachusetts, 1870–1920," *Gender and History* (November 1994): 435–55.

13. Minutes, 16 June 1920, 6 February 1931, Society for the Preservation of Old Dwellings (hereafter SPOD) Papers, Preservation Society of Charleston (hereafter PSC).

14. Ernest H. Pringle, Charleston, to G. Corner Fenhagen, Baltimore, 16 April 1932, Manigault House Papers, South Carolina Historical Society, Charleston (hereafter SCHS).

15. Manigault House Guest Book, Manigault House Papers, SCHS; Miles Brewton House Guest Book, SCHS; Miles Brewton House Guest Books, by permission of the owner, Peter Manigault, 27 King Street, Charleston.

16. See Sidney R. Bland, *Preserving Charleston's Past, Shaping Its Future: The Life and Times of Susan Pringle Frost* (Westport, Conn.: Greenwood Press, 1994), for a recent biography and overview of her career.

17. "Miss Frost Tells History of Her Preservation Work," *Charleston News and Courier*, 24 February 1941. See also Susan Pringle Frost to Nell Pringle, 12 May 1931, Manigault House Papers, SCHS: "I myself have had very heavy losses in business of various kinds. . . . I have lost heavily on Tradd St.; the public thinks I made money and it makes little difference to me what the public thinks; my books will show that on almost every restored house sold I made big losses."

18. Alston Deas, "They Shall See Your Good Works," *Preservation Progress* (May 1962): 1.

19. Bland, *Preserving Charleston's Past*, 81.

20. Susan Frost to William Watts Ball, 8 June 1916, William Watts Ball Papers, Rare Book, Manuscript, and Special Collections Library, Duke University, Durham. Frost relied on the skills of Thomas Mayhem Pinckney, a local African American artisan, whom she hired to "reclaim" several Tradd Street properties from their status as black slums. By the 1930s white residents, including fellow preservationist and artist Elizabeth O'Neill Verner, moved into the area, pushing blacks out and, in most cases, northward to the Charleston Neck. Ironically, the appeal of a home in the historic district to white buyers initiated a significant shift in the downtown racial demographics from a historically, racially integrated residential population to what is today an ahistorical, nearly all-white area of the city. See also Bland, *Preserving Charleston's Past*, 83, 84–86, and Mabel Pollitzer, interview transcript, 19 September 1973, Southern Historical Collection, University of North Carolina Library, Chapel Hill.

21. For historical and architectural details of the Miles Brewton/Pringle House, see "27 King Street," "Information for Guides of Historic Charleston," Tourism Commission, City of Charleston (1985), 285–87, and Susan Pringle Frost, "Highlights of the Miles Brewton House" (Charleston: Privately published, 1944).

22. Susan Pringle Frost to "Nina [Pringle]," 21 January 1919, quoted in Richard Coté, *Guide to the Alston-Pringle-Frost Manuscript Collection*, SCHS, 70.

23. Margaretta Pringle Childs, interview by author, 22 November 1993. See also Susan Pringle Frost, "Highlights of the Miles Brewton House." In this pamphlet, Frost presented her personal memorial to the house and its inhabitants, including African American servants and family pets, through prose, poetry, and photographs.

24. Laura Bragg, typed essay, [1930–31], Laura Bragg Papers, SCHS.

25. In March and April 1929 alone, over 1,300 tourists crossed the double-porticoed

threshold of the Brewton/Pringle House. Ten years later, in April 1939, nearly 20 people visited the home each day. See Miles Brewton House Guest Books, 29 December 1919–March 1931, 29 March 1930–March 1953, by permission of the owner, Peter Manigault, 27 King Street, Charleston.

26. Harvey B. Gaul, "Southern City Combines Attractions of Others," *Pittsburgh Sunday Post*, 24 April 1921, clipping in Miles Brewton House Scrapbook, Alston-Pringle-Frost Family Papers, SCHS.

27. Elisabeth E. Thorne to "My dear Miss Mary," [late 1920s–early 1930s], Miles Brewton House Scrapbook, Alston-Pringle-Frost Family Papers, SCHS.

28. Caroline H. Gaffields to "My dear Hostesses," 10 January 1931, ibid.

29. Elizabeth Covell, essay, 11 April 1937, reprinted in Frost, "Highlights of the Miles Brewton House" (1944).

30. Pringle to Fenhagen, 16 April 1932, Manigault House Papers, SCHS. Ernest Pringle recalled that one of his earliest jobs as a boy was selling newspapers to help raise money for the Colonial Dames' restoration of the Powder Magazine in which his mother participated.

31. Ibid. See also Bland, *Preserving Charleston's Past*, 115.

32. According to Nell Pringle's daughter, Margaretta, the timing of the family's commitment to the Manigault House could not have been worse. Shortly afterward, Ernest lost his job as president of the Bank of Charleston and went to work as a salesman for his younger brother's fertilizer plant. Finally, he established his own investment business to support Nell, their six children, and the Manigault House. Margaretta Pringle Childs, interview by author, 22 November 1993.

33. Ibid.

34. "Society Restores Manigault House, Mrs. Ernest Pringle Is Leader in Work of Preserving City's Beauty," *Charleston News and Courier*, 25 February [1931–32], SPOD Scrapbook, 1932–45, SPOD Papers, SCHS. There is no indication in the historical record that the waxwork was ever produced.

35. Manigault House Guest Book, May 1929, Manigault House Papers, SCHS.

36. Nell McColl Pringle, Untitled short story, [1930], Susan Pringle Frost File, SCHS. Comments written in Nell Pringle's hand on the first page of the story note that "This is my good description of the mental anguish I have gone through about the Manigault house—It was submitted & refused by House Beautiful & others."

37. Ibid.

38. Alice Ravenel Huger Smith, "Reminiscences," in Martha R. Severens, *Alice Ravenel Huger Smith: An Artist, a Time, a Place* (Charleston: Carolina Art Association, 1993) (hereafter "Reminiscences"), 73, 82–83.

39. Ibid., 71, 82–83, 68–69.

40. Ibid., 93; Alice R. Huger Smith and D. E. Huger Smith, *The Dwelling Houses of Charleston, South Carolina* (Philadelphia: Lippincott, 1917).

41. Alice Ravenel Huger Smith to Mrs. Ruby Warren, Orlando Art Association, 22 November 1926, Alice Ravenel Huger Smith Papers, SCHS.

42. "Reminiscences," 97.

43. "Watercolors by Local Artist Shown at Gibbes Art Gallery," *Charleston Evening Post*, 14 December 1936.

44. "Reminiscences," 97–106.

45. Ibid., 97.

46. Alice Ravenel Huger Smith to Mrs. Ruby Warren, Orlando Art Association, 22 November 1926, Alice Ravenel Huger Smith Papers, SCHS.

47. The scholarship of the most prominent historian of the antebellum American South during this period, Ulrich Bonnell Phillips, reinforced this interpretation of slavery as a benevolent institution. See Phillips, *American Negro Slavery* (New York: Appleton, 1918) and *Life and Labor in the Old South* (Boston: Little, Brown, 1929). See also Frances Pendleton Gaines, *The Southern Plantation: A Study in the Development and the Accuracy of a Tradition* (New York: Columbia University Press, 1924).

48. It is important to note that Charleston's African American community boasted several artists who were active during the 1920s and 1930s, such as mortician/painter Edwin Harleston and photographer Michael Francis Blake. They captured on canvas and film images of a competing reality of Charleston that was divorced from a romantic slave past—i.e., the city's thriving African American middle class. See Maurine Akua McDaniel, "Edwin Augustus Harleston: Portrait Painter, 1882–1931" (Ph.D. diss., Emory University, 1994); Jeanne Moutoussamy-Ashe, *Viewfinder: Black Women Photographers* (New York: Dodd, Mead, 1986), 34–39; and Michael Francis Blake Papers, Rare Books, Manuscripts, and Special Collections Library, Duke University, Durham.

49. Herbert Ravenel Sass, "The Rice Coast: Its Story and Its Meaning," in Alice R. Huger Smith, *A Carolina Rice Plantation of the Fifties* (New York: Morrow, 1936), 13.

50. Where convenient to her conception of the past, Smith even modified her revered father's recollections. All of the African American slaves pictured in her series, for example, are dressed in a variety of vivid colors, their clothing perfectly intact, whereas her father's memoirs recount that the slaves were dressed in coarse "blue or grey woolens" on annual allotment which assuredly looked ragged by the season's end. See D. E. Huger Smith, "A Plantation Boyhood," in Smith, *Carolina Rice Plantation*, 59–97.

51. Sass, "The Rice Coast," 42. Sass argues that slavery in the South Carolina Low Country was an exceptionally benevolent familial institution: " 'Slavery' is not a good name for the institution as it existed on the plantations of the Carolina Low Country. The planter did not speak of his negroes as slaves; he called them his 'people' and as he spoke of them so he thought of them—they were his people, not his chattels, and many of them were his loved and devoted friends" (p. 39).

52. "Southern Scenes," *New York Herald Tribune*, 29 November 1936; C. McD. Puckette, "Life on Carolina Rice Plantations," *New York Times Book Review*, 3 January 1937; "Watercolors of a Carolina Rice Plantation to Be Exhibited," *Washington Star*, 9 January 1937; and Henry Seidel Canby, "The Rice Coast in Art," *Saturday Review*, 5 December 1936—all clippings in Alice Ravenel Huger Smith Scrapbook, Gibbes Museum of Art, Charleston.

53. "Reminiscences," 98.

To Keep the Spirit of
Mountain Culture Alive

Tourism and Historical Memory
in the Southern Highlands

C. Brenden Martin

On 16 January 1950 the rough and rowdy behavior of "Slim Jim" Pryor attracted a crowd of curious onlookers at a busy intersection in downtown Chattanooga, Tennessee. Brandishing a hog rifle and a moonshine jug and donning a coonskin cap, Pryor made a spectacle of himself by waving his gun in the air, clogging, and yelling "like a wild man." When a policeman investigated the cause of this public disturbance, Pryor feigned drunkenness and stumbled into the officer's arms. Just as Pryor was about to be arrested, a motorcade arrived with more than twenty people who dressed like hillbillies and Indians. Only then did the officer learn that Slim Jim, this seemingly intoxicated mountaineer, was actually a Gatlinburg booster who had arrived a few minutes in advance of the "Travellin' Hillbillies," a promotional motorcade touring the South to lure visitors to the Great Smoky Mountains with stereotypical depictions of hillbillies and Cherokee Indians.[1]

Slim Jim Pryor's brush with the law is indicative of how tourism has shaped and reflected the collective historical memory of the Appalachian South. Outside visitors constructed the popular perception of the southern

Members of the 1950 "Travellin' Hillbillies" motorcade posed for this picture before embarking on their promotional tour through the South. Kneeling in front is "Slim Jim" Pryor with his coonskin cap and hog rifle. Standing next to him is McKinley Ross, vice chief of the Cherokee Qualla Reservation, wearing a feathered headdress of the Plains Indian culture. Courtesy of Mrs. Fran Stalcup.

highlands as a quaint, primitive region inhabited by white hillbillies and savage Indians. With their identity imposed by outsiders, both Native and white Americans could not easily escape the perceptions created and perpetuated by the media. The residents of the southern highlands, who had limited occupational opportunities, could not easily ignore the modest rewards to be earned by adapting themselves to the marketplace. Thus, many native mountain residents embraced and exploited the stereotypical images of hillbillies and Indians to promote tourism and earn profits. In a conscious attempt to validate America's preconceptions of the region, private entrepreneurs and government agencies developed staged demonstrations of "authentic" culture and other packaged forms of regional identity that, in essence, commodified mountain culture and reinforced inaccurate historical perceptions about mountain whites and Cherokee Indians.

In the early nineteenth century, the mountain South existed as a distinct region of the nation only in physiographic terms. Geologists, botanists, and physicians had long recognized the rugged topography, natural fauna, and healthful climate as distinctive environmental features of the southern mountain ranges, but antebellum visitors rarely regarded southern highlanders as any different from rural residents elsewhere in the South.[2] After the Civil War, however, America's consciousness and conception of the mountain South gradually evolved until, by World War I, the southern highlands existed in the public mind as a distinct region inhabited by contemporary white pioneers. But the emerging perception of the region—a place where "pure-bred" Anglo-Saxon whites lived—inherently marginalized and obscured the lives and history of the Cherokees.

Let us first examine the process of constructing and marketing the historical memory of white Appalachians. The invention of southern Appalachia as a culturally distinct region inhabited by quaint, yet uncivilized whites was a process that involved a wide array of nonindigenous individuals, including local color writers, missionaries, settlement school workers, scholars, journalists, and philanthropists who often focused on the most archaic aspects of life in the region, creating the perception of a static culture.[3] Although scholars have long recognized that a myriad of "outsiders" constructed the complex mythical image of the region, few have fully appreciated the role of tourism and tourists in the process of molding and perpetuating regional identity and historical memory. Many individuals who shaped the public's perception of the mountain South, particularly writers, first gathered their impressions of the region while visiting as tourists. Moreover, travel accounts and tourism promotionals both contributed to and reinforced the idea of regional backwardness.

The notion of Appalachian backwardness was first articulated to mass audiences through the local color literary movement. In the context of post–Civil War cultural nationalism, dialect tales and sketches of the vernacular cultures of America emerged as important literary forms. A new school of writers—including George Washington Cable, Mark Twain, Thomas Nelson Page, Bret Harte, and Joel Chandler Harris—turned away from the stylized romanticism of their predecessors and confronted the phenomena peculiar to their own section of the nation. Searching for a national identity amid the changes brought by immigration, industrialization, and urbanization, Americans were eager to learn about the peculiar and exotic "little corners" of the nation's rural backcountry.

In the 1870s and 1880s magazines such as *Scribner's Monthly*, *Harper's Weekly* and *Atlantic Monthly* published dozens of travel accounts and local color stories that first conveyed the idea of the southern highlands as a unique region inhabited by a quaint people of pure Anglo-Saxon stock living a pioneer existence. Appealing to middle-class readers, publishers encouraged local color writers to focus on regional peculiarities and to ignore the homogeneous features of American life.[4] Since the mountain South appeared to be a perfect source for local color material, a number of notable writers, including Mary Noailles Murfree, Christian Reid, and Charles Dudley Warner, went to the southern highlands as tourists in search of people and places to write about. Consequently, the tourist process shaped their vision of mountain life which, in turn, shaped America's historical memory of the mountain South.

Curiously, the static image of the mountain South arose at a time when the region was experiencing profound economic, social, and cultural changes because of the growth of railroads, extractive industries, and tourism. As railroads became the primary mode of transportation into the region, visitors had less direct interaction with mountain people than ever before. The travel experience became more passively oriented. Whereas earlier generations of travelers often encountered natives in the backcountry, modern travel by railroad prevented these encounters and insulated tourists from the mountain people. Traveling by rail directly to an exclusive resort, tourists crossed paths with but rarely engaged local residents. In addition, because proprietors of exclusive resort hotels often imported their labor force from outside the region, tourists had limited opportunities to interact directly with native mountain residents in these places. Thus, it is not surprising that tourists were able to persist in imagining the southern highlands as a static region, despite the fact that the people of the mountain South were undergoing momentous changes in the late nineteenth and early twentieth centuries. From the visitors' perspective, everything in their insulated tourist experience validated America's perception of the region.

To Americans ambivalent about the rapid changes brought by industrialization, immigration, and urbanization, Appalachia represented a symbolic counterpoint to the progressive thrust of modern urban society. Searching for the source of national uniqueness, many Americans looked to the southern highlands as a source of folk heritage. White Americans increasingly sought out the nation's Anglo-Celtic folk roots in the isolated southern mountains, where there supposedly resided a pure white people whose lives were untouched by modern society. In southern Appalachia, one apparently could find authentic Anglo-American folk traditions untainted by foreign influences.

The few visitors who went to the region looking for an "authentic" cultural experience were disappointed to find that the Old World folkways they had read about seemed to be quickly dying off in the wake of the arrival of railroads and extractive industries. As more and more mountain residents were drawn into the wage economy, they left behind their traditional ways of life and eagerly joined in the American culture of consumption. Some tourists who arrived with preconceived expectations of the region's idyllic folkways lamented what they perceived as the passing of the last vestige of American pioneer heritage. Among the nonindigenous visitors who were disappointed to find that the old mountain folkways were vanishing were Edith Vanderbilt and Frances Goodrich, two prominent leaders in the movement to "revive" the Appalachian handicraft tradition.

Born in New York and raised in Ohio, Goodrich was among the first to realize the market appeal of Appalachian handicrafts. She studied painting at the Yale School of Fine Arts but in the late 1880s decided to devote her life to missionary work for the Presbyterian Church. She traveled to Asheville, North Carolina, for the first time in 1890 as a tourist only to discover that there was a great need for missionaries "to bring some sort of order out of chaos" back in the mountains.[5] Like so many other northern Protestant missionaries in the late nineteenth century, Goodrich discovered that mountaineers were an "exceptional population" who were worthy of social workers' attentions. She decided to stay in the North Carolina mountains "to help them to be good."[6]

Goodrich's first encounters with the rugged life in the mountainous backcountry shocked her as it did many other upper-class visitors. In her words, "I had no conception of such a state of society as exists here. . . . I wish you could see some of the homes where they asked me to stay overnight. I have never seen a whole town of such forlorn wretchedness."[7] In 1892 she began her missionary work in Brittain's Cove, twelve miles from Asheville. After she had gained the acceptance of the local residents, a woman from the cove gave her a forty-year-old woven coverlet as a gift. As an artist, Goodrich recognized the fine craftsmanship of this gift. But she discovered to her dismay that few women in the area still possessed the handicraft skills she had associated with the region. She concluded that here was a "fine craft dying out and desirable to revive."[8]

Goodrich helped to foster the "rediscovery" of the mountain people's cultural roots by opening a shop to teach handicraft skills to women. Founded in 1895 along the old Buncombe Turnpike, Allanstand Cottage Industries allowed tourists to take in local color in a contrived, but nonetheless marketable manner. Most patrons of the shop were tourists who wanted to see the handiworks of the mountain people without actually having to encounter these quaint, yet poor folk. To reach a broader audience, Allanstand held an annual exhibition and sale in Asheville during the peak tourist season. A permanent salesroom in Asheville was later opened in 1908.[9] Appealing primarily to tourists, Allanstand Industries helped to reinforce the static image of the southern highlands by fulfilling tourists' expectations of the region's Old World folkways.

Another tourist dismayed by the apparent decline of the region's handicraft tradition was Edith Vanderbilt, the wife of Biltmore Estate owner George Vanderbilt. During the late 1890s the Vanderbilts and their guests traveled extensively through the Blue Ridge Mountains looking for "authentic" homespun fabric to send as gifts to their northern friends. Perhaps inspired by the success of Allanstand Industries, Edith Vanderbilt in 1901 founded Biltmore Industries, an industrial school that provided handicraft training to young men and women living in and around Biltmore Village. The school offered a number of classes on crafts, but the weaving of fine homespun cloth and the making of wooden furniture and accessories proved to be the most useful, popular, and practical.[10] Proximity to the large tourist market in Asheville enabled Biltmore Industries to operate a popular souvenir shop where visitors could buy "authentic" mountain handicrafts. Its dependence on tourism is underscored by the fact that Grove Park Inn, one of Asheville's most popular hotels, purchased Biltmore Industries and moved its operations to the hotel in 1917.[11]

So began the southern highland handicrafts revival movement, a classic case of cultural selection in which outside interests restructured and reinterpreted the mountaineers' historical memory for the market appeal of tourists. The revival of mountain handicrafts was in part a response to tourists' desire to have their expectations of the region validated. In the absence of an "authentic" mountain experience, handicrafts offered them at least a contrived version of an authentic culture.

While the handicrafts industry helped to perpetuate the pioneer myth long after pioneer conditions ceased to exist in the southern highlands, travel writers continued to reinforce the region's static image. Their articles, which portrayed the region as a land forgotten by time, had a direct and immediate influence on tourists' perceptions of the mountain South. As tourism became an increasingly important leisure activity for middle-class Americans, travel magazines emerged as a vital source for resort owners to inform and attract potential tourists. Articles in *Travel*, the most widely read travel magazine in America in the 1920s, attempted to attract visitors to highland resorts with exaggerated stereotypes of the region.

For instance, in April 1928 *Travel* published an article about Gatlinburg, Tennessee, by Laura Thornborough, entitled "Americans the Twentieth Century Forgot." Thornborough, a Knoxville native who frequently vacationed in the Smoky Mountains, depicted the residents of Gatlinburg as

"descendants of pioneer ancestors, proud of their Anglo-Saxon stock," who
"cling to pioneer ways because of the condition under which they live." In
declaring that "they are dependent upon their own industries for the neces-
sities of life," she gave the inaccurate impression that Gatlinburg residents
were completely isolated from the outside world, when in fact the town was
by then developing rapidly as the premier resort of the Smokies. When
Thornborough described the handicrafts "tradition" of the Smokies, she
failed to mention that the handicrafts industry was a tourist-driven, standardized endeavor introduced by Pi Beta Phi (a women's fraternity that established a settlement school in Gatlinburg in 1912) just a decade earlier. Thornborough noted that "the women weave towels, rugs, draperies, coverlets, and
piece quilts. . . . In and around Gatlinburg there is scarcely a home without a
loom." To readers of *Travel* who longed to escape from the hustle-bustle of
their everyday lives and visit a place where life was simple and quaint, she
offered idyllic images of life in the mountains. For instance, "Stopping at the
home of a weaver you find her singing to a flaxen-haired, blue eyed child of
two or three playing at her knees. You pause to catch the words of the song. It
is an old English ballad."[12]

The editors of *Travel* were by no means alone in recognizing the market
appeal of quaintness in drawing tourists to the region, for there were many
others who used western North Carolina's perceived cultural heritage to
attract visitors. Folk festivals were among the first events that offered staged
versions of regional culture. The earliest and most popular was the annual
Mountain Dance and Folk Festival in Asheville. The person primarily responsible for its conception and coordination was Bascom Lamar Lunsford, a
lawyer and farmer from South Turkey Creek who was concerned that, with
western North Carolina's growing sophistication, the folk songs and dances
of the region were quickly dying out. Also a showman, Lunsford recognized
that regional culture offered an opportunity to attract people and attention. In
1927 he persuaded the Asheville Chamber of Commerce to sponsor a Mountain Dance and Folk Festival. When the first festival was held at the height of
the 1928 tourist season, the Asheville Chamber and the *Asheville Citizen*
vigorously promoted the event as a tourist attraction. While the Chamber's
advertisements promised "the finest folk musicians and dancers ever assembled in one place," the *Citizen* urged visitors to "witness this once in a lifetime
event."[13] Due largely to Lunsford's showmanship and the Asheville Chamber's promotional efforts, the Mountain Dance and Folk Festival was a huge

success. This "once in a lifetime event" became an annual affair that, even to-day, draws tens of thousands of tourists to Asheville every year. Several other tourist-oriented highland folk festivals were produced, such as Jean Thomas's Folk Song Festival in Ashland, Kentucky (1930), and Annabel Morris Buchanan's White Top Folk Festival in southwestern Virginia (1931).[14]

Although individuals and local agencies did much to present staged versions of regional culture, it was the federal government that led the way in preserving and marketing regional identity as a tourist attraction. Indeed, the National Park Service (NPS) was among the first agencies, public or private, to use regional identity in a coordinated manner to draw tourists. In developing and promoting the Great Smoky Mountains National Park and the Blue Ridge Parkway, the NPS strove to portray the region as a land forgotten by time and inhabited by sturdy mountaineers and stoic Native Americans. The Park Service not only built miles of split rail fences and restored numerous log cabins, but it also systematically removed structures that did not fit the frontier image they sought to convey in these parks.

The National Park Service based much of its cultural interpretation of the Great Smoky Mountains on Horace Kephart's *Our Southern Highlanders*. Kephart, a well-educated Midwesterner, had moved to the Smokies to escape his family and alcohol problems. A few years later he wrote his highly acclaimed book, which came to be regarded as the authoritative work on life in the Smoky Mountains. *Our Southern Highlanders* graphically describes many stereotypes associated with the region, including the pioneer lifestyle and Elizabethan dialect of white mountaineers, as well as feuding and moonshining. Directly quoting Kephart, one NPS brochure refers to the mountaineers' "strong and even violent independence that made them forsake all the comforts of civilization." Other NPS promotionals highlight "the great asset afforded the park by the presence of the rough-hewn cabin, the highlander, and the folk-songs and ballads."[15]

Kephart's widely accepted interpretation of life in the Smokies guided the growth of the Great Smoky Mountains National Park in profound ways. For instance, in developing Cades Cove, one of its most popular sections, the NPS sacrificed historical accuracy to create a picturesque pioneer landscape. Durwood Dunn has shown that, contrary to the public view, Cades Cove was by no means isolated from the outside world. In fact, in the early twentieth century it was rapidly modernizing with the coming of better roads, industrial logging, commercial farming, and tourism. Nevertheless, the NPS consciously worked to portray the area as a land of isolated and independent pioneers. After purchasing the land in Cades Cove, the Park Service systematically razed dozens of modern frame houses and stores but carefully restored the primitive log cabins, barns, and churches that captured the pioneer image they sought to project.[16]

To be consistent with the contrived physical environment that they constructed for tourists in the Great Smoky Mountains National Park, the National Park Service launched a cultural preservation effort in the early 1940s that drew heavily from the Kephart paradigm. For instance, in 1941 it published a report entitled *Mountain Speech in the Great Smokies*, which plainly stated that "mountain speech represents a survival of Elizabethan English, as some romantic writers have claimed. One cannot deny that fourteenth, fifteenth, and sixteenth century forms persist in the Great Smokies." In the same year the NPS's *Report on the Preservation of Mountain Culture in Great Smoky Mountains National Park* argued that "every care should be taken to preserve as many of their heirlooms as possible and to keep the spirit of mountain culture alive." Insisting that "there can be no doubt about the fact that mountain culture and the way it appeared when it was first made known to an astonished world, are dying," the report urged the government to take measures to preserve the "pioneer culture that cannot be found in any other part of the country." The reports provided a blueprint for the Park Service's cultural interpretation of the Great Smoky Mountains.[17]

The pattern of interpretation and promotion employed by the National Park Service for the Great Smoky Mountains was much the same for the Blue Ridge Parkway. As with the Smokies, the popular pioneer myth guided the parkway's development and interpretation. To project the pioneer theme, the Park Service built split rail fences along the highway and selectively retained and reconstructed log cabins and old farmsteads. Likewise, it removed or excluded from view all elements that did not fit the frontier myth. Consequently, the major historical and cultural attractions along the parkway revolve around the supposed pioneer lifestyle of southern highlanders—such as demonstrations of grist milling and blacksmithing, a reconstructed pioneer homestead, and displays of regional handicrafts.[18]

As with the Great Smoky Mountains National Park, the Park Service exploited the mountaineer image to promote the Blue Ridge Parkway. NPS officials used the photographs of Earl Palmer in their advertisements to draw tourists to cultural attractions along the parkway. As Jean Haskell Speer points out, Palmer chose to ignore Appalachia's modern elements in his photographs and instead focused on the mythical mountaineer, "the quaint embodiment of cherished American values: independence, pride, self-reliance, loyalty."[19] One of Palmer's favorite subjects was Newton Hylton, who became the poster boy of sorts for Blue Ridge Parkway promotionals. With his long beard, weathered face, and old-fashioned clothes, Hylton looked and acted like the quintessential Appalachian mountaineer. One advertisement explained that their "Uncle Newt" character "was born out of love and admiration for the mountainesque local color he represents."[20]

In using the pioneer myth to draw tourists, the National Park Service sympathetically portrayed mountaineers as hardworking, independent yeomen farmers who represented all that was good about America. Private tourism entrepreneurs, however, were not as committed to depicting mountain residents in a positive light. These promoters, including those native to the region, often chose to entertain visitors with the less flattering, but more recognizable images of the southern hillbilly. Although the contemporary pioneer figure remained a strong selling point for tourists, the hillbilly representation emerged as the most powerful and most popular stereotype of the region primarily because comic strips, hillbilly music, and Hollywood depicted southern highlanders as backward, ignorant, and violent. Reflecting the mountaineer figures in popular culture and at tourist resorts, Americans generally came to believe that life in Appalachia was characterized by feuding, moonshining, ignorance, incest, laziness, and moral depravity.

As the hillbilly image became deeply entrenched in the American mind, it is not surprising that it became a popular theme to attract tourists raised on *L'il Abner* and *The Beverly Hillbillies*. After World War II many private entrepreneurs developed a variety of contrived events, attractions, and souvenirs that projected the hillbilly identity. One might expect such an unsavory representation to be rejected by indigenous mountain residents, but their identity was not their own to create. Facing grim economic prospects in the region, many indigenous entrepreneurs willingly embraced and exploited the hillbilly theme for economic gain. To give the people what they wanted and make more money, many mountaineers played the part of a hillbilly to validate the preconceptions of their visitors.

This phenomenon is obvious in Gatlinburg, where the tourist economy was long dominated by a handful of local families. When Gatlinburg emerged as a popular resort in the 1920s, the community offered relatively primitive accommodations, but it had a thriving handicrafts "tradition" established by the Arrowmont settlement school a decade earlier. Learning by example from the National Park Service and the Arrow Craft Shop, local business leaders gradually adopted the use of regional identity and cultural stereotypes as selling points to tourists. In the 1920s and 1930s, before the onset of major commercial development, promotionals attracted visitors with the quaint images of mountain life that were still readily apparent in Gatlinburg. For instance, a 1927 advertisement pitched the Mountain View Hotel as a "rustic hotel" and included a picture of a typical mountaineer's cabin to illustrate the local color of the area. Prior to World War II, such pastoral ambience reflected the reality of the rural environment.[21] Ironically, the town's success in promoting the *image* of a quiet mountain village helped to erase the *reality* of the people's rural mountain lifestyle. As commercial development gradually erased the bucolic character of Gatlinburg and neighboring Pigeon Forge after the war, many local businesses contrived attractions and projected a false identity that enabled visitors to validate their stereotypical expectations of the region's "primitive" culture.

The "Travellin' Hillbillies" motorcade of 1950 marked a turning point in Gatlinburg's invented hillbilly identity. The promotional tour was the brainchild of Allen Stalcup, a western North Carolina native who had moved to Gatlinburg in the late 1930s and opened the town's first gift shop, the Nut Shop. Hoping to divert Midwestern tourists to Gatlinburg on their way back from Florida, Stalcup convinced most of the town's commercial elite to dress as hillbillies and drive around the South acting like country bumpkins. According to Fran Stalcup, Allen's wife, "we talked just as hillbilly as we could." In early January Gatlinburg's wealthiest business leaders, including mayor Dick Whaley and Rellie Maples, put on shabby clothes and coarse mannerisms and set off for Florida. They decorated their cars with posters of Snuffy Smith and signs reading "Florida in Winter, Gatlinburg on Your Way Home" and "We Ain't Mad with Nobody." Arrow Craft even mounted an antique loom on the roof of a car. The boosters intentionally caused a scene everywhere they went. After Slim Jim Pryor's spectacle in downtown Chattanooga, they proceeded to Atlanta, where they sang "On Top of Old Smoky" with members of the Georgia state senate. As they traveled to and through the Sunshine State, they held impromptu square dances and sang traditional mountain ballads at each stop. Clearly, their spectacles of regional stereotypes demonstrated that native mountain residents were quite willing to portray themselves as hillbillies to attract tourists.[22]

After World War II, the hillbilly motif emerged as a dominant theme for the southern highland tourist industry. In Sevier County, Tennessee, where Gatlinburg and Pigeon Forge are located, tourist attractions often intermingled the hillbilly image with powerful symbols of the Deep South—namely, rednecks and the Confederate flag. These symbols of Dixie grew increasingly apparent in gift shops, restaurants, and tourist attractions after 1960 as more and more whites traveled from the Deep South to spend their vacations in Sevier County. A comparison of the 1956 and 1985 surveys of visitors to the Great Smoky Mountains National Park shows that the total market share of tourists from Deep South states grew by nearly 100 percent over the twenty-nine-year period. This trend during a period of racial turmoil in the South may explain why private entrepreneurs turned to the racially charged symbols of Dixie to attract and satisfy their overwhelmingly white clientele. Ironically, the appeal to Confederate images contradicts the strong pro-Union sentiment of Sevier County during the Civil War. Indeed, the Confederacy is much more popular in Sevier today than it was in 1861, when the county rejected secession by a vote of 1,302 to 1. Nevertheless, in virtually every place involving tourism, including restaurants, museums, gift shops, and entertainment parks, entrepreneurs blended Appalachian stereotypes with symbols of Dixie.[23]

No tourist attraction more clearly illustrates the skewed nature of marketing historical memory than the evolution of Dollywood, Sevier County's premier theme park. An amusement park called "Rebel Railroad" first opened on the site in 1961, just in time for the centennial of the Civil War. Owned by Grover and Harry Robbins from Blowing Rock, North Carolina, Rebel Railroad offered "good Confederate citizens" the opportunity to ride a five-mile train route through "hostile" territory and to help repel a Yankee assault on the train, an experience that must have seemed almost surrealistic to visitors from the North and Midwest. After the Rebels whipped the Yankees in a staged skirmish, the train returned to the village, where tourists could shop in the general store, watch the blacksmith, or eat a sandwich while catching the can-can act in the saloon. Initially, Rebel Railroad was a moderate success, but by the late 1960s the Robbinses were strapped by other investments and opted to sell the park to Art Modell and the Cleveland Browns football team.[24]

Modell reinvented the attraction and created an Old West theme park called "Goldrush Junction." The area received a multimillion-dollar facelift that included the construction of a wood shop, a gristmill, and a sawmill, as well as several children's rides. Tourists still rode the train, but Indians replaced Yankees as the ambushing aggressors. Shortly after the park reopened, the Cleveland investors realized that the quaint images of mountain life were a much stronger selling point than the Old West to visitors to the Smokies. By this time, popular TV shows such as *Hee Haw* and *The Beverly Hillbillies* had reaffirmed the hillbilly stereotypes in the minds of a new

A favorite attraction at Goldrush Junction theme park in Pigeon Forge, Tennessee, was a train ride featuring a staged skirmish between cowboys and Indians. The cowboys always defeated the attacking Indians. Courtesy of Dollywood.

generation of Americans. Consequently, the park's owners abandoned the Old West theme and, by the start of the 1972 season, converted Goldrush Junction to an "ole-timey" mountain pioneer format with "down-home vittles and wholesome family entertainment."[25]

In spite of substantial investments, the park floundered. Mired in debt, Modell and the Browns organization sold Goldrush Junction in 1976 to Jack and Pete Herschend, the pioneers of modern tourism in Branson, Missouri. In Branson, the Herschend brothers had developed a successful mountaineer theme park called "Silver Dollar City," which they sought to replicate in the Tennessee park. At Pigeon Forge employees wore hillbilly garb and were instructed to provide visitors with "down-home hospitality and constant smiles." The tourists arrived to watch craftspeople making "authentic" Appalachian handicrafts and to listen to genuine mountain music. Though craft displays and hillbilly musicians were mainstays for the park, one of the more memorable attractions was a mock reenactment of the Hatfield/McCoy feud. Every few hours a gunfight broke out between the two warring clans and ended with the arrest of the feisty, moonshine-nipping Ma McCoy, played by Blount County native Flo Headrick.[26]

In 1985 the Herschends heard that country music star Dolly Parton wanted to invest in the booming tourist industry of her native Sevier County. After a year of negotiations, she entered the business as a minority partner. The park was rechristened "Dollywood," giving most visitors the impression that she was the sole owner of the park. Since Parton's buxom blonde image was consistent with the "Daisy Mae" stereotype of Appalachian women, she was an appropriate symbol to promote the park. On opening day, Parton proclaimed that "one of the things that I wanted to do with a park like this was to preserve the Smoky Mountain heritage for people to come here and see what we're really all about, rather than just have some Hollywood bunch of people portray Tennessee mountain people in the ways they often do."[27]

Nevertheless, the hillbilly attractions of Dollywood continued to perpetuate many of the region's negative stereotypes. For instance, the *Elwood Smooch Hillbilly Revue* was for several years one of the most popular and visible attractions at Dollywood. Elwood Smooch was the stage name of local entertainer Billy Baker, who dressed, talked, joked, and sang as a stupid hillbilly. Often wearing a toilet seat around his neck, Smooch played on the popular stereotype of the ignorant, lazy hayseed. Some native mountain residents were offended by what one letter to the *Knoxville News-Sentinel* called a "tasteless, degrading portrayal of a Tennessee hillbilly." But judging from the reaction to this letter, the Elwood Smooch act apparently went over well with most of Dollywood's visitors, who expected to be entertained with hillbilly caricatures. In defense of Smooch, a tourist from Chicago wrote to the newspaper that "[w]hen I showed my family from Chicago the pictures [of Smooch] they found them funny." Likewise, a Knoxville resident indicated that many people in the region embraced this stereotype: "we free Southerners can appreciate our hillbilly culture as shown by Elwood Smooch."[28]

Tourism's role in the construction and commodification of white mountaineers, then, shaped the historical memory of the region in profound ways. Not only do tourists apparently believe the hillbilly myth, many longtime mountain residents have embraced it as well. This process of developing, marketing, and reinforcing the identity of white mountaineers closely parallels the experience of eastern Cherokees, whose popular image also was not of their own making. Yet, much like the white mountain residents who embraced the hillbilly stereotype, Cherokees also adapted their image to lure tourists.

The Cherokees who stayed behind in western North Carolina after the U.S. Army forcibly removed their brethren from ancestral lands in the late

1830s are referred to as the Eastern Band of Cherokees. Living on the Qualla Boundary, they saw few tourists until the twentieth century. The age of the automobile and North Carolina's Good Roads Program, however, made tourism a reality for the Cherokee people. As tourism boomed in western North Carolina in the 1920s, more and more visitors traveled to the Qualla Boundary to see "real" Native Americans and to buy "authentic" Indian wares.[29]

The development of the Great Smoky Mountains National Park and the construction of a network of highways in the region set the course for the Eastern Cherokees' economic dependence on tourism. In the 1920s tribal leaders joined an alliance of businessmen, conservationists, and politicians in the movement to set aside land for a national park in the Great Smoky Mountains. By the early 1930s it was clear that the pattern of roads to and through the national park would converge on the eastern side of the park in the town of Cherokee on the Qualla Reservation. In addition, the terminus of the Blue Ridge Parkway led into the town of Cherokee. This situation made "prospects for . . . this place quite attractive," according to tribal superintendent R. L. Spalsbury.[30]

Reinforcing this orientation to tourism was the new federal Indian policy initiated by John Collier, President Franklin D. Roosevelt's commissioner of Indian affairs, who reversed earlier efforts to eradicate Indian cultural identity and encouraged cultural pluralism among Native Americans. The federal government's new policy, coupled with the rise of mass tourism, revived tribal craftsmanship, which had declined significantly with Cherokees' growing participation in the cash economy. Although the Cherokees had held a successful annual tribal crafts fair beginning in September 1914, it was not until the creation of the Great Smoky Mountains National Park that handicrafts emerged as big business on the reservation.[31]

Following the founding of the national park, Cherokee leaders and NPS officials alike recognized that the presence of Native Americans was "a valuable asset to the Park. They will be a big drawing card for it."[32] In the quest to attract tourists to the Qualla Boundary, flair was more important than historical accuracy. Much like the mountain whites, Cherokees proved to be adept at adopting cultural stereotypes to meet the expectations of visitors raised on the images of Indians in popular culture. Most white Americans derived their perceptions of Native Americans from dime novels, Wild West Shows, and, perhaps most important, Hollywood. Since these mediums of popular culture presented primarily the image of Plains Indians, the ingrained stereotype in the American mind was that of a Sioux warrior, wearing a feathered headdress

This page from a 1938 tour book of the Great Smoky Mountains National Park indicates that the National Park Service recognized that Cherokee Indians were a potential tourist draw. Courtesy of the National Park Service Archives.

and war paint, and sitting on a horse holding a tomahawk or a bow and arrow, with his "squaw" and papoose living in a tepee. Some Cherokees adopted these images to lure visitors who wanted to see "real" Native Americans.[33]

One of the earliest examples of a Cherokee playing the role of a Plains Indian was in a 1935 parade in Asheville, when Goingback Chiltoskey garbed himself in the regalia of a Sioux warrior and mounted a horse. Years later Chiltoskey admitted, "I hadn't never been on a horse" before that parade. In 1950 McKinley Ross, vice chief of the Cherokee reservation, accompanied the Travellin' Hillbillies motorcade wearing a feathered headdress and greeting everyone with the ubiquitous Indian salutation, "how!" Perhaps the most visible and popular example of this stereotypical role can be found in the tourist-oriented community of Cherokee, where for the last several decades, several Cherokee men have donned war bonnets and hawked the Pan-Indian Hollywood stereotype along U.S. 441 and U.S. 19. During the tourist season, they stand in front of gift shops dressed in Plains regalia to lure customers into the shops. They often receive tips and charge money to allow the curious to take their pictures. Consequently, for those who look like "real" Indians with copper skin and black hair, "chiefing" can be quite profitable.

The fact that tepees and war bonnets have nothing to do with Cherokee culture does not bother the tourists. One Cherokee "chief" commented: "Ninety percent of the tourists who come here look for Indians who live in tepees and run around naked and hide behind trees, ride horses. Very few of the people who come to Cherokee expect to find the Indians as they live today." Henry Lambert, one of the more popular "chiefs," once experimented by wearing authentic Cherokee clothing and beadwork. To his dismay, the tourists almost without exception passed him by so they could take pictures of "real" Indians in front of nearby stores. "I'm not stupid," Lambert later remarked, "I stuck with the war bonnet." Realizing where their earning potential lay, Lambert and the other "chiefs" simply gave the tourists the fantasy they wanted.[34]

Though "chiefing" suggests that tourism has eroded the Cherokees' cultural identity, the tourist industry has also paradoxically boosted its preservation. Prior to the post–World War II tourist boom, there was not a great difference between the residents of Cherokee and neighboring communities in terms of dress, language, food, housing, jobs, and religion. Little remained on the Qualla Boundary of the Cherokee cultural heritage. But tourism helped to spawn an interest in the cultural and historical legacy of the Cherokees.

Nothing better illustrates this point than the development of the popular outdoor drama *Unto These Hills*. Tracing the historical experience of the Cherokee people, the play originated with the Western North Carolina Associated Communities (WNCAC), a group of white businessmen who organized in 1947 for the express purpose of developing tourism in the North Carolina mountains. Recognizing that increased tourism in Cherokee would benefit communities throughout the region, the WNCAC took on as its first project the production of an outdoor drama on the Qualla Reservation. In 1948 WNCAC formed the Cherokee Historical Association (CHA), a white-dominated organization whose chairman, Harry Buchanan, was a businessman from Hendersonville, North Carolina. CHA hired Kermit Hunter, a drama student at the University of North Carolina in Chapel Hill, to write the play. *Unto These Hills* recounts the story of the Cherokees from their first encounter with Spanish explorers, through their tragic betrayal by Andrew Jackson and the infamous Trail of Tears, to the beginnings of a peaceful life for the Eastern Band of Cherokees. When the play debuted in 1950 at the Mountainside Amphitheater, it was written, produced, and directed by white men. Most of the actors were also white. In spite of some historical inaccuracies and stereotypical characterizations, *Unto These Hills* was engrossing entertainment. It quickly became the most popular tourist attraction on the Qualla Reservation, playing to audiences of over two thousand six nights a week during the tourist season.

The success of *Unto These Hills* inspired the CHA to undertake other projects to attract visitors to the region. In 1952 it opened Oconaluftee Village, a reproduction of a mid-eighteenth-century Cherokee village; peopled with Cherokees who carry out an ancient way of life, Oconaluftee Village offers an authenticity that stands in sharp contrast to the "chiefs" who ply their wares along the highway. A few years later the Historical Association purchased an extensive collection of Cherokee artifacts from a private collector and developed the Museum of the Cherokee Indian, which is now a modern, high-tech facility interpreting the triumphs and tragedies of the Cherokees. Although each of these CHA endeavors has its shortcomings, they offer, among the tourist attractions, the most accurate representations of Cherokee history and culture. Indeed, they helped to inspire a modest revival in the study of the Cherokee language at nearby Western Carolina University.[35]

Cherokee is by no means the only place where tourism has been a catalyst for cultural and historic preservation. Indeed, on numerous instances in the mountain South a burgeoning tourist industry provided the economic rationale to preserve a community's historical structures, such as in Flat Rock, North Carolina, or Townsend, Tennessee. In addition to inspiring historic preservation and sustaining cultural institutions, tourism has also helped to preserve the idea of cultural distinctiveness in the southern highlands. But much of the emphasis is on cultural elements that are overly simplistic or of dubious authenticity, such as log cabins, dulcimer music, and handicrafts.

The relationship between tourism and historical memory in the mountain South is thus complicated and even paradoxical. Tourism has often acted as a catalyst for cultural and historic preservation movements; but the interpretation and presentation of these efforts were often tailored for commercial appeal. Hence, simplistic and romanticized identities of mountain whites and Cherokee Indians fulfill tourists' desires to experience local culture without the messiness and complexities of the real thing. Local residents have been willing to play the stereotypical role of hillbilly or Native American to make money and to preserve the illusion of local color in overly commercialized resorts. At the same time, the growth of tourism in many communities has produced a dramatic shift to an urban commercial lifestyle that belies the rustic, down-home image conveyed by local tourist attractions. And yet tour-

Stereotypical images of hillbillies remain a powerful lure for tourists. This sign uses the hillbilly cartoon character Snuffy Smith to attract visitors' attention. Photo by Brenden Martin.

ism and "cultural preservation" in the mountain South have safeguarded the notion of regional identity, however skewed and fallacious.

NOTES

1. "Coonskin-Capped Smokies Booster Halts Traffic, Nearly Goes to Jail," *Chattanooga Times*, 17 January 1950.

2. Henry Shapiro, *Appalachia on Our Mind: The Southern Mountains and Mountaineers in the American Consciousness, 1870–1920* (Chapel Hill: University of North Carolina Press, 1978), ii–iv.

3. See ibid.; Allen Batteau, *The Invention of Appalachia* (Tucson: University of Arizona Press, 1990); Ronald D. Eller, *Miners, Millhands, and Mountaineers: Industrialization of the Appalachian South, 1888–1930* (Knoxville: University of Tennessee Press, 1982); and David E. Whisnant, *All That Is Native and Fine: The Politics of Culture in an American Region* (Chapel Hill: University of North Carolina Press, 1983).

4. Richard Cary, *Mary N. Murfree* (New York: Twayne Publishers, 1967), 36.

5. Fred Eastman, "An Artist in Religion," *Christian Century*, 6 August 1930, 6.

6. Frances Louisa Goodrich, *Mountain Homespun* (Knoxville: University of Tennessee Press, 1989), 16.

7. Goodrich quoted in Jane Greenleaf, *Home Mission Monthly* 4 (1891): 112.

8. Goodrich, *Mountain Homespun*, 22.

9. Allen H. Eaton, *Handicrafts of the Southern Highlands* (New York: Russell Sage Foundation, 1937), 64–66.

10. Ibid., 69–70.

11. Bruce E. Johnson, *Built for the Ages: A History of the Grove Park Inn* (Asheville: Grove Park Inn and Country Club, 1991), 58.

12. Laura Thornborough, "Americans the Twentieth Century Forgot," *Travel*, April 1928, 1–7, 44–45.

13. *Asheville Citizen*, 23 June 1927; "History of the Asheville Chamber of Commerce," apparently written by the Asheville Chamber [1960], Archives, Asheville Chamber of Commerce, Asheville. The Bascom Lamar Lunsford Scrapbook at Mars Hill College has numerous newspaper clippings about the life of Lunsford.

14. Whisnant, *All That Is Native and Fine*, 185.

15. Horace Kephart, *Our Southern Highlanders* (New York: Outing Publishing Co., 1913); National Park Service, *The Great Smoky Mountains National Park: The Land and Its People* (Washington, D.C.: Department of Interior, 1941), 128–29.

16. Durwood Dunn, *Cades Cove: The Life and Death of an Appalachian Community* (Knoxville: University of Tennessee Press, 1985), 255–56.

17. Charles Grossman, *Mountain Speech in the Great Smokies* (Washington, D.C.: National Park Service, 1941), 12; Hans Huth, *Report on the Preservation of Mountain Culture in the Great Smoky Mountains National Park* (Washington, D.C.: National Park Service, 1941), 3, 8, 26.

18. Phil Noblitt, "The Blue Ridge Parkway and the Myth of the Pioneer," *Appalachian Journal* 21 (1994): 394–408.

19. Jean Haskell Speer, *The Appalachian Photographs of Earl Palmer* (Lexington: University of Kentucky Press, 1990), ix.

20. William G. Lord, *Blue Ridge Parkway Guide Book* (Asheville: Hexagon, 1976), 110, Great Smoky Mountains National Park Archives, Sugarlands Visitor Center.

21. Great Smoky Mountains Travel Bureau, *Tours in the Great Smoky Mountains* (Knoxville: Great Smoky Mountains Publishing Co., 1929).

22. Fran Stalcup, taped interview by Brenden Martin, 12 March 1993, Little River Museum and History Collection, Little River Museum, Townsend, Tenn.; Vic Weals, "'Traveling Hillbillies' Greet Georgia Senate," *Knoxville Journal*, 18 January 1950; "Mountain Folk in Colorful Costumes Pay Tampa a Visit to Plug Their Town," *Tampa Morning Tribune*, 28 January 1950.

23. John D. Peine and James R. Renfro, *Visitor Use Patterns at the Great Smoky Mountains National Park*, Research/Resources Management Report SER-90 (Atlanta: Department of Interior, National Park Service, 1988), 25; Jack Neely, "Where Dolly Meets Dali," *Metro Pulse* 4 (3–17 June 1994): 13.

24. Robert Freeman, "Pigeon Forge: A Progressive Little City," *Tennessee Planner* 23 (December 1963): 1; Neely, "Where Dolly Meets Dali," 13–14; *The Dollywood Story*, pamphlet (Pigeon Forge, Tenn.: Dollywood Publicity Office, 1994), 1.

25. "Goldrush Junction Creating Old Time Atmosphere," *Knoxville Journal*, 13 May 1971; *The Dollywood Story*, 1.

26. "Family Emphasis Planned, Says New Goldrush Owners," *Knoxville Journal*, 8 April 1976; Silver Dollar City Scrapbook, Dollywood Publicity Office, Pigeon Forge, Tenn.

27. *Mountain Press*, 23 July 1985; Lisa Gubernick, "A Curb on the Ego," *Forbes*, 14 September 1992, 418–19.

28. Letters to the editor from Joanie L. Byrd (1 January 1995, F-5), Michelle Shelton

(1 January 1995, F-5), and Melanie Bennett (18 December 1994, F-5), *Knoxville News-Sentinel*.

29. John R. Finger, *Cherokee Americans: The Eastern Band of Cherokees in the Twentieth Century* (Lincoln: University of Nebraska Press, 1991), 54–56.

30. Ibid., 78–79.

31. Ibid., 98; Lawrence C. Kelly, *The Assault on Assimilation: John C. Collier and the Origins of Indian Policy Reform* (Albuquerque: University of New Mexico Press, 1983).

32. Finger, *Cherokee Americans*, 98.

33. Larry French, "Tourism and Indian Exploitation: A Social Indictment," *Indian Historian* 10 (1977): 19–24.

34. Finger, *Cherokee Americans*, 163, 98; Larry R. Stucki, "Will the 'Real' Indian Survive?: Tourism and Affluence at Cherokee, North Carolina," in Richard Salisbury and Elizabeth Tooker, eds., *Affluence and Cultural Survival* (Washington, D.C.: American Ethnological Society, 1984), 65–66; Laurence French and Jim Hornbuckle, eds., *The Cherokee Perspective: Written by Eastern Cherokees* (Boone: Appalachian Consortium Press, 1981), 80.

35. Stucki, "Will the 'Real' Indian Survive?," 65–71.

Le Reveil de la Louisiane

Memory and Acadian Identity, 1920–1960

W. Fitzhugh Brundage

The recent Cajun "revival" in Louisiana is a striking example of the revitalization and reassertion of ethnic identity in the modern South. The music, food, and folkways of the descendants of the French settlers of southwestern Louisiana have become so familiar as to be clichés. Fast-food restaurants sell Cajun-spiced hamburgers, television advertisers use Cajun music to evoke an atmosphere of *bon temps*, and architects crowd subdivisions with faux-Acadian homes. Meanwhile, public authorities have promoted the preservation of the French language in Louisiana, designated Acadiana as a distinct cultural region, and even officially denounced derogatory slang references to Cajuns.

The campaign to preserve and promote Cajun culture during the past three decades has attracted considerable interest. For some observers, the recent Cajun revival demonstrates the possibilities for mobilized communities to slow the erosion of their inherited culture. For other observers, the modest accomplishments of the revival underscore the corrosive and relentless absorption of distinctive communities into modern and mass consumer culture. In a real sense, both assessments are valid. An understanding of the origins of the Cajun revival underscores the ability of a small number of cultural activists to promote consciously and to mold systematically regional culture. It also reveals that the revival of Acadian or Cajun culture, from its inception, has been woven inexorably together with its commercialization.

The contemporary renaissance of all things Cajun may be traced to the activities of a small but prominent group of Acadian enthusiasts active during the quarter century after 1920. The stated goal of the Acadian revival was to make both Acadians and Americans mindful of the Acadian heritage in Louisiana. For all of their professed reverence for traditional culture and their wish to forestall the cultural effects of "progress," the revivalists themselves were powerful instigators of cultural change. By looking upon the residents of southwestern Louisiana as a vulnerable culture whose traditions were tenuous and would persist only through insistent reeducation by cultural enthusiasts sensitive to traditional culture, the Acadian revivalists advocated deliberate cultural intervention. Because of their status and power, they were able to institutionalize their ideas about Acadian identity. They defined what Acadian culture was and adapted decidedly modern means—pageants, films, radio, festivals, and publications—to promote appreciation of it.

In the process, the Acadian revivalists crafted representations of the Cajun past that became tropes—ubiquitous depictions so widely known that their meaning required little if any explanation. Over time their notions took root within Acadians' conceptions of themselves and their culture and precluded consideration of the contemporary realities of Acadia, to say nothing of the dynamics of change in the region. This rendering of Acadian history has had far-reaching consequences for the perceptions of Cajuns. The Acadian "movement" institutionalized a Cajun ethnic consciousness that stressed the "otherness" of white non-Cajun southerners. Cajuns, the revivalists told themselves and others, were not really of the South; the peasantlike Acadians had no place in the familiar narrative of southern history as told by other white southerners. The historical twists and turns of the region's past—slavery, sectionalism, and the traumas of the New South—happened to other people elsewhere. In a real sense, the revivalists placed the Acadian saga outside the flow of southern and, indeed, American history.

The central theme in the Acadian revival of the twentieth century has been the presumption that the Acadians are a people united by a tragic history. Louisiana Acadians trace their origins to peasant settlers who migrated from France to the west coast of "Acadie" or Nova Scotia, beginning in 1604. There they lived in scattered settlements, tended subsistence crops, and raised cattle. Neither their geographic isolation nor their wary attitude toward colonial officials could protect them from the recurring contests between the English, French, and Indians over the surrounding region. After France ceded Nova Scotia to Great Britain in 1713, the British distrusted the loyalty of the French-speaking and Catholic Acadians. During the subsequent half century, British officials endeavored to coerce the Acadians into renouncing their professed neutrality. Finally, at the onset of the Seven Years' War in 1755, British authorities ordered the expulsion of the Acadians.[1]

During the ensuing exile—the so-called *grand dérangement*—about eight thousand Acadians were scattered from Massachusetts to Georgia. Deprived of everything except their movable possessions, the Acadians lost their lands to Anglo-American settlers whom the British trusted. The American colonies received the exiles with open hostility; they, after all, were displaced French at a time of war between the Anglo-Americans and the French. Any realistic hopes of returning to Acadia ended with British victory in 1763. Consequently, Acadians eager to escape their de facto prisoner-of-war status in the British colonies began to migrate to the French colony of Louisiana. Even after Spain acquired Louisiana, the colony continued to welcome the Acadian diaspora from across the Atlantic rim for the remainder of the eighteenth century.[2]

The Louisiana Acadians, like their predecessors in Nova Scotia, sought out isolated regions suited to their agricultural and stock-raising traditions. Their communities clustered along the Mississippi River west of New Orleans, along Bayou Lafourche, and especially around Bayou Teche, the center of "la Nouvelle Acadie." But, as though mocked by fate, the Acadians soon faced growing numbers of Anglo-American and West Indian Creole settlers who, along with their slaves, flooded into southern Louisiana following the Louisiana Purchase in 1803. Acadians responded in various ways to the new settlers. Some, like the Mouton family of Lafayette, clawed their way into the planter elite otherwise dominated by Anglo-Americans and Creoles. Other Acadians occupied a middle ground as small semicommercial farmers and cattlemen. A third group retreated to the fringes of settlement and eked out an existence as subsistence ranchers, trappers, and fishermen.

The Civil War and the subsequent economic transformations of the New South exacerbated these divisions among the Acadians. While the Acadian elites embraced the Confederacy, other Acadians displayed much less fervor, especially after frequent raids by both Union and Confederate troops stripped the region of much of its wealth. At war's end, the Acadian elite united with their Anglo and Creole counterparts in a ferocious vigilante campaign to restore their traditional political and economic control over the region. They joined in welcoming the arrival of railroads, modern rice culti-vation, and oil production. These innovations eroded the cultural cohesive-ness that a shared language, religion, and traditions once had provided the Acadian exiles.[3]

For all of the changes that overtook the Acadians of Louisiana during the nineteenth century, they nevertheless acquired a reputation as tradition-bound peasants. In the eyes of urbane Louisiana Creoles, who took pride in their continued cultural ties with France, the Acadians lacked cosmopolitan refinement. Likewise, Anglo observers ridiculed the rustic Acadians for their purported lack of ambition and resulting poverty. In addition, their alleged hedonism, manifested in dancing, feasting, gambling, and drinking, grated on the sensibilities of many Protestant Anglos.[4]

These negative depictions of Acadians were offset partially by competing, romantic renderings, especially Henry Wadsworth Longfellow's exception-ally popular poem *Evangeline*, published in 1847. Longfellow recounted the exile of the Acadians from their idyllic homeland by tracing the ill-fated romance of two Acadians, Evangeline and Gabriel. Separated on their wed-ding day by the grand dérangement, Evangeline and Gabriel endured the hardships of the Acadian dispersal. Longfellow's resilient heroine subse-quently tracked her Gabriel to Louisiana, where he had fled. To her dismay, she discovered that he had departed shortly before her arrival. After years of fruitless searching for him, Evangeline eventually devoted herself to nursing at a Philadelphia hospital. There, at the close of Longfellow's poem of pa-thetic and unfulfilled romance, she found her fiancé on his deathbed.

However much Longfellow's poetic epic deviated from the recorded his-tory of the Acadians, it nevertheless created a powerful and enduring depic-tion of Acadian culture that reached audiences around the world. The poem revived awareness of the eighteenth-century deportation of the Acadians, and the figure of Evangeline came to personify Acadian tenacity and devotion to tradition and Catholicism. Not surprisingly, those Acadians in Canada and Louisiana who were anxious to refute pejorative stereotypes of Acadians adopted Longfellow's Evangeline as their Joan of Arc.[5]

Louisiana Acadians embraced Longfellow's mythical account of the Aca-dian diaspora, but they revised it to accentuate the purported historical authenticity of Evangeline and her life in Louisiana. If Longfellow's poem depicted the steadfast courage of the Acadian exiles, it simultaneously con-tributed to the idea that they "had abandoned the fatherland and mortgaged their heritage for a new life in an exotic, semi-tropical land."[6] Moreover, Longfellow's Evangeline had lingered only briefly in Louisiana. Intent on claiming the mythical Evangeline for southwestern Louisiana, Felix Voorhies, a St. Martinville judge of Acadian descent, proclaimed in the 1890s that she had been, in fact, an actual person, Emmeline Labiche. On the basis of the purported recollections of his grandmother, published in newspapers and eventually collected in *Acadian Reminiscences*, Voorhies maintained that Labiche had tracked Louis Arceneaux, the Gabriel of Longfellow's poem, to St. Martinville, Louisiana, only to discover that he had married. The real-life heroine, then, had died of grief and, Voorhies reported, was buried in the quaint town.

The impact of Voorhies's account was considerable. It "authenticated the now nationally famous Evangeline myth and planted it firmly in the bayou country," explains Carl Brasseaux.[7] In addition, Voorhies's sentimental vision of traditional Acadian folkways and his admonition to Louisiana Acadians to both remember the grand dérangement and "always be proud to be the sons of martyrs and of men of principle" anticipated the subsequent Acadian revival.[8] Together, Longfellow's poem and Voorhies's quaint "reminiscences" promoted and authenticated the notion of a distinctive Louisiana Acadian heritage and culture.

That members of the white elite in southwestern Louisiana enthusiastically embraced Voorhies's account of Evangeline in part reflected their perception of the waning of Acadian traditions. Members of the regional elite, like their counterparts elsewhere in the country, evinced worry about the threat that rapid economic and social change posed to inherited values.[9] These concerns appear to have been especially acute among elite Acadians—merchants, planters, lawyers, and public officials—who moved back and forth between Acadian communities and the larger Anglo world of Louisiana. Almost certainly their exposure to and assimilation into "American" life made them keenly aware of both the distance that separated them from their ancestors and the condescension of both Creoles and Anglos toward their heritage. Acadian elites, like elites elsewhere, equated culture with ancestry. By resurrecting Acadian heritage and culture they sought to validate their personal and community identity. Thus, their interest in celebrating their heritage did not imply hidebound opposition to modernity or progress. To the contrary, for genteel Acadians, who were clustered in the towns of the region, especially Lafayette, the "Hub City" of Acadian Louisiana, the promotion of Acadian heritage went hand in hand with local boosterism.

That interest in Acadian culture was respectable and "progressive," rather than merely whimsical, was evident in the attention devoted to it by the voluntary associations and clubs of the region. These voluntary associations offered forums in which self-conscious Acadians and their non-Acadian allies could promote commerce and civic pride while also expressing their deliberate idealization of Acadian heritage. The prominence of such associations as outlets for organized contemplation of the local past is hardly surprising. Elsewhere in the nation, clubs, especially women's organizations, assumed the leadership of campaigns to promote an understanding of history and its relationship to the present. In keeping with this pattern, women's clubs in Lafayette conducted several yearlong, systematic surveys of Louisiana history, with special emphasis on the Acadian experience.[10] Similarly, in 1914 the Lafayette Forum, an elite civic club, listened to Judge Julian Mouton, a member of the distinguished Acadian family, describe the history of "pathos, courage, and loyalty" of "the peaceful peasants" who had settled the region.[11]

These genteel civic boosters and antiquarians recognized the need to extend the reach of their nostalgia to the larger Acadian population, whose attitudes were essential to the perpetuation of Acadian culture. Public festivals seemed well suited to this task. As early as 1914 members of the Lafayette Forum established the Acadian Pageant Company, which, by means of a "presentation of history through history, allegory, poetry and the stage," proposed to demonstrate that nowhere in America was there a "more picturesque, romantic, or distinctive history" than in the "land of Evangeline." Their planned pageant, to be staged by a cast of hundreds of the "lineal descendants of the Acadians," would portray a history "of thrift and peaceful contentment" in Nova Scotia and subsequent British "TYRANNY" and forced exile.[12] Like pageant enthusiasts elsewhere during the early twentieth century, the Lafayette planners intended their celebration to be an avowedly didactic spectacle that would yoke the educational innovations of the Progressive Era to the dramatic arts, thereby both promoting community unity and enabling residents to teach themselves and others about their heritage.

Nearly a decade passed before pageant boosters fulfilled their ambition to create a communal spectacle that retold the Acadian past. The centennial celebration of Lafayette Parish in 1923 provided an ideal pretext for their historical production. Intent on applying the latest techniques to the staging of the huge show, centennial organizers enlisted a professional pageant artist to supervise it.[13] On 6 April 1923 between 4,000 and 6,000 spectators (at a time when the population of the town was about 10,000) watched the cast of approximately 2,000, including students from Lafayette's public schools and many of the town's voluntary associations, perform the three-and-a-half hour-

The centennial celebration of Lafayette Parish in 1923 provided an ideal pretext for presenting a historical production retelling the Acadian past. As many as 6,000 spectators watched the cast of approximately 2,000 perform the three-and-a-half-hour Attakapas Trail Pageant. Southwestern Archives and Manuscripts Collection, University of Southwestern Louisiana Archives, N11, Edwin Lewis Stephens Photograph Albums, #1.

long Attakapas Trail Pageant.[14] Initial plans for the pageant, perhaps reflecting the earlier pageant plans, had focused almost exclusively on the romantic tragedy of Evangeline as a personification of Acadian perseverance and valor. The nineteenth-century history of the Acadians and their role in the Civil War apparently merited little attention. One pageant planner had suggested to the pageant supervisor, "How much of the Civil War you want to emphasize, *you* know. I would recommend very little."[15] The performed pageant, however, did incorporate a tableau devoted to the Civil War and even the emblem of nineteenth-century modernity, the railroad. Even so, the Acadian theme remained conspicuous; the third act depicted "the simple village life of the Acadians" and their quaint domestic traditions and old "Village dances." Moreover, to help spectators transcend the chasm of time and to make tangible the connection between the Acadians and their past, one of the performers wore a dress that her grandmother had made a century and a half earlier after arriving in Louisiana from Nova Scotia.[16]

The Lafayette pageant displayed both the nostalgia and the boosterism that would characterize the subsequent Acadian revival. But it remained a single event that could not long sustain a collective identity. In keeping with the tenor of the times, Acadian boosters began to take tentative steps toward

forming organizations to promote their cultural identity. This impulse drew
on many sources of inspiration, including the Catholic Church. Some of the
French Canadian priests who served the region introduced Acadians to the
linguistic and cultural nationalism then developing among French Canadians. As early as 1924, for example, a Canadian priest toured the area
recruiting members for an international society of Acadians. Although he
failed to attract a substantial following in the region, he did increase local
awareness of the quickening international campaign for Acadian unity.[17]

Tourism provided another, albeit decidedly secular and commercial inspiration for the organized promotion of Acadian identity. The Louisiana
landscape immortalized by Longfellow had attracted sightseers throughout
the late nineteenth century, but the inconveniences of rail travel had limited
their numbers. Automobiles now enabled affluent northern refugees from
winter to flock to the region's colorful attractions. At a time of growing
enthusiasm for vacation travel within the United States, residents of southwestern Louisiana embraced tourism as a way simultaneously to promote
their heritage and to pad their wallets. Local boosters, no less than in other
areas of the South, looked with envy at Florida's booming tourist-driven
development.[18]

Growing awareness of the needs and interests of tourists led to demands
for the beautification and promotion of local sites, such as the so-called
Evangeline Oak in St. Martinville where the "real" Evangeline allegedly
glimpsed her beloved Gabriel.[19] Business leaders in the region implored their
neighbors to seize the commercial opportunities that the tourists represented.
C. T. Bienvenu, editor of the *St. Martinville Weekly Messenger*, for example,
urged, "With the increased number of tourists now coming to us . . . I feel
that the time has arrived for St. Martinville to organize and maintain a wide
awake and active organization" to respond to the interest in "the sturdy,
lovable and valiant Acadian pioneers who settled here nearly two hundred
years ago."[20]

No one better appreciated the potential significance of the Acadian past as
a draw for tourists than Susan Evangeline Walker Anding. Although she
could not claim Acadian ancestry, she nevertheless nurtured a strong attachment to all things Acadian that she traced to her lifelong exposure to Acadian
culture and a sentimental bond with her fictional namesake, Longfellow's
Evangeline. The epitome of the industrious clubwoman of the era, she earned
a regional reputation as an irrepressible promoter of civic organizations and
good roads. In 1925 she proposed establishing a permanent national monument to Evangeline and the Acadians in St. Martinville. Not coincidentally,

the monument would be located on the Pershing, the Evangeline, and the Spanish Trail national highways (stretching from California to Florida and from Texas to Canada), which she also promoted.[21]

Susan Anding hitched the apparatus of civic organizing and applied the techniques of advertising to the cause of Acadian cultural identity. Employing her uncanny promotional skills, she coaxed newspaper editors, public officials, and members of the Acadian, Anglo, and Creole elites of southwestern Louisiana to join her Longfellow-Evangeline National Monument Association. As early as 1925 she exploited the latest technology when she broadcast her monument plans to radio listeners across the Deep South. Borrowing an idea from the campaign to fund a monument to the Confederacy at Stone Mountain, Georgia, she appealed to school children in Louisiana to contribute their pennies to the construction fund for the Evangeline Park. She also organized booths at state and local fairs that raised money for the planned monument.[22]

The most successful of her publicity ploys was her use of "charming costumes of the period when Evangeline lived" to arouse interest in and evoke the romance of the Acadian past. She first experimented with representing a lifelike Evangeline in 1926, when she exhibited a mannequin clothed in an Evangeline costume at the Philadelphia Sesquicentennial Exposition. So popular was the exhibit and so well suited to the commercial aesthetic of the era that it subsequently was moved to the window of a New York City department store. In 1928, in what a local newspaper saluted as "a progressive stunt," she chaperoned a group of real-life "Evangeline girls" to the Republican and Democratic National Conventions. Wherever the "Evangeline girls" went, their quaint garb of "prim white hats, tight black bodices, loving blue satin dresses, and wooden shoes" attracted attention.[23] From their quaint convention booths, draped with Spanish moss and outfitted with an old Acadian spinning wheel, the latter-day Evangelines distributed tourist literature and retold the history of "Evangeline Country."[24] The following year Mrs. Anding escorted another group of appropriately clad "girls" to President Herbert Hoover's inauguration.[25]

The success of Evangeline as a motif for Acadian identity was hardly happenstance. Longfellow's Evangeline, of course, was an established literary icon. But the impulse to personify Evangeline bespoke the publicity-crazed tenor of the era. Susan Anding's genius was to adapt the parlor game of tableaux vivant to serve the ends of a modern publicity campaign. By swaddling the "Evangeline girls" in (purportedly) historically accurate attire, she catered to the contemporary nostalgia for the authenticity and charm of yesteryear. If Acadian "girls" induced nostalgia, their "tight bodices" and perky demeanor simultaneously radiated a sex appeal attuned to the modern taste for beauty queens. In addition, there were powerful reasons why the icon of the Acadian revival would be feminine. Like other images of women in contemporary advertising, the idealized Acadian "girls" remained static in time, seemingly sheltering traditions from the forward rush of progress. The combination of their old-fashioned attire and props of domesticity, such as spinning wheels, conjured timeless values of family, community, and heritage that encouraged Acadians and others to acknowledge those traditions even as they withered. Moreover, no mythical male Acadian figure could have evoked romance the way the "Evangeline girls" did. Men powerless to protect their dependents, such as the Acadian patriarchs who were expelled from Nova Scotia, could not easily be turned into heroic figures. But a romantic heroine like Evangeline, who was buffeted by historical forces she could not have been expected to control, actually proved her womanly virtue through her victimization during the Acadian expulsion. Thus, she, far better than any male figure, could become an allegory for Acadians in general.[26]

Susan Anding's campaign was remarkable for the publicity it garnered and for its propagation of many of the tropes of the Acadian revival. But it was less successful at raising funds for the Evangeline Park. She secured a modest contribution of state funds and land, but the park's subsequent slow development prompted her critics to complain in 1929 that she had not conducted the drive "in a business-manner fashion."[27] In 1930 her poor health provided a genteel pretext for easing her out of power and for turning the campaign over to a newly established Longfellow-Evangeline Park Commission.[28] Soon thereafter her ambition for a park commemorating Evangeline came to pass. By the late 1930s park managers boasted that the park housed "more relics and antiques of real Acadian articles [than can] be found anywhere [else]."[29] In addition, they made the convenient (and mistaken) discovery that an old house on the park grounds was the reputed home of Louis Arceneaux, the purported inspiration for Longfellow's Gabriel. The restored home provided a setting of "incomparable and picturesque fascination" in which lecturers and exhibits helped visitors "to understand the pride with which natives keep alive and relive the exploits of their ancestors."[30]

The opening of the Longfellow-Evangeline Park and the resulting tourist interest in it and nearby St. Martinville permanently inscribed the narrative promoted by the nascent Acadian revival onto the landscape. Anding's campaign wed the relentless boosterism of the era with the emerging interest in promoting Acadian self-esteem. She prodded Acadians and non-Acadian sympathizers to organize and present their collective history in new ways and to new audiences. When she invited communities to establish chapters of the Evangeline Park Association, she also encouraged them to imagine themselves as united by their shared Acadian heritage. Thus, when the Chambers of Commerce in the five counties surrounding the proposed Evangeline monument issued public announcements claiming the title of the "Acadian heartland" in 1927, they made manifest the "imagined community" that Anding had helped to inspire.[31]

If Susan Anding helped to fuse a sense of place with the Acadian identity, Dudley LeBlanc, an Acadian raconteur of uncommon ability, strengthened the link between the Acadian identity and the distant past. Unlike Anding, LeBlanc was a descendant of Acadian exiles and had lived in the French-speaking world until he entered Southwestern Louisiana Institute (now the University of Southwestern Louisiana) in Lafayette. After graduating he became rich by peddling everything from patent medicines and tobacco products to burial insurance. His years as a traveling salesman trained him in the use of flamboyant advertising and promotion to appeal to the tastes and traditions of "the people."[32]

When LeBlanc's boundless ambition led him into public life, he applied his well-honed skills of salesmanship to politics. From his first campaign in 1923 until the end of his long political career in the 1960s, he touted his Acadian identity. In 1926, for instance, while representing St. Landry Parish in the state legislature, LeBlanc enthusiastically supported the proposed Evangeline Park by securing $10,000 of state funds for it. He subsequently reminded voters of his concern for Acadian heritage by recruiting members of the Longfellow-Evangeline Association to endorse him at campaign appearances. He also shamelessly employed the symbols of Acadian heritage in his campaigns. In 1926, for example, he delivered a stump speech beneath the branches of the Evangeline Oak in St. Martinville.[33] He sprinkled his speeches with the Acadian patois (when he did not deliver them entirely in French) and incorporated Acadian music and food into his electioneering.[34]

LeBlanc's interest in his ethnic heritage fueled his enthusiasm for forging ties between Acadians in Louisiana and in Canada. Almost certainly his friendship with Father Fidele Chiasson, a French-Canadian priest in Mamou, Louisiana, with a long-standing interest in French Canadian nationalism, was a catalyst for this project.[35] In addition, LeBlanc's knowledge that his ancestors had been prominent Acadian exiles in the eighteenth century inspired his activism. In 1928 he led a delegation of four Acadians and Father Chiasson to a convention of North American Acadians held in Massachusetts.[36] Addressing the six thousand gathered delegates, LeBlanc described the Louisiana brethren as the "most romantic and tragically unfortunate of all the [Acadian] exiles." So well received was his speech that the Democratic National Committee recruited him to campaign in the French-speaking communities of New England on behalf of Democratic candidates. Beyond deepening his appreciation of the uniqueness of Louisiana Acadians, the experience inspired LeBlanc to promote the cultural union of French communities in North America.[37]

LeBlanc's widening ties with the North American Acadian community brought him into contact with F. G. J. Comeaux of Halifax, Nova Scotia, an ardent Acadian activist. In February 1930 Comeaux visited Lafayette and encouraged LeBlanc to organize a "pilgrimage" of Louisiana Acadians to the 175th anniversary commemoration of the Acadian expulsion from Nova Scotia.[38] LeBlanc eagerly embraced the cause and organized mass meetings that drew French-speaking audiences from across southwestern Louisiana.[39] He also founded the Association of Louisiana Acadians, whose membership was limited to descendants of the Acadian exiles. Borrowing from Susan Anding's publicity techniques, he and his association invited each Acadian community to appoint an Acadian "girl" as its representative at the Canadian celebrations.[40]

On 11 August 1930 thirty-eight Louisianans, including twenty-five "Evangeline girls," began a two-week pilgrimage to Canada. The colorfully costumed Acadians attracted widespread publicity. A news service filmed the spectacle that the "girls" presented throughout the trip; national newspapers reported their visit with President Hoover at the White House; banners on the sides of their Pullman cars announced them as "Acadians of the Evangeline Country" and boomed LeBlanc's gubernatorial candidacy (which, not coincidentally, he announced just before the pilgrimage); and radio and public speeches by the "picturesque" Acadians reached audiences across the Northeast and Canada.[41]

Beyond garnering national publicity, the trip intensified the identification of the "pilgrims" with their Acadian heritage. LeBlanc gushed that "the reuniting of this long separated people was most touching. . . . There were many things to be recalled . . . and many common customs and characteristics to be noted."[42] One of the returning "Evangeline girls" raved that the trip "helped to cement us closer to the land from whence we came to the north." To be in Nova Scotia, she continued, "brought back to me the stories of our

In 1930 Dudley LeBlanc escorted twenty-five costumed "Evangeline girls" on a two-week "pilgrimage" to Canada. One of the highlights of the trip was a visit by the colorfully costumed Acadians with President Herbert Hoover at the White House. Southwestern Archives and Manuscripts Collection, University of Southwestern Louisiana Archives, collection 111, Lafayette Photograph Collection.

earlier exile often heard from the older people. . . . I never felt that I was anywhere else but at home."[43]

LeBlanc and his Canadian partners longed to perpetuate this revived sense of shared identity among Acadians. In the following April, LeBlanc organized a visit by 138 French Canadians to Louisiana. Throughout their five-day tour of the major Acadian communities, the Canadians were barraged with images of Evangeline. During visits to all of the shrines associated with the lovelorn Acadian exile, young men dressed as Gabriel and the "Evangeline girls" who had toured Canada the previous year (and other costumed women) greeted the Canadian tourists. The shared faith and language of the Acadians also figured prominently in the celebrations. One measure of the importance attached to Catholicism as a core element of Acadian identity was the 28 Canadian clerics, including a bishop, who joined the pilgrimage. At churches important in the early history of the Louisiana Acadians, the Canadians and their hosts preformed Mass.[44] And at a time of declining French proficiency in Louisiana, the Canadian visitors and their Louisiana chaperones pointedly delivered most of their public speeches in French. LeBlanc scheduled a regionwide French language contest to coincide with the visit.[45]

With the Canadian visitors watching during the unveiling of a monument commemorating Evangeline in St. Martinville, he awarded medals to young Acadian essayists who had recounted "the peaceful life in Acadia before the exile; the cruelties and sufferings of the Acadians when they were exiled; how they settled in Louisiana; [and] their present modes and customs."[46]

The transnational Acadian exchanges continued in subsequent years. In 1936 LeBlanc led another pilgrimage to Canada. He again organized a group of "Evangeline girls" to represent Acadian communities along the gulf coast from Beaumont, Texas, to Pensacola, Florida.[47] As in the past, the pilgrims attracted national publicity. In addition to visiting the hallowed home of the Acadians in Nova Scotia during the two-week, five-thousand-mile tour, the Louisianans stopped for a visit with President Franklin D. Roosevelt, were feted in Baltimore by the governor of Maryland, attended a Mass in their honor at St. Peter's Cathedral in New York City, visited with the celebrated Dionne Quintuplets in Canada, and attended the Texas Centennial. Ten years later, after an interruption caused by World War II, LeBlanc escorted twenty Canadian "Acadian girls" on a grueling tour of southwestern Louisiana. Promoted as part of a "patriotic movement organized to create good will between the Acadians of Louisiana and the Acadians of Canada," the tour highlighted Acadian folk dances and music. The women delivered more than thirty concerts in Acadian communities from the Texas border to Baton Rouge.[48]

The various tours prompted an outpouring of expressions of pride in Acadian identity and heritage. In 1931 the *Opelousas Clarion-News*, for example, saluted the Canadian visitors by affirming that "We are of French descent here. . . . We are proud of our heritages, proud of our accomplishments. . . . These Northern Acadians are part of our French blood and they are related to us by close bonds of sympathy. . . . We trust that the visit of the Acadians . . . will rededicate this romantic bond [between our two sections]."[49] The 1946 tour by the Canadian performers elicited similar sentiments. A St. Martinville audience warmly applauded one of the Acadian "girls" when she urged that "we are all cousins and should preserve our French language and many of our old customs."[50] Similarly, the *Lafayette Daily Advertiser* celebrated the performers' capacity to evoke the "call of the blood" and to demonstrate "the strength of unity that should come from a common heritage."[51]

Beyond promoting Acadian awareness by organizing ongoing contacts between Louisiana Acadians and their "cousins to the north," LeBlanc's signal contribution to the Acadian revival was to codify a historical narrative of Acadian victimhood. In 1927 he published *The True Story of the Acadians*, which he subsequently revised and republished in 1932 and again in 1967. The hardships of exile, of course, had figured prominently in both Longfellow's *Evangeline* and Voorhies's *Acadian Reminiscences*. But neither Longfellow's epic poem nor Voorhies's family lore claimed the precision or credibility of formal historical scholarship. Recognizing the power that the scholarly trappings gave to historical narratives, LeBlanc employed the tools of scholarship, which previously had been used to stigmatize Acadian heritage and folkways, to bolster Acadian pride.

LeBlanc intended his book to be a manifesto of Acadian historical consciousness. He complained that previous accounts of the Acadian experience had "distorted the facts in order to shield the British government from the responsibility of having committed the crime." He, in contrast, insisted on the credibility of his account: "Every controversial statement in this work is supported by authorities with appropriate citations" and "these statements cannot be successfully contradicted." He conceded that his narrative of the Acadian "persecutions" did not rest on new research. Instead, it was a pastiche of lengthy quotations from published histories and primary sources interspersed with breathless celebrations of Acadian heritage. LeBlanc recounted the tragedy of the "simple," "moral," "temperate," "happy," "peaceful," "chaste," and "noble" Acadians who fell victim to a perfidious and cruel British campaign to condemn "a noble race into utter oblivion." Whereas the survival of the Acadians in the decades immediately following their expulsion from Nova Scotia was "a miracle," their subsequent century and a half in Louisiana held little interest for him. He denied any rupture between tradition and modernity and ignored the effects of change. He was satisfied to vouch for the integrity of Acadian culture by pointing to Acadians' continuing fealty to Catholicism. And LeBlanc, like enthusiasts for Appalachian culture who boasted of the purported Elizabethan authenticity of mountain dialects, touted the French spoken by the Louisiana Acadians as "actually classical." "If you are an Acadian," LeBlanc triumphantly concluded, "you have just cause to be proud of your ancestors. . . . No other race of people in the world ever could claim what you can justly and proudly boast for yours."[52]

The significance of LeBlanc's ethnic boosterism should not be exaggerated. In principle, his Association of Louisiana Acadians represented the institutionalization of the Acadian revival. But, in reality, the organization was little more than a vehicle for LeBlanc's caprices. It endured in a state of suspended animation until temporarily revived during his pilgrimages. He displayed little interest in either sustained or comprehensive cultural preservation. Instead, his compulsive hucksterism was always conspicuous in his celebrations of Acadian identity; without fail, LeBlanc's promotion of all things Acadian coincided with either his latest business enterprise or his candidacy for public office.[53] He also revealed condescending attitudes toward the very culture that his association purportedly preserved.[54] Nevertheless, his hagiography of the Louisiana Acadians and promotion of Acadian pride were conspicuous contributions to the nascent Acadian revival. His charismatic personality, shrewd entrepreneurship, and prestige among his fellow Acadians enabled him to extend the reach of the Acadian revival far beyond the private parlors and Chamber of Commerce meeting rooms where it had its origins. His periodic pilgrimages became ritualized expressions of historical memory that explicitly asserted historical continuity. Beyond reminding participants about the past, the elaborate transnational festivities represented the past so that participants became, if only temporarily and symbolically, contemporaries with mythical events. We should not underestimate the power of these performances to diffuse and establish the enduring cultural authority of the Acadian revival.[55]

Without the contributions of Louise Olivier, an Acadian activist, a skeptic might dismiss the Acadian revival as little more than LeBlanc's ethnic chest-thumping and Susan Anding's publicity stunts. Most early promoters of Acadian heritage, including LeBlanc, displayed little concern for preserving traditional folkways. Aside from the mythical attire sported by women dressed as Evangeline and the retelling of some Acadian stories, the marrow of Acadian culture—handicrafts, music, and folkways—had been virtually ignored by previous Acadian boosters. Olivier, in contrast, waged a long campaign to revive "authentic" Acadian folkways. She was, by no means, unique in her deep affection for the French language and Acadian culture. But, unlike other enthusiasts, she was a professional cultural activist who brought specialized training and endless stamina to the campaign to preserve Acadian culture.

Olivier, like LeBlanc, had a deep personal attachment to the Acadian community she pledged to serve. Born in the Acadian village of Grand Coteau and educated at Catholic convents there and in New Orleans, she earned degrees in music and French. After teaching French in public schools and at the Louisiana State University (LSU), she received an appointment in 1938 as the field representative of an LSU-sponsored program to promote the

French language throughout Louisiana. The position called upon her expertise in both music and French while also encouraging her interest in Acadian folk culture.

Her teaching experience made Olivier keenly aware of what she perceived to be the erosion of traditional Acadian culture. "Personally," she explained in 1943, "I feel we are outstanding people saturated with relics of a passing culture!"[56] "Unfortunately," she lamented, "within the last fifty years there has been such a rapid change in the new generations of the descendants of the Acadians brought by modern progress—The customs and even the language of the Acadians are fast disappearing."[57] Traditional Acadians needed to be reinforced in their presumed struggle to hold onto their culture in the face of "progress." Because of her standing as an expert on Acadian folkways, Olivier exerted considerable influence over the value attached to various expressions of Acadian culture. Her self-appointed task was to moderate the destructive impact of modernity by reeducating Acadians to value their traditional culture. She, for instance, advocated purging vulgar modern influences from Acadian music and helped organize a national folk festival to honor the musical traditions she valued. Old Acadian songs were good; newer music was not. Instead of judging new songs or musical styles as evidence of the continued creativity of Acadian culture, she saw them as woeful degeneration. She cautioned an organizer of the National Folk Festival in 1953 that any Acadian bands selected to perform at the festival "would have to be polished, weeded out, advised and directed. They are gradually losing their identity, acquiring cow-boy traits. In other words, they are no longer 'cajun bands' but 'cow-jun bands.'"[58] Her taste and principles similarly led her to value such essentially archaic artifacts as braided palmetto fans and woven baby bonnets above other forms of Acadian handicrafts.

Her early efforts included pioneering one of the first sustained and widespread campaigns to preserve French in Louisiana. Building on LeBlanc's precedent of broadcasting weekly French-language radio programs, Olivier launched an ongoing series of live French broadcasts.[59] She attracted large audiences for these broadcasts as well as to participate in local French programs. Over time, she expanded these "Assemblées" by recruiting public school administrators, teachers, and community activists in Louisiana's French-speaking parishes to help stage festivities that focused on local traditions. In addition, she organized French clubs to perpetuate the use of the language after the conclusion of the "Assemblées."[60]

Her more enduring contribution to the revival was her promotion of Acadian handicrafts during the 1940s and 1950s. Wartime exigencies, espe

Beginning in 1942, Louise Olivier promoted craft demonstrations by Acadian women
dressed in Evangeline attire at local festivals, such as the Crowley Rice Festival and the
Abbeville Dairy Festival. Here unidentified Acadian reenactors add color to a local
festival in the late 1940s. Louisiana Department of State, Division of Archives, Records
Management and History, John B. Gasquet Photographic Collection.

cially gasoline rationing, sharply curtailed her ability to travel and promote
French throughout the state. Consequently, she redirected her energies to an
ambitious campaign to "preserve as a culture the traditional crafts of our
Acadian ancestors," "to furnish an outlet for the self-expression of our
women of Acadian ancestry and to develop initiative and independence
among them," and "to find a market for the handicraft objects produced."[61]
She drew inspiration for her plans from the tradition of handicraft promotion
that extended from the earliest London Settlement houses of the late nineteenth century to the Appalachian handicraft revival movement of the teens
and twenties.[62]

Beginning in 1942, Olivier enlisted traditional weavers, quilters, sunbonnet
makers, and palmetto braiders to produce items for traveling displays of
Acadian crafts that were exhibited at public libraries, club meetings, and
fairs. Convinced of the value of establishing "THIS MOVEMENT AS AN INDUS-
TRY," she installed permanent exhibits, including craft demonstrations by

Acadian women dressed in Evangeline attire, at the Longfellow-Evangeline State Park and other state facilities.[63] She coaxed organizers of local festivals, such as the Crowley Rice Festival and the Abbeville Dairy Festival, to incorporate the preservation of "the French language, customs, etc." into their annual celebrations.[64] Through these measures, Olivier had earned by the 1950s national recognition for her campaign to promote and preserve Acadian crafts and folkways.

Yet Olivier was not entirely successful in imposing her sensibilities or zeal for "authentic" Acadian culture on the Acadian revival. She, like Anding and LeBlanc before her, employed Evangeline outfits to arouse public interest in her campaign. She comforted herself that although the women she recruited to staff the craft displays wore clothes intended to evoke romance, they at least, unlike previous "Evangeline girls," were actual artisans. Although she was largely responsible for the incorporation of Acadian culture in the fairs and festivals that proliferated during the 1940s and 1950s, she nevertheless resented the superficial respect accorded it.[65] Her frustration with frivolous evocations of Acadian heritage mounted during the Louisiana bicentennial celebrations of the Acadian expulsion in 1955, when she complained that "all that seems to count consist of noise and glitter. I am so tired of hearing '*a pretty girl on a shiny float*' and police escorts and brass bands, etc. that I could scream."[66]

The significance of Olivier's labors cannot be measured solely by the actual sales of the Acadian crafts that she promoted. Such sales were never large; in 1956 the total value of woven shirts, napkins, bedspreads, and braided palmetto fans sold totaled less than $10,000.[67] A better gauge was her success at attracting wide publicity for Acadian crafts and encouraging merchants to develop their own sources of these crafts.[68] Her project encouraged thirty-some Acadian craftswomen to revive and perpetuate trades that otherwise had little marketable value. Most important, her signal contribution to the Acadian revival was to institutionalize systematic cultural intervention in southern Louisiana and to introduce there the techniques of cultural preservation that had been applied in various other "folk" communities in the United States and Europe. By doing so, she established a precedent for continuing state funded support for the promotion of the French language and Acadian folkways.

The target of Louise Olivier's sternest criticisms—the Acadian bicentennial celebrations of 1955—was nevertheless the most spectacular expression of the

Acadian revival or what Olivier called "Le Reveil de la Louisiane." The yearlong festivities represented the naturalization of the region's Acadian heritage. They incorporated virtually all of the themes and techniques that had been employed to represent Acadian heritage during the past two decades. Beginning in 1954, the Acadian Bicentennial Commission (ABC), funded with $100,000 from the state, developed extensive plans to commemorate the expulsion of the Acadians. Directed by Thomas J. Arceneaux, a professor and administrator at the University of Southwestern Louisiana who flaunted his direct descent from Louis Arceneaux (the alleged real-life Gabriel of the *Evangeline* tale), the ABC planned a complex, yearlong celebration of Acadian heritage.

The bicentennial opened on 1 January 1955, when Acadian singers and dancers performed at the nationally televised halftime ceremonies of the Sugar Bowl championship football game. Two weeks later residents of Lafayette welcomed a delegation of Canadian Acadians to the annual Camellia Pageant. The Canadians then undertook a "goodwill tour" of southwestern Louisiana. In February the Acadian bicentennial provided the theme for the Lafayette Mardi Gras celebrations. In April, a "pilgrimage to the Mother Church of Acadians" in St. Martinville incorporated the selection of an official "Evangeline" to promote the bicentennial, a nationally publicized reenactment of the first Acadian wedding in Louisiana, and a Mass celebrating the perpetuation of the Acadians' faith. During the summer, the commission's Evangeline toured Louisiana, made radio and television appearances, and performed at Bastille Day festivities near New Orleans. In August, Arceneaux led a two-week Louisiana Acadian pilgrimage to Canada that included radio and television appearances and concert performances. During the fall the Abbeville Dairy Festival, the New Iberia Sugar Festival, and the Ville Platte Cotton Festival incorporated bicentennial themes into their festivities. The culmination of the year's program was the Acadian Bicentennial Climax Celebration held in St. Martinville. During the four-day event, the Acadian folk festival championed by Louise Olivier and directed by Sarah Gertrude Knott, the founder and director of the National Folk Festival, staged performances by Pete Seeger and other musicians of the music of Acadiana and Louisiana. The festivities closed with a pageant, featuring a cast of hundreds, depicting the tragic life of Evangeline.[69]

The influence of the Bicentennial Commission extended beyond fairgrounds and public spectacles. Throughout 1955, the ABC encouraged voluntary associations to participate in the celebrations and to study Acadian culture and history. Intent on incorporating Acadian history and culture into school activities, the commission, along with the Louisiana State Department of Education, published and circulated a booklet entitled *Our Acadian Culture—Let's Keep It!* The aim of the booklet was clear—"to instill a desire in our people to perpetuate our Acadian heritage." Teachers were encouraged to organize activities such as listening to French language newscasts, visiting places "rich in Acadian folklore" like the Evangeline State Park and St. Martinville, and corresponding with French children in Canada and elsewhere. More than a brief primer of Acadian history, folk songs, and cuisine, the booklet represented an important step in incorporating the narrative of Acadian exile and the contemporary defense of Acadian cultural traditions into public education.[70]

The commission also explicitly integrated commercial aims into the bicentennial celebrations. Indeed, the original plans and most of the funding for the ABC came from the Louisiana Department of Commerce and Industry. The priorities of the department were threefold: "to provide Louisiana with a suitable vehicle which will (1) attract new tourist money into the state, (2) display the state's Acadian heritage in the most favorable light and (3) establish Louisiana, for years to come, as a prime tourist vacation spot."[71] Advertising for the bicentennial was linked with the department's burgeoning tourist promotion program as well as with the "Holiday in Dixie" campaign, a private effort to promote tourism in Louisiana. This shameless boosterism and commercialism that so offended Louise Olivier may have been unprecedented in scale or intensity, but it was only the continuation of a tradition that Susan Anding, Dudley LeBlanc, and Olivier herself had contributed to. Strung out over the course of a year, the centennial celebrations fused the spectacle of recurrent invocations of Evangeline and the trauma of the expulsion with tireless appeals to preserve authentic Acadian culture and to promote tourism.

The unfolding of the Acadian revival in Louisiana during the first half of the twentieth century mirrors the evolution of historical memory elsewhere in the South (and the United States). The Acadian boosters, no less than the white "Anglo Saxon" elites of the late-nineteenth-century South, were eager to create a usable past. But they had in mind uses for their past quite distinct from those of earlier historical activists. As early as the 1930s, the tourist brochures, advertisements, and souvenirs that invoked the Acadian and southern past had, in a real sense, commodified it. The locally sponsored pageant in Lafayette presaged the future; it retained some of the solemn ritual that had been conspicuous in previous historical representations, but it also incorporated robust doses of local boosterism and spectacle intended to promote and entertain at least as much as to edify. This mix of boosterism and revelry, which found its fullest expression in the Acadian bicentennial celebration, was an essential element of the emerging tourist industry in Louisiana and the South in general. Since the 1920s the promotion of Acadian culture and consumerism have been inextricably linked. Because Anding, LeBlanc, and their ilk reduced the complexity of Acadian history to a romantic essence, it was ideally suited to adaptation to tourism. They remembered only those events closely linked to the romantic episodes in Acadian history: St. Martinville was a suitably romantic shrine of Acadian memory, Evangeline was an ideal tragic heroine, and Acadian folk traditions were appropriately quaint. Local and state authorities not only have encouraged this romanticization, they also have aided tourists in their pursuit of the romantic by literally mapping history onto the landscape. State agencies in Louisiana and across the South funded parks and historic sites and cluttered the highways and byways with markers that alerted motorists to picturesque historical events and personalities. State tourist bureaus likewise provided curious travelers with brochures that cataloged the historical sites that merited attention; in Louisiana, for instance, the state tourist bureau developed a distinctive promotional campaign for "Acadiana." In these various ways, the marketing methods of the last century have come to be incorporated into the transmission of Acadian historical memory.

The Acadian revival also is a conspicuous example of the increasing role of the state in the promotion of historical memory and revived folkways in the South. Although the voluntary organizations that initiated the revival remain active, their role in the promulgation of memory increasingly has been overshadowed by the state. The extension of state authority into matters past was gradual, beginning with small steps. From a modest beginning when the Louisiana legislature contributed $10,000 to the Evangeline park campaign in 1928, the state's involvement in the Acadian revival has mushroomed to include tourist promotion, state parks, and festivals. (In 1999, for example, the State Department of Culture, Recreation, and Tourism hosted the World Acadian Congress.)[72] Perhaps the most visible demonstration of state commitment is the state-funded Council for the Development of French in Louisiana (CODOFIL). Founded in 1968 by Lafayette-based cultural activists, CODOFIL has aggressively promoted bilingualism and awareness of Cajun (and French) culture in public education.[73] Finally, state largess has undergirded the emergence of the academic study of Acadians, especially at the University of Southwestern Louisiana, the home of the Ragin' Cajuns.

Elsewhere in the South, state promotion of historical awareness followed a similar trajectory, beginning modestly with the establishment of state archives and museums, subsequently expanding to include elaborate historical pageants and festivals, and more recently swelling to embrace countless historical sites and annual festivals. Eventually, all southern states created bureaucracies to study, plan, and market their pasts as tourist attractions. State and local governments now maintain or contribute public funds to operate literally hundreds and hundreds of historic sites. Thus, historical memory has become part of public policy in Louisiana and in the South. Now that the principal responsibility for representations of the past has been assumed by public institutions, debates about memorializing the past necessarily are both public and political.

The legacy of the Acadian revival between 1925 and 1955 is inescapable in contemporary Louisiana. The Cajun identity has attained an influence and a stature far beyond the ambitions of the earliest boosters. A century ago Acadians were obscure if exotic figures overshadowed in the national consciousness by the romantic Creoles of Louisiana. Since then, the success of the Acadian quest for power and social cohesion in the polyglot culture of Louisiana has been so great that much ink now is devoted to informing Louisianans and outsiders alike that the French culture of the state includes white and black Creole as well as Cajun traditions. Indeed, some blacks in southwestern Louisiana openly resent the now-conventional narrative of the region's history that focuses on the Acadians and marginalizes the African American experience. Bemoaning the "cultural piracy" that has appropriated African American traditions as "Cajun," blacks claiming descent from French and Spanish colonists have founded an Un-Cajun Committee and C.R.E.O.L.E., Inc. The group's president, Melvin Caesar, explains: "I'm not against what they (Cajuns) have done. They have marketed their culture very well, and we should learn from them and progress from their success."[74] That these voices of protest, however ineffective, are vented at all testifies to the suffocating achievements of Acadian revivalists.

Yet, despite the apparent success of the marketing of Acadian tradition, Acadian/Cajun identity has acquired the appearance of what sociologist Herbert Gans calls "symbolic ethnicity" or what columnist Maureen Dowd labels "designer ethnicity." Cajun dances, festivals, and exhibits may be commonplace, but these nostalgic leisure activities, some observers contend, comprise the only important and distinctive contemporary expressions of Cajun identity.[75] Otherwise, Acadian/Cajun symbolic references are free-floating and nearly ubiquitous signifiers that have been reduced to mere commercial slogans that adorn every conceivable type of business in Acadiana. Still unresolved more than a half century after the beginning of the Acadian revival is the complex and unstable relationship between the marketplace and Acadian "traditions." Thus, the irony that was evident in the Acadian revival at its origins persists. For all of the distinctive local color of the Acadian "revival," it nevertheless displayed such quintessentially modern American traits as longing for folk tradition, discomfort with "progress," and zeal to commercialize culture and adapt it to contemporary tastes.

NOTES

1. Carl A. Brasseaux, *The Founding of New Acadia: The Beginnings of Acadian Life in Louisiana, 1765–1803* (Baton Rouge: Louisiana State University Press, 1987); Naomi E. S. Griffith, *The Acadian Deportation: Deliberate Perfidy or Cruel Necessity?* (Toronto: Copp Clark, 1969) and "The Golden Age: Acadian Life, 1713–1748," *Historie Sociale—Social History* 17 (May 1984): 21–34.

2. Brasseaux, *Founding of New Acadia.*

3. Carl A. Brasseaux, *From Acadian to Cajun: Transformation of a People, 1803–1877* (Jackson: University Press of Mississippi, 1992); James H. Dormon, *The People Called Cajuns: An Introduction to an Ethnohistory* (Lafayette: Center for Louisiana Studies, 1983), 63–69; Lawrence E. Estaville Jr., "Changeless Cajuns: Nineteenth-Century Reality or Myth?," *Louisiana History* 28 (Spring 1987): 117–40; Donald J. Millet, "The Economic Development of Southwest Louisiana, 1865–1900" (Ph.D. diss., Louisiana State University, 1964).

4. Dormon, *People Called the Cajuns*, 33–43, 55–63.

5. For an excellent discussion of Longfellow's poem and its impact, see Carl A. Brasseaux, *In Search of Evangeline: Birth and Evolution of the Evangeline Myth* (Thibodaux, La.: Blue Heron Press, 1988), 9–14, passim. See also Barry J. Ancelet, "Elements of Folklore, History, and Literature in Longfellow's *Evangeline*," *Louisiana Review* 11 (Spring 1982): 118–26; Naomi Griffiths, "Longfellow's *Evangeline*: The Birth and Acceptance of a Legend," *Acadiensis* 11 (1982): 28–41.

6. Brasseaux, *In Search of Evangeline*, 44–45.

7. Ibid., 19.

8. Felix Voorhies, *Acadian Reminiscences: The True Story of Evangeline* (1907; reprint, Lafayette: University of Southwestern Louisiana Press, 1977), 106.

9. Michael Kammen, *Mystic Chords of Memory: The Transformation of Tradition in American Culture* (New York: Knopf, 1991), esp. pt. 2; James M. Lindgren, *Preserving the Old Dominion: Historic Preservation and Virginia Traditionalism* (Charlottesville: University Press of Virginia, 1993).

10. In 1927, 1928, 1929, and 1954, club members would again undertake lengthy studies of Louisiana and Acadian history. See Annual Programs, Women's Club of Lafayette Papers, box 1, Edith Garland DuPre Library, University of Southwestern Louisiana (hereafter USL).

11. Jerome Mouton, "History of Lafayette," Paul DeBaillon Collection, collection 7, box 3, folder 18, USL.

12. E. L. Stephens Papers, box 6, folder 49, Hill Memorial Library, Louisiana State University, Baton Rouge (hereafter LSU). That such stagecraft and spectacle could convey the long-forgotten past was demonstrated to the satisfaction of the pageant planners during the commencement ceremonies at the Southwestern Industrial Institute in 1914, when the "girl's gymnasium classes" performed traditional "Acadian dances." The dances were intended to prod the audience to recognize the persistence of Acadian culture despite the passing of traditions. The performance conceded the corrosive effects of modernity on vanishing traditions by juxtaposing eighteenth-century and contemporary Acadians. The Acadians of "old" affected "to be greatly shocked by the dress and dancing of their descendants of the present day." But the performance also insisted that a cultural inheritance linked contemporary Acadians with their ancestors. Ibid.

13. David Glassberg, *American Historical Pageantry: The Uses of Tradition in the Early Twentieth Century* (Chapel Hill: University of North Carolina Press, 1990).

14. *Lafayette Advertiser*, 6 March–7 April 1923.

15. Undated, unsigned draft of "Pageant of Attakapas Country," in Attakapas County Pageant Manuscript, MS 16, USL.

16. *The Attakapas Trail: A History of Lafayette Parish with Complete Pageant Score and Prologues* (Lafayette, La.: Community Service of Lafayette Parish, 1923), 37–38.

17. *St. Martinville Weekly Messenger*, 23 February–22 March 1924.

18. With more enthusiasm than accuracy, an Acadian newspaper editor in 1925 forecast that "The time is coming, and soon, when Louisiana will experience a boom similar to that of Florida." *Opelousas Progress*, 7 November 1925.

19. See, e.g., *St. Martinville Weekly Messenger*, 25 February 1925.

20. *St. Martinville Weekly Messenger*, 8 May 1926.

21. Glenn R. Conrad, "Susan Evangeline Walker Anding," *Dictionary of Louisiana Biography* (Lafayette: Louisiana Historical Association, 1988), 14.

22. Susan Anding's campaign may be followed in the *St. Martinville Weekly Gazette* from 1925 to 1931. For a summary of her efforts, see Brasseaux, *In Search of Evangeline*, 36–39.

23. *Opelousas Clarion-Progress*, 14 March 1929. At the Democratic convention the costumed "girls" donated a gavel that a nearly century-old Acadian had carved from a branch of the Evangeline Oak. One of the "girls" recalled, "At times we had to fight our way through the crowd." *St. Martinville Weekly Messenger*, 23 March 1929.

24. *St. Martinville Weekly Messenger*, 7 July 1928; *New Iberia Weekly Iberian*, 12 July 1928.

25. *St. Martinville Weekly Messenger*, 23 June 1928; *New Iberia Weekly Iberian*, 28 June 1928; *New Iberia Enterprise*, 30 June 1928; *Opelousas Clarion-Progress*, 7–14 March 1929.

26. Jackson Lears, "Packaging the Folk: Tradition and Amnesia in American Advertising, 1880–1940," in Jane S. Becker and Barbara Franco, eds., *Folk Roots, New Roots: Folklore in American Life* (Lexington, Mass.: Museum of Our National Heritage, 1988), 103–40.

27. *St. Martinville Weekly Messenger*, 13 July 1929. The charges, brought by a few public officials and businessmen in St. Martinville, were almost certainly an expression of male condescension and grandstanding. As happened during the campaigns to develop the monument at Stone Mountain, Ga., and many other historical sites during the 1920s, professional men yet again asserted custodianship, in the name of "sound business management," over projects that had been initiated and sustained by women.

28. *St. Martinville Weekly Messenger*, 13 July, 3, 17 August 1929, 8 February 1930; *Opelousas Clarion-News*, 23 January 1930.

29. Brasseaux, *In Search of Evangeline*, 46.

30. *Second Biennial Report of the State Parks Commission of Louisiana, 1936–1937* (New Orleans: State Parks Commission, 1937), 65; *Fourth Biennial Report of the State Parks Commission of Louisiana, 1936–1937* (New Orleans: State Parks Commission, 1941), 28. See also Stephen E. McLaughlin, "The Role of the Civilian Conservation Corps in the Founding of Louisiana's State Parks System" (M.A. thesis, Louisiana State University, 1994), 40–45.

31. *St. Martinville Weekly Messenger*, 22 January 1927.

32. Floyd Martin Clay, *Coozan Dudley LeBlanc: From Huey Long to Hadacol* (Gretna, La.: Pelican Publishing Co., 1973), chap. 1.

33. *St. Martinville Weekly Messenger*, 4 September 1926.

34. During his campaign for the position of public service commissioner he delivered, by one count, eighty-two speeches in French. *St. Martinville Weekly Messenger*, 10 September 1926; *Abbeville Meridional*, 27 October 1928.

35. LeBlanc acknowledged "the great part he played in bringing me to an appreciation of my Acadian heritage." Dudley LeBlanc, *The True Story of the Acadians* (N.p., 1932), i.

36. *Lafayette Tribune*, 31 August 1928; *St. Martinville Weekly Messenger*, 8 September 1928; *Abbeville Meridional*, 8 September 1928.

37. *Abbeville Meridional*, 27 October 1928.

38. *Abbeville Meridional*, 1 March 1930.

39. *St. Martinville Weekly Messenger*, 15 March 1930.

40. *Abbeville Meridional*, 28 June, 19 July 1930; *New Iberia Enterprise*, 12–19 July 1930; *New Iberia Weekly Iberian*, 17 July 1930; *St. Martinville Weekly Messenger*, 26 July 1920.

41. *Lafayette Daily Advertiser*, 13, 25 August 1930; *Opelousas Clarion-News*, 14, 21 August 1930; *Abbeville Meridional*, 16 August 1930; *New Iberia Enterprise*, 16 August 1930; *St. Martinville Weekly Messenger*, 16 August 1930; *New Iberia Weekly Iberian*, 4 September 1930.

42. LeBlanc, *True Story of the Acadians*, 90.

43. *Opelousas Clarion-News*, 4 September 1930. The mystical power of the pilgrimage is also evident in the book authored by participant James T. Vocelle, *The Triumph of the Acadians: A True Story of Evangeline's People* (Vero Beach, Fla.: N.p., 1930).

44. *New Iberia Weekly Iberian*, 16 April 1931; *New Iberia Enterprise*, 18 April 1931.

45. The previous year, during the Louisiana pilgrimage to Canada, the French consul in Montreal had given LeBlanc medals to be awarded to Louisiana high school students who wrote the best essays in French on "The Exile of the Acadians." *Abbeville Meridional*, 6 September 1930; *New Iberia Weekly Iberian*, 11 September 1930.

46. *St. Martinville Weekly Messenger*, 4 April 1931.

47. *New Iberia Enterprise*, 19 June 1936.

48. *Lafayette Daily Advertiser*, 9–22 October 1946; *Opelousas Clarion-News*, 10, 24 October 1946; *New Iberia Enterprise*, 10 October 1946; *St. Martinville Weekly Messenger*, 11–25 October 1946; *Abbeville Progress*, 12 October 1946; *New Orleans Times-Picayune*, 12 October 1946; *Crowley Weekly Acadian*, 17 October 1946; *Opelousas Daily World*, 18, 20 (quotation) October 1946; *Abbeville Meridional*, 19 October 1946.

49. *Opelousas Clarion-News*, 16 April 1931.

50. *St. Martinville Weekly Messenger*, 25 October 1946; Clément Cormier, "Tournée

triomphale en Louisiane: Octobre 1946," *Les cahiers de la Société historique acadienne* 17 (October–December 1986): 133–43.

51. *Lafayette Daily Advertiser*, 14 October 1946. LeBlanc's enthusiasm for Acadian exchanges endured into the 1960s, when he led his last group of "Evangeline girls" to the Acadian homeland (and an obligatory visit to the White House and a photo-opportunity with the president).

52. Dudley J. LeBlanc, *The Acadian Miracle* (Lafayette, La.: Evangeline Publishing Co., 1966), viii, 46, 81, 367.

53. The announcements for the 1936 pilgrimage, for instance, proclaimed: "Remember that this tour is intended to advertise the natural resources of Louisiana. It is planned to call the attention of the industrial leaders of the East and of the North to the wonderful resources of Louisiana, to its favorable climatic conditions and to its wonderful labor conditions." *Lafayette Daily Advertiser*, 10 August 1936. For an example of his fusion of politics and Acadian identity, see *St. Martinville Weekly Messenger*, 28 March 1931.

54. For all of his proclaimed attachment to Acadian culture and language, LeBlanc nevertheless announced that he hoped that the 1946 tour of the "Acadian girls" would prod rural Acadians in Louisiana to adapt to progress, including to learn English. "Some of you know," he explained, "that in the interior parishes of Louisiana the Acadian mothers and fathers have not learned the value of education. We felt that by bringing to them those who had the same name and spoke the same language they might become inspired to take more interest, to learn to speak English." *New Orleans Times-Picayune*, 12 October 1946.

55. The tradition of Acadian "pilgrimages" persists. In August 1999 thousands of Acadians from Canada and the United States gathered in "Acadiana" to take part in the second Cogres Mondial Acadien. *New York Times*, 16 August 1999.

56. Louise Olivier to H. B. Wright, 23 April 1943, Acadian Handicrafts Project Records (hereafter AHPR), box 1, LSU.

57. Olivier to Henry D. Larcade Jr., 11 August 1949, AHPR, box 5, LSU.

58. Olivier to Clay Shaw, 23 March 1953, AHPR, box 4, LSU.

59. Elizabeth Mae Roberts, "French Radio Broadcasting in Louisiana, 1935–1958" (M.A. thesis, Louisiana State University, 1959), 88–89.

60. Olivier boasted that "through the medium of the Assemblée, the younger generation became acquainted with and learned something of its French heritage [and . . .] all generations had an opportunity to meet on an equal footing and make practical use of their common language." "Resume of Louisiana State University French Project Activities, 1938–1944," undated [1944?], AHPR, box 1, LSU.

61. Ibid.

62. On the handicraft movement that influenced Olivier, see Jane S. Becker, *Selling Tradition: Appalachia and the Construction of an American Folk, 1930–1940* (Chapel Hill: University of North Carolina Press, 1998), and David E. Whisnant, *All That Is Native and Fine: The Politics of Culture in an American Region* (Chapel Hill: University of North Carolina Press, 1983).

63. Olivier to "Grace," 18 March 1944. AHPR, box 1, LSU.

64. See various festival announcements, AHPR, box 1, 3, LSU.

65. The festivals "bore me," she fumed. "They are getting to be more and more like street fairs—a bunch of society people get together and feast for two days at the Country Club—this is restricted to Fair officials and club members—a parade is held for the

common herd—a French hour is permitted—but not labored on—an ag. [agricultural] Show is held—because that's where you get your money." Olivier to Sarah [Gertrude Knott], undated [1956?], AHPR, correspondence 1955–56, box 7, LSU.

66. Olivier's complaints about the crass commercialism of the bicentennial celebrations hinted at her recognition that her own project also commercialized Acadian culture. Olivier to "Keed," 15 March 1955, AHPR, box 5, LSU.

67. "Sales Records in 1956–1957," [1957?], AHPR, box 2, LSU.

68. See, e.g., "Ways of the Bayou Country," *Recreation* 40 (July 1946): 207–08, 220; *Craftsman* 11 (December 1946): 332–43; *Travel* (January 1947): 21–23; and Marjorie Arbour, "It Pays to Play with Your Family," *Farm and Ranch* 84 (October 1954): 47.

69. The best source for information on the bicentennial celebration is the Acadian Bicentennial Commission Collection (hereafter ABCC), USL.

70. *Our Acadian Heritage—Let's Keep It!* (N.p.: Louisiana State Department of Education, Acadian Bicentennial Celebration Association, and Department of Commerce and Industry, 1954), 3.

71. Edwin L. Reed, Director, Advertising and Promotion, Louisiana Department of Commerce and Industry, 30 June 1954, ABCC, box 3, USL.

72. *New Orleans Times-Picayune*, 30 May, 24 August 1997, 14 January 1998.

73. On CODOFIL, see Robert Lewis, "L'Acadie Retrouvée: The Remaking of Cajun Identity in Southwestern Louisiana, 1968–1994," in Richard H. King and Helen Taylor, eds., *Dixie Debates: Perspectives on Southern Cultures* (New York: New York University Press, 1996), 67–84.

74. *New Orleans Times-Picayune*, 11 August 1997.

75. Herbert J. Gans, "Ethnic Invention and Acculturation: A Bumpy-Line Approach," *Journal of American Ethnic History* 12 (Fall 1992): 44–45 (Gans and Dowd). On contemporary Cajun culture, see Marjorie R. Esman, "Festivals, Change, and Unity: The Celebration of Ethnic Identity among Louisiana Cajuns," *Anthropological Quarterly* 55 (October 1982): 199–210, "Tourism as Ethnic Preservation: The Cajuns of Louisiana," *Annals of Tourism Research* 11 (1984): 451–67, and *Henderson, Louisiana: Cultural Adaptation in a Cajun Community* (New York: Holt, Rinehart, and Winston, 1985), esp. chaps. 10–11.

We Run the Alamo, and You Don't

Alamo Battles of Ethnicity and Gender

Holly Beachley Brear

The Alamo in downtown San Antonio, Texas, has always been an arena of conflict. Built in the eighteenth century with defense in mind, the Mission San Antonio de Valero, which became known as the "Alamo," was the most fortresslike of the five Spanish missions in the San Antonio region. The current battles at the Alamo, which are fought with words rather than guns, have become increasingly complex and ironic. Here the victors of the Texas Revolution celebrate their most famous defeat; here protesters cry out against what they declare to be a symbol of Anglo domination in a city that is almost 60 percent Hispanic; and here, at the nation's most famous site of male sacrifice, a women's group, the Daughters of the Republic of Texas (DRT), holds the reins of power.[1]

The first two incongruities have long been recognized and have received considerable attention. The irony of defeat even attracted the interest of cartoonist Gary Larson, who depicted the fighting at the Alamo occurring around the first Alamo gift shop operator's attempt to sell souvenir T-shirts reading "I kicked Santa Anna's butt at the Alamo"; the price of the T-shirts has been marked down repeatedly as the defenders continue to fall. The less humorous irony of a shrine to Anglos in a majority Hispanic city is of more recent origin, resulting from the steadily rising Hispanic population of southern Texas.

The salience of gender in the controversies surrounding the Alamo is less often acknowledged. Yet considerations of gender lie at the heart of current battles over the site, especially when the women who operate it come under attack from other minority groups. Implicated in the struggle over who should interpret the history of the Alamo and how it should be presented is a complex fusion of gender, ethnicity, cultural authority, and political power (at the state and local levels). These interconnected facets of the conflict, whether or not they are addressed openly, are present in many confrontations over history; the debates at the Alamo over professionalism and expertise have at their base enduring assumptions about the proper roles and relative authority of men, women, and ethnic minorities.

The importance of gender at the Alamo first became clear to me during a private conversation (which is where the social truth of public arguments so often comes to light). A man who had helped me in my research on the Anglo-Hispanic conflict occurring at the Alamo and who is very proud of his Hispanic heritage called to inform me of an uproar that had occurred at the site. He delighted in telling of the "catfight" (his word) among the Daughters as they wrestled to get close to the Queen of England during her 1991 visit to the Alamo. He ended his description by saying, "Well, you know how women can be!"

Abrupt silence followed his comment. Before that, I had, in my informant's eyes, momentarily lost my gendered identity. But during the moment of silence I once again regained it. What had, for a moment in his mind, differentiated me, a female anthropologist (and therefore scholar), from the Daughters? And what, for this man (and many men in our society), defines women and "how they can be"? And who is acceptable in our society to produce and project history, especially at our most sacred memorials?

The Daughters' custodianship of the Alamo has always been inextricably tied to their place in society as Anglo women. In their commitment to preserving the past, the Daughters share many similarities with other women's groups dedicated to safeguarding heritage. Members of the United Daughters of the Confederacy (UDC), the Daughters of the American Revolution (DAR), and the Daughters of the Republic of Texas are all "daughters" via the past, but mothers and wives in the present. These roles are important to the impression each group seeks to convey. The image of daughter, in kinship structure, is a subordinate one: offspring rather than progenitor, the child whose status comes from more famous forefathers. Indeed, one reason the "daughter" kinship groups of the American Revolution, the Confederacy, and the Texas Republic have had greater membership and more prominence than the "son" groups has been that women have long been socialized to accept the subordinate role in our society.[2]

Certainly, the Daughters of the Republic of Texas embraced the subordinate imagery of their public roles. In an 1893 address, President Mrs. Anson Jones outlined to her fellow Daughters the duty of women to remain in the home and the schoolroom, influencing the minds of young children. But men, she explained, were meant to go out into the world and achieve great things. She concluded by transferring women's role to the organization's main purpose: "Daughters of the Republic of Texas, our duty lies plain before us. Let us leave the future of Texas to our brothers, and claim as our province the guarding of her holy past. . . . Let us love to study Texas history and teach it to her children."[3] She presented the Daughters as a group of women performing their duty privately and unobtrusively, properly caring for the home, the past, and the children.

According to the widely accepted precepts of late-nineteenth-century society when the Daughters were founded, white women were charged with caring for men's creations while men moved on to new projects. Throughout the historic preservation movement in the United States, beginning during the mid-nineteenth century, the role of women has been to preserve the "homes" of great men as monuments to heroism, progress, and production. Because such sites of memory were not part of the productive process, they were appropriately the domain of women.[4]

But if the Daughters accepted their subordination to white men, they also endorsed a fervently heroic Anglo account of Texas history. In the Texas "creation myth" that they have promoted, ethnicity and gender are tightly interwoven. They highlight the masculine fortitude of the heroes of the Alamo and the Texas Revolution; Mexicans, in contrast, are depicted as jealous, petty, disorganized, and utterly lacking the self-control that distinguished the Anglo Texans of lore. Anglo men seemingly make progress possible; they bring order to chaos and industry to the wilderness. The mythologized battle scenes depict Anglo men as productive businessmen, focusing on their targets and achieving a high war tally in comparison to their invested losses, whereas the Mexicans appear as self-consumed pleasure seekers, taking siestas and dallying with women when they should be fighting. Anglo women, as complements to their male counterparts, stand on their pedestal as virtuous matrons, whereas Mexican and African American women appear as prostitutes, luring men to bed rather than to battle.[5] Consequently, in the creation mythology surrounding Texas and the Alamo, Anglo men represent the most productive, cultured inhabitants of the region, coming at the end of an evolution that began with Native Americans and was followed by Spaniards and Mexicans. Mythologically, productivity and culture thrive in the region only after the arrival of the Anglos and the victory at San Jacinto of Sam Houston over Antonio Lopez de Santa Anna.[6]

The Daughters of the Republic of Texas, in their official capacity as the state-appointed custodians of the Alamo, in many ways align themselves with this interpretation of the site. Gathering together their overwhelmingly Anglo membership, the Daughters hold a commemorative service annually on 6 March to honor the Alamo defenders. They open the site to only two other private groups: the Order of the Alamo and the Texas Cavaliers. Both are almost exclusively Anglo, all-male organizations. Each uses the Alamo church as a ceremonial site for reproducing themselves in the form of Fiesta San Antonio royalty.[7] Thus the Daughters support the dominant social group in Texas, allowing predominantly Anglo organizations privileged use of the state's most valuable historic property.

Because of their control over the Alamo, the Daughters have served as the primary target for minorities frustrated by their limited access to the site and their subordinate status in the Alamo's interpretation. In the past, the most frequent complaint against the Daughters and the history they present is that the Daughters neglect the Hispanic heritage of the Alamo. Hispanics protesting the Daughters' version of the site's importance describe the group as racially exclusive and claim that the Daughters have used the Alamo to promote a past exclusively absorbed with dominant Anglo Texans.

Yet, in reality, the Daughters occupy a much more ambiguous position in the struggle for cultural authority over memory at the Alamo. Although they are often depicted by their critics as reactionary elite Anglo women whose cultural authority is an extension of their social status, the Daughters' position on the social ladder is actually relatively low. From their inception the Daughters have required that members have ancestral links to at least one of the following groups: colonists brought to Texas by Stephen F. Austin in the 1820s, men who fought for Texas's independence from Mexico in 1835–36, and people who served to maintain the independence of the Republic of Texas prior to its annexation to the United States in 1846. The unsettled conditions of the Texas region during the early 1800s demanded that settlers be rough-and-tumble survivors, so few of the Daughters' ancestors were gen-

teel. Indeed, early in the organization's existence members described themselves as the "widows, wives, daughters, and female descendants of the early
pioneers of Texas who . . . sacrificed life and property for the sake of humanity."⁸ This description, which accompanied the Daughters' bid for custodianship of the Alamo submitted to the Texas legislature in 1904, suggests a more
primitive and primordial ancestry than does the dignified term "Founding
Fathers" associated with the ancestors of the members of such groups as the
Daughters of the American Revolution and the Colonial Dames.

The comparatively modest social status of the Daughters of the Republic
of Texas is evident in San Antonio. Richard Teitz, who served as the first
professional director of the Alamo from 1995 to 1997, noted that most of the
Daughters are not part of the social or cultural leadership of the city. Their
status in society comes not from any connection with the moneyed "old
families" of San Antonio, such as the members of the Battle of Flowers
Association (an organization begun by wives of wealthy San Antonio businessmen in 1891 to organize Spring Carnival, which later became Fiesta) or
the members of the Order of the Alamo (an organization of elite businessmen
begun in 1909 by Virginian John Barron Carrington to elect the queen of the
Battle of Flowers Parade). The status of the Daughters comes primarily from
their role as custodians of the Alamo. Teitz commented on the defensiveness
of some of the Daughters regarding their social status: "Part of the mentality
[of the Daughters] is 'We've been here as long as you people, and we run the
Alamo, and you don't.' "⁹

Ironically, then, DRT members share with some representatives of the Hispanic community in San Antonio the claim that their ancestors preceded the
wealthier Anglo "old families" in the region. Thus, at a time when the
political power of the Hispanic community is relatively strong, the Hispanics
celebrate their control of the city government in much the same way that the
Daughters flaunt their command of the Alamo—in each case, the feeling is
"We run it, and you don't."

Unable to take for granted the resources and social connections available to
elite Anglos in Texas, the Daughters instead have relied on a tactical invocation of their role as women conservators of heritage. The Daughters admit no
doubt as to their mission. The chairman of the Alamo Committee, Mrs.
Edwin R. Simmang, for instance, stated in the October 1959 *Alamo Committee Newsletter* that "the sole purpose to which we are dedicated [is] the
preservation of the Alamo, and the high ideals which it inspires." The tens of
thousands of people visiting the Alamo every year and the reverence expressed by these visitors, she concluded, "is but a re-statement of [the

Daughters's] reason for being."[10] But if their mission is clear, the best strat-
agem to accomplish that end is complicated because the principal charge of
the Daughters, the preservation of the Alamo, differs in important respects
from the self-appointed duties of most other women's groups. The Alamo,
after all, is a battlefield and the mythical sacrificial birthplace of a new republic, not the "home" of great men. It has none of the usual domestic
characteristics of historic properties typically under the care of women's
groups. Second, the Daughters, since their inception, have had to be active in
the public world of politics and business because the Alamo is both a state
property and a money-making enterprise. Thus, the Daughters have long
stretched the boundaries of the gender roles that they themselves proclaim
to uphold.

They also are aware of the unusual cultural authority that they, as members
of a hereditary and voluntary women's organization, exert over an interna-
tionally famous historic site. When the Daughters were founded, they and
sister organizations often entered into partnerships with local and state governments to preserve noteworthy "shrines." But gradually the role of these
women's groups diminished as state and local governments assumed greater
responsibility for representations of the past. The increased involvement of
the state, coupled with the professionalizing of history and museum work,
created "a class of men anxious to wrest the cultural authority over the past
from amateur women historians." Typically, the newly ascendant male public
historians acknowledged the fund-raising capacity of women's organizations
but otherwise viewed them with condescension. The Daughters have bucked
this trend by retaining full control over the state-owned portion of the Alamo
compound in the hands of women.[11]

Intent on buttressing their cultural authority despite countervailing trends,
the Daughters have at times demonstrated an acute sense of the convergence
of etiquette, gender, and power in their dealings with the predominantly male
Texas legislature and the public generally. For instance, in the Spring 1989
issue of *Daughters' Reflections*, a newsletter, Mary Jane Addison, the legislative chairman of the DRT, urged the membership to write letters to the
Texas House of Representatives requesting assistance in the Daughters' battle against a legislative bill to remove them as the state-appointed custodians of the Alamo. In her instructions, Addison explicitly admonished
her colleagues to "remember to be exceptionally polite" in their letters to
the legislators.[12]

Addison's concern for politeness almost certainly derived from members'
reputed unladylike arrogance in many of their public interactions. In 1994, for

example, when the Daughters were in the midst of the fiercest campaign against their custodianship of the Alamo, Sam Dibrell, the son of a Daughter and a former DRT attorney, told the *Dallas Morning News*, "The Daughters are a little like the Dallas Cowboys. They are always under constant attack from critics."[13] Certainly there could be no more telling evidence that the Daughters had acquired an overtly masculine, tough image than that they were compared to Texas's most famous professional football team and the very symbol of all-male athleticism.

This reputation came largely from writers for the San Antonio press who criticized the Daughters in articles and commentaries, especially during the late 1980s and early 1990s. This "negative press" so damaged the Daughters' public image that they finally began to take seriously the possibility that they might lose control of the site. In 1993 they admitted that the organization had an image problem. A *San Antonio Express News* story in that year, for instance, focused on the public perceptions of the Daughters as well as their self-image. Entitled "Under Siege: Why the DRT Thinks It's Doing a Good Job with the Alamo Despite an 'Image Problem,' " the article noted that the Daughters' usual means of greeting criticism—silence—was itself under scrutiny. Their former tight-lipped stance to the media was not working well for public relations since "the frosty-silence defense only helps maintain the us-against-them polarization."[14]

During the mid-1990s the Daughters made a concerted effort to restore their reputation, in part by promoting a gentler (and more feminine) image of themselves. A message from DRT president Carolyn Hilburn in January 1994 trumpeted news of a more positive public image when she asked other members, "Have you noticed all the GREAT PUBLICITY [her emphasis] we have been getting lately? I believe we have had five good [newspaper] articles just recently. Isn't that remarkable?"[15] This "gentler" image, which often betrayed implicitly gendered qualities, became the primary defense of the Daughters, at least to reporters. DRT president general Gail Loving Barnes, for instance, emphasized the feminine nurturance that the Daughters gave the Alamo, declaring, "We lovingly take care of the Alamo." She also noted that they received no money for giving this care.[16] Because the Daughters provided their services at the Alamo for free, such efforts became, in her mind, "loving care." The management of the Alamo was thus presented as a form of altruistic and amateur "home economics" that elevated nurturance and care, not as the aggressive pursuit of profit.

Such maternal rhetoric obscures the fact that the care of the Alamo is not "free." Its upkeep requires substantial maintenance and personnel costs. It is free only in terms of the state's budget. The funding needed for the site's upkeep comes from donations and from profits made in the Alamo gift shop located beside the Alamo church. Contrary to the Daughters' public statements, the money raised by these means goes far beyond "home economics." The Daughters have reluctantly disclosed the amount of money, derived from activities conducted on state-owned property, they spend on the site as well as hold in reserve. Both sums have exceeded one million dollars. Thus, the Daughters, in terms of their financial success, have less in common with their projected image as a group of private homemakers than with successful business*men*.

The finances of the Alamo site have undercut the feminine mystique of the DRT. The Daughters' business and political acumen differentiate them from other women's hereditary and patriotic groups, such as the DAR and the UDC. Most women's organizations interested in the past have been financially independent rather than financially successful. Members typically have money and leisure time at their disposal to commit to historic preservation, but they are not expected to demonstrate enthusiasm or ability for generating a profit. Earning money, after all, implies male aggressiveness whereas giving it connotes female generosity. Yet, even as the Daughters have good reason to hide their financial acumen, they also sometimes boast of it. The Alamo, as the DRT is quick to point out, operates at a profit, whereas many other state sites lose money. A 1994 protest by San Antonio councilman William Thornton, who was evicted from Alamo state property during a photography session, prompted Daughter Anna Hartman to make explicit the subtext for attacks on her organization: "Some of the men attacking us just resent what has been a successful female venture since 1905."[17]

The intensifying protest against the Daughters' control of the Alamo since the late 1980s has forced them to acknowledge the changing political and social context in which they operate. Their new critics now include non-Hispanic opponents. For example, Ron Wilson, an African American state legislator from Houston, introduced a bill in the late 1980s to remove the Daughters from their custodial role. Similarly, the opposition offered by such people as Councilman Thornton reveals that Anglos also are entering the fray. Like Wilson and Thornton, the majority of the public detractors of the Daughters have been men. Increasingly, their attacks have turned on the Daughters' ability (or inability) to be good historians. Questions about the competency of the organization were especially conspicuous during a 1994 dispute over a possible excavation at the Alamo when men of various ethnic affiliations—Hispanic, African American, Native American, and Anglo—faulted the Daughters for improperly interpreting history.

Implicitly, these critics claim history as the domain of men. They share the undisclosed assumption that women do not *do* history; they do not do facts. Women, according to the social dichotomy, do historic preservation (that is, nurturance and care), but they cannot claim historical "truth" as part of their dominion. Historical "truth" belongs to the jurisdiction of men, who, after all, dominate both the pages and the production of history.

In the eyes of these male critics, then, the DRT, as an organization of women, is inherently unqualified to interpret the history of the Alamo. Numerous swipes at the Daughters have underlined this implied "deficiency." Representative Wilson declared that citizens need to make sure that the history offered at the Alamo is "an accurate portrayal of what happened and why." He also contended that the state should resume responsibility for the Alamo because "[w]e probably could pump more money into restoration and promote it a little bit better."[18] The "we" of this statement appears to be state officials, mainly men, who are able to "pump" more male things—history and money—into the site.

Another critic, David Anthony Richelieu, an anti-DRT columnist with the *San Antonio Express News*, dismissed tributes to the Daughters' selflessness by pointing out that their care of the Alamo *has* cost the state something—in his word, truth.[19] Similarly Councilman Thornton complained that "[t]he way the Daughters have done things, there is no way for people to get a real sense of what happened at the Alamo."[20] A month later, in the *Houston Post*, he denigrated the Daughters' approach by suggesting that they also were behind the times: "The way we do things in the world today is to include people and try to be [historically] accurate. I'm certain they [the Daughters] are not interested in inclusion or accuracy."[21]

Thornton's 1994 reference to the inclusiveness of the interpretation of the site pointed to the ongoing controversy over whether a mission cemetery lies under the street located immediately in front of the Alamo. According to Thornton and others, the remains of over one thousand Christianized Native Americans lie buried beneath the street. The Daughters, when alerted to the possible cemetery site, continued to demand that the street remain open to traffic. Their position showed, according to protesters, a disregard for a group intimately tied to the Alamo's missionary past. Hispanic and Native American leaders joined political hands, at least initially, in decrying the DRT's approval of the "desecration of sacred ground."

The street closure was just one of several battles in which the Daughters found themselves confronted by men who believed that the DRT had been both inaccurate and negligent in its portrayal of the Alamo's history. The climax of this controversy over interpretation came in a 1994 proposal (publicized by the *San Antonio Express News* in a special section) to redesign and interpret the city-owned part of the Alamo compound currently known as Alamo Plaza.[22] The newspaper published commentaries by various individuals and groups involved in the debate over the site's history as well as illustrations of the structural suggestions for "a proposal to reclaim history" in which various features of the mission compound existing during the 1836 battle would be reconstructed.[23] So extensive were the reconstruction plans that some critics of the proposal declared that the proponents were trying to turn Alamo Plaza into a theme park, or "Alamoland."

The *purported* aim of the plan was to make the plaza into a more historically defined park, with markers and exhibits to denote where events had occurred at the site. Numerous proposed plaques would explain the daily activities of the compound during the mission period. The master plan for the project also included reconstructing the Alamo fortress as it existed on the city-owned property, leaving the state-owned property containing the famous church unaffected. The implication was that the history of the Alamo was not being presented as accurately and as completely as it should be on the state-owned property run by the DRT.

In response to the intense debate over history on Alamo Plaza, the city of San Antonio created the Alamo Plaza Study Committee, a group of twenty-four people assigned, among other duties, to establish historically factual information concerning the Alamo Plaza. Of this number, twenty were men (83 percent). The committee included six amateur and professional historians who served as authorities for recommendations on how the past should be presented at the Alamo; all were men, and of these, four (67 percent) were Hispanic. Predictably, the Daughters lost their battle to keep the street open.[24]

The San Antonio City Council had not invited any of the historians employed by the Texas Historical Commission to be on the Alamo Plaza Study Committee, despite the commission's expertise in historic preservation. Perhaps this was because the commission is a state agency. As such, it oversees preservation carried out by the DRT, but it has no jurisdiction over the city-owned portion of the Alamo compound. The city councilmen who appointed the committee members presumably wanted to keep the state out of its decision-making process. The issue of jurisdiction also had an underlying ethnic component: San Antonio is predominantly Hispanic whereas

Texas is predominantly Anglo, and the Hispanic community remains suspicious of the Anglo-dominated state government.

Although the Study Committee had no representation from the Texas
Historical Commission, the state agency was asked to offer its opinion on the
proposals for interpreting the plaza. The commission responded by supporting the street closure proposal but did not condone the structural changes
suggested. The commission would approach any replication of missing
structures "cautiously" but did acknowledge that "more [could] be done to
interpret the Alamo site better for visitors." The commission further recommended that one way that the Alamo could remain "a viable historic site that
educates visitors with accurate information" would be the hiring of a "professional firm with a national reputation for interpreting high profile historic
sites" to manage the state-owned portion of the Alamo compound. Moreover,
the Alamo staff should include full-time professionals, possibly under the
direction of the Daughters.[25] The clear implication of these criticisms was
that the Daughters were not sufficiently professional in their presentation of
the site's history.

Caught off-guard by this suggestion, the DRT felt that the Texas Historical
Commission had stabbed it in the back. Previously, the agency had only
guided the Daughters in the physical preservation of the Alamo's buildings; it
had never questioned their interpretation of the site. Recognizing that their
actions were under close scrutiny, the Daughters eventually bowed to the
recommendation of the commission and created the position of director of
the Alamo. The hiring of male managers gave the appearance of a transformation in leadership at the Alamo. Yet, even as the Daughters seemingly de-
ferred to male, professional authority in management and historical interpretation, in reality they retained a firm grip on the reins of power.

That the DRT sought only a male figurehead quickly became obvious. The
expert it selected as the first director of the Alamo came with excellent
credentials. Before accepting the position, Richard Teitz had served for
twenty-five years as director and chief executive officer for various major
American museums. He had received degrees from Yale, Harvard, and the
University of Texas at San Antonio and was a former university professor in
both history and art history. Nonetheless, he proved a most unlikely choice
for the post. Teitz did not grow up revering heroes of the Alamo; he hailed
from Rhode Island rather than the Lone Star State. Moreover, his broad
experience and perspective ultimately worked against him in his dealings
with the Daughters, who opposed any significant changes at the site. They
insisted that its focus remain on the 1836 battle, as it had for the previous

ninety years. Teitz's job was to occupy the most visible office at the Alamo and therefore to remove, at least partially, the spotlight from the Daughters.

Friction between the Daughters and Teitz developed as soon as he began exerting his authority as director. Understanding himself to be a representative of the Alamo, he contacted, on his own, the superintendent of the other four Spanish missions in San Antonio. Eager to interpret the Alamo in the context of the colonial mission culture of the region, Teitz hoped to create links with these federally administered missions. His initiative outraged the Daughters, who were especially angered that he had made these contacts without first consulting them. Teitz suddenly found himself consigned to the ranks of the Daughters' perceived opponents; he became, in the members' eyes, part of the "them" besieging "us."[26] Too independent for the DRT, Teitz was fired by the organization after only a brief tenure. His successor, Brad Breuer (the director as of 1999), was a born-and-reared Texan who appeared to be more in line with the Daughters' way of thinking.

In 1996 the Daughters also created the position of historian and hired Bruce Winders to fill it (he remained in the post as of 1999).[27] In a news release, the DRT described Winders in strictly professional terms, stressing his graduate degrees in history and his teaching experience at Texas Christian University. But its in-group newsletter, *Alamo Mission Chapter News*, presented Winders as "one of us." He himself revealed his allegiance in a telling statement: "History is hereditary. We often learn to appreciate it from our parents and grandparents. . . . Like many men my age, I grew up surrounded by images of David Crockett."[28] Having been "properly" brought up to revere the Alamo heroes, he was unlikely to pose a threat to the Daughters' continuing focus on the 1836 battle at the Alamo.

If the creation of two new positions at the Alamo and the hiring of two professional men at least in part redressed the charges of amateurism, the Daughters still had to rebut criticism about their narrow, ethnocentric interpretation of the site. The anger of protesters over the last two decades has not been entirely wasted on the Daughters. They have been willing, if necessary, to accommodate demands for a broader interpretation of the site's history; they simply have wanted to control that interpretation. One of their recent projects has been the development and installment of the "Alamo Wall of History," which consists of six free-standing panels outlining the history of the Alamo compound from the mission period to the present. This wall was one of the primary focal points of a tour I received during a meeting in March 1998 with Alamo director Brad Breuer, historian Bruce Winders, and committee chair Mary Carmack. The Daughters' insistence on interpretative autonomy was highlighted by Carmack, who remarked that the idea for the Alamo Wall of History originated with the Daughters themselves.[29] In other words, the wall was their choice of how to present history at the site, not a requirement forced on them from the outside.

But some observers who witnessed the protests over the Alamo during the 1990s suggest that the Daughters "conceived" the idea of the wall as a response to movements by various groups to further develop the history of Alamo Plaza, which, since it lies outside the state property line, is beyond the control of the DRT. James Steely of the Texas Historical Commission posits that the Daughters developed the Alamo Wall of History to preempt alternative interpretations by others. Steely, as the commission's chief historian, helped review the history presented on these panels. Early in the development of the project, he and Frances Rickard (also of the commission) contacted the Daughters to express "serious concerns regarding the accuracy of the text" they had prepared for the panels. The text, according to Steely and Rickard, had "many inaccuracies and voids of information." The DRT eventually included these commission representatives in its final meetings on the text for the wall and went along with their suggestions.[30]

Despite their acceptance of advice from the commission, the DRT remained defensive. Daughter Madge Roberts, who served as chair of the Alamo Wall of History Committee, wrote to Steely in December 1996 to thank him for the time he took to review the panels. But she observed, "We found your comments to be very helpful to us. Some of the things we had already discussed and a few [of the errors] we had already caught." The unmistakable implication of these statements is that the Daughters, while appreciative of the commission's concern for accuracy, are fully capable of policing their own historical texts.[31]

This letter also reflects the tension between the Daughters' desire to appear competent and their recognition of the need for professional help if they are to remain the state-appointed custodians of the Alamo. The Daughters needed the credibility of the Historical Commission to secure public acceptance of the project, but they still jealously asserted control over the interpretation of the Alamo's significance.

Curiously, the Daughters as a whole relish outside challenges to their control of the site (as long as those challenges do not come from state agencies). When working with the Daughters, Teitz discerned a fighting instinct among the members even more pronounced than among other preservation groups in the United States. This characteristic became particularly evident during the conflict of the mid-1990s: "They [the Daughters] saw

themselves, in the tradition of the Alamo defenders, as besieged by overwhelming odds [and] by people who were less intelligent, less committed
than they were. And that aspect of the Daughters of the Republic of Texas . . .
has—not altogether fortunately—come down to the present day."[32] The
Daughters' posture and actions are in keeping with the socially constructed
role of women as the torchbearers for historic preservation and evangelists
in the cause of historical memory. And it was this defensiveness that caused
the friction between Teitz and the Daughters as well as their image problems
in general.

Teitz believes that even though the Daughters still enjoy the sense of being
under attack by people who would "destroy" them by taking away their
control of the Alamo, these women, at the same time, fear losing the site,
which is, after all, owned by the state of Texas and by the Texas taxpayers.
State ownership is a major point of protesters: the Daughters act as though
they own the Alamo when, in fact, they are only its stewards. In turn, the
Daughters are suspicious of any group expressing a desire to hold a ceremony at the Alamo, and they want to know the motivations behind each
request. Their repeated denial of access to the site by other groups stems
from the Daughters' jealously guarded identity at the Alamo.[33] The Daughters do not want events held there that would draw attention away from the
era of the Texas Revolution. As a Daughter explained in 1990, all that the DRT
requires of ceremonies held inside the building is that they honor the Alamo
heroes. When explaining why the Daughters, the Texas Cavaliers, and the
Order of the Alamo were the only groups allowed to hold annual ceremonies
inside the Alamo church, she offered the following justification: "We keep it
real special. You can't dilute it down by doing *everything* in there. It wouldn't
mean anything after a while. . . . San Antonio is a city that worships the past,
and this Alamo is the glue that holds it all together."[34] Of course, the past
worshiped is limited to the 1836 battle at the site rather than any preceding or
subsequent history.

Each claim by other groups to the site "dilutes" the Daughters' identity,
which is tied to a twenty-year segment of a history that spans almost three
hundred years (beginning in 1718). When the full history of the site is taken
into account, the Daughters' claim to and interpretation of the Alamo appears
perilously frail. Yet they have no intention of surrendering the Alamo without
a fight.

The fusion of gender and ethnicity in debates surrounding the administration of the Alamo has created an extremely complex political and cultural
struggle over the site. No adequate or nuanced understanding of the contro-

versy over historical memory in San Antonio is possible if gender, ethnicity, or class are ignored. The interpretation of the site, one of the most celebrated historic places in the United States, says much about how the peoples of San Antonio and of Texas choose to represent themselves to each other and to the larger world. The stakes for the Daughters of the Republic of Texas are unmistakable. Challenged on various grounds, the Daughters insist on their "obligation" to preserve the shrine; they brandish their "loving care" of the Alamo to make their opponents appear to be heartless men intent on evicting loyal women—mothers, daughters, wives, and widows—from their self-appointed home. If expelled from their shrine, the Daughters will also surrender a cultural authority and social standing that is almost meaningless unless wedded to the Alamo.

The ongoing struggles over who will control the past remembered at the Alamo reflect much more about our current society than about the events that occurred in Texas during the preceding centuries. Although custodianship was not hotly contested in 1905, the position the Daughters now hold at the Alamo has grown in significance with the growing importance of the reconstructed past in the United States and with the economic success of the Alamo, which is currently the number-one tourist attraction in Texas. Maintaining control of the site depends on public support of the Daughters, both in the press and in the Texas legislature.

To date, the repeated defeat of legislative bills to remove the DRT as the Alamo's state-appointed custodian reveals a quiet approval of the work this predominantly Anglo group of women has done at the Alamo, including the presenting of a past focused on Anglo heroics. The current legislative challenge to the Daughters—Representative Wilson's bill to remove them as custodians—poses no real threat. The measure is one of many that have never even made it to committee. In 1993, when speaking of the upcoming legislative session, Wilson conceded his grudging admiration of the Daughters: "They're definitely a formidable opponent. I have the highest respect for them. Last time they literally kicked my butt."[35] The bill serves primarily to protest the Daughters' administration of the site and to log in the legislative record Wilson's campaign to remove them from their position at the Alamo.

Many officials in the Texas state government, however, believe that other legislative action ultimately will end the Daughters' custodianship. One state employee explained that the issue of finances probably will be the avenue of attack on the Daughters' competence at the site (i.e., how the money is raised and spent at the site and how the financial records are kept). Another, although perhaps unspoken reason for removing the Daughters will be the charge that the organization has not properly administered the Alamo as a museum.

In a 1998 interview, Bruce Winders commented that the "enabling legislation" that awarded the Daughters administration of the Alamo required that the site be maintained as a sacred memorial to the Alamo heroes of the 1836 battle. In other words, the Daughters, in concentrating on that battle, are simply fulfilling a mandate imposed by legislators in 1905. But times have changed. Texas society has changed, and legislation will change the custodianship unless the Daughters are able to move beyond the twenty-year period that has served as the focus at the Alamo. To maintain their control of the site, the Daughters must allow the Alamo to become a museum rather than a shrine created by the Daughters.

There are legitimate complaints that the Daughters have, at times, treated the Alamo as a sacred clubhouse rather than a public museum. Justifiable questions have been raised about the wisdom of allowing a private organization with its own agenda to control the most valuable historic property owned by the state. The charge that the Daughters have not handled history properly is, in a sense, warranted. Yet some of the people hurling these charges represent groups with their own particularistic perspective on the site's significance. Some of the Hispanic community members who protest the DRT's presentation of the past, for example, claim descent from the Canary Islanders sent by Spain to help settle the region in the 1720s. Would they reinterpret the site to dwell on Spain's role in San Antonio? Another group demanding control over the interpretation are reenactors. Interestingly enough, Councilman Thornton, who led one of the protests against the Daughters' handling of the site, has portrayed Alamo hero William B. Travis. Another reenactor suggested that the San Antonio Living Historians Association (SALHA) should have a much larger role in interpreting the Alamo's history. Some members of the association assert what can only be described as a near-spiritual identification with the site. One member even implies that he is James Bowie reincarnated. He will not allow anyone else to portray Bowie in reenactments presented by SALHA, and he speaks of the Bowie knife replica he carries as "my knife." His connection to Bowie became fixed in his mind when he met one of Bowie's female descendants while he was dressed in his Bowie costume. As he presented the woman with a yellow rose, she exclaimed, in awed surprise, that she had dreamed that her ancestor James Bowie had given her a yellow rose. Should, as one reenactor asserted, "men of such caliber" be in control of the Alamo's past? Yet another organization interested in reinterpreting the Alamo is the Catholic Church, which detects valuable religious symbolism in the site. Should it be allowed, as it has publicly suggested, to reclaim the site for Eucharistic services?

Sometime in the future the Daughters will lose control of the Alamo. They may well surrender their authority primarily because the members are unable to meet two conflicting demands: (1) recognize and accept the evolving social composition of Texas by allowing the Alamo to be a museum (which is more politically neutral than a shrine), focusing *equally* on all phases of the site's past, and (2) uphold the static concept of women as subordinate. Such demands require that the Daughters be both contemporary and unchanging, a difficult and unenviable task.

Before my Hispanic informant made his comment about "how women can be," I was intent on viewing the controversy over the Alamo as a symbol of ethnic divisions in San Antonio. Having already concluded that the Daughters were agents of oppression, I was troubled by this man's comments and insinuations and I subsequently have come to appreciate the complexity of the struggle over the Alamo's past, one waged along the lines of class, ethnicity, and, yes, gender. When considering the contemporary controversy surrounding the Alamo, we should remember the often unacknowledged condescension toward women in positions of authority in our society and the strategies that organized women have had to adopt in order to persevere. Seen in this light, there are no innocent victims, no self-sacrificing heroes in the contemporary battle over the Alamo. Such martyrs exist only in each of the combatant's cherished mythology.

NOTES

1. In 1905 Texas governor S. W. T. Lanham officially awarded custodianship of the Alamo to the Daughters under the condition that they would maintain the property, without charge to the state, as "a sacred memorial to the heroes who immolated themselves upon that hallowed ground." But Governor Lanham also decreed that the state-owned property of the Alamo compound would be subject to future legislation by the state of Texas. O. B. Colquitt, *Message of Governor O. B. Colquitt to the Thirty-third Legislature relating to the Alamo Property* (Austin: Von Doeckmann-Jones Co., 1913), 100.

2. See the histories of the various women's historical organizations, including Peggy Anderson, *The Daughters: An Unconventional Look at America's Fan Club* (New York: St. Martin's Press, 1974); Karen L. Cox, "Women, the Lost Cause, and the New South: The United Daughters of the Confederacy and the Transmission of Confederate Culture, 1894–1919" (Ph.D. diss., University of Southern Mississippi, 1997); Wallace Evan Davies, *Patriotism on Parade: The Story of Veterans' and Hereditary Organizations in America, 1783–1900* (Cambridge: Harvard University Press, 1955); Margaret Gibbs, *The DAR* (Holt, Rinehart, and Winston, 1969); Mrs. Joseph Rucker Lamar, *A History of the National Society of the Colonial Dames of America* (Atlanta: National Society of the Colonial

Dames of America, 1934); Lucile E. Laganke, "The National Society of the Daughters of the American Revolution: Its History, Politics, and Influence, 1890–1949" (Ph.D. diss., Western Reserve University, 1951); Stuart McConnell, "Reading the Flag: A Reconsideration of the Patriotic Cults of the 1890s," in John Bodnar, ed., *Bonds of Affection: Americans Define Their Patriotism* (Princeton: Princeton University Press, 1996); and Francesca Morgan, "Home and Country: Women, Nation, and the Daughters of the American Revolution, 1890–1939" (Ph.D. diss., Columbia University, 1998), esp. 151–218.

3. *Proceedings from the Second Annual Meeting of the Daughters of the Republic of Texas* (N.p., 1893), 2–3.

4. On women and historic preservation in general, see Barbara J. Howe, "Women in Historic Preservation: The Legacy of Ann Pamela Cunningham," *Public Historian* 12 (Winter 1990): 31–61.

5. Ibid., 45–63.

6. On the "Texas creation myth," see Holly Beachley Brear, *Inherit the Alamo: Myth and Ritual at an American Shrine* (Austin: University of Texas Press, 1995), 23–44.

7. Out of over 400 members, the Texas Cavaliers organization has only 6 Hispanic members; the Order of the Alamo organization has, at last count (1991), only 1 Hispanic member out of over 800 members. Neither organization has any African American members. The Texas Cavaliers initiate their new members in a secret ceremony inside the church, then go outside to crown their Fiesta royalty King Antonio, who is chosen from among their ranks. The Order of the Alamo, in another private ceremony, selects, via in-person balloting, the queen of the Order of the Alamo (from among the members' unwed daughters) to reign over Fiesta. On these organizations, see ibid., 18–23, 64–83.

8. Adele B. Looscan, "The Work of the Daughters of the Republic of Texas in Behalf of the Alamo," *Texas Historical Association Quarterly* 8 (1904): 81.

9. Richard Teitz, interview with author, San Antonio, 12 March 1998.

10. *Alamo Committee Newsletter*, October 1959, unpaginated.

11. W. Fitzhugh Brundage, "White Women and the Politics of Historical Memory in the New South, 1880–1920," in Glenda E. Gilmore, Jane Dailey, and Bryant Simon, eds., *Jumoin' Jim Crow: Race and Politics in the New South* (Princeton: Princeton University Press, forthcoming).

12. *Daughters' Reflections* 2 (Spring 1989): n.p.

13. "Longtime Defenders of Alamo Engaged in Battle with Critics," *Dallas Morning News*, 5 March 1994.

14. "Under Siege: Why the DRT Thinks It's Doing a Good Job with the Alamo Despite an 'Image Problem,' " *San Antonio Express News*, 16 May 1993.

15. *Alamo Mission Chapter Newsletter*, January 1994, 2.

16. "Rep. Ron Wilson Would Like Texas to Remember a State-run Alamo," *Austin American-Statesman*, 2 March 1993.

17. "For Alamo Defenders, New Assault to Repel," *New York Times*, 29 March 1994.

18. "DRT Gears Up for Another Fight with State over Alamo," *San Antonio Express News*, 3 March 1993.

19. "DRT in New Alamo Battle," *San Antonio Express News*, 3 March 1993. Emphasis added.

20. "Longtime Defenders of Alamo Engaged in Battle with Critics," *Dallas Morning News*, 5 March 1994.

21. "New Battles at the Alamo," *Houston Post*, 24 April 1994.

WE RUN THE ALAMO

22. The city of San Antonio owns about 60 percent of the Alamo compound defended in the 1836 battle. Some of the remainder of the compound is federally owned (the post office) and some is privately owned by independent businesses. The area owned by the state and controlled by the DRT comprises only about 25 percent of the mission compound.

23. "Remember the Alamo: The Growing Debate over the Shrine of Texas Liberty," *San Antonio Express News*, 17 March 1994.

24. But this is not to say that the street closure was based solely on anger at the DRT. The Texas Historical Commission, when asked its opinion, recommended permanent closure of the street for the sake of the physical integrity of the historic buildings at the site.

25. *The Medallion: Preservation News in Texas* (September–October 1994): n.p.

26. Teitz interview, 1998.

27. James Steely of the Texas Historical Commission claims that the DRT employed a historian long before 1996. If this is true, the Daughters probably decided to make the position public in 1996 as part of their attempt to appear more professional in their presentation of history. James W. Steely, telephone conversation with author, 21 May 1998.

28. "Around the Alamo!," *Alamo Mission Chapter News*, September 1996.

29. Mary Carmack, Brad Breuer, and Bruce Winders, interview with author, San Antonio, 12 March 1998.

30. Steely telephone conversation.

31. Madge Roberts to Frances Rickard and James Steely, 18 December 1996 (copy in the author's possession).

32. Teitz interview.

33. Ibid.

34. DRT member who preferred to remain anonymous, interview in San Antonio, 13 September 1990.

35. "DRT Gears Up for Another Fight with State over Alamo," *San Antonio Express News*, 3 March 1993.

Under the Rope

Lynching and Memory
in Laurens County, South Carolina

Bruce E. Baker

In March 1996 the Redneck Shop opened on the town square of Laurens, South Carolina. Selling Ku Klux Klan souvenirs, the shop owner John Howard has emphasized consistently that he "only opened the store so people could better understand a part of the region's history." He tries to carry out this program by operating in the back of the store what he bills as "the world's only Ku Klux Klan museum."[1] Spontaneous protests against the very existence of the shop, sometimes led by Rev. David E. Kennedy, soon degenerated into what everyone involved agrees was a "media circus."[2] And yet, what was really going on here? Is there more to it than the national media's portrayal of a backward southern community filled with anachronistic hate and simmering racial tension? A more complete examination of the situation, such as the one journalist Rick Bragg gave in November 1996, reveals that memory of the "ugly history" of Laurens affects people today; David Kennedy, as Bragg points out, is the great-nephew of Richard Puckett, the victim of the "last lynching in Laurens" in 1913.[3]

By stirring up memories of a time when hate and prejudice produced terrible injustices and cruelties, the shop has become the site of a conflict between differing views of the past. On one side, Howard and the Redneck Shop seek to rekindle racial pride among everyday southern whites. On the other side, black and white citizens warn against the hate and violence they see associated with the ideas the shop espouses. Yet even this survey of the controversy in Laurens is incomplete. For Richard Puckett was hardly the only person lynched in Laurens County. In fact, he was not even the last person lynched there. The use of the memory of Puckett's lynching in Laurens affords an excellent opportunity to examine in detail how the historical memory of lynching, one of the most glaring symbols of black oppression as long as the practice endured, is formed, perpetuated, and used within a particular community.

This essay is not a chronicle of the eight lynchings of African Americans that occurred in Laurens County between 1880 and 1940.[4] Rather, these lynchings serve as a starting point to ask questions about which lynchings are remembered and by whom, how and in what forms such events are remembered, and to what uses the various memories and silences of memory have been put. By examining the historical memory of lynching in Laurens County, we gain a fuller understanding of the phenomenon of lynching and the meanings it held for both those who lived through it and those who have lived with its legacy.[5]

Determining who remembers the lynchings in Laurens County involves defining several "communities of memory."[6] A community of memory may include all those individuals who share a direct or indirect memory of a given event. These individuals, whether in the present or the past, are engaged in what Iwona Irwin-Zarecka terms "memory work"—"concerted efforts to secure presence for certain elements of the past."[7] The creation of such communities of memory is not the result of an event itself, but rather the consequence of "the most basic and accessible means for memory articulation and maintenance—talk."[8] Differing perspectives, based on such factors as race, gender, age, family, or occupation, may influence not only how events are remembered, but also whether events are remembered at all. These perspectives, in turn, create a network of overlapping but distinct communities of memory.[9]

Because communities of memory and oral traditions are sustained through talk, often in small groups, it becomes necessary to distinguish between public and private discourse in order to trace the flow of memory. Public discourse includes all those statements (conceived in a broad sense) made in such a context that the eventual addressees are unknown and uncontrollable. Articles in newspapers, books, legal documents, items deposited in public

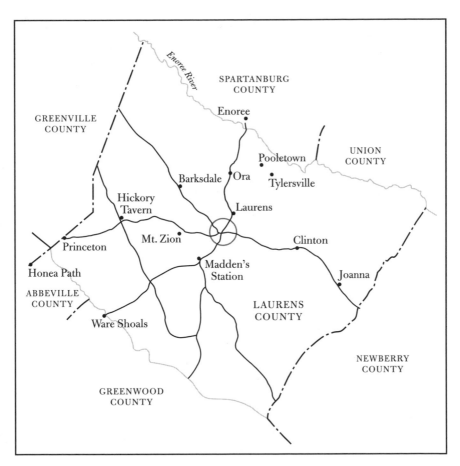

Laurens County, South Carolina

archives, actions in public places, and so forth are all part of the public discourse. People who speak to a reporter for the local newspaper presumably understand that the likely audience will be from the local community, but their remarks pass beyond the reporter's control. No constraints can be tied to the statements that enter public discourse. Private discourse, on the other hand, consists of statements addressed to an audience whose members are known and limited. More control can be exercised over these statements, as when guidelines are given along with the statement about appropriate ways of passing the information along or shielding it.

Statements about lynching in private discourse take several forms. The simplest of these is a general awareness that one or more lynchings have occurred, but without any specific information about the events. Slightly more elaborate is a simple report of a specific lynching that may often contain information about the person lynched, where the lynching took place, or both. In other cases, a more complete, but not necessarily longer, narrative of the lynching may be preserved. These narratives may include additional information such as sequenced events within the story and specific details regarding the means of death and the time of day. Linking the victim to other members of the community through an explanation of his family connections or place of residence is yet another element in private discourse about lynching.

Some statements may cross the boundary between public and private discourse. Preservation of newspaper clippings may be an act within private discourse since it takes statements from public discourse and appropriates them for the collector's use as prompts for both remembrance and perhaps transmission of historical memory to others. Helen Brown of Laurens, for instance, has an extensive collection of clippings dating back to the 1940s, including several articles on the last lynching in South Carolina in 1947. Ed McDaniel, also of Laurens, has boxes of newspaper clippings that he has been saving for thirty years. One of those clippings, given to him by someone else who had kept it for years, contains an account of a lynching in Laurens. Photographs also are items that straddle the border between public and private discourse. A photograph of Richard Puckett was made after he was hanged, and several versions of that photograph exist today, suggesting that it has been copied repeatedly during the intervening decades.

Lynching is largely absent from the local public discourse on the history of Laurens County.[10] Although the original newspaper accounts exist on microfilm at the public library, these sources of information do not seem to inform most people's views of the past.[11] Local newspapers also run features about older citizens reminiscing about the past, but although they may recall the difficulties of the Great Depression or life on the farm, local lynchings are not mentioned. Other published memoirs also are silent about lynchings in Laurens County. The purpose of these books, of course, is to commemorate significant or curious local events, not to perpetuate the memory of the less pleasant aspects of local history. The memory work of lynchings in Laurens County, therefore, falls to various communities of memory operating principally in private discourse.[12]

White residents of Laurens County comprise a broad but more or less coherent community of memory.[13] One event stands out in the memories of the white community: seven of the eight whites I interviewed had heard of the lynching of Richard Puckett in 1913, but most tended to remember it simply

Richard Puckett was lynched for an alleged assault on a white woman in Laurens County in August 1913. The divergent historical memories of this lynching among black and white residents persist to the present. Photographer unknown; photo in author's possession.

as a brief report that a nameless black man had been lynched at a particular location. Puckett was arrested on suspicion of having assaulted a young white woman near Madden's Station. Later that day, he was taken from the jail in Laurens by a mob of nearly two thousand people and hanged from the railroad trestle over River Street. Bill Cooper had "heard a story of where they've lynched at least one person on a railroad bridge not far off the downtown area." It probably also was the Puckett lynching that Cooper was referring to when he said an elderly lady he knew "was talking about being downtown one day and a lynch mob came through, and her father made her get in the store and not look out till it had gone." Bill Cooper's mother, Dorothy Cooper, stated: "There were some lynchings in the county in my lifetime, but I did not see them. I heard about them. I do not remember the names or anything about the lynchings. I just heard they had happened." In some cases, the memory centered primarily on the site where Puckett was lynched but left out any other particular details. Elaine Martin said: "I don't know as I heard about any of them particularly. I just heard about, you know, where they lynched them. You know, it was over there on East Main over at the railroad trestle. That's where they did the lynchings." Only Brock Coggins's account provided any details: "Only one that I ever remember, I mean, hear them talk about it. This colored man raped a white woman. And the lynching took place up there in town. On a railroad trestle. That's the only one I know of. . . . It was in the early 1900s. It happened, I reckon, in 1910 or 1912, somewhere along in there." This account, with its explanation of the reason for the lynching, the place, and the date of the event, is a short but complete narrative.

An event that some whites remember nearly as much as the Puckett lynching was the 1957 killing of a black tenant farmer, Ammon Harris, by his landlord and the landlord's son. Bill Cooper recounted the story while explaining the changes in race relations over time in Laurens County: "A black man that had been a sharecropper with my grandfather Cooper for years and years was working for another man, and they had a fatal altercation which resulted in the man and his son shooting the guy and killing him. And that was in fifty-four. And, of course, there was a trial, but they were let off on self-defense." Dorothy Cooper related the same story: "But we had a man to be killed on my father-in-law's place because he didn't want to work on 4th of July. He had worked for my father-in-law for many years." The Harris killing was memorable partly because of the personal connection to these two consultants, but also because by 1957 this sort of altercation between landlord and tenant had become an anachronism. Dorothy Cooper's comments on what happened to the landlord after the trial suggest a certain level of community disapproval:

> DC: The trial, it was just a "done deal" because he [Harris] was a black man and the man that shot him was white and that man was cleared. But, he did not do well for the rest of his life. He had a lot of trouble.
> BB: When you say "a lot of trouble," what do you mean?
> DC: I don't know. He just didn't do well in business. The people didn't openly condemn him, but they did silently. So things didn't go to well for him after he killed that black man.[14]

Lynchings made a deep impression on the white community of memory only when they were memorable in some regard. For instance, the sheer size of the mob involved in the Puckett lynching made it memorable. If newspaper accounts of two thousand participants and spectators are accurate, over 40 percent of Laurens's population was present at the lynching.[15] Such an event understandably was burned into the local collective memory. By contrast, other local lynchings were not remembered largely because the victims were further removed in time and space from Laurens itself. For the white community, few details of a lynching were usually remembered beyond the site of the execution. In fact, memory of lynchings may be actively discouraged because it reflects badly on the white community at large and perhaps on specific individuals.

As common sense might suggest, historical memory of lynching is generally stronger and deeper among blacks than among whites. Blacks remember more lynchings, and they use those memories in more varied and complicated ways.[16] Virtually every black consultant I spoke to had heard of the lynching of Richard Puckett, and most knew precisely where it had occurred. Even Rachel Watts, who grew up on a farm in the Mount Zion community several miles west of Laurens, had heard of "when they took the man down to the trestle." "When we would go over that trestle," Watts said, "Daddy would say, 'So-and-so was lynched here.' That's all I remember." Those who lived in Laurens offered more detailed accounts of the lynching. Mary Clark explained Puckett's family connections and the year the lynching occurred: "I know about the Garlington family, about a hanging we had in Laurens County. Mr. Garlington . . . [it] was his brother-in-law. And they hung him in 1913 down here in Laurens at one of the trestles."

Lillie Williams-Tims heard about the lynching from her mother, who mentioned it while explaining the family connections of one of Puckett's nieces. Helen Brown, whose mother grew up in Jersey, the largest black community in Laurens, recalled: "Well, they killed, hanged a man on this trestle, used to be a trestle down here on River Street. But that was before my time. He was a Puckett. They lynched him. In fact, my mother said she heard the shots when that happened. She lived up there on the same street, up there on the hill on River Street. And her mother was living, and she said, 'What is it, what is all that noise?' She said, 'You get back in the house. They're killing somebody.' So it was true. He was a Puckett. They killed him." Alice Dendy began by identifying the lynching site: "I can take you to the place where they hung a man right now. . . . Well, it's River Street because it's down there in that swamp." Dendy learned about the lynching and the site of the lynching from members of Puckett's family themselves.[17]

Rachel Watts, drawing on her own memory and consulting her brother, Edward Cunningham, told a detailed story of a lynching that occurred "in [her] father's lifetime." The grandson of Frank and Catherine Simpson was working in the field and

a little white girl twelve or thirteen years of age . . . asked the Simpson man to walk with her and he did. She would pass this black man on her way to school and he would say to her just things like: "What have you got in that lunch box? Give me some of that lunch!" There were some [white] men who saw this black man. In fact, sometimes he would walk a little distance with her. She would ask him, say, "Come and walk with me down to wherever." He didn't have any more sense than to do that. So these white people saw him and they took him and lynched him. Now, Lillie, you know their relatives. Leroy Campbell? His great-grandmother's son, Simpson. They lived right up here off of Highway 76; Gibbs Road, that's where they lived. What happened when they got after the Simpson boy, he ran and hid in a ditch. You know, he was just running away from them, not that he had done anything. He hadn't done anything, but they lynched him anyway.

Two other consultants, Walker Merrill and Willy Eichelberger, when asked, both affirmed that they had heard of a lynching in this location, although neither could remember the circumstances or the victim's name.

None of the lists of lynchings mention anyone named Simpson being lynched in Laurens County, but there was one lynching recorded that bears remarkable similarities to Watts's account. In May 1893 two girls "who live[d] in the neighborhood of Chestnut Ridge Church, about five miles from this city [Laurens], were attacked in a lonely place in the woods by a young negro boy about 18 or 19 years of age."[18] After a couple of false starts, a party of white men headed by the girls' father captured Heyward "Monk" Barksdale early the next morning and brought him before the girls, who identified him as their attacker. That afternoon a mob of four hundred people gathered and hanged Barksdale from a hickory tree alongside the Old Greenville Road. Several details of this story correspond to Watts's account. First, Watts mentions that "the Simpson boy" lived on Gibbs Road, which lies near both the road to Greenville and Chestnut Ridge Baptist Church.[19] Second, both Watts's and the newspaper account mention a girl on her way to or from school. Third, one of the details of Watts's story is the girl's lunch box. According to one newspaper story, "the elder girl, thinking that he [the assailant] only wanted something to eat, offered him her lunch basket."[20] Finally, just as Watts says that Simpson ran and hid in a ditch, the newspaper reported that Barksdale ran from the field where he was working.[21] Given the numerous similarities, it seems probable that Simpson and Barksdale were the same person. A final connection is the fact that Rachel Watts's grandfather, Priest Miller, was a member of the coroner's jury that made a brief investigation of Barksdale's death.[22]

If blacks tend to recall more specific details of lynchings than whites, the families of lynching victims in particular remember lynchings more clearly than either whites or other blacks.[23] In two cases, a family member mentioned a lynching that had occurred within the family but that has been impossible to corroborate through documentary evidence. Walker Merrill told of a relative of his father whom whites drowned near Pooletown, north of Laurens:

> But, you know, you could take a black man off, you know, and hang him if they wanted, you know. But it wasn't so much right in here. But then they would carry you to Pooletown. . . . Some of my daddy's people were living down there. His name was Merrill and he drownded in one of them there, the Pine Hole you call it down there. Yes sir, the Pine Hole down there next to Pooletown. See, the Pine Hole, that's like a suck hole, you know what I'm saying? When they throw you in there, you don't know where you're going. I can't think of his name right now, but he was a Merrill. . . . That was what Dad always told me. And that's why he got drownded in that pool, you know.

Merrill's account may describe the same death that a coroner's jury investigated in 1872, when a man discovered a body on the banks of the Enoree River (about a mile from Pooletown) that "had a rock weighing about thirty pounds tide [sic] to it with a leather strop."[24] Merrill confirmed that the lynching he described did happen near the Enoree River: "Yeah, it was next to the Enoree River." Similarly, Ed McDaniel recalls that his great-uncle was lynched at Madden's Station, just south of Laurens: "I have always heard about a great-uncle of mine who was lynched in the Madden's Station area. And that was why of the McDaniel brothers, my grandfather's brothers, only two remained in this area and the rest left. Now we were always told that that was the reason. He was a McDaniel, but I don't know his particular name. I would never know exactly who he was." In both of these cases, it is entirely possible that the accounts in the family oral tradition of the lynchings are accurate, an example of an event that is preserved in private discourse but that never entered public discourse.

Another lynching that has been remembered primarily within the family of the mob's victim is the last lynching in Laurens County. On 4 July 1933 Norris Dendy of Clinton was arrested for fighting with a white man and lodged in the jail. About nine o'clock that night, four or five men took Dendy from the jail as Dendy's wife and mother watched. The next morning, officers found his bludgeoned body in a churchyard several miles from Clinton. Nearly a year later a grand jury returned no bill on the indictments against five men for the lynching.[25] The indictments elevated the Dendy lynching to a place in public discourse that no previous lynching in Laurens County had attained, and the event remained a subject of public comment for almost a year. It prompted Noah Williams, bishop of the African Methodist Episcopal Church, to cancel an annual church conference planned for 1933 in Clinton.[26] The *Crisis*, the publication of the National Association for the Advancement of Colored People, reported the lynching briefly in the September 1933 issue, and in December it devoted two pages to the story. As late as October 1934, the *Crisis* carried an editorial about the Dendy lynching.[27] After the men indicted for the lynching were not tried, Young Dendy, Norris's father, hired an attorney in Laurens to bring a civil suit against the county under the provisions of South Carolina's 1896 statute that held counties financially liable to the legal representatives of lynching victims. Dendy's attorney, W. R. Richey, presented a claim for two thousand dollars to the Laurens County Board of Commissioners at its 27 December 1934 meeting.[28] The board, which had just paid a man twenty-five dollars for an injury to his mule, unanimously declined to approve the claim.[29] In April 1935 Richey served a summons and complaint in the case on the county supervisor.[30] However, the case does not appear in any contemporary court records, leaving unclear whether it was ever officially filed.[31] Even after this, the family still talked about the lynching among themselves, according to Lillie Williams-Tims.

Perhaps the best illustration of the tenacity of family memory is the enduring memory within the extended Puckett family of Richard Puckett's lynching eight decades later. David Kennedy, as a minister and community activist, acts as an unofficial spokesperson for the family. His account of the Puckett lynching is detailed and moving:

Richard Puckett was my great-grandfather, James Malachi Puckett's brother. And I knew my great-grandfather very well and called him Pop. But the sisters [James Malachi Puckett's sisters, including David Kennedy's grandmother] remembered what was told to them about their uncle. And he was accused, they called him the "would-be rapist." A white lady said something about him. . . . And then they would tell me that my great-grandfather was a bold man because the first time they tried to come and get Richard Puckett, he had his shotgun. And he told the white people [who] came to get him they were not going to take him. And they had to tell the sheriff to come over and get him. And so a mob of over one thousand men came and took Richard Puckett from the jail and brought him down to the trestle over River Street. And according to the *Laurens Advertiser*, the sheriff, chief of police or sheriff at that time, said Richard

Puckett whispered in his ears that he was guilty while the mob was taking him out. And he was helpless. He couldn't do anything. But a reporter said while they were shooting his body up with bullets—and sometimes the black community said they also castrated black men during the lynching process, and they didn't put in the paper about the castration—said that Richard Puckett was crying that he was innocent. While they were lynching him, he was constantly crying that he was innocent. So, we saw the rope.

What is immediately apparent in this account is the unusual level of detail and completeness of the story. Two details, castration and James Malachi Puckett's defense of his brother, were not included in any of the contemporary newspapers. Another interesting feature of this story is the way Kennedy weaves together information from oral tradition with information from newspaper accounts of the lynching.

Kennedy added more detail to the story than others and provided more complex interpretations of those details. Although nearly everyone who recalled the lynching knew the location, Kennedy explained that the trestle was significant because it marked the entrance to Jersey, the largest black community in Laurens. Blacks going to and from the downtown area had to pass beneath the very trestle from which Puckett was hanged. Other consultants mentioned the rope hanging from the trestle, but Kennedy explained that "there was an unwritten law that whoever took the rope down, the same thing that happened to Richard Puckett was going to happen to them." Older people told children that the ghost of Puckett would keep them from taking the rope down to prevent them from meeting a similar fate. (Lillie Williams-Tims, however, felt the rope "was not left there as a reminder"; rather, someone "climbed up to a certain point and just cut the rope and the rest of it just hung there.")

Such stories tended to stay within the family. "In my family," Kennedy said, "the family trusted the family. And they would talk about it to family. . . . But most of the times I heard the story, it was only family present." These stories came primarily from the older members of the family, the nieces of Richard Puckett who had probably learned about it from their father, James Malachi Puckett, or perhaps from firsthand knowledge.

Kennedy related a powerful account of one particular telling of the story when he was in college that had a strong effect on him:

I learned a lot from my grandmother and her sisters, who told the story over and over again when they were with us of the lynching of Richard

Puckett. Sitting around after dinner. Or sitting around sometimes late at night on the porch. And the most memorable time was when I sat with my grandmother and her sisters alone. And my grandfather. And they told the story. And they took me back, and I relived it on that porch that night. It was a strange feeling. And it's overshadowed me. It was like I was really seeing it happen right before my own eyes because they were very descriptive in their language. About what happened. Nobody could tell it like the sisters sitting together telling that story. It was dark, so to a very large extent you could hardly see anything that night. Except for the light shining on their faces. And their expressions that night. As they sit, very still, and the only thing was moving was their mouth, their mouths. And the look they had in their eyes, the anger and the frustration. About the injustice. And also a sense of helplessness that overshadowed. And almost in the words of James Weldon Johnson in *Lift Every Voice and Sing*, "Hope unborn had died." I saw that in their faces. Also their warnings to me. Be strong, but be very careful. They will kill you. [Pause]. Let's talk about something else.

Comparing the lynchings of Richard Puckett in 1913 and Joe Stewart in 1920 helps to clarify how and why some lynchings are remembered and others are forgotten. Although Stewart's lynching happened more recently than Puckett's, it is the Puckett lynching that people still remember. Puckett was lynched at the entrance from downtown Laurens to the main black community, a liminal zone that separated two very different environments. Stewart, on the other hand, was hanged from the North Harper Street bridge over Little River, a place that does not clearly delineate community boundaries. A mass mob lynched Puckett, whereas a much smaller group of people, probably no more than fifty, executed Stewart. The Puckett lynching was a spectacle created for public consumption in a way that the Stewart lynching was not. Finally, Puckett was a member of a large extended family that had roots in Laurens and whose members still live there. Stewart had few such connections. He was born in Virginia and moved to Laurens as a teenager with his family sometime between 1910 and 1917. In 1920, just months before his death in April, he was living with his wife but no children. With no children and no siblings in the community, Stewart's memory simply had fewer minds in which to reside than Puckett's did.[32]

To some extent, the lynchings of Puckett and Stewart have become conflated in the collective memory. Elaine Martin identified the site of the "lynchings" as "over there on East Main over at the railroad trestle." Puckett was lynched on a railroad trestle over River Street, fairly close to East Main Street.

Later Martin describes the trestle as "over Little River on East Main, right after you go over the railroad tracks." Here, she describes a road bridge rather than a railroad trestle going over Little River rather than a street, a description much more in keeping with the site of the Stewart lynching. Similarly, Ed McDaniel had a photocopy of a newspaper clipping on the same page as a separate photograph of a lynching. The photograph is the widely known photograph of Puckett, yet the newspaper story is an Associated Press account of the lynching of Joe Stewart. In both of these cases, the core fact— that a man was hanged from a bridge—remains constant, and the less memorable event is drawn toward the well-known site of the more memorable event.

Whereas private discourse maintains the historical memory of some lynchings in Laurens County, others seem to have disappeared from historical memory, if they were ever there at all. Two of these lynchings happened in the southeastern portion of the county. On 10 April 1881 a black woman named Eliza Cowan who was suspected of burning an outhouse belonging to J. S. Blalock was lynched in Martin's Depot (now Joanna).[33] Several years later a black farmer named Dave Hunter had a dispute with his landlord, Lee Hunter, over the settlement of his yearly account and was beaten to death with a buggy trace by his landlord and others in Clinton.[34] Perhaps because my interviews focused on Laurens and the surrounding communities in the northern half of the county, it is not surprising that no one mentioned these lynchings. Yet no one I interviewed remembered two other lynchings that occurred closer to Laurens. In September 1904 James Calvert Stuart was accused of raping his employer's daughter. A mob of forty to fifty men, including some members of the girl's family, took Stuart into Greenwood County, where they shot him and left his body in the road.[35] In July 1897 Henry Gray was working on a farm near Ora when he was accused of trying to rape a young girl. He was arrested and sent to jail, and the next day a judge arranged to convey him by train to the penitentiary in Columbia. After a gun battle in Joanna, a mob seized Gray from the train. They carried him back toward the site of his alleged attack and hanged him in the presence of several hundred people. Of all the people I interviewed, only David Kennedy had ever heard anything about this lynching.[36]

Discovering why these last two lynchings did not figure more prominently in local memory requires a deeper explanation than does the absence of historical memory of Eliza Cowan and Dave Hunter. (Of course, it is possible that some people do remember these events and I simply did not find them.) The size of the mob involved may affect the way a lynching is or is not remembered. The Stuart lynching was a small affair, carried out by a mob of only forty or fifty people, and the victim was never in legal custody. If a relatively small number of people were involved, most probably from the immediate community and many probably related, the people in the surrounding area may well lack any connection with either the events or the people involved. The Stuart mob was a private mob as opposed to a mass mob, and "the furtive violence of private and terrorist mobs was not (at least in the eyes of whites) so clearly set off from other more mundane and quickly forgotten forms of violence."[37]

The lynching of Gray would seem to be more memorable. A mass mob, numbering in the hundreds, killed him after a drama that had stretched out over most of the day and much of the county. The lynching, moreover, took place near the scene of the alleged crime and the victim had been carried near Laurens itself. Various public officials, including a judge, the sheriff, a deputy, and a mayor, tried to prevent the lynching. Yet it is barely remembered. Even Walker Merrill, who has lived in Ora all of his life, had never heard of a lynching there.

A common thread linking both of these forgotten memories involves the identity and social position of the victims. Stuart was young, only twenty-two, and the reports do not mention a wife or family. One newspaper account states that after the Greenwood County coroner's inquest, the body was turned over to Stuart's father, but the father is not identified further. Henry Gray seems to have had even less substantial connections to the local community. Even his name is in question. One witness testifying before the coroner's jury knew him as John Gray, whereas a news account refers to Jim Gray. The article in the *Laurensville Herald* never listed his name at all. Newspaper accounts provided no further information on him, and witnesses before the coroner's jury stated that they had known him for only two years.[38] Gray lacked an extensive network of kin or long-standing relationships with an employer to provide protection. Such blacks "were vulnerable to the violence of mobs because their character was shrouded in mystery and their reputations were not part of local white memory."[39] Gray's apparent rootlessness may have contributed not only to his death but also to the lack of any memory of his death.

People may not remember some incidents of collective violence for other reasons. The widespread violence, often lethal, of the Reconstruction era in Laurens County seems to be little remembered, perhaps simply because it is more remote in time from the present. Also, during the early 1880s many blacks emigrated from Laurens County, and it is possible that many of those who did had found Laurens too dangerous and violent, like the great-uncles Ed McDaniel mentioned.[40] Moreover, collective violence may have been too commonplace to remember in any specific detail. For instance, when six disguised men whipped two black men living near Tylersville in 1887, newspapers as far away as Hickory, North Carolina, reported the story, but the act was probably not remarkable enough to become part of the local collective memory.[41] In general, individual killings of blacks by whites seem to have been remembered only when they deviated from the general pattern of violence.

A final incident, which occurred within living memory, is conspicuous by its absence from local collective memory in Laurens County. In early March 1933 Barnett Smith, a young black man from Ware Shoals, critically wounded his wife and another woman and then hid in the woods for several days. He stopped at a farm in the Princeton area and asked the white woman there for matches. Frightened, she fled upstairs with her baby, and Smith broke in and threatened her. Greenwood County authorities arrested him later that afternoon just before a mob of one hundred men from Princeton, Ware Shoals, and Honea Path caught up with him. Smith was rushed to Columbia for safekeeping. Within a week after the alleged assault, reports began to appear in local newspapers that night riders were whipping and threatening blacks in the area. After beating black tenant farmers, the night riders ordered them to "leave the country" by Saturday, 18 March. The terror campaign involved approximately fifteen hundred men and covered an area estimated at one hundred square miles in Laurens, Greenville, Anderson, and Greenwood Counties. Investigations by the sheriffs of Laurens and Greenville revealed that at least fifty blacks had indeed fled the area. After about a week of vigorous patrolling, sheriff's deputies and highway patrolmen restored calm to the area.[42]

These seemingly dramatic events appear to have made no impression on the collective memory of the Laurens County residents I interviewed. Thomas Garrett of Hickory Tavern lived closest to the area affected and was himself born in 1933, but he had never heard of the event. No one else, even when asked directly about it, indicated that they knew of the night riding. There may be several reasons for this. First, there were no bodies. Despite the wide scope of the terror, no reports mentioned that anyone was killed, although one terrified, old black man attempted suicide. Second, the night riding took place over a period of at least a week. Rather than remembering a specific event, people would have to remember a series of events over a period of time. If the night riding covered such an extensive area and people's sense of community was often focused on a very small area, it is possible that those involved, both as victims and as perpetrators, may not have connected events happening in different places at different times. Isolated incidents would thus fade from memory over time. Finally, the direct victims of the terror, the blacks who were beaten and forced to flee the area, were no longer in the community. The *Greenville News* reported that of those who had fled, "some are now staying with relatives and friends in Greenville while others are scattered over the state" and there is no reason to think that they returned.[43] As tenants, they probably had precious little to take with them and nothing to return to.

The various memories and silences about specific lynchings in Laurens County reveal some general patterns about the way lynching becomes part of a community's historical memory. Briefly, they are these: memories of lynchings are attached primarily to the families of the victims, lynching victims are more likely to be remembered as part of a genealogical landscape, memories of lynching have a socializing function, and memories of lynching act as covert evidence in private discourse of wrongs that cannot be corrected in the public discourse.

The role of the family in preserving the memory of lynching victims is paramount. In some cases, such as the Merrill and McDaniel lynchings, only the family remembers the event. The reasons why families may often guard such memories so closely lie in the potential danger of such knowledge and the fear that sharing it could lead to betrayal. Walker Merrill's father used the story of the lynching of his relative to warn him against idle talk, saying, "Now, if you know anything don't tell, don't talk about it, because you might get hurt." David Kennedy made the same point when he emphasized that "in [his] family, the family trusted the family." Another reason such memories might be kept within the family is the powerful feeling of vulnerability such memories would create. Kennedy described seeing this effect in his aunts as they told the story of Richard Puckett, and he himself, remembering the experience, used the word "helpless" and decided to "talk about something else."

Those lynching victims who were remembered most clearly were nearly always remembered as part of what folklorist Barbara Allen has described as a "genealogical landscape," an "association of people with place, of kinship with landscape."[44] Walker Merrill made this connection between place (Pooletown), family ("Some of my daddy's people were living down there. His name was Merrill"), and history ("he got drownded in that pool"). The clearest example of placing a lynching victim in a genealogical landscape was in Rachel Watts's identification of the lynching victim at Chestnut Ridge. Watts introduced the story by explaining the victim's family connection: "Cass Simpson's grandson was taken out of his house and killed." As soon as the story of the lynching itself was completed, Watts explained to Lillie Williams-Tims who the victim and the family were by placing them in the genealogical landscape: "Now, Lillie, you know their relatives. Leroy Campbell? His great-grandmother's son, Simpson. They lived right up here off of Highway 76. Gibbs Road, that's where they lived." With that identification complete, Watts went on to elaborate on the story and add details to the account. Next she told a seemingly unrelated story of a time when her father had been cheated out of some molasses by his landlady; the connection was made clear, however, when I asked for some clarification about details of the lynching. Watts explained in more detail who the victim's family was, naming his mother and father and several of his aunts and uncles. When I asked where it happened, Watts responded, "That happened in Chestnut Ridge right up here on Highway 76, right across from that brick house where the lady lived that told Daddy he had to give her the molasses." The event, the family, and the place were all linked.

Even if little information is known about a lynching, that information may be conveyed in this sort of context. David Kennedy explained: "I heard of the last name [of Henry Gray, lynching victim] because Reverend James Gray is our moderator. And some people . . . say that there could have been a relation with Reverend James Gray. . . . They would say Reverend Gray from Enoree. . . . And they would talk about a Gray man from Enoree. So that's the same guy." Here Kennedy links family with place. The "Gray man from Enoree" was lynched, and Reverend Gray was from Enoree, so the not-unreasonable conclusion is that the "Gray man" may well be related in some way. The nexus of genealogy and geography provides an anchor for memory.

Historical memory of a lynching can be a socializing tool, more so for blacks than whites. Primarily, stories of lynchings were used as warnings. Rachel Watts, for instance, said, "So then, my father was forever talking to his boys, telling them, you know, 'Don't get yourselves involved in instances where you could get lynched' for doing things like that." David Kennedy and Walker Merrill also spoke of hearing about lynchings as warnings. It is probably significant that those who were warned were those most in danger of lynching—young black men. Other blacks such as Helen Brown's mother or the children in the photograph of Richard Puckett also learned about lynchings while they were still children, exactly the opposite of white children.[45]

Historical memory of lynchings became the object of an unequal contest between those who could forget and those who could not, or could not afford to, forget. By controlling public discourse—the newspapers, the courts, the books, and, to a somewhat lesser degree, the schools—whites had the luxury of remembering or forgetting the past as they chose. Since lynching certainly did not fit within the narrative of progress so important to American identity at this time, it was in the best interest of white community boosters to condemn lynching in general while forgetting specific lynchings within their own communities. Even those who actively condemned lynchings before, while, and after they occurred may well have chosen to silence the memory of those same lynchings in order to maintain a positive version of local history or to prevent the memory of the lynching from further damaging race relations.[46] Blacks, in contrast, could not so easily forget the sudden and violent death of a family member, a friend, a neighbor. Even if they could forget, it was often wiser to remember quietly the lesson that the lynching was meant to teach. But if blacks remembered lynchings in private discourse, they could seldom break the silence of the public discourse about those lynchings.

Individual lynchings, by their very nature, tended not to be objects of public discourse. W. Fitzhugh Brundage points out that "not every lynching was an event laden with symbolism."[47] If some lynchings, like Richard Puckett's, were elaborately staged and deeply encoded with cultural significance, others, like Joe Stewart's, were quiet, private affairs. Even so, what all types of lynching shared was that they removed an individual from participating in public discourse. As a way of reasserting values about the social order, lynchings acted as silencings. One of the messages communicated by a lynching was that the mob's victim was no longer to be an object of public discourse, either. Someone who made a statement challenging a social order in the realm of public discourse—Joe Stewart standing up for a young black boy who was being threatened by whites, for instance—was removed, silenced. The silence was continued when a coroner's jury failed to name those responsible. Lynching, then, was a self-effacing event. First it silenced an alleged offender; then the anonymity of the mob and the silence of local public discourse muted any attempt to name the lynching as a crime and to exact justice. The effect was amplified when, as in Laurens County, all the lynching victims were black, all the mobs were white, and whites exercised nearly complete control over public discourse for several decades after the lynchings.

The silence regarding lynching within the public discourse divested the victim's family of the means to prove that an injustice was done.[48] The silence of witnesses removed the possibility of proving that specific individuals lynched the victim; without testimony, the mob dispersed into anonymity. And those who had evidence might be intimidated into not coming forward. When Norris Dendy was lynched, the solicitor twice subpoenaed Hugh Mims, a black man who had seen the unmasked lynchers take Dendy from his cell. Ignoring subpoenas, Mims refused to return to Laurens from New York, where he had fled, to testify. There were no trials, and thus the county government could summarily dismiss the lawsuit brought by Dendy's family.

In the era of Jim Crow, my consultants insisted, blacks had no means of recourse when an injustice was done them. Commenting on the killing in 1957, Bill Cooper said, "And even as late as that, the black man had no legal recourse. Or his family. . . . You know, there was that system that the blacks really had no recourse when something like that happened. They had no legal protection." Helen Brown gave a more succinct answer to my question of "What became of that, after [Harris was killed]?": "Nothing. He [Harris's killer] was acquitted." Another example involved the fencing off and theft of land belonging to Rachel Watts's father. When asked, "Why wouldn't they make a noise about it if it was clearly an illegal act," Watts replied, "If whites said they were going to do something, blacks could not try to stop them. Dad and Uncle Ford were those type people that when whites did things to them, they more or less said nothing." With no recourse, the damage became a wrong incapable of being righted. And what could be done in such a situation? As Walker Merrill stated, "You couldn't do anything about it! You had to swallow it and keep it to yourself." Those who suffered the damage of the lynching itself had to add their own silence within public discourse to the silence of those controlling public discourse—to become, in effect, complicit in the final stage of the very injustice being perpetrated against them.

Yet, as we have seen, the memory of the lynching persisted within the private discourse of various communities of memory. This persistence is what gives such memories their power and what fuels conflicts over memory such as the furor surrounding the Redneck Shop. The past that the Redneck Shop seeks to evoke in today's public discourse is one that is purged of any wrongs. When John Howard hands out a copy of the photograph of Richard Puckett, he emphasizes, probably correctly, that the Ku Klux Klan was not involved, that the citizens of Laurens lynched Puckett.[49] Besides, as the newspaper accounts tell us, Puckett confessed to his crime. There was no wrong because the lynching was justified. Even the governor at the time, Cole Blease, supported the lynching and assisted in carrying it out by refusing to call out the militia.[50] As David Kennedy points out when he says that "the family . . . would talk about it to the family," Puckett's family members kept the memory of his lynching in private, not public discourse. It would not have been safe to have insisted on the injustice of the lynching in public. And as the case of Norris Dendy shows, doing so probably would not have accomplished much. This situation created a tension between history as presented in public discourse and memory preserved in private discourse.

But recently the power relationships governing the production and maintenance of public discourse have shifted to such an extent that the memory of a lynching, long sustained in private discourse, can be brought back into public discourse.[51] Although these old wrongs may not be righted, they can now at least be publicly acknowledged. The change that makes this possible, of course, is the civil rights movement. Ed McDaniel emphasized this when he explained that "when integration was coming about, my grandmother would talk about how things used to be. . . . Things were better now than they once were, so you need to capitalize on that. . . . So anytime we would talk about those type of things [lynchings], it would be to show a contrast and to let us know that things could be better." When David Kennedy took the lead in protesting the Redneck Shop, he used the memory of Richard Puckett, even the same photograph that Howard used, as a way of establishing that a wrong had been done; racism and hate were not vague generalities that were merely bad for business but were conditions that had led to real suffering and specific damages. The photograph and its story, previously preserved in private, reentered public discourse.

The situation in Laurens illuminates the fate of historical memory of lynching and other examples of collective, reactionary violence in the South.[52] It is typical in that those who have passed along the stories of specific lynchings are getting older and dying, and there is less and less need to tell the stories today. Unlike the period when Walker Merrill or Rachel Watts's brothers were growing up, the stories are not needed to warn young African Americans about imminent danger. And unlike the era when Ed McDaniel, David Kennedy, and their generation were raised, stories of lynchings are not needed to inspire young people to take advantage of opportunities that were unavailable to their elders.[53] What is atypical about Laurens is that a vocal community activist happens to be directly related to the victim of the town's most spectacular lynching. David Kennedy is in the unusual position of being able to force the memory of a lynching, a terrible wrong buried in his family's past, into the midst of contemporary public debate. Will lynchings in other parts of the South also become part of the public discourse on historical memory? Given similar circumstances, it is possible. But almost certainly it will not be a widespread phenomenon. Instead, lynchings will remain in the public discourse as a vague symbol of black oppression, but the historical memory of specific lynchings probably will gradually fade away.

NOTES

1. *Greenville News*, 28 April 1996.

2. The emergence of the Redneck Shop and the subsequent protests and legal battles were covered in the *Greenville News* in a series of articles by April E. Moorefield in March, April, and May 1996.

3. Rick Bragg, " 'Ugly History' Haunts S.C. Town," *Charleston Post and Courier*, 19 November 1996.

4. My list of lynchings for Laurens County is based on the work of Stewart E. Tolnay and E. M. Beck whose *A Festival of Violence: An Analysis of Southern Lynchings, 1882–1930* (Urbana: University of Illinois Press, 1995) uses what is currently the most comprehensive list of lynchings in the South. Professor Beck kindly supplied me with the South Carolina portion of the list. One of those, the lynching of Dave Shaw in 1892, turned out not to be a lynching after all. See *Charleston News and Courier*, 23 June, 8, 12, 26 July 1892. I also found one prior lynching in 1881 in a local newspaper and was referred to an account of a 1933 lynching in the *Crisis*. Based on these sources, I have documented eight lynchings in Laurens County for this period, but in the course of the interviews, there were references to two or three others that I was unable to confirm.

5. In addition to archival research, this study draws on a series of directed oral history interviews I conducted in Laurens County between Fall 1997 and Spring 1998. Altogether, I conducted approximately twenty hours of interviews with twenty-three different individuals. Of this group, nearly all were over fifty years old, but a few were somewhat younger. Fifteen consultants were black, and eight were white. The black consultants were Helen Brown, John Arthur Brown, Mary Clark, Alice Dendy, Eddie Eichelberger, Willy Eichelberger, Thomas Garrett, Carrie Hunter, Lucy Hunter, David Kennedy, Ed McDaniel, James Merrill, Walker Merrill, Rachel Watts, and Lillie Williams-Tims. The white consultants were Lonnie Adamson, Brock Coggins, Carolyn Coggins, Bill Cooper, Dorothy Cooper, John Howard, Elaine Martin, and Frances Weathers. Of these, all lived in Laurens unless otherwise noted in the rest of the essay. I would like to thank these individuals for their time and assistance with this project. Several scholars interested in lynching have studied memory both directly and indirectly. Arthur Raper's classic *The Tragedy of Lynching* (Chapel Hill: University of North Carolina Press, 1933) includes references to prior lynchings in several communities. Folklorist Richard M. Dorson discussed oral accounts of a lynching in Michigan in "The Oral Historian and the Folklorist," in *Selections From the Fifth and Sixth National Colloquia on Oral History* (New York: Oral History Association, 1972), 48. James McGovern used interviews as an important source for his *Anatomy of a Lynching: The Killing of Claude Neal* (Baton Rouge: Louisiana State University Press, 1990), xi. In the introduction to his *Racial Violence in Kentucky, 1865–1940: Lynchings, Mob Rule, and "Legal Lynchings"* (Baton Rouge: Louisiana State University Press, 1990), 5, George C. Wright notes, "Folk traditions tell of people who were murdered in isolated counties and dumped into rivers and creeks, or who—according to biased white newspapers—escaped from the authorities and simply disappeared." Charlotte Wolf has written about the effects of a lynching in Tennessee in 1900 on the socialization of blacks and whites in "Constructions of a Lynching," *Sociological Inquiry* 62

(February 1992): 83. Although not focusing specifically on lynching, Lynwood Montell has used oral history as a way of documenting and understanding lethal violence in a local community in *The Saga of Coe Ridge: A Study in Oral History* (Knoxville: University of Tennessee Press, 1970) and especially *Killings: Folk Justice in the Upper South* (Lexington: University Press of Kentucky, 1986).

My consultants tended to consider lynching as one item on a broader spectrum of racially motivated violence and injustice. Lynching differs from other examples of what Walker Merrill called "the way the white people treated them [blacks]" more in degree than in kind. Bill Cooper, after mentioning two lynchings he had heard of, referred to the killing of a black tenant by a white landlord, saying, "But that was a case of the same type thing." Rachel Watts, when asked about "violent events in this area that [she] heard about while . . . growing up," recalled that she "sat and listened to my father tell the stories about not so much violence but how blacks were treated." Folklorist Henry Glassie emphasizes the importance of using community ontologies as a guide in his sublime study of an Irish community, *Passing the Time in Ballymenone: Culture and History of an Irish Community* (Bloomington: Indiana University Press, 1983), esp. chaps. 2 and 32. Glassie employs and expands the ideas of Dan Ben-Amos, "Analytical Categories and Ethnic Genres," *Genre* 2 (September 1969): 275–301. Recent historical scholarship has also sought to place lynching within a larger framework of violence and oppression. Nearly twenty years ago, Jacquelyn Dowd Hall's *Revolt against Chivalry: Jessie Daniel Ames and the Women's Campaign against Lynching* (New York: Columbia University Press, 1979) explained how the lynching of black men for alleged crimes against white women worked to keep white women in a subject position. Hall expanded on the ideas in her book in a later essay, " 'The Mind That Burns in Each Body': Women, Rape, and Racial Violence," in Ann Snitow, Christine Stansell, and Sharon Thompson, eds., *Powers of Desire: The Politics of Sexuality* (New York: Monthly Review Press, 1983), 328–49. George C. Wright (*Racial Violence in Kentucky*, 1) claimed that "racial violence in Kentucky [was] evident in many forms" besides just lynching. More recently, Wright has shown the direct continuities between lynchings and "legal lynchings" in "By the Book: The Legal Execution of Kentucky Blacks," in W. Fitzhugh Brundage, ed., *Under Sentence of Death: Lynching in the South* (Chapel Hill: University of North Carolina Press, 1997), 250–70. William S. McFeely, in the afterword to *Under Sentence of Death*, 318, uses examples from Columbus, Ga., to show that "African Americans in Columbus saw" the murder of a civil rights activist in 1956 "as belonging to a chain running back" to a 1912 lynching "and to others still more terrible in detail." This study, however, separates lynching as an analytically useful category from the broader native genres of racial injustice. George B. Tindall, concluding the chapter on violence in his *South Carolina Negroes, 1877–1900* (Columbia: University of South Carolina Press, 1952), 259, writes, "The fear of violence is a basic context in which the history of South Carolina Negroes during the period must be studied to be clearly understood."

6. Iwona Irwin-Zarecka, *Frames of Remembrance: The Dynamics of Collective Memory* (New Brunswick, N.J.: Transaction Publishers, 1994), 47–65.

7. Ibid., 8.

8. Ibid., 54.

9. In folklorists' terms, a community of memory consists of those individuals who share a largely consistent oral tradition about certain events or groups of events. As Barbara Allen and Lynwood Montell point out in their *From Memory to History: Using Oral*

Sources in Local Historical Research (Nashville: American Association for State and Local History, 1981), 92, "Because individuals perceive events from their own personal vantage points, the local history researcher is likely to encounter conflicting attitudes toward the same event from different people within the same community, especially when political, social, or moral issues are involved." Arthur F. Raper gives an example of this in *Tragedy of Lynching*, 94.

10. Many scholarly works mention Laurens in passing while discussing larger topics, but these are not the principal source of local history for community residents, and Laurens does not yet have a county history comparable to that of its neighbor: Archie Vernon Huff's *Greenville: The History of the City and County in the South Carolina Piedmont* (Columbia: University of South Carolina Press, 1995). Lynching is not always absent from the public discourse on local history, however. In contrast to Laurens County, see Stanly County and Cabarrus County, N.C., as discussed in Bruce E. Baker, "North Carolina Lynching Ballads," in *Under Sentence of Death*, 221, 226.

11. An exception to this would be the case of community scholars or local historians. Although many such community scholars rely primarily on oral tradition, some may use old newspapers and other records to go into more detail on particular subjects. Lillie Williams-Tims is a good example of this phenomenon in Laurens. While looking through microfilmed newspapers for something else, she read about the lynching of Norris Dendy, about which she had already heard vague accounts. Two other community scholars in North Carolina who used newspapers to augment their knowledge of lynchings of which they had heard are Eddie Gathings of Wadesboro and George F. Hahn of Mt. Pleasant. Both are mentioned in Bruce E. Baker, "Lynching Ballads in North Carolina" (M.A. thesis, University of North Carolina, 1995), 43–44, 100.

12. William Watts Ball, an influential newspaper editor in South Carolina, was living in Laurens in 1893 when Heyward Barksdale was lynched; although he recorded the incident in his diary years later, he did not mention it in his 1932 memoir, *The State That Forgot: South Carolina's Surrender to Democracy* (Indianapolis: Bobbs-Merrill Co., 1932). Local histories and genealogies, which bring memory and history into the public discourse, are the primary sources of information on Laurens history. Julian S. Bolick's *A Laurens County Sketchbook* (Clinton, S.C.: Jacobs Press, 1973) combines sketches of prominent local houses with brief historical essays about the houses and their occupants. The *Sketchbook* combines brief sketches on a number of historical events, churches, and small communities with histories and genealogies of local families. The purpose of these two books is, of course, to commemorate Laurens County history, not to perpetuate the memory of the less pleasant aspects of local history. The memory work of lynchings, therefore, falls to various communities of memory operating principally in private discourse. See John D. Stark, *Damned Upcountryman: William Watts Ball: A Study in American Conservatism* (Durham: Duke University Press, 1968), 29, and William P. Jacobs, ed., *The Scrapbook: A Compilation of Historical Facts about Places and Events of Laurens County, South Carolina* (Clinton, S.C.: Laurens County Historical Society and Laurens County Arts Council, 1982).

13. One obvious community of memory is the lynchers themselves. Unfortunately, their memories are inaccessible. Lynch mobs are usually anonymous, if not at the time, then at least in the historical record. Even were their identities known, the decades that have passed make it doubtful that many survive. And if they did, interviewing people about lynchings they themselves had participated in would be an extremely difficult task. Will

Gravely, in researching the 1947 lynching of Willie Earle in Greenville, S.C., has had no success in talking to several of the surviving alleged members of that mob. Gravely, personal communication, Denver University, 5 May 1998.

14. Earlier incidents like this would not have been as 'unusual. For instance, in 1899 a white landlord told his black tenant to finish hoeing some cotton. When the landlord reached for a whip, the tenant grabbed an ax. The landlord shot the tenant to death, and the coroner's jury ruled it self-defense. As late as 20 March 1930, the *Laurens Advertiser* reported that a white foreman shot a black farmhand for not working on a Saturday; the employee apparently recovered, and no charges were brought.

15. U.S. Bureau of the Census, *Thirteenth Census of the United States Taken in 1910: Statistics for South Carolina* (Washington, D.C.: GPO, 1913), 577. Distinctions among the types of mobs that carried out lynchings and the reasons for the lynchings are important and affect the way lynchings are remembered. For a thorough consideration of the various types of mobs, see W. Fitzhugh Brundage, *Lynching in the New South: Georgia and Virginia, 1880–1930* (Urbana: University of Illinois Press, 1993), chap. 1.

16. For another example of historical memory of lynching within a black community and the transmission of that information, see David Frost Jr.'s memoir, *Witness to Injustice*, ed. Louise Westling (Jackson: University Press of Mississippi, 1995), 5–8, 12–20.

17. Consultants sometimes knew of other lynchings from outside Laurens County but often remembered them less clearly. Willy Eichelberger, who was ninety-seven years old at the time of our interview, had heard of the 1906 lynching of Bob "Snowball" Davis in Greenwood County. Eichelberger's son, Eddie, explained: "This guy was on the chain gang. They called him Snowball. He used to drive the road scraper. That was his job on the chain gang. And they claimed that he raped a white girl. That's what he was hung for. I think it was in the thirties, or first part of the forties, I think." Terence Finnegan gives an account of this lynching in "'At the Hands of Parties Unknown': Lynching in Mississippi and South Carolina, 1881–1940" (Ph.D. diss., University of Illinois at Urbana-Champaign, 1993), 264–69. David Kennedy had heard about the lynching of Anthony Crawford in Abbeville in 1916 (described in Finnegan, "At the Hands of Parties Unknown," 173–88), and many consultants knew of South Carolina's last lynching, that of Willie Earle near Greenville in 1947.

18. *Laurensville Herald*, 12 May 1893.

19. In Laurens County, and probably elsewhere throughout the South, rural communities are often known by one name to their black residents and another name to their white residents since communities are often centered around churches. The community of Chestnut Ridge, the name of the white church, therefore, is coextensive with the community of Mount Zion, the name of the black church.

20. *Charleston News and Courier*, 11 May 1893.

21. Ibid.

22. Laurens County Coroner's Inquisition Book, 1897–1901, 81, Laurens County Public Library (microfilm). I spoke with Mrs. Watts by telephone on 24 March 1998, and she agreed that Heyward Barksdale probably was the person to whom she was referring.

23. For an intriguing account of memory in the family of a lynching victim, see Will Gravely, "Reliving South Carolina's Last Lynching: The Witness of Tess Earle Robinson," *South Carolina Review* 29 (Spring 1997): 5–17. Doria Johnson, a great-great-granddaughter of Anthony Crawford, who was lynched in Abbeville, has written an account of that lynching and its effects on the Crawford family for an internet genealogy

site. See Johnson, "The Lynching of Anthony Crawford," Christine's Genealogy Website, 1998, ⟨http://www.charity.com/contributors/anthonycrawford.htm⟩.

24. Laurens County Coroner's Inquisition Book, 1872–76, Laurens County Public Library, 15 (microfilm).

25. *Laurens Advertiser*, 6, 13 July 1933, 14 June 1934.

26. Edwin D. Hoffman, "The Genesis of the Modern Movement for Equal Rights in South Carolina, 1930–1939," *Journal of Negro History* 44 (October 1959): 256.

27. *Crisis* 40 (September 1933): 209; " 'Too Rich to Be a Niggar,' " *Crisis* 40 (December 1933): 282–83; "Norris Dendy's Children," *Crisis* 41 (October 1934): 300.

28. *Laurens Advertiser*, 28 December 1934. The 1896 statute is sec. 15-51-210 of the Code of Laws of South Carolina. The county in which a lynching takes place is liable for not less than $2,000 to the legal representative of the victim. The county can, however, recover the amount of the judgement from parties engaged in the lynching, thus offering criminal courts an incentive to convict lynchers.

29. Laurens County Board of Commissioners Minutes, 1934–36, South Carolina Department of Archives and History, Columbia (microfilm) (hereafter SCDAH).

30. *Laurens Advertiser*, 18 April 1935.

31. Taking, or at least considering, legal action against mobs in Laurens County did not begin with the Dendy case. In 1892 Dave Shaw was tortured by a mob near Tumblin Shoals to extract a confession of burglary. Shaw would probably have been lynched but for a lucky escape. After hiding out in Georgia for a few weeks, he returned to Greenville to seek the advice of an attorney. For a brief time, it appeared that Governor Tillman was interested in using the Shaw case as an example to discourage lynching, but he soon abandoned the effort. See *Charleston News and Courier*, 31 May, 1, 5, 23 June, 8, 12, 26 July 1892.

32. Stewart's lynching is reported in the *Charleston News and Courier*, 3 April 1920, and the *Laurensville Herald*, 9 April 1920. Other information comes from Death Certificates, vol. 14, no. 7952, 1 April 1920, SCDAH; 1910 census; *City Directory, Laurens and Clinton, S.C., 1917* (Columbia, S.C.: Southern Directory Agency, 1917), 182; 1920 census, Laurens Township, City of Laurens, Ward 4, Jennings Street, 109.

33. *Pickens Sentinel*, 21 April 1881; *New York Times*, 18 April 1881.

34. Laurens County Coroner's Inquisition Book, 1891–94, Laurens County Public Library, 103 (microfilm). Brief mention of the lynching is made in the *Charleston News and Courier*, 7, 10 January 1898, and the *Laurensville Herald*, 14 January 1898.

35. *Charleston News and Courier*, 25, 27 September 1904; *Laurensville Herald*, 30 September, 7 October 1904; *Columbia State*, 24 September 1904.

36. *Charleston News and Courier*, 24 July 1897; *Laurensville Herald*, 30 July 1897.

37. Brundage, *Lynching in the New South*, 48.

38. Laurens County Coroner's Inquisition Book, 1897–1901, Laurens County Public Library, 81 (microfilm).

39. Brundage, *Lynching in the New South*, 82. Other consultants confirmed the protective role white employers could play for their black tenants. Walker Merrill, whose father always got along well with his employers, the Flemings, claimed that in addition to relaxing the norms of racial interaction, the Flemings would protect the Merrill family from other whites who might be inclined to give them trouble. Thomas Garrett stated that the Wasson brothers played a similar role in Hickory Tavern, where they were among the leading landowners.

40. Tindall, *South Carolina Negroes*, 174–78.

41. *Hickory Western Carolinian*, 23 September 1887.

42. *Greenville News*, 8, 18, 19, 20 March 1933; *Anderson Independent*, 8, 9, 18 March 1933; *Laurens Advertiser*, 9, 23 March 1933; *Charleston Evening Post*, 8 March 1933; *Charleston News and Courier*, 8, 9, 17, 20 March 1933.

43. *Greenville News*, 19 March 1933.

44. Barbara Allen, "The Genealogical Landscape," in Barbara Allen and Thomas J. Schlereth, *Sense of Place: American Regional Cultures* (Lexington: University Press of Kentucky, 1990), 161.

45. Apparently, whites in Laurens County generally heard little about lynchings as children. Even those who were living at the time were shielded from the lynchings. The elderly woman Bill Cooper spoke of was not allowed to watch a lynch mob pass by when she was a girl, and in telling about his mother's recollection of the lynching of Joe Stewart in Laurens in 1920, Cooper said that "she said what she remembered was going to school and they were talking about it. And the teacher had actually gone down there to see it. And, of course, her father would not have let her see something like that." Elaine Martin's mother told her about the Puckett lynching but also said that "when she was a child, grownups wouldn't have talked about things like that where children could hear." For the lessons of lynching for black youths, see Charles S. Johnson, *Growing Up in the Black Belt: Negro Youth in the Rural South* (1941; reprint, New York: Shocken, 1967), 316–18.

46. W. W. Ball's reaction to the lynching of Heyward Barksdale in 1893 is one of many examples of what I am describing here. See also Brundage, *Lynching in the New South*, 32.

47. Brundage, *Lynching in the New South*, 15.

48. This analysis is based on Jean-François Lyotard's idea of the *differend* as explained in his book *The Differend: Phrases in Dispute*, trans. Georges Van Den Abbeele (Minneapolis: University of Minnesota Press, 1988). He writes, "This is what a wrong [*tort*] would be: a damage [*dommage*] accompanied by the loss of the means to prove the damage" (p. 5). Thus, a lynching is itself a damage, but the silence about the lynching within the public discourse imposed on the victim and the victim's family and community removes the possibility of proving that a damage was done, giving the victim no opportunity for redress in the public discourse. This is what Lyotard describes by the term *differend*: "A case of differend between two parties takes place when the 'regulation' of the conflict that opposes them is done in the idiom of one of the parties while the wrong suffered by the other is not signified in that idiom" (p. 9).

49. I saw Howard hand a copy of the Puckett photograph to a customer at the end of a transaction on 22 November 1997, when I spoke with him for a couple of hours about this project. I do not know if Howard always distributes copies of the photograph as he declined a follow-up interview on 21 February 1998. Howard did have many copies of the photograph in November, one of which he generously gave to me when I requested it.

50. Governor Coleman L. Blease to Colonel John M. Cannon, 13 August 1913, box 22, Governors' Papers (1911–15: Blease), SCDAH.

51. An example of the successful use of the memory of lynching as a means of providing recourse for a damage is the case of the lawsuit against the state of Florida brought by survivors and descendants of victims of the destruction of Rosewood in 1923. For a full account, see Michael D'Orso's *Like Judgement Day: The Ruin and Redemption of a Town Called Rosewood* (New York: Boulevard Books, 1996).

52. To take only a few examples from South Carolina of the varied fates of historical

memory of this sort of conflict, we might consider Edwin D. Hoffman's claim that "No South Carolinians could be found [in 1957] who recalled these events [the violent police and Klan suppression of the biracial Greenville Unemployed Council] in Greenville in 1931," made in "Equal Rights in South Carolina, 1930–1939," *Journal of Negro History* 44 (October 1959): 360 n. 20. More recently, the film "The Uprising of '34" has brought the General Textile Strike of 1934 back into public discourse. The *Greenville News* devoted three pages in its Sunday edition to the shooting at Chiquola Mill in Honea Path. Deb Richardson-Moore and Jim DuPlessis, "Generations of Silence: The Chiquola Mill Shootings," *Greenville News*, 28 April 1995.

53. For a similar argument about the decline of ballads about lynchings, see Baker, "North Carolina Lynching Ballads," 240–41.

Southerners Don't Lie;
They Just Remember Big

David W. Blight

I have known few people in my life with a deeper sense of history, and a more profound need to express it, than the Reverend Eugene Winkler, a legendary minister in the Chicago area and currently the senior pastor at First United Methodist Church in downtown Chicago. Gene was born in Dewitt, Arkansas, and grew up the son of an itinerant Methodist minister in towns in Mississippi, East Texas, and Louisiana as well as his native state. For thirty years Gene has pastored churches, punctured complacency, challenged congregations with his progressive politics, and created remarkably civic, urban and suburban ministries in Illinois. He is very much a southerner still, but one who came to the land of Abraham Lincoln with more antislavery and humanist spirit than perhaps any Midwestern abolitionist ever mustered. Winkler is one of the most widely read human beings I have ever known. His sermons, infused with biblical mastery and lessons in tough "grace," are also journeys into the past. A William Faulkner devotee, Gene often fills his sermons with characters such as Thomas Sutpen, Dilsey Gibson, Joe Christmas, or the various Compson children to make his points about ambition and sloth, glory and tragedy, sin and redemption.

Winkler is a storyteller who has been listening all of his life in and around Yoknapatawpha County, and he speaks back. Although his own faith is pure, he understands the mythical power of religion, and therefore of history and memory. Gene embodies some of the wonderful contradictions of southern intellectuals. A learned student of Soren Kierkegaard and an admirer of every freedom fighter from John Brown to Ida Wells, Diedrich Bonhoffer to Martin Luther King and Nelson Mandela, he also loyally keeps portraits of Robert E. Lee and Stonewall Jackson in a corner of his private office wall. In conversation I once asked Gene the abrupt question: "Why do Southerners seem to have a greater sense of history and longer memories than most other Americans?" His quick two-word answer, "The War," gave me a shortened version of Walker Percy's famous answer—"because we lost the war." The Reverend can still become animated about Reconstruction, regaling me, as he once did, with tales of what "carpetbaggers" did to some of his ancestors in Arkansas.

Gene Winkler's South is both a real and a mythical universe, a deep well of local and broader memories, reminders that we are all from some place (or at least yearn to be), as well as part of a larger humanity striving for the same things. This sense of place has been a burden to some southern writers (one thinks of Richard Wright's desperate need to escape the South at the same time that its oppression compelled him to write), whereas most have thrived on what Eudora Welty called "the blessing of being located."[1] But where the Gene Winklers of the world know that we cannot ever fully escape our pasts, many Americans, southerners included, devote considerable exertion to doing just that. As Fitzhugh Brundage makes clear in his introduction to this volume, the South is not necessarily richer in history and memory than any other region of the United States. The sense of social memory in any region or group depends on how much of its collective, cognitive energy is devoted to the work of selecting and imposing meaning on the past, how much effort it extends in remembering and forgetting as social units. The South's history, inherently part of the national story, but also peculiarly apart from it, has given it a special place in America's collective memory. As Winkler once quipped in a sermon, "Southerners don't lie; they just remember big."

A good deal of history has happened *to* the South, as in that lost war, and not merely *in* it. The South has been both the author of its own fate and, at times, blamed its condition on every kind of outside force. Unlike most parts of the United States, with Native Americans the obvious exception, the South was conquered and had to be reimagined and re-created. Just how much it changed in that reimagining has been one of the most persistent questions in southern history—the old perennial about continuity and discontinuity. And, as C. Vann Woodward pointed out in 1960, in *The Burden of Southern History*, the South had not shared equally in the national self-image of innocence, moral superiority, abundance, progress, and invincibility with other parts of the country. Yet, as a white memory community, southerners (with much northern help) have fashioned their own myths of innocence and victimization in the "Plantation Legend," the "Lost Cause," and various racial theories. The Lost Cause seems to have an eternal life in American culture, reviving again and again in relation to changes in race relations. The Confederacy, that unique southern experiment in independence and the preservation of a slave society, seems to invoke eternal fascination in our culture for its "rebellion," its heroes and causes, its cult of fallen soldiers, its battle flag as source of regional identity and racial icon. Southern writer Allan Gurganus, author of *Oldest Confederate Widow Tells All* (1983), speaks for the many white southerners resisting the current Confederate revival. Ruefully, he chides his fellow southerners to give up on the battle flag and other symbols, especially what he calls the South's "secret power: our habit of anticipating defeat while never accepting it." Urging southerners to officially relegate the Confederate flag to museums, Gurganus warns: "Trust me. The South is no place for beginners. Its power of denial can turn a lost war into a vibrant, necessary form of national chic."[2]

The essays in this book demonstrate that a great deal can be at stake in conflicts over memory. Every group of southerners we encounter seeks some form of a usable past, some degree of control over the social memory of their town, state, or region. A lesson of virtually every piece is that those who can create the dominant historical narrative, those who can own the public memory, will achieve political and cultural power. Sometimes that control emerges in intensely personal or familial ways, as in the tale of how homosexuality is remembered and forgotten in a Mississippi county, or how white women in Charleston created a narrative of that city's history rooted in domestic and architectural traditions, ordered social hierarchies, and a benign racial regime of slavery. Memories also survive in the personal ways lynchings are remembered in black families and communities—through sites, icons, and oral tradition. Often, though, the struggle to control memory emerges from public rituals, acts of commemoration, political conflict, and commercial practice.

In every case in this book we observe the human quest to own the past and thereby achieve control over the present. Artisan patriots in Georgia used their Revolutionary republicanism to claim their place in society as planters and slaveholders. Antebellum black Virginians, too, claimed their Revolutionary heritage, by both public acts, including emigration, and private expressions of memory. The great divergence, as well as dependence, in southern memory is clear from Confederates who claimed their new revolution of

1861 as the true preservation of the legacy of the Revolution of 1876, while freed blacks in 1865–66 made long treks on dusty southern roads to attend Emancipation celebrations where they expressed their own revolutionary "rebirth."

The problem of historical memory is essentially one of competing narratives, marshaled often to high political ends. We encounter a generation of black religious writers who fashioned a new, redemptive narrative and destiny for their people, a millennial sacred drama in which blacks would rise to historical dominance over time. We are still only beginning to learn just what a decisive break Emancipation was in America's national memory. All black efforts to deal with their servile past and to compete for control of new national or southern narratives encountered such violence as that in Wilmington in 1898, revealed here as a white supremacist crusade to take back political control of North Carolina by dominating the state's official memory. And finally, this volume offers multiple examples of the commodification of memory through heritage tourism, one of the world's largest growth industries. The invention of a mountain folk heritage in the southern Appalachians, a narrative of victimhood and diasporic survival among the Acadians, and the story of all the groups who would like to control the memory of the Alamo demonstrate how susceptible historical memory is to the whims of the market.

At the heart of many of the stories in this book is the relationship of memory to identity. As Brundage contends, a southern identity will disappear only when people no longer "imagine themselves within a southern historical narrative." That clearly has not yet happened. But in 1963, Flannery O'Connor mused eloquently on just such a prospect. She worried that southern writing might soon read as though it came merely from "some synthetic place that could have been anywhere or nowhere." She feared that television would soon be the greatest influence on southern as well as other writers. Too much "phony-Southern" had already crept into literature for her taste. O'Connor acknowledged that in "the present state of the South . . . our identity is obscured and in doubt." In complicated ways, many of them dealing with race, O'Connor's fears of a lost southern distinctiveness may be just what has in later decades bred an increased consciousness of the multiplicity of southernness.[3]

But before leaving the subject, O'Connor had wisdom to impart about just what constitutes an individual or social identity. "Southern identity is not really connected with mocking birds and beaten biscuits and white columns," she said, "any more than it is with hookworm and bare feet and muddy clay roads." Nor was that identity to be discovered in "the antics of our politicians," she contended, since "power obeys strange laws of its own" in every society. "An identity is not to be found on the surface," O'Connor instructed; "it is not accessible to the poll-taker; it is not something that can become a cliche. It is not made from the mean average or the typical, but from the hidden and the most extreme. It is not made from what passes, but from those qualities that endure. . . . It lies very deep. In its entirety, it is known only to God." Speaking for her trade, O'Connor argued that the "greatest blessing a writer can have" is to "find at home what others have to go elsewhere seeking." When people share a past, however tragic and conflicted, she concluded, then they possess a special thing: "the possibility of reading a small history in a universal light." Is this not what the best of southern storytellers have always done? It certainly is the case with O'Connor and Faulkner. As Joel Williamson wrote of Faulkner, "the stage happened to be the South, the subject was the human condition, and the play was on-going and without end."[4]

The introduction to this book takes its title from the final lines of the late autobiography of W. E. B. Du Bois, a southerner for a time. All of the essays and the one short story in Du Bois's classic, *The Souls of Black Folk*, were written while he was a young professor in Atlanta between 1897 and 1903. Du Bois wrote *The Autobiography* in 1958–59 as he reached the age of ninety. In the last chapter, after reflecting at length on aging, death, and the repression of free thought in America during the Cold War, Du Bois concludes with what amounts to a prayerful appeal to the dead and to memory. "I whisper to the great Majority: To the Almighty Dead," he says, "into whose pale approaching faces, I stand and stare." He invites the dead to "outvote" the living with their wisdom. "Let your memories teach these wilful fools," he implores the dead, "all which you have forgotten and ruined and done to death." As though reaching back to books, to story, to an ancient, time-enriched sense of the past, Du Bois seeks collective guidance for the species during its travail of nuclear fear and its struggle to face and conquer the color line as the civil rights movement begins to take hold. He pleads for counsel from the past and ends his own life story with the words: "Teach us, Forever Dead, there is no Dream but Deed, there is no Deed but Memory."[5]

Du Bois acknowledges that there can be no aspiration without dreaming, but no imagination without knowledge. We cannot act without memory. But here in the elder African American scholar's prayerful vision, we face the riddle of memory, whether individual or collective. As humans, we are the only animals capable of knowing our own history. But that knowledge can both liberate and paralyze us. Memory, therefore, is the thing—the power—we cannot live without, but at the same time, it can be excruciating to live with it. By preserving and cultivating memory, we might understand both our capacity and our incapacity for action. Too much memory can consume and kill us; without it, though, we risk being ignorant creatures of fate. As Du Bois implores, one of our greatest tasks is to turn memory (experience, knowledge, and the stories from which we draw identity), whatever its burdens, into humane action.

An extraordinary southern case in point is Katherine Du Pre Lumpkin, the youngest among three sisters in a prominent Georgia family. As Jacquelyn Dowd Hall has demonstrated, Lumpkin, the author of a classic autobiography, *The Making of a Southerner* (1946), grew up thoroughly indoctrinated with Lost Cause ideology by her family, especially her father, William Wallace Lumpkin, a Confederate veteran and bitter custodian of a noble, victimized, racially superior white South. Indeed, Katherine Lumpkin was raised amid a family obsession with the rituals of the Lost Cause tradition, including Confederate veterans' reunions and parades and explicit instructions by her father as though part of catechism classes. For the Lumpkin sisters, white supremacy, the image of the South potentially ruled by outsiders, the prospect of black domination, and their region as the defender of racial and gender order were the organizing truths of life embodied by the Ku Klux Klan.[6]

Here was a burden of memory seemingly impossible to overcome. Yet, as Hall argues, the very contradictions embedded in the Lost Cause tradition, coupled with her education outside the South and a growing political consciousness after World War I, saved Katherine Lumpkin and rendered her "capable of freedom." Eventually taking a Ph.D. in sociology and embracing the emancipatory message of the Social Gospel, Lumpkin became a reformer. She wrote traditional sociology, became fascinated with the black experience in her native South, and through the *I* narrative of autobiography, found a personal voice in which to contest virtually every element of the memory community in which she was raised. Through the course of the upheavals of the 1930s and 1940s, Lumpkin discovered what Hall calls "a new regional past," breaking free from the types and the melodramatic narrative of the Lost Cause. Echoing Du Bois, Hall's re-creation of Lumpkin's struggle to "rewrite . . . and spring free from," while also "honoring," her past becomes a compelling story of how, for African Americans surviving the age of Jim Crow, as well as a daughter of the planter class, "remembering was a conscious political act."[7] Some authors in this century have found their way to revise history by challenging social memory (even their own) in fiction, some only in the freer use of autobiography, and some still by logging months in the archives and writing traditional historical analyses of new peoples and new sources, all rooted in both new and old questions. To continue to understand the riddle of history's fascinating confluence with memory, we must continue to read and write in all of these modes. And we must continue to make memory that power that we think *about* as much as *with*.

NOTES

1. Welty quoted in C. Vann Woodward, "The Search for Southern Identity," in Woodward, *The Burden of Southern History* (1960; reprint, New York: New American Library, 1969), 30.

2. Ibid., esp. chaps. 9, 10; Allan Gurganus, *New York Times*, 8 December 1996.

3. Flannery O'Connor, "The Regional Writer" (1963), in *Flannery O'Connor: Collected Works* (New York: Library of America, 1988), 846–47.

4. Ibid., 846–47, 844; Joel Williamson, *William Faulkner and Southern History* (New York: Oxford University Press, 1993), 6.

5. W. E. B. Du Bois, *The Autobiography of W. E. B. Du Bois: A Soliloquy on Viewing My Life from the Last Decade of Its First Century* (New York: International Publishers, 1968), 422–23.

6. Jacquelyn Dowd Hall, "'You Must Remember This': Autobiography as Social Critique," *Journal of American History* 85 (September 1998): 439–53.

7. Ibid., 455, 458–59, 461, 464. On Du Bois's own struggle to use history as a weapon to dislodge dominant historical memories in America, see David W. Blight, "W. E. B. Du Bois and the Struggle for American Historical Memory," in Geneviève Fabre and Robert O'Meally, eds., *History and Memory in African-American Culture* (New York: Oxford University Press, 1994), 45–71.

contributors

Bruce E. Baker received his M.A. in folklore from the University of North Carolina at Chapel Hill, where he is currently enrolled in the Ph.D. program in history. He has contributed to *Under Sentence of Death: Essays on Lynching in the American South* and the *Handbook of North Carolina History*.

Catherine W. Bishir is the architectural survey coordinator for the North Carolina Division of Archives and History. She also teaches architectural history at North Carolina State University and Duke University. She has published in *Southern Cultures* and is the author of *The Unpainted Aristocracy: The Beach Cottages of Old Nags Head* and *North Carolina Architecture*, and the coauthor of *Architects and Builders in North Carolina: A History of the Practice of Building*, *A Guide to the Historic Architecture of Eastern North Carolina*, and *A Guide to the Historic Architecture of Western North Carolina*.

David W. Blight is the Class of 1959 Professor of History and Black Studies at Amherst College. He is the author of *Frederick Douglass's Civil War: Keeping Faith in Jubilee* and *Race and Reunion: The Civil War in American Memory, 1863–1915* (forthcoming).

Holly Beachley Brear received her Ph.D. in anthropology from the University of Virginia and is the author of *Inherit the Alamo*. She has taught at George Mason University and the University of Virginia.

W. Fitzhugh Brundage received his Ph.D. from Harvard University and is professor and chair in the Department of History at the University of Florida. He is the author of *Lynching in the New South* and *A Socialist Utopia in the New South* and the editor of *Under Sentence of Death: Essays on Lynching in the American South*.

Kathleen Clark received her Ph.D. from Yale University. She is an assistant professor in the Department of History at the University of Georgia.

Michele Gillespie received her Ph.D. from Princeton University and is an associate professor of history at Wake Forest University. She is the coeditor of *The Devil's Lane: Sex and Race in the Early South* and the author of *Fruits of Their Labor: White Artisans in Slaveholding Georgia, 1790–1860.*

John Howard, the former director of the Center for Lesbian, Gay, and Bisexual Life at Duke University, is an associate professor of history at the University of York in England. He has published in *Callabo, Radical History Review, Southern Changes,* and *Southern Historian;* has edited *Carryin' On in the Lesbian and Gay South: Historical Essays;* and is the author of *Men Like That: A Southern Queer History.*

Gregg D. Kimball is assistant director of publications at the Library of Virginia. He received his Ph.D. from the University of Virginia. Previously, he was a curator and historian at the Valentine Museum in Richmond, where he curated numerous influential and highly regarded exhibitions on life and labor in Richmond and coauthored the exhibition catalog *In Bondage and Freedom: Antebellum Black Life in Richmond Virginia, 1790–1860.* He is also the author of *American City, Southern Place: A Cultural History of Antebellum Richmond.*

Laurie F. Maffly-Kipp is the author of *Religion and Frontier Society in California* and numerous articles about African American religion. She received her Ph.D. in American history from Yale and is an associate professor of religious studies at the University of North Carolina at Chapel Hill.

C. Brenden Martin received his Ph.D. from the University of Tennessee. He was a historian at the Museum of the New South in Charlotte, North Carolina, and is now associate professor of history at Northwestern State University in Natchitoches, Louisiana.

Anne Sarah Rubin is an assistant professor of history at the University of Maryland, Baltimore County. She has published articles in the *Virginia Magazine of History and Biography* and *Southern Cultures.* She also has been the manager of the Valley of the Shadow Project, an interactive history of the Civil War in two communities, and is the coauthor (with Edward L. Ayers) of a CD-ROM version published by W. W. Norton.

Stephanie E. Yuhl was a Lilly Fellow in History at Valparaiso University and is now assistant professor of history at Holy Cross College. She received her Ph.D. in history from Duke University. She is revising her dissertation, "High Culture in the Low Country: Arts, Identity, and Tourism in Charleston, South Carolina, 1920–1940," for publication.